Also by Yvette Taylor

WORKING-CLASS LESBIAN LIFE: Classed Outsiders

LESBIAN AND GAY PARENTING: Securing Social and Educational Capital

CLASSED INTERSECTIONS: Spaces, Selves, Knowledges (*ed.*)

THEORIZING INTERSECTIONALITY AND SEXUALITY (*co-edited with Hines, S. and Casey, M.*)

SEXUALITIES: REFLECTIONS AND FUTURES (*co-edited with Hines, S.*)

EDUCATIONAL DIVERSITY: The Subject of Difference and Different Subjects (*ed.*)

FITTING INTO PLACE? Class and Gender Geographies and Temporalities

MAPPING INTIMACIES: Relations, Exchanges, Affects (*co-edited with Sanger, T.*)

Queer Presences and Absences

Edited by

Yvette Taylor
London South Bank University, UK

and

Michelle Addison
Newcastle University, UK

First published 2013 by
PALGRAVE MACMILLAN

Palgrave Macmillan in the UK is an imprint of Macmillan Publishers Limited,
registered in England, company number 785998, of Houndmills, Basingstoke,
Hampshire RG21 6XS.

Palgrave Macmillan in the US is a division of St Martin's Press LLC,
175 Fifth Avenue, New York, NY 10010.

Palgrave Macmillan is the global academic imprint of the above companies
and has companies and representatives throughout the world.

Palgrave® and Macmillan® are registered trademarks in the United States,
the United Kingdom, Europe and other countries.

ISBN 978–0–230–30254–9

This book is printed on paper suitable for recycling and made from fully
managed and sustained forest sources. Logging, pulping and manufacturing
processes are expected to conform to the environmental regulations of the
country of origin.

A catalogue record for this book is available from the British Library.

A catalog record for this book is available from the Library of Congress.

10   9   8   7   6   5   4   3   2   1
22 21 20 19 18 17 16 15 14 13

Printed and bound in Great Britain by
CPI Antony Rowe, Chippenham and Eastbourne

Contents

List of Figures and Tables

Figures

Tables

Notes on Contributors

Michelle Addison is an ESRC funded Ph.D. student at Newcastle University and a Visiting Scholar at the Weeks Centre for Social and Policy Research, London South Bank University. Her thesis looks at workplace identity (re)formation, (mis)recognition, and resistance, querying which identities come to be valued and rewarded whilst giving attention to those that are silenced and marginalised. Her research explores the classed and gendered contours of employee's workplace experiences as they come to be mediated, expressed and realised through emotion. During 2007, Michelle worked as a research assistant on the ESRC funded study: 'From the coal to the car park?' with Yvette Taylor (PI) (see Taylor. Y and Addison, M. (2011) 'Placing Research: "City Publics" and the "Public Sociologist"' *Sociological Research Online* 6(4)).

Carsten Balzer wrote hir Ph.D. thesis on transgender movements and subcultures in Brazil, Germany, and the United States. S_he carried out fieldwork in Tanzania and the Brazilian Amazon region, as well as in Rio de Janeiro, New York City, and Berlin, taught courses at the Free University Berlin, and has published a book and various chapters in anthologies and articles in peer-reviewed journals in the U.S., Brazil, Germany, and Spain. S_he is a member of the steering committee of the international human rights NGO Transgender Europe (TGEU), chairperson of the Scientific Advisory Board of the Transgender Network Berlin (TGNB) as well as a founding member of the academic online magazine 'Liminalis – Journal for Sex/ Gender Emancipation and Resistance'. Currently Carsten Balzer is the lead researcher and project manager of TGEU's 'Transrespect versus Transphobia Worldwide' (TvT) research project, which s_he initiated in 2009.

Chiara Bertone is Assistant Professor in Sociology of the Family at the University of East Piedmont, Italy. She holds a Ph.D. in Women's and Gender Studies in the Social Sciences from Aalborg University, Denmark. Her main interests lie in sexuality and family change, explored from a gender perspective. She has worked on a national survey on sexuality in Italy, and coordinated a European project on the families of origin of lesbian and gay people. Publications include the books *Whose Needs? Women's organisations claims on child care in Italy and Denmark* (2002) and *Le omosessualità* (2009), and the article, written with Raffaella Ferrero Camoletto, 'Beyond the sex machine? Sexual practices and masculinity in adult men's heterosexual accounts', *Journal of Gender Studies*, 2009.

Max Biddulph is a lecturer in the Centre for Research in Schools and Communities in the School of Education, University of Nottingham,

UK. Prior to working in Higher Education, his experience of working in a number of UK secondary schools provided the grounding for some strong themes that weave through his career, namely performance, community, and empowerment. At a national level he has worked to develop inclusive sex and relationships education curricula and most recently his research interests have focused on dimensions of narrative and autoethnography as mechanisms for exploring and communicating queer experience. Max also has a strong interest in activism, LGBT and HIV politics and in 1997 he was one of the founder members of SWAN – the National Association of Assertiveness Trainers of Gay/Bisexual Men. Outside of work he is proud to be a member of the gay men's leather community.

Mark Casey is a lecturer at Newcastle University where he teaches the modules 'Understanding Everyday Life', 'The Sociology of Tourism' and 'Regulating Sexuality'. He is the current degree programme director for Politics and Sociology. His research interests cover a wide range of areas from sexuality, gender, space and place, social class and travel, tourism and mobilities. He is currently undertaking research funded by Newcastle University on the island of Mallorca focused upon meanings of home and belonging for the British expatriate community in light of the economic downturn.

Youngsook Choi is an independent researcher and artist/curator with a particular interest in the relationship between gender and space. Her doctoral thesis was on how the gender control of the state and its institutional practices have affected spatial occupation by gender differences, especially with reference to transgendered people's points of view (2011, King's College London). Choi had been involved in public arts and culture projects such as the Women and Space Festival and Sexuality Museum for Youth in Seoul, Korea. She also ran the creative workshops with young queer people about hetero-centric dating culture enforced by commercial sectors and its influence on their everyday lives. The outcome of workshops has been published in the arts collection *Very Special Valentine's Day* (2011, Youthvoice). Choi is currently part of the advisory group for the Seoul Community Arts Creation Center, designing cultural programmes for immigrant women and working class children.

Jen Jack Gieseking Ph.D., is a visiting assistant research professor at the Graduate Center of the City University of New York (CUNY). Her research as a cultural geographer and environmental psychologist focuses on how everyday co-productions of space and identity support or inhibit social, spatial, and economic justice. She is working on her first book, *Queer New York: Lesbians' and Queer Women's Experiences of Social and Spatial Justice in New York City, 1983–2008*. Her website is www.jgieseking.org.

Andrew Gorman-Murray is Lecturer in Social Sciences (Geography and Urban Studies) at the University of Western Sydney. He is a social and cultural geographer who focuses on lesbian, gay and sexual minority experiences of belonging and exclusion in everyday spaces, including homes, neighbourhoods, suburbs and country towns. His work analyses the intersections of queer politics, everyday experience, material culture, and urban and regional geographies, seeking to enhance social inclusion alongside scholarly thinking. He has published in *Environment and Planning A*, *Social and Cultural Geography, Gender, Place and Culture, Journal of Rural Studies, International Journal of Urban and Regional Research, Emotion, Space and Society, Antipode, Australian Geographer, Geographical Research*, and *New Zealand Geographer*. The current chapter is based on research conducted for an Australian Research Council Discovery Project (DP0986666), *Men on the Home Front*, on changing relations between masculinities and domesticities in inner Sydney.

Beatrice Gusmano holds a Ph.D. in Sociology and Social Research at the University of Trento; her thesis won the first prize of the Maria Baiocchi Award (2009) as the best doctoral dissertation research in LGBT studies. She is member of the Centre for Interdisciplinary Gender Studies at the University of Trento. She is currently carrying out a research on workplace best practices on the grounds of sexual orientation and gender identity. She has been involved in studies concerning the construction/management of sexual identity in the workplace (*Forms of Resistance to the Organization's Symbolic Heteronormative Order*, Oxford 2010; "Coming out or not?", *Journal of Workplace Rights* 2008); local and European public policies aimed at fighting discrimination against LGBT people ("Presentation and replicability of LGBT best practices at local level", Rome 2011); diversity management; gender education; illness narratives by parents with disabled children.

Jan Simon Hutta works for the research project "Transrespect versus Transphobia Worldwide" (TvT) of the activist network Transgender Europe. He teaches courses on queer politics and migration at Humboldt University Berlin and is co-founder of the German transdisciplinary journal 'sub\Urban'. He received his Ph.D. in human geography from The Open University, Milton Keynes, UK, and conducted ethnographic research in Brazil and Germany. His publications on sexual and gender politics and the relations of subjectivity, neoliberalism and space have appeared, among others, in *Environment and Planning D: Society and Space* and the edited volumes *Rethinking the Public: Innovations in Research, Theory and Politics* and *Queer Futures: Reconsidering Normativity, Activism and the Political*.

Kateřina Lišková is Assistant Professor in the Gender Studies program at the Faculty of Social Sciences, Masaryk University, in the Czech Republic. Her research is focused on gender, sexuality, and the social organization of intimacy. She was affiliated with the New School for Social Research as a Fulbright Scholar, as a Visiting Scholar with New York University, and as a Marie Curie Fellow with Columbia University. She has lectured at various U.S. universities and her papers have appeared in several monographs published by Routledge, Sage and Blackwell. In the Czech Republic, her book *Good Girls Look the Other Way, Feminism and Pornography* was published by Sociological Publishing House (2009).

Karina Luzia is a social geographer and a lecturer in academic development at Macquarie University in Sydney, Australia. Her current research projects include the geographies of same sex parented families in Australia and the role of casual and sessional teachers in higher education. Her research interests are diverse and diffuse, and include cultural geographies of home, work and family; higher degree research scholarship and teaching; academic development and identity; feminist theory and methods; gender and sexuality; and work/life balance.

Nick Rumens is Senior Lecturer in Management at the University of Bristol, UK. His current research interests include Queer Theories and the disruptions they might generate within the field of organisation studies. Nick's research has mobilised queer theories to examine workplace friendships and intimacies, genders and sexualities in organisation and critical management research. He has published articles on these topics in journals such as *Human Relations, The Sociological Review, Human Resource Management Journal and Equality,* and *Diversity and Inclusion: An International Journal.* He has also published a number of books, including *Queer Company: Friendship in the Work Lives of Gay Men* (2011) and, co-authored with Mihaela Kelemen, *An Introduction to Critical Management Research* (Sage, 2008), which includes a chapter on queer theory and management research. He is currently co-editing (with Fiona Colgan) a book, titled 'Sexual Orientation at Work: International Issues and Perspectives', to be published by Routledge.

Yvette Taylor is Professor in Social and Policy Studies and Head of the Weeks Centre for Social and Policy Research, London South Bank University. She was previously a Senior Lecturer at Newcastle University, a Fulbright Distinguished Scholar at Rutgers University (2010–2011) and a Visiting Professor at the University of California, Berkeley (2012). Her most recent book, based on ESRC funded research, is *Fitting Into Place? Class and Gender Geographies and Temporalities* (Ashgate, 2012). Other books include *Working-class Lesbian Life: Classed Outsiders* (Palgrave, 2007) and *Lesbian and Gay Parenting: Securing Social and Educational Capital* (Palgrave, 2009), as well as edited collections *Classed Intersections: Spaces, Selves, Knowledges* (Ashgate, 2010), Theorizing *Intersectionality and Sexuality* (Palgrave, 2010) and *Sexualities: Reflections and Futures* (Palgrave, 2012). Yvette is currently conducting an ESRC project 'Making Space for Queer Identifying Religious Youth' (2011–13) and is PI on an ESRC seminar series 'Critical Diversities@ the Intersection: Policies, Perspectives, Practices (2012–2014). She regularly writes on the BSA's Sociology and the Cuts blog and on the Gender and Education Association (GEA) forum. She directs the MA in Gender and Sexuality at the Weeks Centre.

Acknowledgements

Thanks to all contributors for their efforts throughout. A version of Chapter 8 'That's not really my scene': Working-class lesbians in (and out of) place' was originally published in *Sexualities*, 11(5): 523–46 and thanks are given for allowing reproduction.

Queer Presences and Absences: An Introduction

Yvette Taylor and Michelle Addison

Queer Presences and Absences explores changes and continuations in lesbian, gay, bisexual, transgendered and queer lives, identities and spatial practices in the twenty-first century. Queer pasts, presents and possible futures are situated across local, national and international spaces including Brazil, the Czech Republic, Italy, Russia, the UK and the USA. Using a range of methods, including interviews, ethnographies, diary and mapping exercises, auto-biographical fictions and archival research, authors connect pasts, places and policies with contemporary times, linking individual and social presences (and absences) affectively and materially. As contributors variously show, different realities do not emerge from nowhere: histories are carried and contested in (re)making queer lives, identities and spaces on and off the (queer) academic page (Hines and Taylor, 2012). The shifting nature of these contestations is apparent in theorising sexuality beyond a 'queer niche' placement (Richardson et al., 2006; Taylor, Hines and Casey, 2010; Taylor, 2012a). Considerations of sexual lives, identities and experiences are now central to much work across a broad range of academic disciplines and to contemporary public interest and policymaking. So, what does it mean to chart the queerness of presence and absence at a time when Queer *is* appearing?

Arrivals and departures – or absences and presences – point to different locations inhabited and the various claims made upon places. Of importance is the concerns (and capitals) enacted in being, doing and denying 'queer'. Several authors reflect on whether we are 'queer enough' or 'post-queer', combining disciplinary engagements with professional and personal dis-identifications. As editors, we have been compelled to think through our own 'queer' engagements and appearances: in occupying institutional positions of employee, research assistant, Ph.D. student, mother, visiting academic, professor, we have felt variously present and absent. Educational and personal trajectories intersect with – and sometimes 'fail' – anticipated employment expectations (Addison, 2012; Taylor and Addison, 2011,

Taylor, 2012b). These queer labours persist and resist in being present, in feeling absent.

Issues of loss and gain, absence and presence, continuity and transformation are explored here through diverse empirical perspectives. An extensive body of sexualities research now exists but there is a persistent need to be attentive to inequalities across places and positions. In spite of burgeoning social sciences literature in sexualities studies, most existing empirical and theoretical work has focussed on Anglo-speaking or Western European countries (Binnie, 2004; Puar, 2007; Rahman, 2010; Kulpa and Mizieliñska, 2011). Research on postcolonial sexualities highlights deeply embedded ethnocentrism which fails to account of the lived experiences of queers from the global South (Santos, 2012). Similarly, comparatively little has been written about sexualities in post-communist Eastern Europe and the former Soviet Union (Stella, 2010). There is an enduring tendency to focus attention upon the lives of *certain* sexual subjects: Anglo-speaking, urban, white, middle-class, able-bodied lesbians and gay men in the global North. Such a focus moves certain lives from a previously 'othered' status to one of recognition and inclusion. Queer theory in particular has been accused of abstracting and effacing the materiality of queer presence even in changing contexts (Taylor, Hines and Casey, 2010; Browne, 2011).

With some noise generated by, for and about queers, quieter spaces and subjects of, for example, the home, family and neighbourhood, can be sidelined: so do these locations have a queer potential or presence? We now hear of emerging *homo*normativies as well as *hetero*normativies in the re-construction of sexual landscapes. Across different times and places, 'family' is used as a return to a 'straight and narrow' version of belonging, a political threat of valuelessness and as a claim for a familial difference in, say, 'friends as family' (Weeks, Heaphy and Donovan, 2001; Taylor, 2009). In all of these competing sentiments the 'queerness' of social life is ironed out, regulated and celebrated, suggesting more presences and absences than can be charted here alone. But the intention is not to finalise and capture LGBT lives as queer-in-themselves, now written into academic collections as well as into changing international social policies. Rather the hope is to reflect on the different places and publics of 'queer' as intersecting private and public realms, where varied claims for, on and through queer citizens are situated across time and place (Puar, 2001, 2002; Binnie, 2004; Taylor and Addison, 2011).

There are urgent debates on queer lives – and queer deaths – as the capacity of LGBT activisms and citizenship claims are seen as fulfilled and failed, as excessive and limited (Weeks, 2007; Hines and Taylor, 2012; Taylor, 2011). Sexuality shapes educational, leisure and legislative fields, where, for example, issues of queering the curriculum, the classroom, the city and the country are articulated as issues of regenerative potential or degenerative failure. Future lives and 'best interests' are urged *and* disputed where certain presences are *capacitated* and *incapacitated* in claiming (queer) citizen, consumer, caring and parental positions (Edelman, 2004; Vitellone, 2008; Taylor, 2009, 2011, 2012b).

Within forms of activism, some bodies/citizens/families/futures are already lost to queer terrain and some simply do not get imagined as having a presence. Shifting terrains of 'winning worlds' (Weeks, 2007) sit alongside critique of such 'worlds' as always *particular* and not easily mapped out linearly, constructed rather than completed in ongoing class, racial and gender inequalities (Hines, 2007; Taylor, 2007; McDermott, 2010; Stella, 2010). The queer subject as an intervention/alternative/challenge is resituated here not as *automatically* capacitated as subversive but as a subject worthy of careful consideration. In thinking through the where and when of queer arrivals, authors variously ask 'what has to be in place for 'arrivals' to be visible as academic efforts, political projects and everyday lives?'

There is deliberateness in this collection in the placing of 'early career' scholars from the UK, Australia, the USA, Italy, Brazil and the Czech Republic: this is necessary in order to attend to 'queer presences and absences' as perspectives that are often marginalised. It is important that these inclusions are not tokenistic or fixed in the insertion of the 'early' academic, as the researcher from 'elsewhere'. To posit an arrival or an inclusion can involve the uneasy assertion of abilities to chart histories and futures through a particular queer lens. Subjects, spaces and citizens can be measured as advanced, progressive or abject in claiming queerness here, there and everywhere.

Rather than capturing and evidencing queer terrains, chapters provide a range of varied vantage points on queer, casting a wide conceptual net upon this as a theoretical framing, practical engagement (or failure), methodological approach and lived experience: the differences between these chapters reveals the breadth of (dis)engagements with debates on queer, where, for example, 'absence' may be read as subversive and 'presence' positioned as mainstreamed. This collection examines the intersection of diverse identities and realities, across multiple geographical sites. In so doing it answers calls to diversify 'geographies of sexualities' (Browne, Lim. and Brown, 2007) beyond limited and geographically specific contexts by looking at sexualised lives and realities and the socio-spatial practices they make claims to. It asks, 'where do these articulations take us in expressing queer presence and absence across time and place?'

In Part I, 'Queer Movements, Marginalities and Mainstreams', contributors engage with multiple ways of being and the diverse realities of sexualised individuals, communities and global cultures. In 'Against the Dignity of Man: Sexology Constructing Deviance during "Normalisation" in Czechoslovakia', Kateřina Lišková explores the shaping of sexualities and gender during 1948–89. Through analysing sexological texts written and published during 'normalisation' (1969–89), Lišková attempts to situate *normalisation* as a historical era that is juxtaposed against a temporally located scientific understanding of *deviance*, drawing out tensions in the production of the sexual citizen in Czechoslovak sexological discourse. Interestingly, Lišková also looks at the situatedness of sexology as a discipline during this communist period; sexology was regarded as an obscure and niche specialty and as such was afforded little concern by the Communist Party, allowing it to develop. This time period in Czechoslovak history, Lišková argues, seen the propagation of new stories about the body, erotic and intimate life. This chapter brings together questions of discipline formation in an East European context and its connection to state (de)legitimation of 'sexual citizens', as legally codified bearers of 'pathological' sexualities; such an absence is seen to nonetheless afford a limited presence in the margins.

In 'Community at the Backstage: Gays and Lesbians in the Czech Republic', Kateřina Nedbálková focuses on the representation and positioning of gay and lesbian communities in the Czech Republic 1980–2010. Drawing on empirical data collected from diary entries and interviews, Nedbálková examines the forms in which stratification was embodied and spatialised by mapping the alternative geographies gay men in pre-1989 communist Czechoslovakia. Nedbálková moves to contemporary formations of lesbian community in the Czech Republic, focussing on mothers who actively dis-identify as lesbian, despite being in same-sex relationships. Instead of challenging embedded heterosexual normativities, some lesbian-parented families are assimilating in order to claim respectability and displace 'otherness' elsewhere. This new moment of 'homo-normalisation' contrasts with the earlier, 'alternative' periods of resistance and again we are forced to think through opportunities and constraints in resisting *and* complying. Claims to belonging vary across different historical periods in the same place and Nedbálková argues that regime changes in the Czech Republic have significantly impacted on the claiming of and taking up of space by lesbian and gay communities and how they become recognised and established in wider civic society.

In 'Lesbian lives and real existing socialism in late Soviet Russia', Francesca Stella focuses on a notable absence in both queer and Russian studies, namely that of women involved in same-sex relations in Soviet Russia (1917–89). This chapter is an important contribution to queer studies, widening efforts beyond white, Western, middle-class experiences. Stella draws on biographical interviews with women who talk about their same-sex attraction and the dangers, difficulties and tensions that they experienced during the Soviet period. In common with previous chapters, and echoing Lišková in particular, Stella argues that there has been a professionalised and expert editing and narrating of queer lived experiences. The hegemonic linking of queer subjectivities with science has drawn on clinical discourse to explain queer practices as 'perverse' and deserving of punitive regulation. Prison camps and clinical discourse sets the historical scene for Stella's research, where current expressions of same-sex desire are profoundly shaped by gendered inequalities.

In 'Identities and Citizenship under Construction: Historicising the "T" in LGBT Anti-Violence Politics in Brazil', Jan Simon Hutta and Carsten Balzer actively engage with growing calls to connect critically with sexual cultures and identities beyond the global North. Discussion is based on ethnographic research involving interviews with 100 Brazilian Trans People which highlights some uneasy alignments with LGBT activism. In this chapter we gain a complex understanding of Brazilian trans cultures and identities, situated alongside a (mis)positioning of these as 'new' identities, possibilities and queerness (Hines, 2007; Sanger, 2010). Hutta and Balzer argue that contemporary problems of transphobic violence need to be viewed in relation to contingent practices and identifications that have *historically* evolved in response to violence, oppression and discrimination, as ever-responsive to and fulfilling of ongoing practical enactments of citizenship. Hutta and Balzer shed new light on the lives of Brazilian trans people and simultaneously foreground political challenges in contemporary LGBT activism in the global South.

Moving on to Part II, 'Queer Mediations and (Dis)locations', the chapters centre around claims to 'private' and public spaces, mediated through consumption, possession and entitlement, alongside dispossession, poverty and un-entitlement. In 'Liminal Subjects, Marginal Spaces and Material Legacies: Older Gay Men, Home and Belonging', Andrew Gorman-Murray considers the positioning of older gay men in contemporary Sydney asking, 'what does it mean to feel 'at home' as a gay man living in a city with a vibrant gay culture?' Gorman-Murray begins to answer this by linking gerontology literatures with geographies of sexualities research, providing insights into the spatial presences and absences of older gay men. The place of home as a site of identity and wellbeing is considered against a straightforward assumption of home as refuge or closet. Instead 'home' is re-evaluated as having political potential. Homes carry possessions which themselves constitute records of domestic material cultures that convey the collective histories of gay pasts. Through these material legacies, older gay men become present to contemporary gay cultures, whereby domestic material cultures are placed as part of a constitutive, everyday and visible politics of identity.

Youngsook Choi's chapter, 'The Meaning of Home for Transgendered People', considers the constant negotiations with – and a battling against – a pervasive hetero-normative matrix, landscaping how 'home' is made and lived in. For Choi, the feeling of home can be far from comfortable, being instead a claustrophobic and closeted space where many facets of gendered identity are hidden to safeguard traditional binary roles of gender. For Choi's transgendered participants the home is often seen as a space of relentless and painful gender policing, which reinforce and reproduce heteronormative gender binarism. These public-domestics have devastating effects on personal wellbeing and feelings of belonging in one's own home, which travel beyond the confines of domestic spaces. Choi calls for a greater queering of gender conventions both in the home and in a wider social context.

Mark Casey takes up this call in considering the significance of resources needed to navigate certain landscapes in 'Belonging: Lesbians and Gay Men's Claims to Material Spaces'. Looking at transitions across a life course, Casey attends to (dis)connections between various geographical spaces across the urban city, as public space, and in the home, as a contested and claimed 'private' space. He highlights how claims are made to a normative sexual identity, seen as legitimate and 'safe', fulfilled in part through income and possession of local knowledges. Such capitals and connections facilitate navigation of city space, in surfing realms of respectability. By looking at classed and gendered strategies, Casey moves between 'home' and 'scene' space, troubling a neat location of sexual geographies. Clearly, a queer presence is not easily available and may be restricted to those who perform an increasingly sanitised, professionalised and (homo)normalised identity within the Western cityscape.

Following on, Yvette Taylor in '"That's Not Really My Scene": Working-Class Lesbians In (and Out of) Place' reflects on LGBT scene space in the UK as shaped by changing economies of place and personhood, which re-produce class as a central point of exclusion, even as inclusion is celebrated, visible and announced. The re-production of such space via city regeneration, as newly carved out and promoted terrains indicative of city sophistication (the 'pink triangle'; the 'merchant quarter'), mediates both place and people and often queerly so. The felt experience that such places were 'not really their scene' is suggestive of varied queer (working-class) absences within a limited queer-present. Working-class lesbians both participated in and felt excluded from scene spaces, often criticising them as 'pretentious' and 'unreal' for their superficiality and cosmopolitan gloss. This fractures the celebration of queer visibility and a commercial viability based on a regenerated 'coming-forward' of queer consumer-citizens in 'global gay' cities. In the aesthetic upgrading of LGBT scenes, a politicised perspective was often believed to have been sacrificed and jeopardised by gendered and classed based inhabitations which interviewees themselves were part of.

In 'Queering the Meaning of "Neighbourhood": Reinterpreting the Lesbian-Queer Experience of Park Slope, Brooklyn, 1983–2008', Jen Gieseking discusses a queering of conventional models of neighbourhoods. Drawing from inter-generational group interviews with lesbians and queer women who came out between 1983 and 2008, Gieseking takes the LGBT neighbourhood of Park Slope, New York City, as her fieldwork site. She deploys mapping exercises, coupled with archival research, to discuss and explore feelings of belonging in place. The prevalence of lesbian and queer culture is an important celebration of queer presences, but often this is contingent on the mobilisation of particular cultural and economic capitals, which are of course, not easily claimed by all. Gieseking suggests that the meaning and survival of Park Slope, as a predominantly affluent, lesbian-queer neighbourhood, is not grounded in spatial boundaries that would be identifiable on a physical map. Rather her findings indicate that Park Slope's longevity as an LGBT space is rooted in lives and cultures which breathe through people who are mobile, transient, politically active and often financially secure. The history of Park Slope then is reproduced by the lesbian and queer subjectivities able to comfortably inhabit visible and recognised places. Outside of this neighbourhood, in differently classed and more ethnically varied spaces, the story is not so celebratory: we get glimpses of other queer identities beyond this variously visible and hidden map.

In Part III, 'Queer Presences and Absences: Everyday and Everywhere?', the chapters reflect on the everyday aspects of queer lives, from 'hidden geographies' across changing institutional and parental spaces, which sometimes don't make it onto the map of the queer city/neighbourhood. Reflecting on recent studies of queer families and communities, Karina Luzia in 'Present Absences: Hidden Geographies of Lesbian Parenting' investigates the everyday experiences of women parenting in same-sex relationships, with children under five years old. This chapter responds to calls to fill in theoretical and empirical gaps in the work on queer lives, arguing that there is work to be done around particular mundane realities that continue to complicate the lives of 'privileged' queer families. Lesbian parent families who are often represented as comfortably professional, educated, employed, white, Western and middle-class identity nevertheless relate parenting experiences that do not fit neatly, if at all, into mainstream representations of same-sex parenting (see also Taylor, 2009). Making more complex the narration of advantage and disadvantage, Luzia highlights the role of unplanned pregnancies, where 'planned parenting' through reproductive technologies is placed as 'ideal, active and thoughtful' (Taylor, 2009). More broadly, this chapter reflects on accounts by queer families that, despite the real privileges of a '(homo)normative' status, respondents nonetheless struggle in a variety of ways and are thus not-so-comfortably 'present' or privileged. Mundane everyday practices and experiences reveal how queer family forms are lived, with tension and discomfort, as well as with privilege.

In '"Queer" and "Teacher" as Symbiosis? Exploring Absence and Presence in Discursive Space', Max Biddulph continues a focus on generational realities, where various presences are constituted as threatening or protective, with the rhetoric of the 'best interests' of children carving out a divisive educational landscape. These tensions are expressed through the 'fictionalised fact' of queer identifying, male teacher (Taylor, 2009; Inkle, 2010). Biddulph considers the daily tensions in navigating professional educational space, oscillating between the roles as a regulated educator and an ageing gay man. Excerpts from imagined, felt and recalled interactions with students convey the ambivalence of institutional occupation, colliding with care, protection, homophobia and gendered expectation. The themes of regulated masculinity and anticipated homophobia continue outside classroom conversations and into cruising spaces, characterised by markedly different sexual cultures. Yet Biddulph shows how educational and sexual communities re-compose complex webs of social relations in which individuals, such as educational professionals *and* students, are profoundly exposed and regulated on a daily basis. The imperative to change, adapt and hide aspects of one's identity in tightly policed spaces raises questions about the complexity of queer lives and queer space in considering absences and presences. Biddulph exposes such questions in weaving fictionalised facts into his auto-ethnographic account based on his experienced as an educator and on research interviews with male teachers.

In 'Organisation Studies: Not Nearly "Queer Enough"', Nick Rumens discusses the queering of organisation studies. Queer theory appears to have little relevance or value to managers and organisations where, in turn, not many queer theorists have shown interest in the study of organisations and contemporary work life. Importantly, Rumens explores the role of queer theory within university business schools and to its relevance in understanding worker identities. Importantly, this chapter illustrates how queer theory is a vital tool in problematising the hetero and homo-normativity of organisational life, making space for new possibilities and different futures for queer identifying individuals in neoliberalism times.

In 'Queerying the Public Administration in Italy: Local Challenges to a National Standstill', Chiara Bertone and Beatrice Gusmono examine the contradictions, possibilities and emergent struggles connected with representing a positive queer subject in the context of citizenship rights and a neoliberal political agenda. They draw upon empirical data and present five case studies from Italy. Focussing on local networks built by different administrations, they trouble the construction of the queer subject foregrounded in local LGBT policies. As the category 'LGBT' emerges in policy as part of an equality and diversity agenda, so too does the desire for the neoliberal active, invested and visible subject. In making this *particular* subject present and political, where does this leave those who do not engage in such articulations and activisms? In answering these questions, Bertone and Gusmono interrogate the politics of inclusion embedded within the development of new social policies and in doing so, draw attention to how the LGBT subject can be deployed as an all-encompassing diversity benchmark. In a time where Italian local authorities are in transition, there seems to be awkward moves between a politicised queer collective to a rhetoric of individualised 'urban safety', responsive to meet the needs of a victimised and marginal queer individual. By working closely and *listening* to the ideas and rich experiences cascading in LGBT communities and organisations, Bertone and Gusmono call for the development of social policy that works in dialogue with LGBT organisations and individuals, and acknowledges the complexity of representing, accounting and doing a queerer diversity politics.

This volume historicises legacies, gains and emergent struggles and how they map onto the past, present and the future. collectively, it questions what experiences and geographical locations are recognised as worthy for academic study, as well as who and what is legitimised as visible, worthwhile and possible. The strength of this collection is rooted in its international diversity and interdisciplinary reach, which is not to assert a capturing, encompassing vision of *everywhere*. All contributors critically engage with the multiplicity of sexualised lives and realities often in the peripheral margins of academic discourse. In doing so, this collection hopes to reflect on the different places and publics of 'queer' as intersecting private and public realms, where varied claims for, on and through the queer citizen are situated across time and place.

Bibliography

Addison, M. (2012) 'Feeling your way within and across classed spaces: The (re)making and (un)doing of identities of value within Higher Education in the UK' in Y. Taylor (ed.) *Educational diversity: The subject of difference and different subjects*. Basingstoke: Palgrave Macmillan, pp. 236–56.

Binnie, J. (2004) *The globalization of sexuality*. London: Sage.

Browne, K., Lim, J. and Brown, G. (2007) *Geographies of sexualities: Theory, practices and politics*. Farnham: Ashgate.

Edelman, L. (2004) *No future: Queer theory and the death drive*. Durham, NC: Duke University Press.

Hines, S. (2007) *TransForming gender: Transgender practices of identity and intimacy*. Bristol: Policy Press.

Hines, S. and Taylor, Y. (eds) (2012) *Sexualities: Reflections and futures*. Basingstoke: Palgrave Macmillan.

Inkle, K. (2010) 'Bent: Non-normative embodiment as lived intersectionality' in Y. Taylor, S. Hines and M. Casey (eds) *Theorizing intersectionality and sexuality*. Basingstoke: Palgrave Macmillan, pp. 255–73.

Kulpa, R. and Mizielińska, J. (eds) (2011) *De-Centring Western Sexualities. Central and Eastern European Perspectives*. Farnham: Ashgate.

McDermott, E. (2010) '"I just want to be totally true to myself": Class and the making of the sexual self' in Y. Taylor (ed.) *Classed intersections: Spaces, selves, knowledges*. Farnham: Ashgate, pp. 199–216.

Puar, J. (2001) 'Global circuits: Transnational sexualities and Trinidad', *SIGNS: Journal of Women in Culture and Society*, 26(4), Summer: 1039–66.

Puar, J. (2002) 'Circuits of queer mobility: Tourism, travel, and globalization', *GLQ: A Journal of Lesbian and Gay Studies*, 8(1–2), Winter: 103–39.

Puar, J. (2007) *Terrorist assemblages: Homonationalism in queer times*. Durham: Duke University Press.

Rahman, M. (2010) 'Queer as intersectionality: Theorising gay Muslim Identities', Special issue on Sexuality, *Sociology*, 44(5): 1–18.

Richardson, D., McLaughlin, J. and Casey, M. (2006) *Intersections between feminist and queer theory*. Basingstoke: Palgrave Macmillan.

Sanger, T. (2010) *Trans people's partnerships: Towards an ethics of intimacy*. Basingstoke: Palgrave Macmillan.

Santos, A. C. (2012) *Social Movements and Sexual Citizenship in Southern Europe*. Basingstoke: Palgrave.

Stella, F. (2010) 'The language of intersectionality: Researching "lesbian" identity in urban Russia' in Y. Taylor, S. Hines and M. Casey (eds) *Theorizing intersectionality and sexuality*. Basingstoke: Palgrave Macmillan, pp. 212–34.

Taylor, Y. (2007) *Working class lesbian life: Classed outsiders*. New York: Palgrave Macmillan.

Taylor, Y. (2009) *Lesbian and gay parenting: Securing social and educational capital*. Basingstoke: Palgrave Macmillan.

Taylor, Y. (2011) 'Queer presences and absences: Citizenship, community, diversity – or death', *Feminist Theory*, 12(3): 335–41.

Taylor, Y. (2012a) 'Queer encounters of sexuality and class: Navigating emotional landscapes of academia', *Emotion, Space and Society*, published on http://dx.doi. org/10.1016/j.emospa.2012.08.001, accessed on 30 September 2012.

Taylor, Y. (2012b) 'Future subjects? Education, activism and parental practices', *Graduate Journal of Social Science*, Special Issue of Futurities and Social Science 9(2): 65–85.

Taylor, Y. and Addison, M. (2011) 'Placing research: "City publics" and the "public sociologist', *Sociological Research Online*, 16(4) [not paginated].

Taylor, Y., Hines, S. and Casey, M. (eds) (2010) *Theorizing intersectionality and sexuality*. Basingstoke: Palgrave Macmillan.

Vitellone, N. (2008) *Object matters: Condoms, adolescence and time*. Manchester: Manchester University Press.

Weeks, J. (2007) *The world we have won*. New York: Routledge.

Weeks, J., Heaphy, B. and Donovan, C. (2001) *Same sex intimacies: Families of choice and other life experiments*. New York: Routledge.

Part I
Queer Movements, Marginalities and Mainstreams

1
'Against the Dignity of Man': Sexology Constructing Deviance During 'Normalisation' in Czechoslovakia

Kateřina Lišková

Introduction

Normalisation is the official name for the period following the failure of Czechoslovakia's Prague Spring of 1968, which had a tangible impact on the ways in which citizens were able to identify and express their sexuality. The 1960s were a time of changing political climate not only in Western Europe and the United States, but also in some Soviet 'satellites'. In Czechoslovakia, calls for reform and political emancipation went hand in hand with cultural awakening and artistic experimentation. The prevailing political effort was to 'humanise' socialism and steer it away from rigid post-Stalinism. This social upheaval and hopeful anticipation culminated in the Prague Spring; however, the Soviet tanks came on 21 August 1968 and quashed the hopes of millions of people wishing to live under 'socialism with human face' (Křen, 2005). A reconstructed political cadre came to power with a new slogan – 'the normalization of conditions' (Křen, 2005). Its aim was to eradicate any opposition and extinguish any spark of revolt. The regime oscillated on 'the border between authoritarianism and (exhausted) totalitarianism' (Křen, 2005: 874), requiring conformity from its citizens and their political obedience.

The re-established communist order enforced a regimentation of public life that encouraged retreat into private life. Contrary to the previous decades, active participation and belief in communism were no longer expected, it sufficed not to protest and to blend into the crowd. Citizens were to become uniform and deviation from the norm was not tolerated (Holý, 2001: 21). This social contract was 'based on (mutual) hypocrisy and lies' (Křen, 2005: 875). The emerging atmosphere of normalisation, characterised by stillness and hopelessness, and described as 'the Eastern iceberg, because life in those countries was ossified and motionless and as if frozen' (Ouředník, 2006: 68), lasted with only few changes until November 1989.

13

Various scholars have since analysed what was happening politically in this time period (Kaplan, 1993; Vykoukal, Litera and Tejchman, 2000; Holý, 2001; Křen, 2005); activities of protest have been well documented by historians, there are oral histories of key political figures, dissenters as well as those persecuted by the regime in their everyday lives.[1] Interestingly, what is absent are analyses of the scholarly disciplines, especially those pertaining to the everyday lives of people. Two decades after the regime change, we still lack accounts of how science functioned in communist society, particularly a science directly affecting one of the most intimate areas of people's lives – that of sexuality. This absence can be partially explained by the fact that communist power curtailed science and research with the exception of deploying it to serve the needs of the Party and the state.

Today it might seem that 'communist' scholarship would simplistically mirror the Party line, resulting in superficial and thus analytically uninteresting research. These days normalisation is customarily presented as 'the Eastern iceberg' – a period in which nothing changed, social life – including science – stood still and was limited to mere reproduction. I want to challenge this view. Unlike disciplines studying people and their relationships that were banned or severely restricted, such as sociology or philosophy, sexology enjoyed a special status under communism. Never banned by the Party, sexology continued to exist throughout the whole communist period. However, the object of its study invoked a certain marginalisation; since its beginnings in the nineteenth century, sexology was at risk of being ridiculed both for its 'lowly' object and exclusion from public understanding and scrutiny via its inaccessible language (Weeks, 1985). The combination of official tolerance and relative obscurity created a niche that granted sexology not only uninterrupted development but even space for the formation of a field relatively free of constraining oversight.

In this chapter, I will analyse sexological texts written and published during 'normalisation' (1969–89). My aim is to juxtapose *normalisation* as a historical era with the scientific understanding of its opposite, *deviance*. Analysing the discursive renderings of sexual deviance as articulated by the discipline of sexology, I will explore the ways in which sexual (and implicitly gender) normalcy was constructed. Also, I hope to capture tensions between the categories of the normal and deviant and its presence and absence in Czechoslovak sexological discourse.

I ask the following questions: What kinds of sexual practices and gender identities did Czechoslovak sexology diagnose as pathological or deviant,[2] and what forms were deemed normal? How stable were the categories of normal and deviant? What deviant sexualities were rendered visible by sexological accounts? What was the supposed origin and genealogy of deviance? What was the role of the family in the genealogy and definition of deviance? What attributes were ascribed to deviants beside non-normative sexual practices? How was gender understood and connected with deviance?

What was the extent of sexology's disciplining drive? And to what extent did it allow for agency, reflexivity and change? These issues have remained unexplored, to the detriment of understanding the specificities of discursive constructions of gender and sexuality in the Eastern European context. My chapter thus attempts to redress Western-oriented scholarship and suggest possible queering moments in sexology, which is usually understood as a disciplining force. However, the normalising drive of sexology seems to be strengthened by the fact that the discipline analysed here operated under an authoritative regime.

Framing sexology

Western sociological research into sexology has shown the great extent to which sexuality is a product of sexological discourse (Weeks, 1985, 2003; Hall, 1995; Bland, 1995; Bland and Doane, 1998a/b; Duggan, 2000; Oosterhuis, 2000; Irvine, 2005; Marcus, 2007; Bauer, 2009). This stream of thinking follows Foucault's analysis to explore the key concepts of disciplining, regulation and governmentality asserting itself via the proliferation of discourses on sex in the Western regime of *scientia sexualis* (Foucault, 1980) – which is in fact sexology and the neighbouring disciplines of forensic medicine and psychiatry.

My chapter is informed by a Foucauldian approach and by the work of Judith Butler. It is her focus on the axes of sex-gender-desire (Butler, 1990) that structures my analysis of sexological disquisitions written during the last two decades of state-socialist Czechoslovakia. Butler pointed out the quintessential connectedness of socially intelligible subjects, heterosexual men and women, with the heteronormative status quo based on the socially regulated family (i.e. Butler, 1997). Guided by her 'question of how normative sexuality is reproduced to the queer question of how that very normativity is confounded by the non-normative sexualities' (Butler, 1997: 272), I want to challenge the seamless equation between normal and heterosexual on the one hand, and non-normal and non-heterosexual on the other. I suggest that exploring deviant heterosexualities, as captured by the sexological pen, might bring new insights into the construction of sex-gender-desire and subvert an easy alliance between family-normal-heterosexual.

Sociologists and historians of sexuality tend to agree that sexology reasserted the modernist notion of difference defining people as varying in their anatomy, physiology and intellect (Oosterhuis, 2000) and linking this difference, as along with sexuality, to biological imperatives (Weeks, 2003). It was the Darwinian paradigm shift that 'encouraged the search for the animal in man, and found it in his sex' (Weeks, 2003: 43). The sexual and the biological were thus inextricably linked, finding their expression and codification in sexology. Contrary to this established understanding, I argue that the Czechoslovak sexology during normalisation identified social phenomena rather than biology as underpinning sexuality, especially in its deviant forms.

The discipline of sexology has constituted an unusually strong tradition in the Czechoslovak republic. The Sexological Institute has been an integral part of Charles University's Medical School in Prague. It was founded as the first university-based sexological department in the world in 1921.[3] Sexologist Raboch, however, claimed that the institute was founded after World War II 'as a manifestation of the progressiveness of our socialist society' (Raboch, 1977: 227). As much as the 'true' origins of the Sexological Institute are unclear, it seems that sexology during normalisation was reluctant to attribute its own genealogy to the democratic First Republic[4] but rather professed itself a component of a communist system. This nevertheless attests to the willingness of the official discourse to include sexology in its tradition. As a result of the East/West divide after World War II, Czechoslovak sexology was to a large degree cut off from discussions and developments occurring within Western sexology and related disciplines. Up until the present, however, there is no analysis of its operation.

Sexology in Czechoslovakia did not vanish. Compared to other disciplines studying people, it even flourished. In my analysis, I will focus on scholarly presentations from annual Sexological society conferences and on transcripts of sexological scholarly gatherings from the normalisation period (1969–89). The chief reason for choosing these kinds of materials instead of books was their semi-official character. In the Janus-faced society of normalisation, where nearly everything and everyone had their 'official' non-contradictory side as well as the 'unofficial' one, I believe more candid insights and open discussions can be found in materials meant only for internal purposes. I unearthed these documents in the archive of the Sexological Institute in Prague. They are not available in libraries – not intended for the public eye they were published in small mimeograph prints of about 500 copies, typed on typewriters. These edited volumes ('sborník') published from 1978–87 (analysing 'cases' and 'data' since the early 1970s) consist of short conference papers given by sexologists as well as psychiatrists, psychologists and forensic scientists. Especially invaluable were the literal transcripts of discussions among presenters included in some of the volumes. Virtually all the authoritative figures speaking (and writing) during this period here are sexologists and psychologists who are still influential today – publishing medical textbooks and often quoted in the popular media.

These volumes cover a wide range of topics from fertility disorders and their cure, teenage sexuality, sex education, contraception and abortion, venereal diseases, victimology in case of sexual offences, orgasm in women, sexual performance disorders in men, to minority sexualities such as homosexuality, transsexualism, sexuality of the mentally ill and sexual pathology and deviance. I will focus on those papers discussing deviance in all its forms.[5]

To make sense of the written sexological texts, I will use the methods of discourse analysis. The discursive approach works on the assumption that language does not mirror some outside-existing reality but that it productively constitutes reality; a methodological approach in line with the poststructuralist theories of Foucault and Butler. Discursive methods focus on structures of meaning – the forms, orders and patterns – present in a text, to reveal meaning-making processes and offer rich interpretations (Jaworski and Coupland, 1999).

Understanding deviation and the norm

Sexology was founded in the nineteenth century as a medico-forensic science,[6] and close cooperation between sexologists, forensic scientists, criminologists and psychiatrists was still visible at sexological conferences during the period analysed. Presenters often discussed deviance in terms of various sexual 'state of facts' that resulted in varying legal qualifications. Typically, sexual offences belonged to the category 'against the dignity of man' (Máthé, 1982: 39). However, other legal framings were used in communist law, ranging from infringement of personal liberty through disorderly conduct to disruption of socialist relations. Thus non-conforming sexual acts were deemed as aimed against individuals (and against oneself) sometimes the communist legal system identified them as directed against the whole of society.[7]

Sexologists during normalisation seemed to be aware of the social forces forming sexualities. The sexologist Kočiš in his paper 'Evaluating sexual delinquents' states that: 'The perception of sexual delinquency is in every society burdened by a disorganised web of fixed and flexible attitudes, values and norms. The perpetrator of such criminal acts arouses different attitudes in society compared to perpetrators of other offences. Every sexual delinquent is understood as a manifestation of deep alienation from social norms' (Kočiš, 1982: 15). Similarly the psychiatrists Molčan and Žucha claim 'such manifestations are deviant which psychogeneity is almost exclusive' (Molčan and Žucha, 1982: 395). These authors thus identify social, mostly changeable phenomena as constructing a sexually deviant act. Placing deviance fully in the social and mental realm contradicts the established sociological perception of sexology as deeply rooted in biology. Weeks in his analysis of sexology unequivocally claims that 'sexual theorists adopt[ed] a firmly essentialist idea of sexuality' (Weeks, 1985: 80) while 'their achievement has been to *naturalise* sexual patterns and identities' (ibid., italics in original).

The normative social fabric defining deviance is difficult to navigate, especially for the expert. As Kočiš explains: 'On a daily basis while creating expertise, we get into situations when we have to – not only for ourselves but also for other experts – time and again define basic psychopathological terms, examine the concepts of psychopathological, psychiatric and sexological theories. [...] Nowhere are the borders between health and illness, norm and abnormity so indistinct where the medical and especially social consequences of expert diagnosis so grave as in these cases' (Kočiš, 1982: 16). Sexological evaluation is perceived as fluid, constantly (re)defining its own apparatus. These shifting grounds, though, have serious consequences for the diagnosed person. Often, Kočiš says, 'the expertise reflects the ideology of the expert' (Kočiš, 1982: 20) and is filled with prejudices, moralising and pseudo-theories. Moreover, the situation is difficult for the expert himself as he encounters problems that question his competence and pose a high risk of misdiagnosis. Medical experts in court often discuss 'problems and conflicts that should be dealt with on an academic level, in a small circle of experts' (Kočiš, 1982: 16). Despite such diagnostic errors and even pseudoscience, the legitimacy of sexological experts was not being doubted. Despite terminological fluidity, misgivings were to be covered and debated out of the public view. Sexology thus posed the potential to disrupt the normalisation order by shifting its own apparatus, with repercussions for the legal apparatus. This possibility is, however, limited by the closeted operations characteristic of sexology as a discipline.

The expert scientific methods of sexology replaced the guilt and absolution of religion as the chief authority deciding the truth and being of subjects (Foucault, 1980). However, Czechoslovak sexologists realised that medical diagnosis to a large extent exonerated the deviant– it is not his fault, he is ill. Instead of imprisonment, protective treatment of deviants was often ordered in specialised psychiatric facilities. In many of these cases, sexologists deemed the treatment inefficient. It led some of them to re-introduce guilt (and the subsequent need for punishment) into sexological lexicon: 'Taking away the experience of guilt leads inevitably to relapse and closes the way to correction' (Hubálek and Zimanová, 1982). Moreover, exculpation brings about 'the feeling of victory over authority' (ibid.) which is uncalled for, especially in an authoritative society such as normalisation Czechoslovakia. Disease is faultless; breaching human dignity by sexual deviance was to be viewed as a moral issue that must not go unpunished. In another register, guilt is connected to confession. Foucault (1980) translates the Christian logic of guilt-confession-absolution to modern Western *scientia sexualis* where it functions as guilt-confession-truth. Where Foucault presupposes disciplination through the truth of sex, normalisation sexologists called for the ultimate disciplining through imprisonment. Sentenced sexual deviants whose conduct was deemed dangerous or simply objectionable were institutionalised in psychiatric facilities. The duration of their sojourn was unlimited and their treatment fully in the hands of psychiatrists (Hubálek and Zimanová, 1978) who were explicitly aware of their disciplining power: 'The situation resembles that of a pediatrician's waiting room: the patient is not expecting efficient help, someone more powerful in a white coat is about to dispose with his time and body' (Brichcín and Hubálek, 1987, unp).

However typically referring to particular diagnoses and legal 'state of facts', deviance is occasionally expanded to include non-normative lives such as those of unmarried lone men. Normalcy, abnormality and deviance merge and diverge in the following discussion (Sborník, 1985: 149–155) of a paper by the psychologist Tichá on the lives of men who live alone (Tichá, 1985):

Zvěřina:	We always a priori suspect these lone men of deviancy. Well, it might not be right to a priori suspect deviancy. But when a man is older that 30 and is alone, then we have to first exclude deviancy. [...] I don't know what the percentage is, it is probably complicated, but certainly there are deviants.
Finková:	But there are divorced, not only single men?
Zvěřina:	Yeah, I get that, well but a divorced man, he is a guy who has problems ...
[Bohumila] Tichá:	[...] I would like to react to the question if they are deviant or not. This is not – Věra is shaking her head at me and I am not sure exactly why?
[Věra] Capponi:	... they are weird.
Tichá:	I, they are weird. Well, they are, there is something else. I work in counseling, I don't work with pathology much. I don't mean that the people wouldn't be weird but I don't work with pathology in my own thinking. [...] And that they are not having intercourse, well it needs to be said there is a great level of identification with the mother's view that sometimes almost feels like these guys are homosexual. When I started doing the get-together dancing lessons I felt like there were 90% latent homosexuals and these are usually guys fixated on their mother. Věra, you are shaking your head again? [...]
Capponi:	... but I'm afraid, Bohumila, that there is some deviant focus in many of them – or more or less we should work therapeutically with them in the sense that loneliness is not a defect, that it's not a disease.

The statements of each discussant in this exchange shift from refusing abnormality (of lone men) to suggesting their deviance, or the other way around. None are unambiguous in their diagnosis. The sexologist Zvěřina starts by questioning the sexological practice of assuming deviance in lone men only to finish by surmising their deviance, even in those who had not been alone all their lives. The psychologist Tichá, who presented the paper on lone men, strives to defend the normalcy of such men only to then slip into admitting her presumption of these 'weird' men's homosexuality, thus equating homosexuality with deviance. The psychologist Capponi fervently counters Tichá's belief in her subjects' normalcy but ends equivocally by suggesting that they are not deviant or pathological. Ambiguity thus seems to be the defining feature of these sexologists' attempts at defining deviance. The ambiguity is even stronger in efforts to delineate the border between deviance and aggression.

Deviance, aggression and its significance

Sexually deviant behaviour equals neither sexual deviation nor psychological disorder: there are various ways in which sexologists approach deviation. Kočiš (1982: 18) muses:

> Considering the increasing dissonance between the experiential and reproductive character of sexuality, we can recognise as normal, from a biological as well as medical perspective, such sexual behavior which aims at the mutual satisfaction of consenting mature individuals of the opposite sex. Sexual conduct labeled as normal in this way has prevailed in all known cultures. [...] Sexual conduct labeled as normal has an advantage over other forms of sexual conduct for biological reasons – it contributes to procreation.

This definition starts out very open-minded, reflecting the non-reproductive character of most sexual encounters and stressing mutuality and satisfaction as key factors. The legitimacy of normalcy defined this way is confirmed by biology and medicine – interestingly, biology functions to define the normal while pathology is defined through the social, as shown previously. However, the inclusiveness of normalcy under this definition is breached by the invocation of heteronormativity. Kočiš contradicts his opening 'sex is for pleasure' by concluding that 'sex is for reproduction'.

Deviance is often conflated with aggression; aggression can be both deviant as well as non-deviant. Sexologists Zvěřina and Pondělíčková open their paper 'Diagnosis of sexual deviance in sexual aggressors' (Zvěřina and Pondělíčková, 1982) by stressing the importance of distinguishing between 'true sadists' and 'pathological sexual aggressors'. The authors analysed 264 forensic evaluations made throughout the 60s and 70s by 11 sexologists. The diagnosis of sexual deviance was made in 74 men; this number includes both 'sadists' as well as the 'pathologically aggressive' because 'both terms are used in insufficiently unified meanings and both essentially mean the same as the sexual motivation of an examined man is deviant, that is qualitatively changed' (ibid.). The authors thus effectively undermined their opening statement insisting on the necessity of distinction. Moreover, they found that the diagnosis of sexual deviance varies widely with various forensic scientists – it ranged from 15 to 77%. The authors, puzzled by the dispersion in expert evaluations, attribute this disparity to the lack of a unanimous definition of sexual deviance. The (il)logic comes full circle.

Sexologists present some characteristics distinguishing sexual deviants from non-deviant sexual aggressors. The authors mention their age first. Deviants were younger, mostly in their twenties. That would suggest that deviance disappears later in life. The authors state that 'the third decennium is the time when socio-sexual defectiveness peaks' (ibid.). Sexual deviance is thus not a lifelong defect but is 'somehow connected to the process of socio-sexual maturation in men' (ibid.).

The generic anticipation of violence in men combined with their perceived lustfulness offers itself as an explanation for both sexual excessiveness as well as sexual aggression. As such, sexual deviancy in young men is not disruptive to social order but rather quite affirmative of it in its re-enactment of the already expected (especially since it will pass with time). Normative gender characteristics of masculinity are diagnosed here as deviant. In Butlerian terms, male sex combined with pronounced masculine gender characteristics brings about, surprisingly, deviant desire. The only redeeming feature of this combination is its transitory character.

While age is the first characteristic of a deviant, according to sexologists there is another, possibly age-related: the deviant's partnership status. Deviants did not have a partner and were deemed more inept in their relationships with women. Having a partner is considered a sign of normalcy, connecting (normal) sexuality with (possible) procreation. And the proper scene for normal procreative sexuality is the family.

It's all in the family

In search of etiology, the deviant's family of origin is primarily identified as the culprit. Again, it was not biological characteristics that were examined but exclusively the social attributes of the deviant. According to Brichcín and Koubek (Brichcín and Koubek, 1982), aggressive non-deviants typically grew up in a family with an aggressive and alcoholic father, generally from the lower echelons of society. Deviants were dominated by a hostile mother as children while their father was weak or missing. Similarly Drdková identifies the 'incomplete and dysfunctional family' as the cause of deviance, namely 'exhibitionism, pedophilia and homosexuality' (Drdková, 1987). Parents of future deviants had somatic diseases; over 80% of them completed only primary school and 9% had been prosecuted and charged with criminal offences. Fathers often had a mental diagnosis and suffered from alcoholism while mothers were 'benevolent and inconsistent in their upbringing' or raised children alone (ibid.).

Deviance develops when the gendered and heteronormative assumptions of the two-parent family characterised by a feminine woman and masculine man are disrupted. Deviance can be triggered by a family where the sex and gender attributes of parents are mismatched. The unhealthiness of such conditions is underscored by illness and criminality, connoting the undesirable. Yet, as with aggressive deviants whose sex-gender characteristics were excessive/hyperbolised, sexual non-normalcy might develop from a mixture where parental sex-gender features line up and even are exaggerated.

'Normal' family of origin is believed to foreground the future normalcy of an individual. The psychologist Weiss and sexologists Hubálek and Zimanová (Weiss, Hubálek and Zimanová, 1985) stress the role of the father. Their sample of 100 patients hospitalised in the sexological ward of the psychiatric facility in Horní Beřkovice between 1976 and 1981 was divided into three groups: patients who grew up in a complete family, patients with an alcoholic father, and patients without a father. The second and third groups constituted 18 and 16% respectively, which the authors sum up as 44%. Despite the authors' claim, this number in fact indicates that more than half of their patients come out of families that conform to the norm of 'complete', without a problematic father figure. This inconsistency goes unnoticed and unresolved by the authors. They admit not being able to identify 'the specific pathogenic mechanism' (ibid.: 133) distinguishing between those who grow up healthy despite their 'maladapted' family of origin and those who do not. Zimanová, Weiss and Fuka point out the 'mutual interaction of both sexes in family life' (Zimanová, Weiss and Fuka, 1985: 137) as the main condition for 'healthy sexual development' since children tend to reproduce their parents' marriage model in their own future families.

This concept of mimetic heteronormativity functions solely to reproduce the norm discursively, as it explains neither why there are 'deviants' brought up in 'normal' families, nor why there are 'normal, healthy' individuals brought up in 'maladapted, dysfunctional' families. As in the previous study, the authors assert 'up to 50% of sexual delinquents come out of divorced or incomplete families' (Zimanová, Weiss and Fuka, 1985: 137). However high this proportion might seem, the chances of future sexual distortions still resemble those of a coin flip.

Moreover, the authors linked the level of family pathology to particular diagnoses. Exhibitionists, heterosexual paedophiles and sexual aggressors show the lowest levels of family pathology while 'a group of homosexual individuals comes out of this comparison as significantly worse in all observed factors' (Zimanová, Weiss and Fuka, 1985: 138).[8] Decidedly worst are homosexual paedophiles deviating both in sex as well as age of their preferred object. Whatever the criteria for their deviance acceptability scale, it betrays the authors' heteronormativity. Only in a heterosexually-centered universe can aggressors and paedophiles (as long as they are heterosexually oriented) score better than homosexuals (irrespective of their age preference). Family distortion, possibly alongside the axes of sex and gender, instigates deviant desire in children. The deeper the distortion, the further away it pushes one from the hetero-centre.

The psychologists Plaňava, Capponi and Weiss discussed the topics of nature vs. nurture and (dys)functional families. Plaňava challenged the 'linear and mono-causal model' (ibid.: 149) of the absent father model presented by Weiss, Hubálek and Zimanová. He deems it both well-known as well as insufficient, lacking any role for the mother and the individual himself in the explanation. Having disclaimed the mono-causal social model, he concludes his exposé by reasserting the biological one, asking 'to what extent the deep delinquency of the father transfers genetically' (ibid.: 150). Biology as referred to by Plaňava implies inevitability as did the social causation model presented originally by Weiss,[9] Hubálek and Zimanová. The psychologist Capponi also disagrees with the father-son social transfer claiming that dysfunctional and incomplete families are not synonymous. She claims 'divorced families adapted [to the new situation] are actually of the same quality as the harmonious families. And I am afraid it is so' (ibid.: 150). Although manifestly disproving the good-evil binary of complete/harmonious-incomplete/dysfunctional, Capponi tacitly reinforces the two-parent married family model by signifying the undivorced families as harmonious as well as by sighing at the end of her contribution. Capponi attributes this otherwise 'completely abandoned model [of father-son social transfer] as valid especially in very low and socially pathological groups in the population' (ibid.). Weiss accepts his colleagues' comments limiting the explanatory power of his original model: 'Essentially, it is proven they fail but we cannot say in what realm the failure will take place' (ibid.). Stereotypical genealogies of abnormality (linearity, biology, incomplete unhealthy family) are challenged and even abandoned in favour of unaccustomed ones (complex causation, social factors and new family models). Despite these innovations, the discursive constructions of sexologists reveal an undying effort to reach definitive answers, which would work with the force of gravity. Their cursory remarks hint at the impossibility of this task.

Sex, gender and normativity

In the psychiatric hospital Horní Beřkovice, there were 87 men diagnosed with sexual deviance who were institutionalised consecutively between 1975 and 1978. Among them, there were heterosexual paedophiles, exhibitionists, homosexual paedophiles, sexual aggressors, fetishists and '4% of atypical deviant behavior'. Hubálek and Zimanová describe their inmates: 'Their defective sexual behavior is usually the only obvious pathological element in their personality and thus out of all diagnostic groups of patients treated by psychiatry they externally come nearest the norm' (Hubálek and Zimanová, 1978). The line between normalcy and deviance is precarious and remains invisible outside the context of sexual conduct. Doctors thus support their diagnoses with observations unrelated to sex:

> Regarding their value system, they are as a group more conservative compared to their peers; they usually maintain the value system of their parents' generation. They come from disharmonic families, an absent father authority in their upbringing is prevalent. [...] Overall, the behavior of these patients is shifted towards infantility and femininity.
>
> (ibid.)

The sexual pathology of these incarcerated men manifests as gender deviance. Since desire does not offer itself for immediate inspection, it is gender as its stand-in that is examined by sexologists. Desire can be substituted for gender as long as it is expected that sex, gender and desire are linked in a binary fashion, allowing for only two distinct and obvious outcomes: feminine women and masculine men desiring the opposite sex. It is femininity that is indicted in the cases of these sexually deviant men: beginning with the predominant mother figure in their childhoods, who is implicitly blamed for their future failure, and represented by their own femininity in adulthood.

Similarly, deviants' gender deviance shapes their partner relationships (Weiss and Zimanová, 1984). The authors, to their surprise, found that the marriages of deviants are stronger and more permanent than those of the 'normal population' (ibid.: 156). Their original explanation was 'pathological equilibrium' of the couple or a 'social or other handicap of the wife' (ibid.). Next the authors decided to study the wives more thoroughly and applied a 'role in/consistency test' based on the 'traditional stereotype of a woman and man' (Weiss and Zimanová, 1984: 157). This test works on the assumption of binary oppositions between men and women and the necessity of consistency of perceived levels with the self-identified ones of masculinity and femininity in the couple. The authors identified high consistency in masculine and feminine roles in their patients' relationships; women scored even higher than the population average. However, women scored lower in their femininity index compared to the general female population while men scored higher in the masculinity index. The authors ascribe these findings to their patients' deviance: 'Due to their defect, they perceive women with all the feminine attributes as endangering and anxiety inducing because of their possible failure, they prefer partners whose behavior does not show such traits. High levels of perceived masculinity of men in couples could be explained through the mechanism of hypercompensation' (Weiss and Zimanová, 1984: 158).

This sexological explanation circumscribed a circular arc from (sexual) pathology through a hint at (sex-gender) discrepancy to (gender) pathology. Diagnosed sexual deviants and even their close ones are inadvertently labelled as deviant in other social characteristics. While men deviate in their sexuality (which endangers their masculinity), women deviate in their gender (which strengthens their relationships). Male sexual non-conformity has its counterpart in female gender non-conformity. This sex-gender-desire mismatch has the potential to disrupt the sexological status quo of binary embodied existence. This inconsistency is even more intriguing for the couple cohesiveness it brings about, because it is precisely the heterosexual coupled norm that is the archetype and legitimisation of the sex-gender-desire binarism. However, if, a queer gender-sexuality mix works better for the stability of partnerships than normal settings do for the 'normal' population, then it questions the presupposed heteronormative foundations and furthermore contests the family as a site where these foundations are seamlessly lived and reproduced.

Normative expectations included bodily attributes. Some deviants were treated with synthetic female hormones after preventive roentgen radiation, which was supposed to prevent 'undesirable gynecomasty'. Feminisation of a male body was deemed deeply undesirable because the main aim of the treatment was 'the adaptation to heterosexual non-deviant activity' (Hubálek and Zimanová, 1978), which implicitly presupposes two opposite genders with appropriate bodies. Pharmacotherapy for others consisted in the administration of lithium to suppress sexual potency (Bártová et al., 1984). Deviant men were treated through attenuation of their sexuality while their gendered bodily characteristics were upheld. Behavioural therapy was recommended in cases where deviation coincided with conventional heterosexuality. Treatment thus lay in punishing deviant sexual practice and curing by 'heterosexual performance-related incentives' (Molčan and Žucha, 1982: 397). This heteronormative frame propelled the re-construction of binary gender characteristics together with normal heterosexual practices. Such sexological limitations on sexual practice are worth noting. Heterosexuality in itself is not enough: it is the particular practices deemed normal that make one a healthy individual.

The subversion of sexual norms, however, is not accompanied by general non-conformity among deviants. These sexologists describe their patients as conservative and, interestingly, point out characteristics that were normally highly valued by communist society. Patients are characterised as diligent workers with positive evaluation of their 'civic-work duties'[10] who took on various posts in communist societal organisations. The authors label these activities as 'hypercompensation', 'cover-up' and 'mimicry' (Hubálek and Zimanová, 1978). A question remains whether these sexologists dismissed their patients' characteristics because no deviant could pride himself on such qualities (and be this well integrated into society) or whether sexologists knew only a deviant would publicly present himself with attributes normal people did not aspire to (because to be integrated into society, to its public realm, was looked down on and ridiculed during normalisation).

Whatever the reason, these authors structured their therapy in an unconscious consonance with communist practices: 'Individual communication
with a patient is reduced to a minimum. All decision-making has to pass
through the community. The senior doctor has the right to veto' (ibid.). As
in the rest of society, rules seemed to be democratic and decision-making
processes collectively shared. And as in the rest of society, there was a strong
limiting factor to it.

Conclusion

Was sexology under normalisation normative? There is no unequivocal
answer. It certainly resorted to heteronormativity as the gold standard for
all sexuality and gender identification, extended deviance from non-normative sexualities to non-normative lives, conflated deviance with violence
and connected it with crime. On the other hand, the structure of the
texts reveals ambiguities, occasionally even tendencies towards openness
and inclusiveness of non-normal sexual conduct and its bearers. At times,
sexologists seem to be aware of the instability of diagnoses and their consequences, particularly for those who could end up behind bars as a result
of diagnosis. Sexologists insisted on clear distinctions, while providing con-
founding definitions. As a discipline, sexology approached reflexivity, yet
refused to unveil its discussions to the public eye.

Sexology surely provided valuable expert knowledge that the 'normalised'
state could use. It also strengthened the secular character of the communist
state. The discipline of sexology brought about emancipatory discourses of
breaking taboos and affirming pleasure, which stand as a powerful antidote
to religious doctrines that have restricted sexuality for centuries. But again,
the situation is equivocal: sexology has propagated enlightenment against
the obscurantist approaches of the church while also effectively appropri-
ating its discourse of guilt, discipline and redemption as I have shown in
the case of normalisation sexology. However, while mainstream Christian
doctrines preach procreative sex and abstinence, sexology prides itself on
exploring and understanding various practices of bodily pleasures. Often
retreating to clandestine operations, which put its godly powers out of
reach for ordinary mortals (where nineteenth-century sexology used Latin,
normalisation sexology publishes volumes 'for medical personnel only'),
sexological discourse has been contested by sexologists themselves; there is
everything but general unanimity among sex doctors.

Sexual deviance, mostly unavailable for direct observation, was for the
purposes of diagnosis implicitly substituted by gender deviance. Deviant
men exhibited feminine gender traits and if they had wives these tended
to be less feminine compared to the norm. Queer gaps are thus revealed
in a normal sex-gender-desire line-up. Moreover, deviance can break out
not only in situations where the set sex-gender-desire is disrupted but also,

and not infrequently, where these axes are coherent according to a classical heterosexual matrix.

There are certain silences in the texts analysed; the desire of women is not discussed. This oversight is not entirely negative, given that what is being scrutinised is deviant desire. Women, traditionally perceived as desire-less, might have escaped the sexological gaze as desiring subjects. They, however, were present discursively through the notion of femininity. It is femininity in men and/or the femininity of their mothers that is blamed for their deviancy.

Therapy was structured along the lines of sex-gender-desire while upholding proper bodily characteristics (in the case of hormonal treatment) and encouraging appropriate gender attributes (in the case of behavioural therapy). In terms of desire, the whole notion of deviance points to a further narrowing down of the hetero-norm: having sex with a partner of the opposite sex is not enough; what matters are (normal) practices. Deviant heterosexualities trouble the 'normal' that heterosexuality seems to signify.

The almost exclusive reliance on social factors while attempting to explain the origin and genealogy of sexual deviance is striking. In the accounts analysed here, sexologists identify non-normative family arrangements as the generator of future sexual deviance in children. Similarly, deviance manifests itself by living out of the coupled norm. The regime that initially strived to dissolve the nuclear family is, in its normalisation phase, back to normal: only the conventional two-parent family begets (sexual) normalcy. However, sexological accounts normatively advocating the normal family reveal that the so-called normal family does not guarantee (sexual) normalcy nor explain non-normalcy. It serves solely to reproduce itself as the golden rule against which anyone can be measured at any time to account for their deviancy. Contrary to sexological (and often sociological) claims, family does not provide a venue for the inescapable reproduction of strictly heteronormative sex, gender and desire. This understanding has the potential to queer the equation of family-normal-heterosexual.

Sociology usually points to sexology's naturalising and biologising drive when accounting for sexual conduct and its motives. The essentialising drive in sexology, identified by Weeks (1980), is characteristic of the discipline as practiced during normalisation in Czechoslovakia. But there, the ultimate cause shaping (deviant) sexuality was not biology. Natural causation connotes rigidity, unchangeability and in the case of deviance an air of degeneration. Social genealogy, on the other hand, promises to inject openness and malleability into our understanding of sexual traits. In the materials analysed, however, social explanations functioned as rigid schemata possibly reflecting the stale climate of the normalisation 'iceberg'.

The power of definition in sexological (and subsequently juridical) hands is paramount. But vocabulary, evaluation and diagnoses, as I have shown, are not fixed. Sexology constantly redefines its own apparatus. Sexological discourse is up for grabs, possibly by those who are subjectified by it. The reclaiming might start as the 'silent ignoring and disguised mocking' typical of life during normalisation (Křen, 2005: 875) and then continue in its subversion and our emancipation.

Notes

This research was supported by a Marie Curie International Outgoing Fellowship within the 7th European Community Framework Programme.

1. The 'Memory of the nation' project gathers and analyses the oral histories of survivors of both totalitarian regimes, Nazism and communism, available at http://www.pametnaroda.cz/?locale=en_GB, accessed on 1 October 2012.
2. Throughout this chapter, I will use the term 'deviant' and 'deviance' as used in analysed materials. It is not only for a lack of another umbrella term for all non-normative sexualities and subjectivities or just for the sake of authenticity; I decided to keep the term 'deviant' for its striking contrast with the term 'normality' that pertains to the analysed period. 'Deviance' seems to be the term that replaced 'perversion' typical of the nineteenth and early twentieth-century sexological lexicon.
3. The year 1921 as the founding one is indicated at the Sexological Institute contemporary website http://www.sexuologickaspolecnost.cz/historie, accessed on 1 October 2012.
4. The First Republic is the period of 1918–38, marking the establishment of independent Czechoslovakia on the ruins of the Austro-Hungarian Empire and its end with the Munich Treaty.
5. Thus this chapter is not primarily focused on same-sex desire because it was not at large regarded as disease or deviance. Homosexuality only sometimes resurfaces into disquisitions on deviance and only then I will discuss it. As I will show, sexology is ridden with ambiguity, which applies to homosexuality as well.
6. Krafft-Ebing's *Psychopathia Sexualis*, published in 1886 and generally perceived as sexology's founding text, carried the subtitle *A Clinical-Forensic Study*.
7. Similarly variable was the medical diagnosis of sexual deviance. A man who intruded into the bedrooms of older women at night to grope their breasts was diagnosed by different sexologists as a feeble-minded sadist, psychopathic pythiatic personality, alcoholic sadist or constant atypical fetishist-frotteur acting against adult women (Zimanová and Hubálek, 1982: 35). The same court consecutively adjudicated the same criminal activity of this man on varying legal grounds, using the whole spectrum of legal definitions mentioned.
8. Again, in their account, the authors refute 'the legitimacy of some categorical claims of organically conditioned etiology in the origin of sexual deviations' (Zimanová, Weiss and Fuka, 1985: 139). Biological causation is rejected and social explanation accepted as the most influential factor. The social, usually understood as fluid and amenable to change, is here treated as a rigid cause-effect entity.
9. Ironically, Weiss, still active and well-known today, has switched sides. These days he is a self-proclaimed biological essentialist. The 'postmodernist relativization of health and illness, function and dysfunction that we can witness in opinions based on social constructivist disputing of scientific facts [...] is essentially ideological and antiscientist' (Weiss, 2002: 17).

10. Such evaluations were regularly made for each individual since the beginning of their schooling. Schools, workplaces and even street committees kept records concerning one's involvement with various communist institutions and one's attitudes towards the 'communist system of government'.

Bibliography

Bártová, D., Burešová, A., Hajnová, R. and Tichý, P. (1984) 'Farmakoterapeutické ovlivňování deviantního sexuálního chování. Aspekt klinický a spermiologický' in *Sborník 1984*. Ústí nad Labem: Česká sexuologická společnost a KÚNZ, pp. 146–50.

Bauer, H. (2009) *English literary sexology: Translations of inversion, 1860–1930*. Basingstoke and New York: Palgrave Macmillan.

Bland, L. (1995) *Banishing the beast: English feminism and sexual morality, 1885–1914*. London and New York: Penguin.

Bland, L. and Doane, L. (1998a) *Sexology in culture: Labelling bodies and desires*. Chicago: The University of Chicago Press.

Bland, L. and Doane, L. (1998b) *Sexology uncensored: The documents of sexual science*. Chicago: The University of Chicago Press.

Brichcín S. and Koubek, K. (1982) 'Projekce některých rysů osobnosti sexuálních agresorů v kresbě lidské postavy' in A. Stančák (ed.) *Sexualita ženy*. Bratislava: KÚNZ a Slovenská sexuologická spoločnost', pp. 135–43.

Brichcín S. and Hubálek, S. (1987) 'Psychoterapie parafilních osob' in *Sborník 1987*. Ústí nad Labem: Press Erwa, unpaginated.

Butler, J. (1990) *Gender trouble: Feminism and the subversion of identity*. New York: Routledge.

Butler, J. (1 December 1997) 'Merely Cultural'. *Social Text*, 53, 265–77.

Drdková, S. (1987) 'Význam rodinného a výchovného prostředí na tvorbu sociálně-patologických faktorů sexuálních deviantů' in *Sborník 1987*. Ústí nad Labem: Press Erwa, unpaginated.

Duggan, L. (2000) *Sapphic slashers: Sex, violence, and American modernity*. Durham: Duke University Press.

Foucault, M. (1980) *The history of sexuality, Vol. I*. New York: Vintage Books.

Hall, L. A. (1995) *The facts of life: The creation of sexual knowledge in Britain, 1650–1950*. New Haven: Yale University Press.

Holý, L. (2001) *Malý český člověk a velký český národ: národní identita a postkomunistická transformace společnosti*. Praha: Sociologické nakladatelství.

Hubálek, S. and Zimanová, J. (1978) 'Psychoterapie sexuálních deviantů' in *Sborník 1978*. Ostrava: KÚNZ, unpaginated.

Hubálek, S. and Zimanová, J. (1982) 'Otázky viny po sexuálním deliktu' in *Sborník 1982b*. Ostrava: KÚNZ, unpaginated.

Irvine, J. M. (2005) *Disorders of desire: Sexuality and gender in modern American sexology*. Philadelphia: Temple University Press.

Jaworski, A. and Coupland, N. (1999) *The discourse reader*. London: Routledge.

Kaplan, K. (1993) *Sociální souvislosti krizí komunistického režimu v letech 1953–1957 a 1968–1975*. Praha: Ústav pro soudobé dějiny AV ČR.

Kočiš, L. (1982) 'Posudzovanie sexuálnych delikventov' in A. Stančák (ed.) *Sexualita ženy*. Bratislava: KÚNZ a Slovenská sexuologická spoločnost', pp. 15–23.

Křen, J. (2005) *Dvě století střední Evropy*. Praha: Argo.

Marcus, S. (2007) *Between women: Friendship, desire, and marriage in Victorian England*. Princeton: Princeton University Press.

Máthé, R. (1982) 'Psychiatricko-psychologická spolupráca pri znaleckom posud-zovaní sexuálnych delikventov' A. Stančák (ed.) *Sexualita ženy*. Bratislava: KÚNZ a Slovenská sexuologická spoločnost', pp. 39–51.

Molčan J. and Žucha, I. (1982) 'K behaviorálnej terapii sexuálnych deviácií' in A. Stančák (ed.) *Sexualita ženy*. Bratislava: KÚNZ a Slovenská sexuologická spoločnost', pp. 395–9.

Oosterhuis, H. (2000) *Stepchildren of nature: Krafft-Ebing, psychiatry, and the making of sexual identity*. Chicago: University of Chicago Press.

Ouředník, P. (2006) *Europeana. Stručné dějiny dvacátého věku*. Praha – Litomyšl: Paseka.

Raboch, J. (1977) *Očima sexuologa*. Praha: Avicenum.

Sborník (1978) *Sborník prací přednesených na celostátní vědecko-pracovní schůzi České sexuologické společnosti červen 1978 v Opavě*. Ostrava: KÚNZ.

Sborník (1982a) *Sborník prací přednesených na celostátní vědecko-pracovní schůzi České sexuologické společnosti 18.–19. února 1984 v Ústí nad Labem*. Ústí nad Labem: KÚNZ.

Sborník (1982b) *Sborník prací přednesených na vědecko-pracovní schůzi České sexuologické společnosti s mezinárodní účastí, červen 1982 v Opavě*. Ostrava: KÚNZ.

Sborník (1985) *Současné problémy výchovy k partnerským vztahům. Metodický materiál. Sborník z II. konference v Uherském Hradišti 6.–8.3.1985*. Brno – Olomouc: Krajská manželská a předmanželská poradna.

Sborník (1987) *Sborník prací přednesených na celostátní vědecko-pracovní schůzi České sexuologické společnosti 12.–13. března 1987 v Ústí nad Labem*. Ústí nad Labem: Press Erwa.

Stančák, A. (ed.) (1982). *Sexualita ženy – Forenzné aspekty sexuality. Zborník referátov prednesených na V. a VI. Košických sexuologických dňoch*. Bratislava: KÚNZ a Slovenská sexuologická spoločnost'.

Tichá, B. (1985) 'Sexuální život osamělých mužů' in *Sborník 1985*. Brno – Olomouc: Krajská manželská a předmanželská poradna, pp. 141–4.

Vykoukal, J. P., Litera, B., and Tejchman, M. (2000) *Východ: Vznik, vývoj a rozpad sovětského bloku, 1944–1989*. Praha: Libri.

Weeks, J. (1985) *Sexuality and its discontent: Meanings, myths, & modern sexualities*. London and Boston: Routledge and Kegan Paul.

Weeks, J. (2003) *Sexuality*. London: Routledge.

Weiss, P. (2002) *Sexuální deviace. Klasifikace, diagnostika, léčba*. Praha: Portál.

Weiss, P., Hubálek, S. and Zimanová, J. (1985) 'Role otce ve výchově ve vztahu k sociální adaptaci sexuálních delikventů' in *Sborník 1985*. Brno – Olomouc: Krajská manželská a předmanželská poradna, pp. 132–4.

Weiss P. and Zimanová, J. (1984) 'Konzistence sexuálních rolí v partnerských vztazích sexuálních delikventů' in *Sborník 1984*. Ústí nad Labem: Česká sexuologická společnost a KÚNZ, pp. 156–9.

Zimanová, J. and Hubálek, S. (1982) 'Neobvyklý případ – kazuistické sdělení' in *Sborník 1982a*. Ústí nad Labem: KÚNZ, pp. 32–5.

Zimanová, J., Weiss, P. and Fuka, J. (1985) 'Rodinné prostředí v dětství v sexuálních delikventech' in *Sborník 1985*. Brno – Olomouc: Krajská manželská a předmanželská poradna, pp. 137–40.

Zvěřina, J. and Pondělíčková, J. (1982) 'Diagnóza sexuální deviace u sexuálních agresorů' in *Sborník 1982b*. Ostrava: KÚNZ, unpaginated.

2
Community at the Backstage: Gays and Lesbians in the Czech Republic

Kateřina Nedbálková

The following chapter focuses on the gay and lesbian community in the Czech Republic between 1980 and 2010 (including the time before the regime shift in 1989). This time frame plays a key role in regards to the main analytical frame of the text, which is the inspection of the positioning of the gay and lesbian community[1] within wider social structures. I attempt to interpret the limits and possibilities created through the intersections of class, gender, ethnicity and sexuality in the context of the LGBT community. The time period with which my research is situated witnessed a shift from a society forcibly levelled off in terms of wages and property to a society which, as a result of liberalisation and market privatisation, transforms itself into a society setting up and reproducing a multi-layered range of social inequalities (Večerník, 2010). Regime change also meant the gradual establishment of civic society institutions which affected conditions for the re/establishment and re/organising of gay and lesbian space and community.

In this chapter I focus my analysis on two seemingly utterly disparate contexts: it begins with the description and interpretation of gay and lesbian communities during the 1980s in the Czech Republic and ends with the first decade of this century. In its first part, the text focuses on the meaning and role of the gay and lesbian community mainly for gay men in the totalitarian Czechoslovakia. The second part of the text concerns itself with the place of the lesbian community in the lives of contemporary lesbian families. I also turn attention to the diary entries of a public toilet employee; these narratives point to the axes and contours of the stratification of the Czech society after 1989, and, at the same time, enables the introduction of some of the key analytical concepts with the aid of which I interpret the excerpts of data. I focus on different types of actors in a different time period and a specific context. I hold that the value of interpretation of the comparison of gay men in totalitarian Czechoslovakia with contemporary lesbian mothers in the Czech Republic lies in the possibility to examine questions pertaining to the social structuring, legality/illegality, formal and informal organising, private and public expressions, and power execution of these communities of gays and lesbian. While these two subgroups can be perceived either as entirely distinct or as a unified community I attempt to rank in this regard with texts offering 'critical treatment of the differences between sexual dissidents (Binnie and Valentine, 1999). I focus on the connections and disconnections between these groups as these dis/connections appear and disappear in various settings and contexts.

To contextualise the LGBT community in the Czech Republic, I begin with a short overview of the attitudes toward homosexuality and legal rights of gays and lesbians in the country. Long-term research has shown that, in comparison with other Central and Eastern European countries, the Czech Republic has been relatively tolerant of same-sex marriages and same-sex child adoption.[2] In the Czech Republic, public perceptions of homosexuality have been primarily associated with medicine and sexology. During the socialist regime (as early as 1961), homosexuality ceased to be punishable by law, yet homosexuals continued to be targeted by the state secret police, routinely blackmailed and persecuted. In 1989, with the shift in regimes, the situation changed, and the first official institutions and organisations for gays and lesbians were established. In 2006, the Czech Republic was the second post-Communist country to legalise registered partnership for same-sex couples.

Methods

I combine data from various settings (fragmented gay and lesbian community sites under communism, public toilets and lesbians in domestic and family settings). I have conducted 12 interviews with gay men and two interviews with lesbians around the theme of the presence or absence of the gay and lesbian community in the Communist era. I have used the diaries of Ms Marta, a public toilet employee, from between the years 1991– 2005, and I draw on my interviews with 17 lesbian families (with 34 women), conducted as part of my post doctoral research, from the years 2004–9. In terms of social position the respondents can be (with the exception of Ms Marta) classified as middle class and white.[3]

Interview respondents for the topic of g/l community under communism were selected based on their age. To make the interviews relevant for the chosen topic, I was looking for people over 45 years of age. Thanks to my 15 years of experience of the Brno[4] gay and lesbian community, I was able to contact the potential respondents either directly, or through a contact person, who would enable me to access circles of people I would not have been able to reach on my own. The lesbian family interviews have been conducted on the basis of a snowball effect of contacts. The first lesbian couple was one participating in a public debate on parenthood, and through them I was able to contact two other families, until I reached the final number of 17. The fact that I conducted only two interviews with lesbians for the 'community in communist regime' research is not merely a descriptive detail of my research, but points to a more general fact of lesbian invisibility in public places (Taylor, 2008; Valentine, 2000). I would like to use this potential 'deficit' , then, as a chance to point analytically to the status of the gay and lesbian community within the more general gender and class structures of society.

Underground community

The gay and lesbian community has been approached from many different perspectives and paradigms in social sciences. If we understand the community as places where gays and lesbians spend time or meet,[5] the pre-1989 community can be found primarily in the following locations, which, according to one of the respondents, divide into two basic groups:

> Gay life happened on two basic levels, the first was one that I particularly love reminiscing on and will never forget, these home gatherings. There were groups of people who would agree to get together on Saturdays for partying: dancing, drinking, chatting. It is obvious, or evident, that the bonds between people were a whole lot tighter then than they are today. There are so many gathering places these days. And the second level of community formation was the underground level (and I have experienced that type of community even abroad, in England and Australia), those cruising areas where people would make fleeting encounters. The public toilets, I suppose, were among them, but there, one did not simply act on sexual urges or the promise of anonymous sex, of tea-rooming, cottaging, as they say, which, of course, was made possible there and widely happened, too, but one also used it as an opportunity to meet someone like oneself. Every boy growing aware of his homosexuality would suddenly see these pornographic and vulgar inscriptions there at the public toilets. There had been one like that there, one of them had peed here. Gradually, it would dawn on the boy.
>
> Václav

The preceding quote points to the interconnection of two seemingly incompatible platforms of the community: on the one hand, private parties organised in people's apartments, and on the other hand, public spaces enabling anonymous sex (public toilets, saunas, public swimming pools.) Public toilets[6] were an important part of the gay subculture in the Czech Republic before 1989, at a time when officially, no gay and lesbian bars, clubs or organisations existed, a time when the State Security kept a record of homosexuals in order to blackmail them. Public toilets – and other such places, like saunas, swimming pool showers, parks and railway stations – functioned partly as cruising areas, but also presented one of the few opportunities (for men) to meet a person of the same sexual orientation.

This second type of gay community environment was particularly prone to the enactment of homosexuality, as a place where it was possible to gain visibility as a gay person in the eye of the other, where it was possible to make oneself discernible, decodable, intelligible and accessible as a gay male.

> At the urinal, you show each other who is able to do what [laughter] and then you either nod to the other that you will go someplace together or you do not. You could enter the stall then, or we would go to the university library or other public toilets. Something could happen right at the urinal, too. That was attractive to some people because someone could watch, or there was a potential that a new person would arrive.
>
> Marek

It was a place that provided the chances of sex without further commitment, but also one of the very few opportunities for meeting others and getting initiated into smaller private groups and networks.

> In front of the Brno main railway station there was a huge meeting place for homosexuals who would stroll the area day and night. One person introduces you to another. In this way, I got hooked with a group of boys. It took an almost anti-state form, as I learned to listen to the 80s hippies who were forbidden, it was illegal to play them out loud. The initiation is always crucial, these men taught us about the culture and the music of the 60s, this stuff that is again so popular now, they taught us how gay people could live in the socialist structures, how one could keep their own homosexuality a secret, how to put ads in the papers [looking for a boy for a to go vacationing].
>
> Michal

Through newly made connections, a person was gaining cultural capital in the form of cultural taste, be it in music, film or literature, and was learning highly practical skills, such as how to avoid mandatory military service, or how to put ads in the papers at a time when openly same-sex ads were forbidden. Here I am referring to the theory of social structuring developed by Pierre Bourdieu (1998). Social actors are differentiated (and differentiate themselves) based on their share in the four basic types of capital: the cultural, the social, the economic and the symbolic. The amount of capital is reflected in the habitus, internalised form of the class condition, a lifestyle, taking place in various social fields such as education, culture, consumption, the market, the family, politics, etc. (Bourdieu, 1998).

The selected interview excerpt is quite telling in its monogendered quality. Homosexuals, in Michal's narrative, are the synonym for gay men. While it can be asserted that gay men and lesbians were invisible in the communist Czechoslovakia, (lesbian) women were disadvantaged doubly: they were not granted even the handful of unofficial spaces that were so readily colonised by (gay) men. I find rather surprising the non-normative view of gender that some of the male respondents expressed in their accounts and memories of the gay and lesbian community under the totalitarian regime.

> I think that the demand for masculinity is a trend ... a fairly recent one. Replay your complete porn collection and see who stars in those films and videos, the way those people look. In the recent years there is a clear preference for more masculine types, even in porn, and it didn't used to be so. During socialism, I cannot remember meeting even one single guy who would prefer bears.
>
> Kamil

In the part of the interview that immediately followed this narrative, Kamil, with significant nostalgia, recounts a home party of the homosexual therapeutic group which he was a member of in the 1980s. As a joke, all the men present at the party took turns trying on the dresses of Kamil's mother. Robert, who is present at the interview (and was present at the party) immediately adds that it was simply an impromptu piece to make others laugh, rather than a transvestite performance.

In Roberts's narrative, there is importance given to the difference between transvestism and entertainment. At the party described, the people were not participating in transvestism, but in entertainment, even though, at least theoretically, the two may not represent mutually exclusive categories. Robert was probably referring to the difference between institutionalised transvestism represented by organised public performances (an expression of transvestism not possible in the pre-1989 Czechoslovakia) and informal, unscripted, non-rehearsed gender play. What other forms of gender performance (Butler, 1990) are suggested by the polarity between formal and informal transvestite play? There is the difference in setting and in audience (a get-together of friends vs. performance in front of the anonymous public crowd), in spontaneity (an impromptu event vs. a performance that is rehearsed, planned, staged and paid for) or in the perspective from which the performance is being put on. Spontaneity, amateurism and momentary entertainment seem to be viewed as somehow superior here over transvestitism in the sense of a more long-term interest or even occupational. Gender identity functions as a normative ideal (Butler, 1990: 16), and the possibilities/options of not reaching this ideal are always contextually specific.

Men colonising the so-called gay spaces in the totalitarian Czechoslovakia were reluctant to see the association of gays and lesbians as a community.

> K: I don't really feel it to be a community.
> R: There are people who are ill and it is as if one referred to them as a community, too. What do we have in common? The range of these folks

is so wide, each one has their own interests, and the only common denominator is that we are 'bent' [...]. That's as if we were saying that people on wheelchairs were a community, because they give each other tips on fine-working wheelchairs to be had. I think it is a community only if and when people act together in some common interest.

K: I don't think so, it could be people with common interests but there may be no end result. The people have to feel they belong together, be ready to stick up for one another. But if you go to the public toilets and some gypsies assault you, will the others at the urinals stick up for you? They won't. Homosexuality itself is not a community, as much as it may get presented as such, these days.

To be a part of the community used to equate to belonging and even cultural capital (Bourdieu, 1998; Skeggs, 2003; Taylor, 2007, 2010). Gays and lesbians shared tips, ideas, experience on how to live a day-to-day and fairly common life (even) as a homosexual person, where to look for potential life or sex partners, or how to avoid military service and police raids. The feeling that 'people used to be there for each other more', was closely related to the fact that there used to be a stronger need to hide one's homosexuality if one did not wish to run the risk of being stigmatised and discredited. Also the female respondents were remembering the pre-1989 times with nostalgia and stressed out the underground character of an anti-establishment rebellion, which, with the change in political regime, the women I interviewed find no more need for.

The only legally existing and formally established 'gay' group under communism was the network of 'sociotherapeutic clubs', a type of therapeutic groups led by a sexologist or a similarly trained 'expert', where people would discuss topics and concerns related to homosexuality. It was well known that having gone through a therapeutic group of this sort was one of the few officially accepted ways to secure the so-called blue book, a document that excluded a person from the obligation to complete the mandatory two year military service in the Czech Republic. Just as I have shown in cases of informal gay scenes, men have dominated also this formally established and scientifically sanctified institution.

Public toilets and a broader social structure

It is possible to perceive the stronger bond within the gay and lesbian community prior to the year 1989 to be the result of more general social circumstances. The society of socialist Czechoslovakia, compared to the situation within the contemporary Czech Republic, was definitely more homogeneous, and there was a more clearly defined polarity especially along the lines of the communist establishment vs. the resistance against it. The shift of regimes naturally resulted in a shift within the social structure.

The following section will focus on the differentiation of social spaces and while the theme of public toilets will remain, I will focus on it with the use of different empirical material: the diaries of the employee of a public toilet. My goal in the following section is to suggest that the post-89 society was heavily socially structured, and also, to suggest the ways power is exercised within this society. Here, power does not work primarily as a tool of absolute repressive surveillance any more. Instead, it is established in and through disciplining, and especially self-disciplining, which is performed as part of day-to-day interactions (Foucault, 1978).

In 1998, during my first research trip to the public toilets, I encountered Marta, the 75-year-old female pensioner who had been working in the public toilets since 1991. To my great surprise, at the end of this first trip Marta handed me her diaries. She had kept a diary for 14 years, and her diary entries were revolving primarily around the topic of her work. Marta's diaries revealed a social space full of interaction, limits, rules, norms and values, a space inhabited by specific types of social actors. The institution of public toilets can be understood as an example of a gendered organisation (Acker, 1992), and also as a place where modern power manifests itself through unrelenting surveillance and disciplination (Foucault, 1978; Skeggs, 2004).

Located in Brno city centre, the public toilets of my research were situated under the street level, designed so as to allow entry to from the street via two separate gates marked *WC Gentlemen* and *WC Ladies*. The male toilets were divided into two rooms, one with urinals and the other with cubicles. In the women's toilets there were only individual cubicles. The male and female sections were separated by a hallway. The hallway lead to an 'office', a room with two counters and two windows, one on each side, designed for two (female) employees to collect payment for the use of the toilet.

> When I started working as a toilet lady [in 1991], after having responded to an ad in the papers, I had no idea what the job would involve and what to expect, what kind of people I would be meeting every day. I got to know people who were good, bad, drug addicts, Gypsies, homeless, skinheads, thieves and, above all, homosexuals. [2002]

> […] we're in Brno, the city full of tough guys, Gypsies, fags, the homeless who would occupy the cubicles and only vacate them after police intervention, and where would the women go then? [1995]

These quotes introduce us into Marta's classificatory world, into a world structured according to age, social class, gender, ethnicity, into a world that may lack all order, at times, but consistently divides individuals into two basic categories: conformists and deviants. When the label 'deviant' is applied, the attached stigma multiplies: as a means of further stereotyping attention (i.e. explanation of a certain conduct) is drawn to additional characteristics of the deviating individual. And so, children who appear undisciplined while using the public toilets are labelled Gypsies and described as individuals who had been suspicious from the moment they had appeared at the premises. Marta relates her fear in seeing a group of Roma people at the entrance to the toilets. She expects trouble, which, undoubtedly, materialises in some form or another by the end of the diary entry. We find a multiplication of deviation in the following excerpt: It is an account of gender rule transgression by a woman involved in 'deviant conduct'. She is described as young, drugged up, and a Gypsy.

> In the morning, a young Gypsy woman came. Without paying, she walked into the urinals that were full of men. I shouted at her not to enter the men's section, and she replied she was a man. Later, two gentlemen on their way out said the woman was drugged up and did not know where she was. They asked me to kick her out. I shouted 'OUT at once, go throw up in the park!' She got out. [1998]

Erving Goffman describes toilets as places of surveillance that allow some men and women to discipline others (1997). This is achieved, for example, by the already-mentioned separate entrances for men and women. Such a division is not necessary for the function of the toilets per se. However, it has a very important social role which involves surveillance over expected male and female appearances. Women who enter through the 'female' entrance into the section reserved for females are reminded that they are women, not men, and vice versa. At the same time, appearance-based stereotyping takes place. Thus, at first sight, a woman may be identified as a man (and vice versa), and, subsequently, banished from the area reserved for 'normal' women and relegated to 'the other half' of the premises, where they belong according to the stereotypical reading of their gender expression. The individual banished from entering the toilet section of their choice is humiliated for not having passed, at first sight, as a legible representative of 'their' gender category. They are faced with the option of either presenting themselves (through the use of their voice or their body) as a 'real' member of the appropriate gender, 'proving' that they have been misidentified, 'misread', or, leaving the premises. Appearance at the public toilets is very important, men and women are evaluated and scrutinised based on appearance (Skeggs, 1997). And while the effort to remain intelligible permeates both the private and the public sphere, I hold that it is also significantly gendered. I will examine this more closely in the last part of this text, one that deals with lesbians.

In addition to gender-based division, the space of public toilets is split into an employee and a visitor section, each generating different views of the rules of operation of the institution of the public toilets. The two forces struggling against each other at the public toilets are represented by the status of an employee and that of the customer. The differentiated colonisation of the space of the toilets is embodied, for example, by conflicts over the employee-created sign stating that 'the customer is forbidden to stay at the premises longer than absolutely necessary'. Such a sign is an unspoken acknowledgment of the fact that there exists a community of men who use public toilets for anonymous sex with other men. It is men like that, says Marta's diary, who spend hours and hours on end at the premises. They fail to respect even the 6pm closing time. The toilets' female employees reprimand such rule-breakers and refer them to other places, most typically to a brothel. Despite offering services for heterosexual sex only, brothels are classified by Marta in the same category as public toilets, as 'places of male sex'. Sexual desire is thus channelled to a proper object (heterosexual) and a proper place (a brothel).

In their struggle for domination over the space allotted them, and for establishing that which is 'normal' and 'moral', the female employees often try to create allies, as a diary note shows: 'The homeless hated "B"s[7] and they harmed them whenever and however they could.' Marta describes how the homeless poured water on those they called 'fags', splashing a bucket of water through the opening at the bottom of the cubicle in which there were two men together.

In Marta's diaries, the toilets' female employees are portrayed as targets of male derision and easy targets for children and exhibitionists, to whom they represent an anonymous and thus safe objects onto which to vent anger, desire, annoyance, weakness or excitement. The women involuntarily find themselves in the position of working-class therapists. Their work underground is, metaphorically, a kind of struggle with the unconscious and the suppressed. In the toilets, people get rid of that which is considered dirty and excessive, and the employees' task is to supervise this process and ensure that order is installed, that people emerging from the dark underground enter a world that seems clear, bright, correct and normal.

Although Marta does not provide her 'clients' with interpretations that are sanctioned by expert knowledge, long-term study and experience, and although her social background distances her from the mental health care culture that pertains to the social classes she does not belong to, she manages to take on the weight of projected emotions and ground them like a lightning rod. The 'toilet lady' is a job with distinct class and gender connotations. It is the prototype of a female-coded profession and, at the same time, the representative of a low-prestige, low-status job. If Goffman calls the secretarial job a dead-end position for someone who dresses well and is not interested in career-making (1997), the toilet lady is a similarly low-prestige version for an older woman unafraid of manual labour, bad smell and of dressing down in a way appropriate to such a job. The job of a toilet lady is another example of the over-representation of women in low-status, low-prestige professions, and also illustrates the close link between class and gender structures.

Space is divided into the stage and the back stage (Goffman, 1999). The public toilet employees' 'office' is exactly such a back stage, where common, daily action takes place: coffee-making, lamenting the feeling of tiredness, sharing anger, fear, private information, food consumption. The totality of this back stage is underscored by the fact that the employees cannot leave the place until their shift ends. They work, rest, talk and have lunch at a confined space which – due to its underground location and constrained character – resembles another total institution, the prison. The women protect the relative safety of this space with imaginary props, such as a fake telephone (there is no landline on the premises and the employees, at their age, as is typical for this country, are unlikely to own or use mobile phones) which they threaten to use in cases of necessity, to summon up the higher and formal authority of the police. From this room, women stage an enactment of self-confidence and determination, as they collect money and enforce rules. Men, on the contrary, attempt to invade the employees' privacy through acts of verbal, physical or sexual violence.

The position of the 'toilet lady' thus in many ways resembles that of lesbian women: we tend to find them as if in the private sphere, they keep in the background, watching from the distance a space dominated by men. Femininity (much more likely than masculinity) can function as a class of its own kind. It is an investment and an achievement especially for women who have been marginalised and excluded in various ways, and thus made to prove their credibility and work to gain their respect, over and over (Skeggs, 1997). I will turn to this aspect of femininity in more detail at the end of this chapter.

The institution of public toilets incorporates seemingly contradictory influences. On the one hand, toilets are enabling spaces where desires and wishes kept under control elsewhere can emerge and arise. On the other hand, toilets operate within the mechanisms of control and regulation as spaces of repression. This regulatory function clearly surfaces when police authority is being invoked:

> The police now come here during the day, and especially at night. It is good that they are seen around here. Once, two came and one of them shouted: 'How many fags do you have down here today, missus?' At once, five of such guys ran up the stairs. The police are always surprised that we don't have a phone here. [1998]

The task of the police is not repressive intervention or law enforcement. Instead, they act as a symbolic power referred to, imagined, visualised. In everyday life, even without the embodiment of authority, we too come under the forces of surveillance and control, in our efforts to become decipherable and comprehensible to others. As Michel Foucault (1978) argues, power in modern societies does not function as an authoritarian repressive force that enforces order through the use of violence. It works, instead, rather as a wide-spreading net of relationships that have no clearly identifiable source or origin. Although in the underground of the public toilets, we encounter practices that we would label inappropriate or outright 'perverted', the fact that such conduct occurs precisely there may signify that the actors are aware of their own inappropriateness, aware that they engage in activities that 'should' be hidden. The never- and ever-present control that gains its strength from the kind of self-disciplination that involves bodies and souls makes toilets a 'good' example of the working of modern power. It is precisely the working of power through self-disciplination that I will deal with in the following section, which focuses on one of the subgroups of the lesbian and gay community, lesbians in families.

Lesbians on their private stage

As I have indicated, the focus of the following section will be on women, that is, on lesbians bringing up children in the context of the lesbian family.[8] I chose this subgroup because I see it as an illustrative example of the (process of) differentiation within the l/g community (in the Czech Republic) in the past decades. It is a case in point that reveals hierarchies that are created (and recreated) in the community as a part of larger social structures. I focus only on how such families relate to the lesbian community and whether, or in what way, the manner in which they relate to it is similar or different to the attitude of gay men that I have described in the first part of the chapter.

When the topic of conversation turned to the lesbian community, one of my respondents immediately raised the question 'Who is a lesbian, anyway?' To the women in this particular family, both of the terms, 'lesbian' and 'community' had fairly negative connotations, a situation which, as I was to find out later, was characteristic of those I encountered in other participating families. The position of the family of Dita and Kamila, however, was quite extreme.

Despite the fact that Dita had been in the relationship with her partner for years, and that she is the biological mother of the children the two women are bringing up together – children whose birth into the relationship had been planned – Dita herself, as she said, would not call herself a lesbian. It is as if, in this case, neither sexual orientation nor day-to-day partnership played a primary role in the establishment of the status of the 'lesbian': Let's consider what specifically lesbianism meant to Dita and Kamila, what image of lesbianism they referred to when they chose to distance themselves from it.

> Personally, I am not sure I am a lesbian at all. I do not see myself that way in terms of my appearance, and also, I find the word offending. I would

not use the term to refer to myself. I would be ashamed to. [...] Those girls seem to me to be some kind of sub-species, neither a man nor a woman. They are going through an internal struggle. [...] The lesbian is closer to those transsexuals, she is a split personality.

Dita

The lesbian woman, as described by Dita, was sort of a man trapped in the female body, a body disavowed and hidden in baggy clothes. It was one that cannot be but a ridiculous imitation of the real man. Based on Dita's logic, the masculinity of a lesbian can never be authentic, as it is not supported by the possession of the penis. The lesbian is not being characterised solely by her physical appearance, however. She can also be recognised by her 'significantly lesbian gestures'. Adjectives such as 'typical', 'classic', 'obvious', or 'clear', were an indisposable part of Dita's account of lesbians, malehood and femalehood, because stereotypical categorisations result in a perceived obviousness in the comprehension of such entities.

You can smoke in a female or a male way. Smoking is just not the same. You can sit as a woman or as a guy, put clothes on, take 'em off in a female or male way, everything can be done differently.

Dita

Not only can various activities, practices and gestures be performed 'in a male or female way', but also, according to Dita, they *should* be performed as such. The appeal to coherence of sex, gender and gendered practices can be perceived as striving for intelligibility. Persons become intelligible while being gendered (West and Zimmerman, 1987; Butler, 1990). To be a lesbian, thus to be 'insufficiently female', is, to Dita, an obvious impediment, something that casts one into a 'lower-category' of humanhood. Lesbianism in their view was contradictory to femininity (Taylor, 2007; Gabb, 2004). The images of lesbianism and femininity found in respondents' accounts do not refer only to people, but also to specific locations or environments. Inge, another of the narrators, connected lesbianism with the gay and lesbian bar scene, and, just as in the case of the previous couple, there was a pronounced contempt attached to it.

When I see those girls [in bars], you see these lost souls, you are sorry for them. I am such a sensitive person and so I say to myself jeez, and then I run home as fast as I can and tell myself well thank god. [laughs]. The fact that there really are such people there, some real losers, right. Or those, a bunch of those exhibitionists that more likely than not just pretend they are after girls. [...]. I tell myself: 'Gosh, what am I doing here?' Either there are those gypsies, or those like Rambo-types in leather jackets.

Inge

To her, the community represented by the bar is not a place of the new-found home or pride, but, on the contrary, a place described as the very contradiction of home. It is not a place where masks are discarded, a place where one can be who one really is, but instead a place of pretence and exhibitionism. Inge's partner, Mirka, only confirms such an image when she says that the environment of the lesbian bar seemed to her 'strange and dirty' (Taylor, 2008). Here, the community does not represent a platform for embracing a uniting category or identity, but serves instead as a negative frame of reference, a fact which the women indirectly pointed to when they said: 'We've got nothin' in common with 'em. We are depressed by the community, makes us sad. We are somewhere else.'

Classification and reviewing based on the normative gender is joined with additional categories such as truth and authenticity of the sexual orientation, ethnicity, class and marital status.

> Let those people get it, finally, that really, this is no 'just for the kicks' trick, it's not like we do it 'cause we're just plain bored with whatever else, not like we just tryin' to think up whatever, or what not.
>
> Irma

In Irma's view, homosexuality is a clear cut, definite and fixed, unchanging characteristic. Such a perspective is in full accord with sexological discourse, which, in the Czech Republic, remains the determining and dominant type of knowing and knowledge-making in the field of human sexuality (Sokolová, 2005; Lišková, 2009, 2011). Irma had applied such knowledge to herself as well, when she perceived herself as someone who was absolutely 'honest with oneself', positively evaluating her own clear-cut sexual orientation. In contrast, she expressed distance and contempt when she narrated stories of women making bisexual choices. Honesty in terms of sexuality did not mean that Irma would have had intimate relationships with women exclusively, but that relationships with men would retrospectively be framed as unsatisfactory, especially on the level of sexual expression.

> Bisexuality is like sitting on two chairs at once. And one either is or is not true to oneself. Perhaps there really are some people who get turned on by both, I don't know. But in those types I know there is always either some profit being made, personal, or really, immaturity, ambivalence. There simply always is some impure element that makes them be both sides, right. And that's why I have a term, and I know I have a reason for the term, a pure, pure-breed, all that. When it is a lesbian that has got it figured out, right. She wants only a woman and there are no ifs and buts. Like I was expected to get married, right. And of course I could've pulled such an act, 'course I could. For him. Even in bed. Like any woman can,

right. But it was simply unthinkable for me. Like, to him. To act so shitty. Yeah, two-faced like that, right.

Irma

In the previously quoted excerpt from Irma's account, it is a reflection of Foucault's thesis connecting sexuality and truth (1978). Here, sexuality is presented as a source of authenticity that characterises a person and determines them. It becomes a person's duty to find the truth about their own sexuality, and such a truth should be of an unchanging, definite kind. This normative image of a true, proper gay person is an illustrative example of homonormativity discussed elsewhere (Valentine, 2000; Bell, 2001b; Taylor, 2008).

Gays and lesbians are not a monolithic community, then, the 'homosexual identity' is more a socially created representation than the expression of some internal characteristics that form a particular type of behaviour or lifestyle (Binnie and Valentine, 1999). On the level of activism, however, it is practical to refer to unity and uniformity, because through them, that which is seen as common goals is reached more easily. During negotiations that preceded the passing of the Czech registered partnership law, there was a push, on the part of some of the activist, to silence efforts that demanded the inclusion of parental rights for gays and lesbians. There were fears that any mention of childbearing and gay and lesbian parenting would spoil the chances of getting the law passed.

In the accounts of my respondents, it seems as if identifying with the community was often perceived as a stigma of sorts, and the declaration of normality and conformity offered a way to free oneself from this stigma (Gabb, 2004; Taylor, 2009). Identification with the common, the known and the expected (thus, 'normal') may take the form of expressing one's inclusion within the aggregate of 'normal' families.

No, really, y'know, we don't like make differences here, and I think it exactly is awfully wrong to, you know how some girls would close themselves really somehow, around that movement, and that's like so friggin' not right, because really, overall, people have pretty much the same kind of concerns as some married friend and her husband do.

Marie

For the respondents, it was as if the community was a sect of sorts (not conspiratorial underground anymore), in which one tended to include others, rather than oneself. It was the space of those 'other' gays and lesbians with whom the women in the sample, based on their own accounts, had little in common. The declination carried often also the class dimension. According to some women participation in the community (active or passive) was an alternative for those who don't prove successful anywhere else (at work, in the family).

In the following interview excerpt Kamila and Dita relate how important earning a good reputation with their new neighbours was to them as they moved in from a city. To fit in well, they tried to do what they perceived to be the most valued for the village folk, which was manual labour.

Kamila: It's not like some exhibitionists arrived who would walk around holding hands here. We were particularly careful about that and came into the village expecting that there would be, might be, problems, and that because of that we had to act even more proper. We would be particularly careful about what we had been doing before we greeted these old village folk. And of course the whole village, the common and, moreover, the communist, have a certain lifestyle and then some strangers arrive from Brno/a city/, rolling in dough, right. Well, what helped us most was that in order to build a house for ourselves here we worked all year from spring to winter, here at the plot.

Dita: … and we slaved off, believe me. Really, we would come weekends, and those Christians would pass this place, those families, and we would be here in all this dust and would work all year round. All year in overalls.

Both Kamila and Dita had enough financial capital to hire paid workers for the completion of the construction work on their house, yet they deemed it highly important to be seen labouring at the site in person. The quoted part of the interview revives a number of stereotypes that come to mind as a polarity between the village and the town is drawn. The village folk are labelled Christian and Communist (no matter how mutually exclusive these categories happen to be). Kamila and Dita, as women coming from a big town, imagine being seen through the eyes of the villagers as 'exhibitionists', and, through their actions, try to distance themselves from this imaginary stigma. Exhibitionism is being connected here with openness about one's intimate connection (manifested through public hand-holding) and is subsequently substituted with a socially more desirable and normative exhibitionism embodied through hard manual labour. The stereotyping of city and village contained a class aspect as well. The two women were very much aware of the fact that their economic capital ranked them, financially, way above their new neighbours.

Awareness of difference can be seen in the accounts of two of my other respondents, Agata and Eva, as well. They run a coffee house, which they occasionally utilise to host meetings of lesbian or feminist groups. The two women comment on their own position in the community as follows:

They are shocked by us and we are shocked by them, because we are quite different from all those girls that come to our coffee house, they are so terribly promiscuous, or just y'know so terribly … really!

Eva

Another stereotype is being added to the already created picture of the masculine lesbian, one all too often tagged to homosexuality: promiscuity. Stable partnership and family lifestyle are this way set in opposition to the promiscuous lifestyle where the former is perceived as more valuable than the later.

Conclusions

Prior to the year 1989 (in the atmosphere of public nonexistence of homosexuality), all energy would be consumed by the effort to secure a common life (even) as a homosexual person. The process of learning, finding and gathering necessary information, and general knowledge-making used to be laborious and happened face-to face. Today, largely due to Internet access (see also Wincapaw, 2000; Gruszczynska, 2007), it can be done privately, can turn into a solitary act, even though the what and the how of an Internet search still requires a certain cultural capital and other not-so-obvious competences. Since 1989, a number of dating webpages have appeared where personal ads could be posted, a number of LGBT servers have been created, several LGBT organisations have been stated and establishments opened. Studies and books of non-fiction as well as fiction (of varying quality) have been published, university courses dealing with the topic of sexuality and homosexuality have been taught and attended, and, (since 2001) even an annual queer film festival[9] has been organised. A growing multiplicity of lifestyles and cultures is a more general characteristic of the transition from a totalitarian to a more democratic society, and brings, on the one hand, a weakening of the previously tighter bonds within the community, and on the other hand, a potential for forming stronger alliances, confirmed through contexts and dimensions other than sexual orientation.

One of the more surprising conclusions is the realisation that gender seems to structure the LGBT community more significantly than it used to. Whereas in the stories recounted by out male respondents, the use of female names as nicks for other homosexual men appeared to be quite frequent, in the interviews with lesbian women, intentional play with or subversion of gender identity was mentioned only very rarely, whether on the level of language or performance.

To return, in conclusion, to the difference between the stage and the backstage, where, as suggested by Goffman (1999), social life takes place, perhaps one could make the assertion that during communism, the community took place mostly at the backstage, with no prospect of legally backed-up change or visibility. A regime shift has not, however, brought the back staged community up on the stage. It is the context of lesbian families that illustrates quite clearly the persisting tendency towards a dissolution in the expectable and the sanctified, (the family), which, despite the innovation in the type of actors cast, leaves lesbians in the sphere of the private, and, at the same time, also normative.

Lesbian families in their day-to-day acts, then, balance between the stigmatised stereotype of 'the lesbian', which they try to escape, and the picture of an autonomous family that is not a simple copy of the so-called mainstream model, yet still proves itself good enough, not only in securing loving family background for its children, but also in being legible, comprehensible and undoubtable. A 'good' family, in this case, also equals an invisible family, one that does not draw attention to its untypical and emphasised other. The respondents, mostly, were not proud champions of the rights of gays and lesbians, or the rights of parents and children in general. If the term 'coming out', some sort of coming-to-terms, signifies the process of accepting one's homosexual orientation, a successful g/l family could be characterised by an expression 'coming in'. It is as if lesbian women, through their family lives, were authentically entering the world of the 'normal', 'expected', 'common' others and most importantly respected.

Notes

1. Even though the acronym LGBT is usually applied I use mainly the terms 'gay' and 'lesbian' (or 'l/g') because I focus mostly on gay men and lesbians in this chapter.
2. *Češi jsou vůči sňatkům a registrovanému partnerství homosexuálů vstřícnější než Poláci, Maďaři a Slováci* (2005). Public Opinion Research Centre of the Institute of Sociology of the Academy of Sciences of the Czech Republic (CVVM) Press release. Retrieved on 11 November 2006 from http://www.cvvm.cas.cz/upl/zpravy/100533s_ov51128.pdf.
3. The Czech Republic (as a post socialist country) presents in terms of class a specific context. The communist regime was characteristic of homogenous social structure with the working class put on a pedestal and seen to deliver the political and economic goals of the regime. This is in in contrast to the construction of the contemporary working class in the West (Skeggs, 2004, Stenning, 2012). The change of regime in in 1989 brought a distinctive re-making of class based on the differing positions of people within the system of the ownership of production, and then varied by other economic, cultural and social capitals (Machonin 1994).
4. Brno is the second largest city in the Czech Republic (with 400,000 inhabitants).
5. For more detailed theoretical and empirical framing of LGBT community, see Stein (1997), Binnie and Valentine (1999), Binnie and Skeggs (2004), Bell and Binnie (2004), Švab and Kuhar (2005), Taylor (2007), Béres-Deák (2007), Gruszczynska (2007) and Jorgens (2007).
6. For interpretatively rich accounts of public toilets in the relation to broader social structures, see Skeggs (2001) and Bell (2001a).
7. Probably the abbreviation of 'buzerant' ('bent') It should be noted that the term 'b' to indicate 'gay man' is being used by people both within and outside the g/l community.
8. Lesbian and gay families have been researched extensively during the last six decades (see Green, 1978; Golombok, 1996; Stacey and Biblarz, 2001; Almack, 2008; Sullivan, 2004; Taylor, 2009).
9. See the festival webpage at http://www.mezipatra.cz/.

Bibliography

Acker, J. (1992) 'Gendered institutions: From sex roles to gendered institutions', *Contemporary Sociology*, 21(5): 565–9.

Almack, K. (2008) 'Display work: Lesbian parent couples and their families of origin negotiating new kin relationships', *Sociology*, 42(6): 1183–99.

Bell, D. (2001a) 'Fragments for a queer city' in D. Bell (ed.) *Pleasure zones: Bodies cities, spaces.* Syracuse: Syracuse University Press, pp. 84–102.

Bell, D. (ed.) (2001b) *Pleasure zones: Bodies, cities, spaces.* Syracuse: Syracuse University Press.

Bell, D. and Binnie, J. (2004) 'Authenticating Queer Space: Citizenship, Urbanism and Governance', *Urban Studies*, 41(9): 1807–20.

Béres-Deák, R. (2007) 'Values reflected in style in a lesbian community in Budapest' in R. Kuhar and J. Takás (eds) *Beyond the pink curtain: Everyday life of LGBT people in Eastern Europe.* Ljubljana: Peace Institute, pp. 81–93.

Binnie, J. and Skeggs, B. (2004) 'Cosmopolitan sexualities: Disrupting the logic of late capitalism', *Sociological Review*, 52(1): 39–62.

Binnie, J. and Valentine, G. (1999) 'Geographies of sexuality – a review of progress', *Progress in Human Geography*, 23(2): 175–87.

Bourdieu, P. (1998) *Teorie jednání.* Praha: Karolinum.

Butler, J. (1990) *Gender trouble: Feminism and the subversion of identity.* New York: Routledge.

Foucault, M. (1978) *The history of Sexuality, Volume One.* New York: Pantheon.

Gabb, J., 2004. 'Critical differentials: Querying the incongruities within research on lesbian parent families', *Sexualities*, 7(2): 167–82.

Goffman, E. (1999) *Všichni hrajeme divadlo: Sebeprezentace v každodenním životě.* Praha: Nakladatelství Studia Ypsilon.

Golombok, S. and Tasker, F. (1996) 'Do Parents Influence the Sexual Orientation of Their Children? Findings from a Longitudinal Study of Lesbian Families', *Developmental Psychology*, 32(1): 3–11.

Green, R. (1978) 'Sexual identity of 37 children raised by homosexual or transsexual parents', *American Journal of Psychiatry*, 135(6): 692–7.

Gruszczynska, A. (2007) 'Living la vida Internet: Some notes on the cyberization of Polish LGBT community' in R. Kuhar and J. Takács (eds) *Beyond the pink curtain: Everyday life of LGBT people in Eastern Europe.* Ljubljana: Peace Institute, pp. 95–115.

Jorgens, F. (2007) 'East Berlin: Lesbian and gay narratives on everyday life, social acceptance, and past and present' in R. Kuhar and J. Takács (eds) *Beyond the pink curtain: Everyday life of LGBT people in Eastern Europe.* Ljubljana: Peace Institute, pp. 117–39.

Marta (1999) *Marta's diaries* (Personal diaries of employee of the public toilets in Brno).

Lišková, K. (2009) 'Defining pornography, defining gender: Sexual citizenship in the discourse of Czech sexology and criminology' in E. H. Oleksy (ed.) *Intimate Citizenships: Gender, Sexualities, Politics.* New York: Routledge, pp. 147–56.

Lišková, K. (2011) 'Released from gender? Reflexivity, performativity, and therapeutic discourses' in M. Benson and R. Munro (eds) *Sociological routes and political roots.* Oxford: Blackwell, pp. 189–204.

Machonin, P. (1994) 'Social and political transformation in the Czech Republic', *Czech Sociological Review*, 2(1): 71–87.

Skeggs, B. (1997) *Formations of Class & Gender: Becoming Respectable*. London: Sage Publications Ltd.

Skeggs, B. (2001) 'The toilet paper: Femininity, class and mis-recognition', *Women's Studies International Forum*, 24(3): 295–307.

Skeggs, B. (2003) *Class, Self, Culture*. New York: Routledge.

Sokolová, V. (2005) 'Identity politics and the (b)orders of Heterosexism: Lesbians, gays and feminists in the Czech media after 1989' in J. v. Leuween and N. Richter (eds) *Mediale Welten in Tschechien nach 1989: Genderprojektionen und Codes des Plebejismus*. München: Kubon und Sagner, pp. 29–44.

Stacey, J. and Biblarz, T. (2001) '(How) Does the sexual orientation of parents matter?' *American Sociological Review*, 66(2): 159–83.

Stein, A. (1997) *Sex and sensibility: Stories of a lesbian generation*. Berkeley, LA and London: University of California Press.

Stenning, A. (2012) 'Where is the post-socialist working class? Working-class lives in the spaces of (post-)socialism', *Sociology*, 39(5): 983–99.

Sullivan, M. (2004) *The family of women: Lesbian mothers, their children and the undoing of gender*. Berkeley: University of California Press.

Švab, A. and Kuhar, R. (2005) *The unbearable comfort of privacy: The everyday life of gays and lesbians*. Ljubljana: Peace Institute.

Taylor, Y. (2007) *Working class lesbian life: Classed outsiders*. Basingstoke: Palgrave Macmillan.

Taylor, Y. (2008) '"That's not really my scene": Working-class lesbians in (and out of) place', *Sexualities*, 11(5): 523–46.

Taylor, Y. (2009) *Lesbian and gay parenting: Securing social and educational capital*. Basingstoke: Palgrave Macmillan.

Taylor, Y. (ed.) (2010) *Classed intersections*. New York: Ashgate.

Valentine, G. (2000) *From nowhere to everywhere: Lesbian geographies*. New York: Routledge.

Večerník, J. (2010) 'Střední vrstvy v české společnosti a výzkumu: Mizející, nebo zapomenuté?' *Lidé města*, 12(3): 475–97.

West, C. and Zimmerman, D. H. (1987) 'Doing gender', *Gender and Society*, 1(2): 125–51.

Wincapaw, C. (2000) 'The virtual spaces of lesbian and bisexual women's electronic mailing lists', *Journal of Lesbian Studies*, 4(1): 45–59.

3
Lesbian Lives and Real Existing Socialism in Late Soviet Russia

Francesca Stella

Introduction

This chapter contributes to current debates about queer presences and absences by focusing on a notable absence in both queer and Russian studies, namely that of the lives of women involved in same-sex relations in Soviet Russia (1917–89). Until very recently, in existing accounts of Soviet society, queer lives, and lesbian lives even more so, have been notable by their absence and invisibility. Since the 1990s, a handful of pioneering studies has begun to uncover their hidden history; however, existing work has almost exclusively focused on state-enforced mechanisms of regulation of same-sex desire by exploring medical and legal discourses on homosexuality, or same-sex desire in Soviet prison camps (Engelstein, 1995; Zhuk, 1998; Healey, 2001; Kuntsman, 2009). While offering very valuable insights into the lives of Soviet queers, existing research has mostly been based on archival and documentary sources such as police records, court documents, medical studies and the memoirs of GULag prisoners. Thus, with few exceptions (Rotkirch, 2002), the literature has privileged the perspective of professionals or witnesses, rather than queers themselves, and focused very heavily on the environments of the clinic and the prison camp, where homosexuality was symbolically confined by the Soviet state.

This chapter shifts the focus to the everyday lives of women experiencing same-sex desire beyond the confine of the clinic and the prison camp, drawing on biographical interviews with 24 women who were socialised and became aware of their attraction to women during the Soviet period. The aim of the chapter is to reflect on what made these lives so invisible, and what an exploration of these lives can tell us about the social regulation of same-sex desire in Soviet society more broadly. Findings point to the need to reassess the extent to which the Soviet medical establishment attempted to 'cure' women of their desires, and emphasise instead the role of the Soviet gender order (Ashwin, 2000) and of the socio-economic organisation of Soviet society in shaping women's experiences and in making expressions of same-sex desire invisible. In the conclusion, I argue that an empirical exploration of Soviet queer lives can do much more than uncover a little known page of Soviet history: by broadening the geographical breadth of empirical enquiry, it invites a critical reassessment on the dominance of Western-centric theoretical perspectives, which have emphasised the links between capitalist modernity and the emergence of lesbian subjects.

Invisible subjects: The regulation of same-sex desire in Soviet Russia

The socio-legal and medical regulation of sexual and gender 'deviance' by the Soviet state have featured prominently in virtually all the existing literature on Soviet and post-Soviet Russian homosexualities. The Soviet penal code criminalised consensual sexual relations between men, making them a crime punishable with up to five years in jail, while the medical profession widely regarded both male and female sexuality as a perversion or a personality disorder. The influence of Soviet legislation and medical guidelines continued to be felt after the demise of state socialism and the break-up of the Soviet Union in 1991: anti-sodomy legislation was repealed in 1993, and homosexuality was struck off the official list of illnesses issued by the Ministry of Health in 1999 (Stella 2008).

While the physical and symbolic violence perpetrated by the Soviet state against queers through medicine and the law is sometimes portrayed in the literature as evidence of Russian exceptionalism, it should be noted that the view of same-sex desire as an illness or a crime was by no means unique to Soviet Russia. Indeed, this view was also prevalent in many other European countries since the nineteenth century, although most decriminalised and de-medicalised same-sex desire much earlier than Russia (West and Green, 1997). Healey (2001) notes that 'modernising' discourses of sexuality, which aimed to control the health and growth of the population by policing and disciplining practices deemed 'deviant' and 'immoral', penetrated into Russia during the late nineteenth century. However, one of the key questions faced by scholars of Soviet Russia is how modes of biopower mediated through the law, medicine and education, and theorised by Foucault as a constituent feature of modern liberal capitalist societies (Foucault, 1978), were articulated under state socialism in Soviet Russia (Healey, 2001).

Hoffmann sees the Stalinist period (1928–53)[1] as crucial in consolidating the key features of state socialism in the Soviet Union and indeed of Soviet modernity, which he identifies as social interventionism and mass politics (2003: 7); it is perhaps no coincidence that research on gender and sexuality has also singled out the Stalinist period as a key moment in establishing a distinctive Soviet gender order (Buckley, 1989; Ashwin, 2000), and in defining laws and policies regulating same-sex desire (Healey, 2001; Engelstein, 1995; Karlinsky, 1989). The Stalinist period marked a retreat from the utopian optimism and social experimentation of the early Soviet years, and saw the introduction of legislation restricting access to divorce and abortion, the recriminalisation of male homosexuality (1934) and the unequivocal endorsement of the nuclear traditional family as the founding unit of Soviet society (Healey, 2001; Buckley, 1989), alongside the introduction of the command economy, rapid industrialisation, the collectivisation of agriculture, and the consolidation of a heavily centralised political and administrative system. Both state-sponsored homophobia and monogamous heterosexuality harnessed to the reproductive needs of the socialist state became institutionalised in Soviet society. The nuclear heterosexual family was co-opted into Soviet ideology in a new capacity, namely to serve the needs of the socialist state for an extensive army and labour force, and state policies remained staunchly pro-natalist throughout the Soviet period, while discussion of sex and sexuality in the public domain were constrained by strict censorship (Ashwin, 2000; Shlapentokh, 1989; Temkina and Zdravomyslova, 2002). In spite of the Soviet state's formal commitment to gender equality and the emancipation of women, the Stalinist period also saw the emergence of a distinctive Soviet gender order which still defined citizens' rights and duties to the state on the basis of their gender (Connell, 1987; Ashwin, 2000). Male privilege in the public sphere was largely preserved, as men were imagined as soldiers (defenders of the Motherland) and workers (builders of socialism), while women were expected to be 'working mothers' and contribute to society both through paid employment and through reproduction (Ashwin, 2000).

Existing literature points out that social control of same-sex desire in Soviet Russia was also gendered. Although both male and female homosexuality were defined in similar terms as a perverted attraction to persons of the same sex, only sexual relations between men were punishable with a prison sentence. Healey (2001) indicates that during the early Soviet years medical experts had neglected female homosexuality; however, from the late 1950s the resurgence of Soviet sexology, which focused mostly on 'deviant' and 'pathological' sexuality, also marked a renewed interest in lesbianism, which was to be cured through forced hospitalisation, the use of psychiatric drugs and psychological therapy (Healey, 2001: 244). Same-sex desire was stigmatised not only through its association with crime and mental illness, but also through the 'conspiracy of silence' (Kon and Riordan, 1993: 93) that surrounded the issue for decades: while the heavily censored Soviet media barely allowed for an open discussion of issues related to sex and intimacy, any mention of homosexuality, deemed a particularly shameful topic, was conspicuously absent from it until the late 1980s (Kon, 1997).

Much of the empirical research into Soviet queer lives has focused on the clinic and the prison camp, the two environments where homosexuality was symbolically confined to by the socialist state and where its existence was indirectly documented in reports by medical and legal experts and through the accounts of eye witnesses such as the memoirs of prison inmates (Healey, 2001; Kozlovskii, 1986; Zhuk, 1998; Kuntsman, 2009; Engelstein, 1995). Interestingly, although lesbianism was never criminalised, much of the existing research on the topic has focused on prison camp subcultures (Kozlovskii, 1986; Zhuk, 1998; Kuntsman, 2009), an environment where same-sex relations among women gained a degree of visibility since they were tolerated as a surrogate of heterosexual relations in an 'unnaturally' same-sex environment. It is not surprising, therefore, that much of the existing literature has emphasised the punitive and repressive role of the Soviet state in enforcing heteronormativity (Healey, 2001; Essig, 1999; Engelstein, 1995; Gessen, 1994). The focus on the harsh realities of the clinic and the prison camp, however, conveys a very uneasy presence, making queerness visible only on the margins of Soviet society. This uneasy presence seems to be reflected in collective memory: for Soviet generations, images of queerness, marginality and criminality have become metonymically entwined through repeated association (Kuntsman, 2009), while the expression 'nontraditional sexual orientation' [*netraditsionnaya orientatsiya*], commonly used in contemporary Russia to refer to homosexuality, reflects the perception of queer subjectivities and lifestyles as a novel, post-Soviet phenomenon (Baer, 2009). While the prevailing focus on the clinic and the prison camp is unable to challenge selective queer presences in Russian collective memory, many questions about the lives of Soviet queers remain unanswered: for example, how did queers live in more ordinary environments under real existing socialism? What made their lives so invisible? Which spaces allowed the emergence of forms of queer solidarities and communities[2]? While the literature traces the roots of Soviet institutionalised homophobia to the Stalinist period, would a focus on the late Soviet period reveal significant shifts in expert and societal views on same-sex desire?

This chapter, based on biographical interviews, contributes an alternative perspective to debates on the regulation of female same-sex desire in Soviet Russia by foregrounding the experiences of women whose romantic and sexual relations with other women took place outside of the environments of the clinic and the prison camp (see also Rotkirch, 2002). The analysis here focuses on the reasons behind the invisibility of same-sex desire in Soviet society: while most of the literature has emphasised the importance of Soviet punitive medicine in erasing queer lives from Soviet history, this chapter considers the role of more pervasive and subtle mechanisms of everyday surveillance and shaming in making female same-sex relations invisible.

Researching 'lesbian' lives through biographical interviews

This chapter is based on interviews with 24 women born between 1946 and 1969, and who lived in the cities of Moscow, Ul'yanovsk and St Petersburg at the time when the research was undertaken. Interviews were collected for two separate research projects: an ethnographic study (2004–5) on lesbian identity in post-Soviet Russia uncovered significant generational differences in the experiences of the women interviewed (Stella, 2008, 2010); these preliminary findings were further explored in a follow-up study (2010), based on 13 biographical interviews, and focussed more specifically on the experiences of women who were socialised and were involved in same-sex relations during the Soviet period. All the participants were recruited through snowball sampling with the help of community activists and acquaintances. All participants identified as ethnic Russian [*russkaia*], although a minority had a mixed heritage (one of the parents being, for example, Tatar, German, etc.). Most women in the sample had higher education and were employed in white collar or professional jobs[3]; the higher than average levels of education reflect the general characteristics of the social networks formed around the community settings through which potential participants were approached.[4]

The gender-specific 'lesbian', rather than the gender-neutral 'queer' is used here to collectively refer to the women interviewed; this reflected general language usage among participants, who predominantly utilised the word lesbian [*lesbiianka*] as a shorthand for women experiencing same-sex desire, alongside other, more colloquial terms. The term 'queer' [*kvir*], a recent borrowing from English, did not feature at all in interviews and more casual conversations, although at the time when fieldwork took place it was beginning to appear in Russian queer consumer culture. While the label 'queer' has been used elsewhere to mark Russian sexualities as exceptional vis-à-vis supposedly 'Western' binary categories of homosexual/heterosexual (Essig, 1999), I deliberately use 'lesbian' as a way to play down Russian exceptionalism and soften polarised notions of 'East' versus 'West' (see Stella, 2010). Even as I write a reflexive account of my research design and methodology, I acknowledge that reflexivity does not do away with difference or power, and that it is an instrument through which research subjects are categorised, 'fixed' and appropriated by the researcher (Skeggs, 2002; Adkins, 2004). I acknowledge the power involved in naming research subjects, particularly the discrepancy between research categories and terms of self-identification, and the voices that were missed out in the process. Not all the women interviewed identified as lesbians, as some used other terms of self-identifications such as 'ex-heterosexual' or 'bisexual', and others were reluctant to label themselves at all; moreover, two male-identifying women declined the invitation to take part in the study, as they felt that their experiences would not be captured by the notion of lesbian or same-sex desire.

The picture is further complicated by the fact that interviewees' retrospective accounts of their lives often contrasted their 'lesbian' present to their 'heterosexual' past, where same-sex desire was not acted upon or not explicitly articulated as 'lesbian'. Fourteen women in my sample had been married at some point in their lives, and nine women had children from previous heterosexual relationships. Institutional endorsement of heterosexual marriage in Soviet society upheld heterosexuality as the norm (Healey, 2001), and the last section of the chapter will revisit the theme of heterosexual relations by exploring the relationship between the invisibility of lesbian desire and married status as a marker of respectable femininity in Soviet society. What is of interest here, however, is that many women indicated that they started to identify according to their attraction to women only later in life, while in the past their marital (married/unmarried) and family status (mother/childless) seemed to be more important to their sense of self and to how they were perceived by others. Some, like Aleksandra[5], retrospectively rationalised their marriage with the constraints put on them by dominant social norms, while also explaining that coming to identify as a lesbian was a gradual process:

> I started to have sexual relations exclusively with women rather late. Soon after I separated from my husband, at 27 or 28. With my partner we've been living together for more than 30 years. We never talked about this, we never talked about being lesbians. We just loved each other and started living together, that's all. At the time our social circle was heterosexual, our friends were heterosexual. And then, little by little, some gay men appeared around us, then others. And our friends, our social network, began to change. In general, most of our closest friends are now gays and lesbians. And all the more now. And only later, by degrees, I got to the understanding that I am a lesbian.
>
> Aleksandra, Moscow, b. 1946

Aleksandra's experience shows that women's identifications are not only a reflection of their sexual practices or romantic involvement with other women, but they are also shaped by their social networks and by their engagement with subcultural environments. This illustrates Plummer's (1995) point that sexual identities are social and relational, and that they are created and sustained by shared narratives and by a sense of belonging in queer communities. It has been pointed out that shared sexual stories are grounded in specific configurations of class, gender, race/ethnicity and generation, and that narratives of community (re)produce both presences and absences, inclusions and exclusions (see, for example, Taylor, 2011). While I acknowledge that some of these complexities are bracketed in the present analysis, the notion of 'imagined community' (Anderson, 1991; Valentine, 1995) as a reference point is important here, since, at the time when the interviews took place, all interviewees socialised at least occasionally at community events or in informal lesbian networks, and talked about the lack of such reference point in the past.

Findings from this study indicate that significant generational differences emerged from interviews, and suggest that older women's reluctance to identify on the basis of binary notions of sexual orientation reflected Soviet censorship and stigmatisation of same-sex desire in the public sphere, but also mirrored more broadly their experiences of isolation. Younger women who came of age during the 1990s and early 2000s had access to a variety of information about same-sex desire and relations through the media, popular culture and the Internet. They had rarely experienced prolonged periods of isolation, once they had become aware of their attraction to women, since finding other like-minded women, gaining access to and socialising in lesbian networks was relatively easy, especially for women living in Moscow. By contrast, for women socialised during the Soviet period, censorship on sexual matters and the invisibility of same-sex desire in the public sphere impacted negatively on their ability to find other queers, and to give a collective name to their desires and relations (see also Rotkirch, 2002). With one single exception[6], the older women I interviewed were unaware of places where queers socialised until the 1990s, even if there is some evidence that such places existed in big cities such as Moscow and Saint Petersburg. For some, this resulted in long periods of isolation, and in the inability to find a partner. Galya (Moscow, b. 1959), for example, had her first lesbian relationship in 1977, when she was 18; she went to university in Moscow and subsequently lived in different Soviet cities, but was unable to meet other gays or lesbians until she came across a letter to the editor from a lesbian woman in a mainstream magazine in 1996; through the magazine she was able to trace the address of the letter's author, a woman very active in the Moscow lesbian community, and started a correspondence with her. This contact played a big role in her decision to move back to the capital, where she became very involved in the activities of local community organisations.

The late 1980s and the early-to-mid 1990s were often mentioned in interviews with older women as a time that opened up new possibilities to access information and be introduced to lesbian circles. This period corresponds to the more liberal political climate initiated by Gorbachev's policy of openness (*glasnost'*, 1985–91) and to the immediate aftermath of the demise of state socialism (1991); by all accounts this time marked a significant shift in public discourses on sex and sexuality in Russian society, as they became much more pluralistic, liberal and market-driven (Baer, 2009). It was during this period that many women came across for the first time press articles discussing male and female homosexuality and personal ads. The wider availability of more diverse sources of information also offered new possibilities for socialising: personal ads, for example, provided (and still provide) not only a means to find a sexual partner, but also a way of being introduced to 'lesbian' networks, as illustrated by Zhanna's experience in the late 1980s:

> There was this silly personal ads paper. It had a section called 'She plus she'. I wrote a personal and got it published. And I got lots of letters. More than a hundred. I made a selection. If there were grammar mistakes,

I just replied 'no'. I tried to reply to everyone. I wrote, 'sorry'. I met four or five of the women who wrote. I understood that there was a *tusovka*.[7] One of these women took me there.

Zhanna, Moscow, b. 1962

Gaining access to community organisations and scene space and being able to socialise in 'lesbian' networks represented for many women a significant shift: while their previous relationships had mostly resulted from lucky encounters, and had developed in isolation from a community, the more liberal climate of the late 1980s and early 1990s offered greater opportunities to meet potential partners, to share experiences and to rearticulate their identity on the basis of new discourses which started to reclaim 'lesbian' as a positive marker of identity. In this respect, the last years of the Soviet Union and the immediate aftermath of the demise of state socialism emerge as a watershed of sorts in women's lives. Women's narratives confirm the relevance of the notions of 'Soviet' and 'post-Soviet' generations (see also Yurchak, 2006), as interviewees stressed the importance of having grown up in a country and under a social system that no longer existed, and how this had influenced their experiences and their ability to form same-sex relationships in comparison to younger generations of lesbians. At the same time, many interviewees talked about the last years of the Soviet Union and the turmoil which characterised its aftermath as an undistinguished period in which Russian society was undergoing huge political and socio-economic transformations, which affected all aspects of their lives beyond their sexuality. Stories of resilience, survival, forced career changes, unemployment, loss and ill-health, newly found freedoms and success framed women's accounts of what was happening in their intimate lives. While many accounts of post-Soviet transition have portrayed the events of 1991 as the sudden replacement of state socialism with a completely different political and economic model (Burawoy, 1999), women's narratives indicate that change manifested itself in their lives as a much more gradual process. This is a point worth bearing in mind when considering the impact of broader social and cultural changes on women's experiences and identifications.

The threat of medical treatment

As discussed earlier, most of the literature on Soviet homosexualities has foregrounded the role of the Soviet medical profession in regulating and disciplining female same-sex desire. In a report on the rights of gay men and lesbians in the Russian Federation compiled in the early 1990s, Gessen (1994) relates that women acting on their lesbian desires could be committed to a psychiatric hospital on the initiative of their parents or relatives; they were forced to take psychiatric medication and, after having been discharged, had to register with a psychiatric clinic for periodic checks. Being formally diagnosed as a lesbian also entailed the loss of some civil rights, such as being banned from some professions and from obtaining a driving licence (Gessen, 1994: 17–18). The importance of medical treatment as a key mechanism of social control is also emphasised by Essig, who argues that the diagnosis of mental illness and the ensuing forced treatment 'worked primarily at a symbolic level' as a threat that was meant to deter women from enacting homo-erotic desires (Essig, 1999: 28–9).

Both Gessen (1994) and Essig (1999) report a few cases of women who had, indeed, been subjected to psychiatric treatment because of their sexuality. While it is not my intention to dismiss the devastating effects that forced treatment had on these women's lives, it is not clear to what extent this practice was widespread, whether there were any dissenting voices among medical practitioners, or whether official medical guidelines changed over time during the late Soviet period. Findings from this study indicate that the extent to which medical practitioners actually interfered with 'deviant' sexual practices needs to be researched in greater detail. Medical treatment to cure women of their desires did not feature in the narratives of the women I interviewed; although three women came into contact with medical experts, their experiences show that forced treatment was not the unavoidable fate of all the women who came into contact with Soviet medicine. Lyuba, for example, recalled going to see a doctor in the late 1980s when she was going through a period of severe depression, and being referred to a sexopathologist:

I went to a psychiatrist first […]. She referred me to a sexopathologist. She took me to the Psychiatric Institute. I remember there was a laboratory there, with the writing 'sexopathology'.

And they never tried to cure you?

No, absolutely not. As I understand it, they treated me for depression. […]. The worst thing is that they never gave you any information. It's impossible that sexopathologists didn't know about lesbians. They didn't say anything. Apart from nonsense such as 'show an interest in men'. In the same vein, they mentioned that they had this guy [*presumably a patient*] who liked men, and they supposedly re-educated him, and he started showing an interest in women.

Lyuba, Moscow, b. 1962

Although there was no attempt to forcibly cure Lyuba of her desires, her referral to a sexopathologist clearly signals that her sexuality was seen as abnormal and pathological. The consultants never 'treated' Lyuba for her attraction to women, although they hinted at the possibility of heterosexual 're-education', a technique practiced on a male patient, allegedly with some success. Disappointingly for Lyuba, who was not sexually active or aware of the existence of others like herself at the time, experts did not offer any information about lesbianism, out of ignorance or perhaps in order to avoid stimulating her 'unhealthy' interest in women.

The non-interventionist attitude shown by the medical professionals in Lyuba's story are echoed in Sofiya's conversations with a psychiatrist, which took place in the late 1970s, when she was a policewoman and worked with juvenile offenders in a small town in the Urals. Sofiya related a conversation about a young ex-convict involved in a same-sex relationship:

> There was a girl who had just come back from an all-female institution where she had served a prison sentence. She came back, she was 17 and a half, she came back with another girl and she started to show quite openly that they lived like husband and wife. [...] I went to see a psychiatrist because the girl's mother became very anxious about her; she took her to a psychiatrist and told her exactly what was happening. And the psychiatrist told her: 'I can prescribe some medications, but they won't be any use'. [...] And when I understood that this cannot be cured, I started to ask the psychiatrist more questions, supposedly about that girl, but in reality I was asking about myself. She told me that you have to accept this for what it is, and added that until the age of 25 an individual's sexuality is still not rigidly defined, [sexual] orientation can change before the age of 25.
>
> Sofiya, St Petersburg, b. 1953

Like the consultants Lyuba met in Moscow, the young doctor from Sofiya's hometown in the Urals adopted a hands-off approach and did not forcibly cure the young offender. Unlike them, however, she did not suggest the possibility of 'heterosexual re-education', arguing instead that human sexuality is not something that can be artificially 'corrected' [*neispravimo*]. These two stories show that different protocols and personal views concerning the medical treatment of female homosexuality must have existed among Soviet medical professionals; however, they also indicate that the dominant view was that female same-sex desire was abnormal and deviant, and went against social norms of 'respectable', 'proper' and desirable behaviour. The image of same-sex desire as pathological was conveyed even when the possibility of treatment was denied.

While medical discourses were important at symbolic level in pathologising same-sex desire, the 'threat of the Cure' (Essig, 1999) itself may not have been the primary mechanism through which same-sex desire was regulated and made invisible in Soviet Russia. Indeed, interviews show that women were not necessarily aware of the threat of forced therapy, while more ordinary and subtle mechanisms of scrutiny, marginalisation and shaming featured in women's narratives. Some of them are well illustrated by Yulya's experiences as a young woman; having moved to the Saint Petersburg region to train as a plasterer and tiler, Iuliya worked on construction sites and lived in hostel accommodation with her workers collective on the outskirts of Saint Petersburg. At the age of 20 Yulya was caught having sex with another girl by the hostel's administrator. The pair had to undergo a trial of sorts at the hands of their comrades for their 'morally corrupt behaviour' [*moral'noe razlozheniie*]; the outcome of the 'trial' was the shunning of the two women by their co-workers and the threat to report them to the Communist Youth League[8] if they did not end their affair:

> We had what was called a hostel 'commandant', who could enter the room without knocking, to say for example 'be quiet' and the like. They caught us ... They caught me with a girl, and they even had a comrades' court [*tovarishcheskii sud*] [...] We used to have criminal courts and comrades' courts: the workers' collective gathered and listed the offences committed by the person on trial, and the other comrades from the collective decided, for example, to deprive the worker of their salary, or some production prize, or voucher, or another popular option was to shun them [*boikotirovat'*]. This meant not talking to the convicted person for a while, ignoring them. We had a comrades' court and they decided to ignore us. And they told us that they would bring the case to the Communist Youth League if we didn't stop this nonsense [*zanimat'sia erundoi*]. The most horrible thing was that I had to split up with that girl after the trial. Because it was a major blow for her. I had different friends, who at work did what they were told for the benefit of the management, but outside they continued to socialise with me as they always had. She had different friends, and she freaked out. Women were not put in jail for that, criminal law only concerned men. But she was worried that she may end up in jail, and so on. [...] Everyone knew about us, but again the word 'lesbian' was never uttered, this was referred to as bad behaviour. [...] Morally corrupt behaviour [*moral'noe razlozheniie*]: members of the Communist Youth League do not behave like that.
>
> Yulya, St Petersburg, born 1966

Iuliya's story illustrates the amount of scrutiny that the institutions of the socialist state were able to exercise on its citizens' private lives, as well as the importance of more informal and subtle mechanisms of social control. Comrades' courts, conceived as a way to involve ordinary Soviet citizens in the running of the justice system, were typically composed of selected members of housing and work collectives, and were called on to consider minor criminal offences, violation of local ordinances, as well as 'offences which did not contravene written laws but breached accepted norms of social behavior or otherwise undermined social cohesion' (Gorlizki, 1998: 406), ranging from arguments between neighbours to disrespectful behaviour towards spouses or parents. As Gorlizki (1998: 406) notes, comrades' courts brought under public scrutiny relations that in liberal Western societies were seen as belonging to the private sphere, and therefore beyond the reach of legitimate legal and societal intervention. As many scholars have noted, different configurations of private and public existed in Soviet society, and the private sphere was only weakly protected from the scrutiny or interference of the authorities (Oswald and Voronkov, 2004). Indeed, individuals had to protect their private and intimate lives both from the arbitrary intrusion of state institutions and from collective scrutiny (Oswald and Voronkov, 2004; Kharkhordin, 1995; Shlapentokh, 1989).

The very public exposure and shaming of the young couple was initiated by representatives of Soviet officialdom (in this case, the commandant of the hostel, the members of the comrades' court, and potentially the Communist Youth League), but the trial and punishment involved the participation of the couple's co-workers and even of Iuliya's mother, who was notified of her daughter's 'immoral' behaviour by letter, and asked to exert influence on her, in spite of living miles away. Punishment by public exposure and shunning was clearly a form of social pressure to conform to heteronorms, and extended beyond the work environment to the two women's social circle and families. As Yulya's experience shows, the effect of public shaming is the silencing of same-sex desire: the public trial did not offer an opportunity to name and define the relationship between Iuliya and her girlfriend, since the word 'lesbian' was never uttered. More importantly, Yulya came to the realisation that, in order to protect herself, she would have to hide the real nature of her relationships in future.

> When my mum received the letter [about Iuliya's 'immoral' behaviour, following the trial at the comrades' court], we had a serious talk, and she told me, 'If you have decided to live like this, fine, but there is no need to force society to see your life'. She thought that I should not be open [*about her attraction to women*], because society would never accept this, and I would be a pariah [*izgoi*]. You need to keep it quiet, find yourself someone and keep it quiet, there is no need to broadcast it. She can just be introduced as a close friend. [...] She [her mother] was against any kind openness, to avoid trouble. I agreed with her, because I had quite a hard time.
>
> Yulya, St Petersburg, b. 1966

As the experiences of other interviewees confirm, secrecy and dissimulation were paramount to the ways in which women negotiated their lesbian relationships, which were mostly hidden under the semblance of 'friendship' or disguised by other signs of respectability, such as marriage and motherhood. The awareness that these relationships could not be publicly displayed usually came from more subtle mechanisms of shaming than in

Yulya's case; these included the disapproval expressed by family and peers of 'excessive' interest they showed in women, disparaging remarks on lesbian relations and the stigmatisation of childless and unmarried women, seen as not fulfilling their potential as women and their duties towards Soviet society. Secrecy and dissimulation are closely associated to lack of privacy: as the next section will show, the private sphere of the home did not necessarily represent a space where same-sex desire could be safely expressed and articulated.

Private space, 'compulsory heterosexuality' and the invisibility of same-sex relations

Specific Soviet configurations of private and public spheres outlined earlier also affected women's experiences in terms of their relationships and patterns of cohabitations. As already mentioned, most of the women interviewed had been married at some point in their lives, and the notion of marriage as every woman's destiny and as a marker of respectable womanhood featured prominently in women's narratives, whether they had been married or not. This reflected the prevalence of marriage over other forms of partnership and cohabitation in Soviet Russia (Kaz'mina and Pushkareva, 2004: 211–13). On the other hand, cohabitation with a female partner during the Soviet period was extremely rare among research participants, and often not even contemplated as an option; this was not necessarily linked to fear of exposure but to very practical reasons related to the availability of housing and the ways in which it was allocated, as Tamara explained:

> During the Soviet period the majority of the women I dated eventually got married and lived a heterosexual life, I mean, same-sex relations had no prospects. For two women, well, you could of course live sort of together [*kak-to vmeste*], but at the time there were huge problems with housing, and it was difficult to explain to your parents why your girlfriend was staying. There was no way around it, lesbian couples simply had nowhere to live.
>
> Tamara, Moscow, b. 1952

The housing shortage mentioned by Tamara concerned mainly urban areas, and lasted throughout the Soviet period[9]: severe overcrowding meant that homes offered little privacy, as most Soviet citizens lived in very cramped conditions, in spite of the regime's promise to give every Soviet family their own apartment. The housing shortage and overcrowding were not a problem that concerned predominantly the working class, since, until the mid-1980s, virtually all Soviet housing was socialised. Single-family apartments were allocated to citizens through their workplace or city councils according to rigid criteria which prioritised married couples with children (Attwood, 2010); mechanisms of housing allocation clearly reflected institutional endorsement of the nuclear family as the 'founding unit' of Soviet society. Single parent families were not prioritised in the allocation of housing until the early 1980s, while single unmarried individuals were expected to live either with their family of origin, in communal flats or in hostel accommodation (Attwood, 2010). Tamara herself, as an unmarried woman who had four children from short-term heterosexual relationships, while being romantically involved mainly with women, lived with her mother until the latter's death.

The fact that 'lesbian couples had nowhere to live', as Tamara put it, contributes to explain their invisibility, as living in the parental home or sharing accommodation in communal flats and hostels meant women's private lives were under constant scrutiny, and they often hid the real nature of their relationships. At the same time, lack of long-term prospects of sharing a home with a female partner and starting a 'proper' family contributed to the perception, widespread among research participants, of same-sex relations as unviable. Same-sex relations were often contrasted to heterosexual coupledom, seen as offering better prospects to settle down and to receive social approval by conforming to the key markers of respectable femininity and adult womanhood – getting married, moving out of the family home and starting a family. Both Larisa (St Petersburg, b. 1951) and Aglaya (St Petersburg, b. 1957), for example, explained that their first relationship with a woman ended when their respective girlfriends, under pressure from their parents, decided to get married, a decision which Aglaya understood and supported at the time because, as she explained, 'with a man you can start a family'.

Before the 1990s, in the absence of lesbian community and scene space, for the vast majority of the women interviewed sexual and romantic relations resulted from lucky encounters, and involved correctly reading the signs of mutual attraction. While women who were predominantly or exclusively involved in same-sex relations recalled that many of their partners in the past had been 'straight' women, who would eventually get married and lead a heterosexual life, lesbian affairs where one or both partners were married, or involved in a parallel heterosexual relationship, were common. While it is tempting to read heterosexual marriage as a case of false consciousness, and a way to passively give in to pressures to conform, women gave a variety of reasons for getting married. Some women had had a meaningful and loving relationship with their husband, others retrospectively saw it as a rational choice taken in order to settle down and have a child, and for some it was a way to solve practical issues, such as obtaining a *propiska*, a residence permit required to live in certain Soviet cities (Stephenson, 2006), or finding a living space. The fact that previous heterosexual relationships and marriage were common in Soviet women's narrative has been interpreted in some of the literature as evidence of the exceptional fluidity of Russian sexual practices and identities vis-à-vis binary Western constructions of sexuality as either gay or straight (Essig, 1999). I argue, however, that these recurring narratives should not necessarily be read as a specific to Soviet Russia. In a recent study on gay and lesbian parenthood in the UK, Taylor (2009) found that the majority of her interviewees had children from previous heterosexual relationships, and that many of them had previously been married. The British women (and men) interviewed by Taylor, particularly those from a working-class background, also spoke of previous heterosexual relationships in a very matter-of-fact way, as inevitable and not necessarily problematic.

While some women presented their heterosexual past as inevitable, their narratives also show that they had agency in negotiating the terms of their marriage or ways to become a mother. Both Katya (Moscow, b. 1956) and Margarita (Ul'ianovsk, b. 1962), for example, emphasised that they got on well with their husbands, who were reliable family men and were also very tolerant of their lesbian affairs, of which (unusually) they were aware right from the start of their relationship and did not perceive as threatening. After accidentally becoming pregnant with her first child, Tamara found a married man who was willing to conceive and parent 'from a distance' two more children with her, while Yulya conceived her son with a male friend who was about to emigrate, with the mutual agreement that he would not be involved in the child's upbringing. However, jostling family responsibilities, heterosexual relations and lesbian desires was not always unproblematic, as conflicting loyalties, needs and affections could be a source of conflict and pain. On the other hand, women who had been married, or had children from previous heterosexual relationships, also stated that married or divorcee status, as well as having children, could serve as a useful 'front' to mask same-sex relationships and to reaffirm a respectable heterosexual image. Although marriage and motherhood were rarely pursued with this aim in mind, several women stated that their status as a mother or a wife could come in handy in keeping suspicion of being sexually 'deviant' at bay and in protecting their intimate lives from prying eyes. I argue therefore that 'compulsory heterosexuality' (Rich, 1980), understood as hegemonic discursive practices endorsing heterosexual romance, marriage and the nuclear family as the 'natural' norm, was more important than the 'threat of the Cure' (Essig, 1999) in making same-sex relations both unviable and invisible. As this section has shown, however, institutionalised heteronorms operated in specific ways in the context of Soviet socialist society, which was characterised both by different configurations of private and public and by a distinctive gender order (Ashwin, 2000), based on the working mother gender contact.

Conclusions

This chapter has contributed to debates about queer presences and absences by identifying a blind spot in the literature on Soviet queer sexualities: while most of existing literature focuses on the clinic and the prison camp, this chapter offers an alternative perspective by foregrounding the experiences of women whose lives and relationships took place outside of these environments.

While most of the existing literature has emphasised the key role of Soviet punitive medicine in regulating and silencing same-sex desire, I have argued for the importance of examining other, more subtle and quotidian mechanisms of stigmatisation and shaming. Their essence and effects may not be substantially different from those operating in other societies (Goffman, 1963); however, different configurations of private and public, restricted access to private personal space and institutional endorsement of marriage and the nuclear family under state socialism are key to understanding what made lesbian lives so invisible in Soviet Russia. While I acknowledge the importance of situating research data within the broader socio-historical context of Soviet Russian society, I argue against an overemphasis on Russian uniqueness, a perspective which is present in some of the literature which portrays either Russian queer sexualities or state regulation of same-sex desire in communist Russia as exceptional vis-à-vis the West. I propose instead that furthering the empirical exploration of queer lives under state socialism in Soviet Russia, and more broadly in communist Central and Eastern Europe, can challenge the ethnocentric assumption of much queer studies literature, and advance theoretical conceptualisations able to soften and complicate assumed divisions between 'Eastern' and 'Western' sexualities, and sensitive to geographical and cultural variations.

Queer studies have been widely critiqued for producing selective visibilities: for example, as Jackson (2009) notes, the global proliferation of queer identities is often read as a process emanating from the global 'West', a perspective which has contributed to bracket and marginalise non-Western queer sexualities as 'derivative' and 'underdeveloped'. Similarly, Wilson (2006) notes that 'discussions of "modern" Asian queer subjectivities share the general framework of an import-export calculus: the assumption that legible queer sexualities derive from US-inflected Western modes of sexuality or from Western-based systems of modernity, such as capitalism'. Kulpa and Mizielińska (2011: 23) show how Central and Eastern European sexualities are discursively positioned between 'East' and 'West', as '"European enough" (geographically) but "not yet Western" (temporarily)'. They note that, while the experience of state socialism sets the region apart from linear Western trajectories to modernity, 'Eastern European' and 'Western' temporalities have converged again after the fall of communist in the region, and the 'transition' to 'Western' models of political and economic development. This 'temporal disjunction', however, is problematically interpreted against paradigmatic Western models of progress, in order to (re)configure Central and Eastern Europe as the post-communist 'other', which is lagging behind and is yet to achieve the Western 'present'. The communist past, often portrayed as an instance of 'failed modernity', is key to the perceived temporal disjunction between 'Russian/Eastern European' and 'Western' sexualities; therefore, an empirical exploration of generational sexualities and state socialism in the former communist world can productively foreground diversity in the region, uncover alternative genealogies of queer sexualities, and ultimately make a substantial contribution to 'de-centring' Western temporalities within queer studies.

Notes

This chapter is dedicated to the memory of Raya T., a friend and one of the women who took place interviewed for the study, who passed away in 2011.

I gratefully acknowledge the financial support received for two periods of fieldwork in the Russian Federation from the Carnegie Trust for the Universities of Scotland (2005 and 2010), the British Association for Slavonic and East European Studies (2005) and the University of Glasgow (2005).

1. The period when the Soviet Union was under the leadership of Iosif Stalin (1878–1953).
2. Whilst Healey's work (2001) examines male subcultures in early Soviet Russia, there has been no systematic attempt as yet to research female networks, possibly owing to the difficulty of locating relevant documentary sources and eyewitnesses (Zhuk, 1998).
3. Socio-economic background no doubt shaped women's experiences and subjectivities (Rotkirch, 2002), and the representation of same-sex desire in the Soviet Union was markedly classed (Kuntsman, 2009) and racialised (Healey, 2001). However, an examination of how ethnicity and class impacted on women's experiences is beyond the scope of the present chapter, given the complexities of debates over race, ethnicity, national identity and class in Soviet and post-Soviet Russia. The concept of class, for example, is not easily transferred to Russia, not least because the profound socio-economic transformations which have followed the demise of the communist system were followed by the emergence of a new class structure.
4. In both Moscow and Ul'ianovsk, gatekeepers who facilitated the recruitment of potential participants were linked to the Moscow Gay and Lesbian Archive and the Moscow community group *Klub Svobodnogo Poseshcheniia* [Free attendance club]. Most of my Saint Petersburg interviewees were contacted through a woman who was very active in the local LGBT community, and who organised *kvartirniki* [concerts held in private flats] in her own apartment. These community initiatives were conceived as a more 'civilised' alternative to the 'rowdy' and youth-oriented commercial scene, and aimed to cater for the needs of more mature women; events organised revolved around specific interests in literature, the arts and acoustic songwriting [*bardovskaya pesnya*], and were more likely to appeal to a more educated audience.
5. Not her real name. In the interest of preserving anonymity, pseudonyms are used throughout, and other identifying details have been changed.
6. Liza, who had moved from provincial Ul'ianovsk to Saint Petersburg as a young woman to enter higher education, had been introduced to a queer network by new acquaintances she had met entirely by chance.
7. *Tusovki* can be translated as informal networks or 'in-crowds', whose members are linked by common interests and bonds of friendship and solidarity (Pilkington, 1994: 236–8).
8. *Komsomol*, a state-sponsored youth organisation whose membership numbered tens of millions.

9. By 1986 17% of the population still lived in communal apartments or hostels, and every fifth family was on a housing list, awaiting to be allocated their first apartment or a bigger one, more suited to the needs of extended or expanding families (Attwood 2010: 200). It was not uncommon for newly married couples to wait for several years before being allocated a flat and to continue living in the parental home after their marriage.

Bibliography

Adkins, L. (2004) *Revisions: Gender and sexuality in late modernity*. Buckingham: Open University Press.

Ashwin, S. (2000) *Gender, state and society in Soviet and post-Soviet Russia*. London: Routledge.

Anderson, B. (1991) *Imagined communities: Reflections on the origin and spread of nationalism*. London: Verso.

Attwood, L. (2010) *Gender and housing in Soviet Russia: Private life in a public space*. Manchester: Manchester University Press.

Baer, B. J. (2009) *Other Russias: Homosexuality and the crisis of post-Soviet identity*. Basingstoke: Palgrave Macmillan.

Buckley, M. (1989) *Women and ideology in the Soviet Union*. Hemel Hempstead: Harvester Wheatsheaf.

Burawoy, M. (1999) *Uncertain transitions: Ethnographies of change in the postsocialist world*. Oxford: Rowman and Littlefield.

Connell, R. W. (1987) *Gender and power: Society, the person and sexual politics*. Stanford, CA: Stanford University Press.

Engelstein, L. (1995) 'Soviet policy towards male homosexuality: Its origins and historical roots' in G. Hekma, H. Oosterhuis and J. Steakley (eds) *Gay men and the sexual history of the political left*. Binghamton, NY: Harrington Park Press, 155–78.

Essig, L. (1999) *Queer in Russia: A story of sex, self, and the other*. Durham, NC: Duke University Press.

Foucault, M. (1978) *The history of sexuality. Vol. I: The will to knowledge*. London: Penguin.

Gessen, M. (1994) *The rights of lesbians and gay men in the Russian Federation*. San Francisco: IGLHRC.

Goffman, E. (1963) *Stigma: Notes on the management of a spoilt identity*. London: Penguin.

Gorlizki, Y. (1998) 'Delegalization in Russia: Soviet comrades' courts in retrospect', *American Journal of Comparative Law*, 48(3): 103–25.

Healey, D. (2001) *Homosexual desire in revolutionary Russia: The regulation of sexual and gender dissent*. Chicago: University of Chicago Press.

Hoffmann, D. (2003) *Stalinist values: The cultural norms of Soviet modernity, 1917–1941*. Ithaca: Cornell University Press.

Jackson, P. (2009) 'Global queering and [global] queer theory: Thai [trans]genders and [homo]sexualities in world history', *Autrepart*, 49(1): 15–30.

Karlinsky, S. (1989) 'Russia's gay literature and culture: The impact of the October Revolution' in M. Duberman, M. Vicinus and G. Chauncey (eds) *Hidden from history: Reclaiming the gay and lesbian past*. London: Penguin, 347–64.

Kaz'mina, O. and Pushkareva, N. (2004) 'Brak v Rossii XX veka: Traditsionnye ustanovki i innovatsionnye eksperimenty' in S. Ushakin (ed.) *Semeinye uzy: modeli dlia sborki*, Vol. 1. Moscow: Novoe literaturnoe obozreniie, 185–218.

Kharkhordin, O. (1995) 'The Soviet individual: Genealogy of a dissimulating animal' in M. Featherstone, S. Lash and R. Robertson (eds) *Global modernities*. London: Sage, 209–26.

Kon, I. and Riordan, J. (eds) (1993) *Sex and Russian society*. Bloomington: Indiana University Press.

Kon, I. S. (1997) 'Russia', in D. West and R. Green (eds) *Sociolegal control of homosexuality: A multi-national comparison*. New York: Plenum Press, 221–42.

Kozlovskii, V. (1986) *Argo russkoi gomoseksual'noi subkul'tury: materialy k izucheniiu*. Benson, VT: Chalidze Publications.

Kulpa, R. and Mizielińska, J. (2011) *De-centring Western sexualities: Central and Eastern European perspectives*. Farnham: Ashgate.

Kuntsman, A. (2009) '"With a shade of disgust": Affective politics of sexuality and class in memoirs of the Stalinist Gulag', *Slavic Review*, 68(2): 308–28.

Oswald, I. and Voronkov, V. (2004) 'The "public–private" sphere in Soviet and post-Soviet society: Perception and dynamics of "public" and "private" in contemporary Russia', *European Societies*, 6(1): 97–117.

Pilkington, H. (1994) *Russia's youth and its culture*, London: Routledge.

Plummer, K. (1995) *Telling sexual stories: Power, change, and social worlds*. New York: Routledge.

Rich, A. (1980) 'Compulsory heterosexuality and lesbian existence', *Signs* 5(4): 631–60.

Rotkirch, A. (2002) '"Liubov" so slovami i bez slov: Opyt lesbiiskikh otnoshenii v pozdnesovetskom periode' in E. Zdravomyslova and A. Temkina (eds) *V poiskakh seksual'nosti*. Sankt-Peterburg: Dmitrii Bulanin, 452–68.

Shlapentokh, V. (1989) *Public and private life of the Soviet people: Changing values in post-Stalin Russia*. New York: Oxford University Press.

Skeggs, B. (2002) 'Techniques for telling the reflexive self', in May. T. (ed.) *Qualitative research in action*. London: Sage, 349–74.

Stella, F. (2008) 'Lesbian identity and everyday space in contemporary urban Russia'. Unpublished Ph.D. thesis, University of Glasgow.

Stella, F. (2010) 'The language of intersectionality: Researching "lesbian" identity in urban Russia', in Y. Taylor, S. Hines and M. Casey (eds) *Theorizing intersectionality and sexuality*. Basingstoke: Palgrave Macmillan, 212–34.

Stephenson, S. (2006) *Crossing the line: Vagrancy, homelessness and social displacement in Russia*. Aldershot and Burlington, VT: Ashgate.

Taylor, Y. (2009) *Gay and lesbian parenting: Securing social and educational capital*. Basingstoke: Palgrave Macmillan.

Taylor, Y. (2011) 'Queer presences and absences: Citizenship, community, diversity – or death', *Feminist Theory*, 12(3): 335–41.

Temkina, A. and Zdravomyslova, E. (2002) *V poiskakh seksual'nosti*. St Petersburg: Dmitrii Bulanin.

Valentine, G. (1995) 'Out and about: Geographies of lesbian landscapes', *International Journal of Urban and Regional Research*, 19(1): 96–111.

West, D. and Green, R. (eds) (1997) *Sociolegal control of homosexuality: A multi-national comparison*. New York: Plenum Press.

Wilson, A. (2006) 'Queering Asia', *Intersections: Gender, History and Culture in the Asian Context*, issue 14, http://intersections.anu.edu.au/issue14/wilson.html, accessed on 31 January 2012.

Yurchak, A. (2006) *Everything was forever, until it was no more: The last Soviet generation*. Princeton: Princeton University Press.

Zhuk, O. (1998) *Russkie amazonki: Istoriia lesbiiskoi subkul'tury v Rossii XX-go veka*. Moskva: Izd-vo Glagol.

4
Identities and Citizenship under Construction: Historicising the 'T' in LGBT Anti-Violence Politics in Brazil

Jan Simon Hutta and Carsten Balzer

Introduction

> What's in the media is this: repression against homosexuals – very plainly nowadays, right? In the past, it used to be something more covered, something more ... occult. Nowadays not. Nowadays, people openly say: 'I don't like gays!' People openly pass by and slap someone in the face, or do this or that. Which I think, erm ... in the favela I think it's stronger, right? Because there are no laws that protect the individual. They exist – but in here they don't work! If I'm subject to a homophobic attack and get a lamp in the face, that's how it will have to be, done and over! I'll have to ... I can't go to the reference centre and make a denunciation. I can't, because I live here. I have family here.
>
> Gilmar[1]

This statement by the activist Gilmar, who identifies as *travesti* and lives in Rio de Janeiro's favela complex Maré, highlights a set of issues around violence that this chapter will scrutinise. (The identity '*travesti*' is among these issues.) As we will explain shortly, the statement points to the need to gain a historicised and spatialised understanding, not only of violent manifestations that have gained renewed public attention over the past decade, but also of the subjectivities that have suffered from violence and the forms of political activism that have been developed in response. We are referring to violence directed at people whose gender expressions and performances is perceived as challenging hegemonic norms, an issue that over the past 15 years has gained prominence in both trans and LGBT activisms[2] in Brazil. The burgeoning genre of victimological studies, for instance, has been mobilised to highlight the prevalence of verbal and physical aggression against lesbian, gay, bisexual and trans people[3], the latter's particular vulnerability frequently being underlined.[4] Gay Group of Bahia (*Grupo Gay da Bahia*,

GGB), which documented murders of LGBT people since the 1980s, has repeatedly highlighted the high share of *travestis* among the victims. In a report from 2009, the activists suggest that based on their findings *travestis* are 256 times more likely than gay men to be murdered (Grupo Gay da Bahia, 2009). In international LGBT activism and public debate, lethal violence against Brazilian trans people has received attention due to the Trans Murder Monitoring (TMM) project of the organisation Transgender Europe, which the authors are conducting in collaboration with local organisations like GGB. In absolute numbers, Brazil has had the highest share of the reported murders of trans people worldwide documented by the project, amounting to 256 reports since 2008 as of September 2011 (Balzer and Hutta, 2011).[5]

While there has thus been a growing awareness of violence against Brazilian trans people in activist and academic contexts both nationally and internationally, attempts to understand and find viable political responses to this issue have encountered a number of challenges. In this chapter, we engage with two of them. Firstly, in the wake of Don Kulick's (1998) book on *travesti* sex workers, Anglophone academic debates have tended to treat *travesti* subjectivity in the singular and to focus on very specific forms of embodiment and gender performance. The actual multiplicity of Brazilian trans identities has largely been neglected, as has their wider social and historical context, eclipsing from view how these identities have been shaped by discrimination, oppression and violence. Secondly, violence against trans people has often been considered detached from political responses to such violence, or only by making generic and undifferentiated references to LGBT activism. The historical transformations in both LGBT and trans activisms resulting especially from a shift towards state-centred, biopolitical activism in the late 1990s, and the potentials and limitations that have ensued, have thus gone unnoticed. As a result, there has been a poor understanding of trans people's, partly denied, capacities to gain and enact 'citizenship', in both a state-directed and a quotidian sense.

This chapter has thus three main objectives. The first is to gain a complexified and historicised understanding of Brazilian trans cultures and identities. We argue that contemporary problems of transphobic violence need to be viewed in relation to contingent practices and identifications that have historically evolved in response to violence, oppression and discrimination. Secondly, we want to draw attention to political responses to such violence, which gained new momentum with the biopolitical activisms that emerged in the late 1990s, leading to new challenges. Following on from a consideration of these challenges, we finally want to highlight trans people's practical enactments of citizenship, which call for renewed political endeavours to effectively counter violence. We will use empirical research that was conducted between 2000 and 2011 in Brazil and had both historical and current dimensions, as will be described later on.

Let us come back to the quoted statement by Gilmar, who was one of our interviewees. Gilmar is 26 year-old and the co-founder of Brazil's first LGBT group based in a favela, *Grupo Conexão G*, which is directed mainly towards issues of *travestis*. '*Travesti*' refers to persons who were assigned a male gender at birth and live their lives or large parts of their lives in a female, partly female, or different gender, using often various expressive and body-modifying practices without necessarily aiming to assume a 'full female' body and identity by means of gender reassignment surgery or an endeavour to plainly 'pass' as woman. A particularity of the identification of many *travestis* is that they *also* identify as homosexual/gay, using 'homosexual' (*homossexual*) as a more generic term. It is of note that such a conflation of concepts that are viewed as detached in Anglo-American discourse is characteristic of queer identities in Rio de Janeiro's subcultures. Balzer showed that – contrary to the prevalent Western habit of differentiating and combining sexual orientation and gender identity (as, for instance, in the differentiation into gay, lesbian or straight trans persons) – among Rio's diverse subcultural identity concepts there is also one that assigns specific trans identities to a particular sexual identity. Many of Balzer's informants defined themselves as 'homosexual of the gender *travesti*' or 'homosexual of the gender *transformista*' (*homossexual do gênero travesti/transformista*) (Balzer, 2007: 342–71). In contrast to many other *travestis*, however, Gilmar retains a male name, which suggests the use of the male pronoun, *ele*. As Gilmar simultaneously uses female grammatical endings (such as *cansada*, 'tired'), we will use the pronouns 's_he' and 'hir' to take account of the simultaneity of male, female and further or undeterminable identifications.

A note on Gilmar's use of the term *homofobia* might be useful here. Given Gilmar's identification as *homossexual*, the fact that s_he uses the term *homofobia*, while addressing in particular violence against *travestis*, might not surprise. 'Homophobia' is also a generic standard term used in globalised lesbian, gay, bisexual, trans and queer (LGBTQ) activism. Over the past decade, there has however been a growing recognition, both in Brazil and elsewhere, of the need to specify 'transphobia', in the sense of violence, hostility and injustice related to non-normative gender identity and expression, against 'homophobia', which is generally understood as relating to sexual orientation. This is because trans people face specific, and often particularly problematic and extreme, forms of violence, discrimination and oppression.

Interestingly, after highlighting the problem of open 'homophobia' in Brazil, Gilmar points out that this problem is aggravated by the fact that in a context like Maré, 'there are no laws that protect the individual' – or rather, such laws 'exist – but in here they don't work!' Gilmar seems to consider in particular the mobilisation of state security in the form of police and criminal justice not viable, as aggressors might take revenge on hir and hir family, which in turn the state would not be able to prevent. This points to the intricacies activists have faced due to the mentioned turn to biopolitical forms of activism, raising the question of the kinds of agency and citizenship that trans subjects like Gilmar might be able to enact – or, in fact, already *do* enact.

Our discussion intervenes into current queer debates on various accounts. It aims to give new presence to certain issues that have been largely absent in these debates, and, simultaneously, strives towards a new kind of queer presence. We understand 'queer' as a political and analytical term that challenges norms around sexuality and gender along with associated power relations that take shape in historical and spatial context. 'Queer' moreover suggests an affirmation of certain practices, bodies and identities that have been marked as deviant, unnatural, or immoral (see Halberstam, 2005; Hutta, 2010a: 33–5; Muñoz, 1999). Much of the 'queer' debate that has proliferated since the 1990s has concentrated on performative, embodied acts and their norm-challenging potentials. Visual and textual representations as well as practices developed within subcultures have formed privileged sites of engagement. While we retain the critical and affirmative aspects of a 'queer' project, we aim to situate performing subjectivities more thoroughly within space and time, considering subcultural and representational phenomena along with discourses and practices that unfold in formal politics and every-day contexts as part of societal power dynamics. Our approach differs significantly, for instance, from Kulick's mentioned discussion of embodied *travesti* subjectivity, which has become a standard reference in queer debates beyond North America and Western Europe. Where Kulick is concerned with the formation of a *travesti* subjectivity (in the singular!) through intimate and sexual relations, we wish to highlight the emergence and transformation of manifold trans identities in historical and political contexts that have been violently constraining and simultaneously politically contested. We thus want to give stronger presence to a set of historical and political issues that have tended to be absent in prevalent queer debate.

On another level, by addressing the Brazilian context, this chapter troubles the genealogy of 'queer', a term that has emerged in Anglo-American activist and academic contexts, and is now also used in many non-English-speaking European contexts. In Brazil, by contrast, the use of 'queer' has been limited to academic debates, even if in recent years some activists and artists have started mobilising it as well. While our approach can be said to constitute a 'queer analysis' in its concern with gender, sexuality and power, the subjectivities we are concerned with have largely defied interpellation into the semantic universe of 'queer', insisting on their singularity. When we use 'queer people' or 'queer identities' in relation to the Brazilian context, we are hence making a particular translation, summoning a notion of 'queer' that is not fully in shape. As the presence of 'queer' is contested and under construction, what our discussion strives towards is thus a queer presence that is yet to come.

The empirical methods we rely on comprise interviews, group workshops, participant observations and archival work. Balzer's data were collected during six months of ethnographic fieldwork in Rio de Janeiro between 2000 and 2001. This fieldwork was based on multi-local research with participant observation and concentrated on street sex work, nightlife and show business, social activism, as well as informants' daily lives. A transgender person hirself, and due to friendships in these subcultures Balzer was welcomed very heartily in all places. From the over 80 transgender persons s_he came to know during participant observation and informal talks, s_he interviewed 31 individuals in total, focusing on biographical aspects, self-images, self-organisation, and political strategies. Moreover, analyses of historical documents (video tapes, flyers, underground publications) and current publications (transgender and gay magazines, weekly magazines, tabloid newspapers) were conducted (see Balzer, 2007: 36–54). Hutta conducted nine months of fieldwork in Brazil between 2007 and 2009 (Hutta, 2010a: 235–47). Central were two participatory workshop series conducted in Rio de Janeiro's wider metropolitan region. The focus was on people's experiences of various spaces inhabited in daily life. Activities also comprised city walks and visits and lead to recordings of 45 individuals, including five *travestis* and various subjects who identified with local genderqueer terms like *bichaboy*. As a gay and queer person whose social, political and research activities frequently intersected, Hutta moreover gained insights in a range of less formalised contexts. A second research strand targeted LGBT and trans activisms and involved participant observations, document analyses and 17 interviews, which included four trans activists. We will moreover make use of research we jointly conducted as part of an activist research project of Transgender Europe, which is called 'Transrespect versus Transphobia Worldwide' (TvT)[6]. The aforementioned Trans Murder Monitoring forms part of the TvT project. As part of the TvT project, we have also conducted further interviews with activists, including Gilmar. Due to the focus of our research, in what follows we will mainly focus on the extended metropolitan region of Rio de Janeiro. As will become clear especially in our discussion of anti-violence activism since the late 1990s, Rio also played a paramount role in the development of newer political strategies.

Identities and activisms shaped in the context of dictatorship, violence and oppression

The complexity and diversity of Brazilian trans identities that evolved in the twentieth century is often reduced to a single and simplified identity: the *travesti* (see for instance Silva, 1993; Oliveira, 1994; Kulick, 1998). *Travesti* is however only one identity in a spectrum of Brazilian queer and trans identities, and the meaning of the term changed over the course of the past decades and bears its own complexity. Reductive understandings of Brazilian *travestis* as 'prostitutes' have also proliferated outside Brazil due to Kulick's mentioned book as well as waves of *travesti* migration and travel from the dictatorship and post-dictatorship Brazil to European cities like Paris and Milan in the 1980s and 1990s. However, this concerns a very specific set of experiences that are directly connected to historical formations of violence, repression, discrimination, as well as a sexualised consumer culture that all in different ways targeted or took shape around *travestis*. In order to understand the diversity of Brazilian trans identities as they evolved over the last five decades, as well as the context in which they were shaped, it is necessary to look backwards, starting in the times before the last Brazilian dictatorship. In particular, such a historically situated approach is crucial to contextualise the question of transphobic violence and political strategies that have been developed in response. The following brief historical review serves to better understand the connections and detachments between the LGBT movement and trans organisations, and to reconsider the meaning and significance of the 'T' in the prevalent acronym 'LGBT'.

During Brazil's democratic period after WW II and especially in the late 1950s and early 1960s, identifiable gay bars opened in Rio de Janeiro's Copacabana. What, in places like New York City, was known as female impersonation or drag, and in Brazil used to be closely linked to certain carnival balls, acquired acceptance by a wider public outside Carnival (Balzer, 2007: 312). The historian James Green informs us that 'glamorous cross-dressers emerged from these drag balls to perform in mainstream theatre productions that attracted a wide audience' (1999: 148). Among these so-called cross-dressers was Rogéria[7], who became Rio de Janeiro's first drag star in the early 1960s and is nowadays known as Brazil's most famous *travesti* or *transformista*. At that time, people like Rogéria were called *travestis*, meaning travesty performers. However, what people like Rogéria were doing was not simply 'female impersonation'. In an interview with Balzer, Rogéria explained that since childhood she always felt 'female'. In the late 1960s and early 1970s, like most of Rio's *travestis* at the time, she took female hormones. In the early 1960s, however, many different female identities evolved in the increasingly open and organised gay scene, which published their own journals. In one of Rio de Janeiro's gay journals, '*O Snob*' ('The Snob'), a discourse started in 1963 on the variety of the different gender identities that could be observed in Rio's gay scene: the *bichas*, *bofes*, *bonecas* and *entendidos* (Balzer, 2007: 312–14). Rogéria's *travesti* identity was thus expressive of only one of a set of multiple trans and queer identities.

Rogéria's career brings into relief how trans cultures and identities changed since the 1960s in the context of social transformations in Brazil. Her becoming famous coincided with another event that was going to have a strong impact on Brazil's culture in the following decades, namely the 1964 coup d'état, which resulted in 20 years of military dictatorship. The military repression that started in the late 1960s and reached its peak in the 1970s had two main targets: anyone who was seen as part of the 'communist threat', and anyone who was said to pose a threat to 'Brazilian family morals'. The latter 'threat' was associated primarily with gay people and of course with *travestis*, who were the most recognizable gays at that time. Military censorship prohibited any *travesti* show on television and in the theatre, and males were imprisoned for looking gay, that is, feminine. Judy and Theo, for instance, two of Balzer's informants, explained that during the military dictatorship they were prosecuted and arrested several times by the police due to their female appearance. In 1972, 25 *travestis* dressed in bikinis were arrested at once on a beach in Rio's South Zone (Balzer, 2007: 315–19; Green, 1999: 251).

Rogéria and others who could afford to do so left the country.[8] A great part of those who stayed to worked as sex workers to sustain themselves and formed marginalised subcultural groups and networks. For instance, in 1974, 15 year-old Rebecca from Rio de Janeiro left her family because of being homosexual and *travesti*. As a consequence, she lived on the street with other *travestis*, taking female hormones and learning how to do sex work. In an interview, Rebecca explained that she started to do sex work out of necessity as she had no other option and did not want to starve. Another example is Cora, a *travesti* from Rio de Janeiro who left her family as an 11 year-old kid in the mid-1970s. Cora said she started to do sex work because she wanted to wear a skirt and be independent. Most of Balzer's informants who had their coming-out during the military dictatorship told similar stories of hardship.[9] The own family was often part of the problem and sometimes even became a threat, as the report of one *travesti* powerfully demonstrates. Being committed by her parents to an insane asylum, she was treated with drugs and 'electric shock therapy' 'to lose the desire to be a *travesti*'. In the early 1980s, almost at the end of the dictatorship, up to 5000 *travestis* lived from sex work in Brazilian cities like São Paulo and Rio de Janeiro (Balzer, 2007: 315–29; Penteado, 1980: 2; Oliveira, 1995: 92).

While in the early 1960s sex work did not play a prominent role in *travestis'* lives, during the dictatorship one could observe the formation of an independent sexual market for *travestis*. The increase in *travesti* sex work is directly linked to the repression of the dictatorship in various ways. First of all, drag performances, *travestis'* primary profession, were forbidden, and *travestis* were excluded not only from the labour market, but also from the housing market, which led to self-organisation in the emergent sex work scene. This development was intensified by the dictatorship's orientation towards international capitalism and consumer culture as well as the promotion of urbanisation, which was supposed to project Brazil into the world market.

With the developing *travesti* sex market, dynamics of demand and supply provoked changes in the identities and bodies of *travestis*, who were of course themselves entangled within emerging consumerism and shifting imaginations around gender and beauty. For instance, in order to better attract their clients, as well as sometimes to satisfy own desires, *travesti* sex workers transformed their bodies with female hormones and injected industrial silicone, but did not want to have gender reassignment surgery. They thus had to take enormous health risks to survive and find their roles in the newly emerging sex market. Apart from the risk of serious liver damage as a side effect of taking female hormones without medical supervision, it is above all the injection of industrial silicone lead, and still leads, to serious health problems and sometimes death. Rebecca, who survived the injection of industrial silicone, explained: 'That's the story of silicone injection: many already died from injecting silicone' (Balzer, 2007: 331–2).[10]

By the end of the dictatorship in the mid 1980s, the formerly positive term *travesti* had become associated with 'prostitution' and crime, and *travestis* were often seen as *marginais*, a term signifying a shady, marginal, immoral and criminal existence. When Rogéria returned to Brazil and started a comeback in the 1980s, she dissociated herself from 'street *travestis*' by calling herself a *transformista*. In the early 2000s, many of Balzer's informants agreed that Rogéria was the first to use the term *transformista*, which had not been known before the 1980s. Thus, Rogéria, who had previously made the term *travesti* famous, later popularised the new and less prejudicial term *transformista*.

In the last ten years of the Brazilian dictatorship, from 1975 to 1985, a phase that is known in Brazil as the so-called *abertura* or 'opening' of the dictatorship, various liberation movements (such as students, trade unionists, women, *negros*, and gays) emerged. The slight reduction of the ongoing repression made it possible for alternative media to come into life again. During the *abertura*, however, *travestis* experienced even more repression and police brutality than before. In the mid-1970s, in Sao Paulo, a systematic hunt for *travesti* sex workers started that lead to the arrest of 2000 *travestis*, who faced the same treatment as the political prisoners. In 1981, a military operation called 'operation Rondão', which was directed mainly against *travestis*, who were called 'human trash' (*lixo humano*), led to the arrest of 1500 *travestis* in one week. The fact that *travestis* faced the starkest repression led to a wave of solidarity of the developing *Brazilian LGBT movement*. One of the most important and influencing journals in this movement was *Lampião da Esquina* (street corner lamp). Various articles addressed the sufferings of *travestis* and the repression they faced, and authors bemoaned the absence of *travesti* participants in the '1st Brazilian Meeting of Homosexuals (*I Encontro Brasileiro de Homossexuais*) in 1980 (Balzer, 2007: 324–6).

After the end of the dictatorship in the second half of the 1980s, the situation for *travestis* became even worse. Military police kept hunting down *travestis*, now being supported by the so-called death squads and vigilante groups. 'Disgusted' citizens were not prosecuted when they ran a car into a group of *travesti* sex workers at night or when they hunted *travestis* down with iron rods and planks. In the late 1980s and the early 1990s, the number of murders of *travestis* as well as on gays increased enormously. In the early 1990s, when the AIDS hysteria had its heyday and let to an increase of homophobia and transphobia, *travestis* had not only become associated with 'prostitution', crime, and drugs, but also with AIDS (Balzer, 2007: 333–4).

While in the 1980s homecoming exiled *travestis* like Rogéria reinvented themselves as *transformistas*, and *travesti* sex workers transformed their identities in the context of the sex market, in the 1990s, some younger *transformistas* benefitted from the global drag queen hype and reinvented them as 'non-sexual', fun-making drag queens, adding a new persona to the spectrum of Brazilian trans identities (Balzer, 2005: 120–3). At the same time, the professionalisation of *travesti* self-organisation in the context of civil rights started in 1992 with the founding of the first *travesti* NGO in Brazil, ASTRAL (*Associação de Travestis e Liberados*) in Rio de Janeiro. Rebecca, one of the ASTRAL activists in the 1990s and early 2000s explained that ASTRAL was founded by five *travestis*, who started by writing protest letters to the General Command of the Military Police and organised demonstrations to complain against police violence.[11] ASTRAL also started to organise national *travesti* congresses[12], which led to the formation of new *travesti* NGOs throughout Brazil. In 1995, ASTRAL members participated in the 7th National LGT meeting, during which the ABGLT (*Associação Brasileira de Gays, Lésbicas e Travestis*), the Brazilian Gay, Lesbian, and Transgender Association was founded. (Today, the acronym is placeholder for *Associação Brasileira de Lésbicas, Gays, Bissexuais, Travestis e Transexuais*). While ASTRAL continuously conducted HIV/AIDS prevention and counselling, anti-violence and justice were the main focal points of its political agenda. At a trans demonstration in 1999 in front of the city council, ASTRAL members declared: 'The *travestis* of Rio de Janeiro and Brazil affirm: The police kill more than AIDS!' (Balzer, 2007: 340–1).

At this time, in 1999, in Rio de Janeiro an institution called *Disque Defesa Homosexual* (DDH) was created within the State Office of Public Security in collaboration with LGT activists and researchers (Ramos and Carrara, 2006). Activists had three representatives of the LGT movement. A main focus of the DDH was the transformation of the civil and military police from an institutional menace for LGT people into an institution that protects them (Balzer, 2007: 384–5; Hutta, 2010a: 315–20; Soares, 2000: 155–6). This transformation was a challenge, which is highlighted by the late Hanah Suzart, who was the first *travesti* representative within the DDH and gave trainings to the military police of how to respectfully address trans people:

And when I went to give a talk at a group from the military police, a policeman said: 'How do I refer to you? Mister? Misses?' And that's always a big laugh, right? Very funny. [...] I said to him: 'I am dressed [*estou travestido*] as a woman, I would like you to refer to me using the feminine form, I prefer 'Misses', because I am single.' He said: 'Misses, it is strange what is happening to us, who are old policemen, who have been in the military police for 20 years. It's funny for people and difficult for ourselves, because formerly we used to catch the *bichas* at Campo de Santana [a popular park] and took them to through the backdoor to the police station. [...] And today, these gays can come entering the station through the main entrance and say 'the policeman, did this and that, he touched me and took that many Reais off me', and when the policeman comes to the battalion the next day, he gets arrested.[13]

The creation of the *Disque Defesa Homossexual* in Rio in 1999 marks the beginning of a new formation of knowledge and political practice in relation to homo- and transphobic violence in Brazil. Having outlined the trajectory in particular of *travesti* as both embodied subjectivity and political identity that has been shaped by acute violence as well as by desires and struggles to live happily and gain respect, we will now turn to recent activist responses to violence.

Contemporary LGBT and trans activisms against violence and discrimination

While in the early 1980s anti-violence activism focused on denouncing and protesting violence committed by the police, the state and society (for instance, in a legendary protest march against the aforementioned 'operation Rondão' in 1981), with the new collaborations between state and social movement actors that arose in the context of the DDH, activists started to see the police and the state as potential resources in the struggle against violence. These resources consisted both in being able to mobilise the police for the prevention and repression of violence, and in accessing means for educating the police themselves, which continued to be responsible for a great share of violence (Ramos, 2007). Rebecca, the ASTRAL activist, who in the 1990s became subject to violence from the police many times, stated in 2000 that although police violence was decreasing, it still existed and remained a challenge.[14] In 2007, Roxane pointed out that arbitrary and illegal practices of 'collective punishment' of *travestis* – very common up to the 1990s – largely stopped, at least in Rio's Central and South Zones. Spatial differences, however, are indicated by Sasha, who lives in a small town in Rio de Janeiro's peripheralised Baixada Fluminense region, and states: 'You can count on your fingers who [of the police] from here respects us, because in the early morning [*na madrugada*], if they can do it, they do it.'[15] By 'they can do it', we take Sasha to mean abusive behaviour. In the twilight between night and day the police can do whatever they want, no matter what formal laws and policies might exist. This statement highlights one of the challenges for anti-violence activism we want to discuss, in particular with respect to spatial differences. Moreover, while the police violence against trans people decreased, the general violence against trans people, including extreme forms remained and still remains a major problem, as the studies and data cited in the beginning illustrate (see also Balzer, 2007: 130–1; 2009: 148).

The now 50-year-old *travesti* Marcelly Malta from Porto Alegre was among the first activists who, in 1999, started to teach courses on human rights, sexual minorities and sex work for trainees of the civil and military police (Böer, 2003). After having been in an abject-like position during decades where, lacking the opportunity of formal employment, she worked as a sex worker and was detained, humiliated and maltreated time and again by the police, Marcelly was now able to step into the position of an expert, even if her living situation continued to be precarious.[16] Hanah's account of her experiences in the context of the DDH highlights the kinds of issues this shift provoked on the part of public institutions. Many trans people, in the early 2000s as today, still fear(ed) to report crimes to the police. As a DDH representative, Hanah went to the police for *travestis* who feared to make a denunciation. When she went to the police one time and the responsible officer was not willing to listen and take any action, she took her mobile phone and called her contact person within the State Office of Public Security. A couple of minutes later, her contact in the Office called the police officer in question, reminding him of his duties and threatening with sanctions. From the moment on, Hanah said, she was treated very respectfully, able to make her denunciation, and even offered a cup of coffee.[17]

The broader discursive backdrop to this re-orientation of activism was provided by on-going debates around a 'democratisation' of the country and an increasing awareness on the part of the political left that the Brazilian police, with its separation of civil and military police, maintained the grossly undemocratic design and martial macho ethos it had acquired during the military dictatorship (Soares, 2006). Debates around 'democratisation', 'human rights' and 'citizenship' opened up practical possibilities for lesbian, gay and trans activists to start engaging with securitisation and the police from within the polity, which had formerly been limited to activities in the area of HIV/AIDS (Hutta, 2010a: 175–80). Of particular importance were attempts by leftist scholars and politicians to re-appropriate and re-define the Brazilian notion of *segurança pública* ('public security') – which in the 1970s meant the aversion of 'the communist threat' and of the 'threat to Brazilian family values' – in terms of the 'security of the public', the security of 'the collective, of citizens' (Souza, 2008, 150; emphasis in the original) (see Hutta, 2010a: 207–16). But not only did activists see new possibilities of political engagement emerging in relation to the field of *segurança pública*, on the part of state actors, leftist politicians like Luiz Eduardo Soares, who was coordinator of public security of the state of Rio de Janeiro when the

DDH was set up, saw in anti-homophobic activisms a resource for democratising state security. The notorious problems of the Brazilian state security apparatus were for Soares directly linked to its violent macho ethos that brought with it a devaluation of everything deviating from hegemonic masculinity. Engaging positively with sexual minorities, for him, bared a potential of countering this ethos, epitomising and synthesising the broader project of democratising security (Hutta 2010a: 317).

In the DDH, activists' desire to educate the police thus conjoined with the desire of leftist politicians like Soares to democratise Brazilian public security, paving the way not only for a proliferation of DDH style *centros de referência*, or 'reference centres', throughout Brazil, but also for the elaboration of detailed LGBT public security agendas on municipal, state and national scales on the basis of hybrid state-activism ensembles. In 2007, Rio's LGBT movement organised the 1st National Seminar on Public Security and Combating Homophobia (*I Seminário Nacional de Segurança Pública e Combate à Homofobia*), which was funded by the Brazilian government and was followed by numerous further seminars on the level of states. The much vaunted 1st National LGBT Conference of 2008 in Brasília, which was the first state-organised national conference and opened by President Lula da Silva, contained a thematic block on public security which articulated into a set of concrete proposals (see Secretaria Especial dos Direitos Humanos, 2008). On the level of public campaigns, the LGBT movement placed a great focus on an (as yet unsuccessful) 'hate crime' legislation that criminalises various kinds of discrimination and prejudice in relation to sexual orientation and gender identity. The proposal was originally issued in 2001 and then turned into the law project 'PLC 122/2006' in 2006.

The ascendency of engagements with *políticas LGBT de segurança pública*, or LGBT public security politics, coincided with, and contributed to, the consolidation of a new approach and self-conception of the Brazilian LGBT movement, which we already indicated in relation to 1990s trans activism. From the mid 1990s, NGO-style and increasingly professionalised advocacy came to replace earlier forms of consciousness-raising and street protest, a process that already started in the 1980s, yet gained new momentum in the mid and late 1990s (De la Dehesa, 2010; Facchini, 2005; Hutta, 2010b). The term *MHB*, *movimento homossexual brasileiro* was in this process gradually replaced, first, in the early and mid 1990s, by *MGL* (movement of gays and lesbians) and *movimento GLT* (movement of gays, lesbians and *travestis*), and, more recently, by the label *movimento LGBT*.

This re-naming is also expressive of changes on an epistemological and discursive level. As political engagements increasingly circulated around policies in the field of public security, as well as in fields of health, employment, family life, and so on, what was previously affirmed as the political collectivity of 'homosexuals' that gained unity through a common struggle against oppression and violence, now had to be differentiated according to the 'demands' of the specific 'sub-populations' that lesbians, gays, bisexuals, and trans people articulate in relation to the state, such as access to institutions, the guarantee of securitisation and various forms of care. The epistemological and discursive framing of 'LGBT people' as minority populations demanding access to institutions and state securitisation and care announces an insertion into what Michel Foucault (1998; 2008) characterises as 'biopolitics' – a politics of liberal-democratic states that is centred on the various dimensions of the 'lives' of populations and their constituting bodies. Foucault argues that such a biopolitics, enables the state to increase these populations' productivity and comes along with certain formations of knowledge and practice. For only through knowledge of which sub-population is subject to which kinds of risks and vulnerabilities can state institutions make interventions in the various fields concerning the population's lives. Importantly, such knowledge is not being produced simply by 'the state' in order to 'control' the populations in question, but rather in the context of LGBT activism itself, that is, hybrid ensembles of social movement and state actors, as well as various public, private and activist loci of knowledge production.

The acronym 'LGBT', then, serves simultaneously as a unifying shorthand for a group of 'minorities' in need of special care of the state, and as a placeholder for the very different demands the different populations composing this 'minority' articulate. The letter 'T' has occupied a simultaneously prominent and precarious position within this acronym and within the political activities running under its banner. As mentioned earlier, already in the context of the meeting of *homossexuais* in 1980, the absence of *travestis* was lamented, indicating simultaneously their marginalisation in relation to lesbians and gays and their presence in some political debates. The tripartite representation in Rio's DDH, as it was set up in 1999 (one lesbian, one gay, one trans person), indicates the important position trans activists had in LGT (later called 'LGBT') public security activism right from the start. Hanah Suzart explained that there had been discussions in the late 1990s within the *carioca* LGT movement that led to the consensus, that 'we need three representatives, a gay representative, a lesbian representative and a *travesti* representative'.[18] A press release published by the Brazilian LGBT Association (ABGLT) in July 2010 again expresses a great investment in trans issues. It mentions the high number of homicides of trans people in Brazil and proposes a campaign around several issues, including, apart from the aforementioned legislation against homophobia, for instance also the support of a campaign for the use of trans people's social name, the approval of a project for enhancing trans people's employment opportunities, and the implementation of an anti-violence and service hotline. At the same time, however, the 'T' has frequently been marginalised, as several of our interviewees reiterated. Tensions around such marginalisation also became clear during various activist events Hutta participated in. During the National

LGBT Conference of 2008, for instance, a trans activist intervened into a discussion on public security by expressing her irritation with the way in which some gay activists used the term 'homophobia', which in her view did not address the issues she was facing as a trans person.

This paradox of acknowledgement/participation and marginalisation also reappears in the concrete forms of knowledge that have emerged in the discursive field of public security, such as victimological studies.[19] This strand has been of particular relevance to the constitution of a biopolitical reorientation in activism. A specificity of the use of a victimological methodology is that it is not limited to victims of discrimination and violence, but aims to provide an overview of the populations studied. Ramos and Carrara (2006) point out that this approach helps in opening up the view, beyond the martial scenario of murders, to everyday forms of violence and discrimination that affect greater parts of the population. Moreover, a variety of forms of discrimination and violence is considered that can be related to differences such as gender, age or racial identity, thus providing a more nuanced picture of how violence affects the lives of certain social groups. Studies like this one by Carrara, Ramos and Caetano (2003) suggest the prevalence of diverse forms of physical, verbal and structural violence and discrimination in public and private spaces, institutions and work or school environments. Trans as well as Black people report such experiences disproportionately often across a range of domains. Nonetheless, in their research reports, the authors tend to subsume trans experiences under the label 'sexual orientation', contributing to the prevalent discourse on 'homophobia'. While due to the inclusion of trans people's experiences overall rates of violence and discrimination turn out to be worse than they would be if only lesbians, gays and bisexuals were taken into account, these experiences, and related demands tend then to be invisibilised in the generic talk about 'homophobia'.

Outside the LGBT acronym, autonomous trans activism – which is constituted by a multitude of local organisations and, since the year 2000, also organised in the National Articulation of *Travestis,* Transsexuals and Transgenders (ANTRA) – has only sporadically translated into political projects that address public security and transphobic violence.[20] Apart from the aforementioned police education by trans activists, various demonstrations and the projects of several local trans groups, it is worth mentioning an initiative by trans activist Valkyria from Minas Gerais. Valkyria in 2009 successfully campaigned for a separate prison wing for trans and gay people, who suffered from trans- and homophobic violence within the prison. As a result of public funding, autonomous trans activism has during the past decade tended to focus on health issues as well as, more recently, on positive visibility of trans people more generally and trans people's possibility to use their social name in official documents (which we will come back to).

Contemporary activist engagements around trans- and homophobic violence and public security are oriented primarily towards changes at the level of the biopolitics of the state. They target institutions such as the police and mechanisms of securitisation on municipal, state and national scales of the state. The relevance of biopolitical, state-oriented approaches ensues from discursive and practical political possibilities that have opened up as LGBT people started to become a recognised population whose life matters to the state; and simultaneously from the fact that interventions can now be made directly on the biopolitical level of institutions that are meant to securitise and care for this population, but fail to do so in practice. Yet, state-related, biopolitical activisms in the area of public security simultaneously introduce some conundrums that elicit unease and ambivalences within and vis-à-vis activism. These conundrums ensue from two common experiences. First, in particular the Brazilian civil and military police are often regarded as hopelessly undemocratic, arbitrary and macho institutions that nice-sounding debates around trans and LGBT rights will not be able to modify in any substantial way. Secondly, and more importantly in our present discussion, the biopolitical state institutions targeted by activism have only limited purchase on the actual lives of lesbian, gay, trans and other marginalised people, especially in contexts where the state does not assume a *de facto* role of sovereign agent of government. In the municipality of Rio de Janeiro, for instance, there are over 1000 favelas,[21] a great number of which are being governed by either drug gangs or para-policing groups that are composed of former or off-duty police officers, firemen and soldiers (the so-called *milícias*; see Ribeiro, Dias and Carvalho, 2008). In a range of further contexts, the government of the liberal state is either radically limited or interwoven with non-liberal technologies. In the following section, we want to further interrogate the practical relevance of biopolitical activism by looking at some of the practical strategies trans people have engaged where they do not feel able – or are not willing – to rely on state power for their securitisation.

Practical enactments of citizenship

Hutta conducted research in the Baixada Fluminense region adjacent to the north of the city of Rio, where especially trans people have experienced a high level of violence. The Baixada Fluminense is characterised by idiosyncratic power relations that are framed around clientelist and 'coronalist' relations of dependency, as well as the activity of 'extermination groups' (*grupos de extermínio*) that are paid by merchants to annihilate 'disorder' or challenges to the status quo, forming intricate ensembles with state institutions (see Hutta 2010a, forthcoming). Political concerns with a democratisation of the police or public technologies of prevention face particular challenges in such contexts, where the liberal state does not have a *de facto* sovereignty of government and securitisation. This issue does not only concern LGBT politics or the contexts mentioned. Chatterjee (2004) argues that liberal governmentality, as it has emerged in Western modernity, has always been complicated by political practices that exceed the liberal framework in what he calls 'most of the world'. He directs attention to the intricate forms of politics that emerge at the intersections of formal and informal, legal and illegal, liberal and non-liberal government. In our present discussion, we want to highlight especially how trans and queer people manage to assert a legitimate presence, enacting practical forms of agency and citizenship. While state-oriented activisms are still of relevance, these are forms of agency that differ from the idea of an L/G/B/T citizen mobilising state institutions of securitisation whenever personal rights are being infringed on. The very notion of 'citizenship' needs to be reconsidered here so as to include manifold ways in which claims to collective spaces are concretely enacted, beyond formal laws and institutions that are linked to the biopolitics of the state (securitisation, voting, health services, etc.).[22] It is such concrete enactments of 'citizenship', in a processual sense that we want to turn to.

An issue that Gilmar, along with several other trans and gay people we spoke to in our research, have repeatedly highlighted concerns the necessity of gaining respect and acknowledgement in both the public imagination and concrete contexts of cities, communities and neighbourhoods. Gaining respect is a practical way of developing citizenship, as it entails the possibility to assert legitimate presence and to stake claims to collective space. Even where such claims do not directly entail a stake in state institutions, they might serve as precondition or as a first step. As we ask Gilmar about what could be done to improve the situation, s_he replies:

> We talk a lot about mobilising the SUS [public health care system], but I think the community needs to pass through a process of humanisation, of understanding that this individual is a human being, like any one, right? And deserves to be respected. I always talk about the question of respect, because I think that it's the principal ... the principal step to be taken [...] so we can construct a, a space of better quality of life. If I respect, I have other eyes, and so it goes, and then gathering other benefits. That's why I consider education to be important.[23]

Gilmar challenges prevalent political discourses where 'We talk a lot about mobilising the SUS', which is the Brazilian Unified Health System (*Sistéma Único de Saúde*) that is in theory responsible for numerous practical issues of relevance to trans people, including hormones, treatments related to silicone, surgeries, prevention against and treatment of sexually transmittable diseases, and so on. Gilmar believes that even if formal regulations are in place, whether these will be applicable in actual practice is an entirely different question. What is 'the principal step to be taken' is to gain respect within the community, which can eventually lead to 'better quality of live' and 'other benefits'.

We would like to scrutinise the intricacies involved in the process of gaining respect by zooming in on a conversation with Sasha and Josué in a small town in the Baixada Fluminense region. Josué identifies as *bichaboy*, a term used for young, feminine gay men, and Sasha as *travesti* and *bicha*. At the time of the interview, Sasha's gender presentation is pronouncedly male, which is related to the fact that s_he has started training as a nurse, and hir environment sets up norms regarding gender presentation. This already indicates the social pressures at work that Sasha adapts to in order to earn a living. Brazilian activist director Vagner de Almeida has in his films *The Butterflies* (*Borboletas da Vida*, 2004) and *Living Day by Day* (*Basta um Dia*, 2006) documented some of the acute problems of violence in particular *travestis* and feminine gays (*monas, bichas boys, homossexuais, gays*) suffer in Baixada Fluminense. Many are afraid of leaving the house and need to do sex work on the President Dutra highway that connects Rio with São Paulo, where they are exposed to insults, violent attacks and rapes. Sasha also mentions various homo- or transphobic attacks as well as murders near the place where s_he lives.

Interestingly, though, in a number of everyday contexts, Sasha and Josué openly assert a *travesti* and queer presence. Sasha convened activist gatherings at hir house, which lead to the organisation of the first local LGBT parade. Despite warnings Sasha had received ('they are gonna throw tomatoes at you!'), they went ahead with the event, and Sasha enthused over the positive reactions and the joyful atmosphere. Sasha, however, also indicates that they had to assume a rather intrepid posture ('We're gonna take the tomatoes right in our face!'), and that such appreciation cannot be taken for granted. Josué, who used to live in Sasha's town for several years, points to the contestations that are often necessary, stating 'When we go out, we all go out in a group', and 'We command respect'. This also highlights the significance of subcultural groups, which, as described earlier, began to form especially during the repressive backlash of the military dictatorship. Respect is framed here as something that needs to be 'commanded' in a contested and confrontational way.

For Sasha, it has however at the same time been important to achieve more solidary forms of respect within the community and to reach out beyond 'ghetto'-like in-groups. Achieving this has taken years and is something s_he refers to as a 'struggle'. It also involved the mobilisation and re-articulation of affective interpersonal relations and moral registers, for instance through work of care and assistance. As s_he is training as a nurse, Sasha has special access to doctors and medication, which s_he uses to help people in the neighbourhood. Significantly, due to the fact that this kind of care work is traditionally coded as female, Sasha attains respectability *as travesti*. Josué even states that the community 'don't see themselves without Sasha anymore'. The 'struggle' of achieving respect for Sasha thus entails practical work that responds to the gendered moral landscape. While there is no space here to discuss this any detail, it is interesting to note that this moral landscape is simultaneously being rearticulated in the process. Sasha mentions numerous erotic adventures and relations with young men in the community, for instance when there are barbeque parties at Sasha's house, and after women and children leave, *travestis* and gays start making out with the remaining men, who would ordinarily perform heterosexual family lives (see Hutta, 2010a: 297–8).

Despite the fact that s_he lives in a region that is infamous for its violence, then, Sasha has over the years managed to gain respect within the local community, which even enabled hir to claim public visibility. Solid as the local relations of respect seem to be in many regards, they are nonetheless highly contingent and precarious. Not only has it taken Sasha years to gain respect, s_he also needs to perform a respectable (care-taking) subject, and feels obliged to adopt a masculine persona for the sake of professional education. Moreover, acts of violence occurring on a daily basis are a sad reminder of the fact that one incidence of brutality is enough to end years of positive and respectful community relations.

It is of note that Afro-Brazilian and mestiza (*afro-brasileira, negra, parda*) *travestis* are particularly vulnerable. Rebecca reminds us that they face multiple discriminations insofar as they experience not only homophobia and transphobia, but also forms of Brazilian day-to-day racism. In an interview, and in various informal talks, she explained that for her gaining respect involves multiple levels, including respect of her afro-brazilian identity.[24] Interestingly, however, like some other *travestis* – for instance the aforementioned Cora and also Hanah – she simultaneously fulfilled a significant role in establishing links between *travesti* groups that belonged to different social classes, neighbourhoods, or professional categories. The friendship-based, informal *travesti* networks resulting from such linkages, provided the individuals with mutual respect despite their differing ethnicities, classes, or locations (Balzer, 2007: 388–91). Community structures thus turned out to provide and enable the demanded relations of respect in multiple ways.

Conclusions: Towards a presence to come

In our research, we found that Brazilian trans activists are often precariously situated, both within the unified 'LGBT' movement, and with respect to prevalent state-oriented approaches that seem to have limited relevance in underprivileged contexts. At the same time, acting from a multiplicity of contingently situated positions and identities, which are linked to each other, they have early on developed formal and informal political articulations and strategies to respond to fierce and historically shaped relations of violence. Even in apparently peripheral contexts like Rio de Janeiro's Maré or Baixada Fluminense region, trans activists have created social and political groups and networks, giving visibility to acute problems that are often sidelined in political debates. On the national level, it is worth mentioning that the trans network

ANTRA has since 2006 focused on a campaign for a legislation enabling trans people to use their social name in official documents, which is a particularly interesting campaign as it also affects people who do not enter formalised (and pathologising) processes of *transgenitalização* ('gender reassignment surgery').[25] If activists succeed in gaining an according legislation – which they already did in the state of Rio de Janeiro in 2011 – this would be conducive to gaining respect on various local and institutional scales.

While we pointed out trans activists' precarious position within Brazilian LGBT activism, from an international perspective, their positive presence and acknowledgement still strikes us as extraordinary. Trans people in EU countries, for instance, while facing a different intensity of violence than trans people in Brazil, experience transphobic hate crimes three times as often as lesbians and gay men experience homophobic violence, as recent studies suggest (Turner, Whittle and Combs, 2009: 19). In view of this fact, it is astonishing that it is only in recent years – and partly due to the efforts of the European trans network Transgender Europe – that the situation of trans people and transphobic hate crimes and incidents are duly acknowledged in European LGBT hate crime reports and studies by international NGO's and institutions, such as ILGA-Europe, the DIHR (Danish Institute for Human Rights), the FRA (Fundamental Rights Agency of the EU), the OSCE, or the Commissioner for Human Rights of the Council of Europe. On the national level, trans people in many European countries are still fighting hard to become visible in LGBT anti-violence and anti-hate crime activism. This absence could be exemplarily observed in the 'Tracing and tackling hate crimes against LGBT persons' project, which was conducted from 2010 to 2011 in nine European cities. None of the participating LGB(T) NGOs sent a trans activist to the project conferences and meetings, and most organisations failed to include transphobia and the situation of trans people into the local framework of the project.

If Brazilian trans identities and activisms took shape in a violently constraining social and spatial context, in international perspective, political articulations in Brazil have nonetheless, or rather for this very reason, achieved remarkable discursive and bodily presence. In the 1990s self-organisation started to become partly professionalised, and especially since the late 1990s the issue of transphobic violence has also been tackled in many contexts of LGBT activism. Trans activists have formed an integral part of political debates, even if their position within the 'LGBT' continues to remain ambivalent and precarious.

Notes

1. Interview with Gilmar, 12 January 2011.
2. In Brazil, the acronym 'LGBT' usually stands for '*lésbicas, gays, bissexuais, travestis e transexuais*' (lesbians, gays, bisexuals, *travestis* and transsexuals).

3. We use the term 'trans people' to denote those who have a gender identity that is different from the gender they were assigned at birth, and/or express their gender through language, clothing, accessories, cosmetics and/or body modification in a different way than the gender they were assigned at birth. This definition includes, among many others, transsexuals, transgender, cross-dressers, and genderqueer people, and many more local Brazilian identities like *travestis, transformistas* etc.

4. Carrara, Ramos and Caetano's (2003) survey conducted in collaboration with Rio's *Arco-Íris* group provided a milestone in this victimological strand of research. The authors point out, for instance, that 16.6% of their interviewees reported physical aggression, trans people, however, considerably more often (42%) than gay males (20%) and lesbians (10%).

5. For details regarding the TMM see http://www.transrespect-transphobia.org/ en_US/tvt-project/tmm-results.htm, last accessed on 7 December 2011.

6. For details regarding the TvT research project see the bilingual website: www. transrespect-transphobia.org.

7. Apart from Gilmar, Rogéria, Hanah Suzart and Keila Simpson, all informants' names have been changed for the sake of anonymity.

8. This led to a kind of exodus of Brazilian *travestis*. Shortly after Rogéria and other famous *travestis* went to Paris, around 200 *travestis* followed. In the late 1970s, already up to 500 Brazilian *travestis* lived in Paris, increasing to 1–2000 in the 1980s (Balzer, 2007: 319–20).

9. This continued to be a sad story in the 2000s as Catia explained, a trans activist who cared for *travesti* minors, who left their families and lived on the streets doing sex work. Interview with Catia, 6 February 2000.

10. Here, it is necessary to note that Gender Reassignment Surgery was illegal in Brazil until 1997, and that in 1978 a surgeon who performed GRS was sentenced to two years imprisonment (see Balzer, 2007: 479–80; Balzer, 2010: 83, 89).

11. Interview with Rebecca, 16 December 2000.

12. Already in 1993, 100 *travestis* met at the first of these congresses.

13. Interview with Hanah Suzart, 30 January 2001.

14. Interview with Rebecca, 16 December 2000.

15. Recording in Baixada Fluminense, 2 August 2008.

16. This precarity became evident in May 2008, when Marcelly was beaten and severely injured by the security guards of a public health centre, where she had professional contacts (which became through an open e-mail message sent by the LGBT organisation SOMOS from Porto Alegre to the State Ministry of Public Affairs of Rio Grande do Sul on 15 May 2008). See also Böer (2003) for an account of ongoing prejudice on the part of the police and public officials Marcelly was subjected to after starting to teach courses for the police.

17. Interview with Hanah Suzart, 30 January 2001.

18. Interview with Hanah Suzart, 30 January 2001.

19. Several studies, can be accessed on the homepage of the ABGLT, http://www. abglt.org.br/port/pesquisas.php, accessed on 20 July 2010.

20. This observation is based in particular on an interview with ANTRA president Keila Simpson, 8 December 2010.

21. A project of Rio's city government specialised on irregular and precarious settlements (SABREN) in 2010 listed 1021 favelas, based on more recent satellite images (SABREN, 2010). Favela and formal city spaces have however over the past decades become increasingly interwoven in social and infrastructural terms (Perlman, 2005: 9–10).

22. Our processual approach to citizenship is inspired by Isin's (2008) notion of 'acts of citizenship' (see Hutta, 2010a: 30–1, 166–7).
23. Interview with Gilmar, 12 January 2011.
24. Interview with Rebecca, 16 December 2000.
25. This information is partly based on an interview with ANTRA president Keila Simpson, 8 December 2010. See also ABGLT (2011).

Bibliography

ABGLT (2011) 'Associação Brasileira de Lésbicas, Gays, Bissexuais, Travestis e Transexuais', http://www.abglt.org.br/port/nomesocial.php (home page), accessed on 1 September 2011.

Balzer, C. (2005) 'The great drag queen hype: Thoughts on cultural globalisation and autochthony', *Paideuma*, 51: 111–31.

Balzer, C. (2007) *Gender outlaw triptychon – Eine ethnologische Studie zu Selbstbildern und Formen der Selbstorganisation in den Transgender-Subkulturen Rio de Janeiros, New Yorks und Berlins*, Ph.D. thesis, Free University Berlin, Germany (www.diss.fu-berlin.de/diss/receive/FUDISS_thesis_000000005722).

Balzer, C. (2009) 'Every third day, the murder of a trans person is reported – Preliminary results of a new Trans Murder Monitoring Project reveal more than 200 reported cases of murdered trans people from January 2008 to June 2009', *Liminalis – Journal for Sex/Gender Emancipation and Resistance*, 3, July: 147–59.

Balzer, C. (2010) 'Eu acho transexual é aquele que disse: "eu sou transexual!" Reflexiones etnológicas sobre la medicalización globalizada de las identidades trans a través del ejemplo de Brasil' in M. Missé and G. Coll-Planas (eds) *El género desordenado: Críticas en torno a la patologización de la transexualidad*. Barcelona: Egales Editorial, pp. 81–96.

Balzer, C. and Hutta, J. (2011) 'Again alarming figures: Transgender Europe's Trans Murder Monitoring project reveals 681 reported murders of trans people since 2008', Press release from 30 September 2011, available from TvT Project, www.transrespect-transphobia.org, accessed on 27 December 2012.

Böer, A. (ed.) (2003) *Construindo a Igualdade: A História da Prostituição de Travestis em Porto Alegre*. Porto Alegre: Igualdade.

Carrara, S., Ramos, S. and Caetano, M. (eds) (2003) *Política, direitos, violência e homossexualidade: Pesquisa oitava parada do orgulho GLBT*. Rio de Janeiro: Pallas.

Chatterjee, P. (2004) *The politics of the governed: Reflections on popular politics in most of the world*. New York: Columbia University Press.

De la Dehesa, R. (2010) *Queering the public sphere in Mexico and Brazil: Sexual rights movements in emerging democracies*. Durham: Duke University Press.

Facchini, R. (2005) *Sopa de letrinhas? Movimento Homossexual e Produção de Identidades Coletivas nos Anos 90*. Rio de Janeiro: Garamond.

Foucault, M. (1998) *The history of sexuality, Vol. 1: The will to knowledge*. London: Penguin.

Foucault, M. (2008) *The birth of biopolitics: Lectures at the Collège de France 1978–1979*, edited by M. Senellart, translated by G. Burchell. Basingstoke: Palgrave Macmillan.

Green, J. N. (1999) *Beyond carnival: Male homosexuality in twentieth-century Brazil*. Chicago: University of Chicago Press.

Grupo Gay da Bahia (2009) 'ASSASSINATO HOMOSSEXUAIS NO BRASIL: 2008: Relatório anual do Grupo Gay da Bahia', Press release dated 13 April 2009, www.ggb.org.br/assassinatosHomossexuaisBrasil_2008_pressRelease.html, accessed on 1 May 2009.

Halberstam, J. (2005) *In a queer time and place: Transgender bodies, subcultural lives.* New York: New York University Press.

Hutta, J. S. (2010a) *Queer geographies of Geborgenheit: The LGBT politics of security and formations of agency in Brazil*, Ph.D. thesis, Faculty of Social Sciences, The Open University, Milton Keynes.

Hutta, J. S. (2010b) 'Paradoxical publicness: Becoming-imperceptible with the Brazilian lesbian, gay, bisexual and transgender movement' in N. Mahony, J. Newman and C. Barnett (eds) *Rethinking the Public: Innovations in Research, Theory and Politics.* Bristol: Policy Press, pp. 143–61.

Hutta, J. S. (2012) 'Beyond the right to the governmentalized city: Queer citizenship in a Brazilian context of peripheralization' in A. Fischer-Tahir and M. Naumann (eds) *Peripherization: The Making of Spatial Dependencies and Social Injustice.* Wiesbaden: Springer VS, pp. 222–46.

Isin, E. F. (2008) 'Theorizing acts of citizenship' in E. F. Isin and G. M. Nielsen (eds) *Acts of Citizenship.* London: Zed Books, pp. 15–43.

Kulick, D. (1998) *Travesti: Sex, gender and culture among Brazilian transgendered prostitutes.* Chicago: The University of Chicago Press.

Muñoz, J. E. (1999) *Disidentifications: Queers of Color and the Performance of Politics.* Minneapolis: University of Minnesota Press.

Oliveira, N. Z. de (1994) *Damas de Paus: O Jogo Aberto dos Travestis no Espelho da Mulher.* Salvador: Centro Editorial e Didático da UFBA.

Penteado, D. (1980) 'Um apelo da traditional família Mesquita: Prendam, matem e comam os *travestis!*' *Lampião da Esquina*, No. 24: 2.

Perlman, J. E. (2005) 'The myth of marginality revisited: The case of favelas in Rio de Janeiro' in L. M. Hanley, B. A. Ruble and J. S. Tulchin (eds) *Becoming Global and the New Poverty of Cities.* Washington, DC: Woodrow Wilson International Center for Scholars, pp. 9–53.

Ramos, S. (2007) *Respostas Brasileiras à Violência Urbana no Campo da Segurança Pública: Os Movimentos Sociais e as Organizações Não-Governamentais*, Ph.D. thesis, National School of Public Health, Oswaldo Cruz Foundation, Rio de Janeiro.

Ramos, S. and Carrara, S. (2006) 'A constituição da problemática da violência contra homossexuais: A articulação entre ativismo e academia na elaboração de políticas públicas', *Physis*, 16(2): 185–205.

Ribeiro, C., Dias, R. and Carvalho, S. (2008) 'Discursos e práticas na construção de uma política de segurança: O caso do governo Sérgio Cabral Filho (2007–2008)', *Segurança, tráfico e milícias no Rio de Janeiro.* Rio de Janeiro: Justiça Global, pp. 6–15.

SABREN (2010) 'Sistema de Assentamentos de Baixa Renda', http://portalgeo.rio.rj.gov.br/sabren/index.htm (home page), accessed on 19 February 2010.

Secretaria Especial dos Direitos Humanos (2008) 'Conferência Nacional LGBT. Propostas aprovadas: Relação preliminar', Brasília.

Silva, H. R. S. (1993) *Travesti: A Invenção do Feminino.* Rio de Janeiro: Relume Dumará.

Soares, L. E. (2000) *Meu Casaco De General: Quinhentos Dias no Front da Segurança Pública.* São Paulo: Companhia das Letras.

Soares, L. E. (2006) *Segurança Tem Saída.* Rio de Janeiro: Sextante.

Souza, M. L. de (2008) *Fobópole: O Medo Generalizado e a Militarizaç da Questão Urbana.* Rio de Janeiro: Bertrand Brasil.

Turner, L., Whittle, S. and Combs, R. (2009) *Transphobic hate crime in the EU.* Manchester: Press for Change.

Part II
'Queer Mediations and (Dis)Locations'

5
Liminal Subjects, Marginal Spaces and Material Legacies: Older Gay Men, Home and Belonging

Andrew Gorman-Murray

Introduction: Older gay men on the home front

Neil identifies himself as an older gay man.[1] He is in his mid-60s, retired, and lives alone in a semi-detached one-bedroom villa in Sydney's inner southern suburbs. He wrote the following entry to conclude the reflective diary I asked him to complete as part of a study on the relations between men and the home in inner Sydney:

> Tuesday 16 June 2009. 9:30 pm. I turned on my computer and reviewed the *Men on the Home Front Diary*. Looking at the seven days of the diary, I could see that I was a person whose days were very regular – I tend to do the same things at similar times each day. On reflection I am very happy with life and I would make few changes. My little home is filled with the things I like – CDs, books and very nice furniture and pictures et al.

In this brief assessment, Neil highlights several elements that are instrumental in generating intimate bonds between people and their homes: embodied routines, cherished possessions, and the capacity of both these routines and possessions to facilitate self-reflection, self-recognition, a sense of happiness, and a feeling of belonging. These dimensions are important for relations between self and home generally, but are especially highlighted in work on older people, whose lifeworlds often become focused on the home and its immediate environs (Percival, 2002; Oswald and Wahl, 2005; Cristoforetti, Gennai and Rodeschini, 2011). Neil shows their importance for older gay men, intimating the need to consider how the intersection of sexual identity with ageing shapes, and is shaped by, attachments to home.

Knowledge collected and produced about older gay men (and other sexual minorities) is a notable gap in our understanding of the links between self, home and ageing. I contend that older gay men, such as Neil, have specific life experiences that warrant a discrete focus on their engagements with

93

home and belonging in the context of ageing, and which could contribute to policy on ageing for sexual minorities in contemporary Western societies like Australia. Accordingly, this chapter addresses older gay men's experiences of belonging and exclusion – of presence and absence, in terms of this collection – in domestic environments, as well as public spaces. With few exceptions (Jones and Pugh, 2005; Waitt and Gorman-Murray, 2007; Slevin and Linneman, 2010), older gay men's spatial and environmental encounters have been generally absent from the disciplinary concerns of geography, gerontology and their overlap in the field of geographical gerontology. This chapter thus seeks to 'queer' geographical gerontology through highlighting older gay men's lives, particularly their relations to their home spaces.

To do this, I draw together the concerns of geographical gerontology with insights from the fields of geographies of sexualities and queer gerontology. Geographies of sexualities recognise the heightened spatial exigencies of gay men's life experiences, while queer gerontology elicits the sexualised dimensions of ageing and critiques heteronormative framings of ageing policies. For its part, through examining experiences of space and place in the process of ageing, geographical gerontology has highlighted the vital meaning of home for older people, as noted previously, drawing attention to the significant function of the domestic environment in sustaining their senses of self and identity, and their physical, social and emotional wellbeing (Chaudhury and Rowles, 2005). This chapter brings these insights about place, home, belonging, wellbeing and ageing into conversation with the lifeworlds of older gay men. I articulate the particular textures of the meaningful connectivity between older gay men and their homes, and attempt to show their importance both for the men and wider gay communities. Of course, older gay men are not a unified demographic, but differentiated by intersecting social categories and experiences. For instance, class position affects the financial and material resources available to 'make home'. In this case, I am largely dealing with middle-class men who are able to acquire goods, retain possessions, and attain a semblance of control over their living environment.

The chapter is arranged as follows. I begin by reviewing the bodies of literature that inform this analysis, simultaneously building a conceptual scaffold for interpreting the empirical material. I then introduce the case study, including the project, its aims, methods and data collection. The material is from the project *Men on the Home Front*, which sought to understand the multifaceted relations between men, home and neighbourhoods in inner Sydney. From the initial planning and design stage of the project, I intended to include older gay men as a cohort in the study. This cohort was recruited from Mature Age Gays (MAG), an organisation based in inner Sydney that provides support and advocacy for older gay men. I introduce MAG, and then focus on the six men, aged 55–73 years old, who participated in the intensive qualitative study of men, home and belonging, which included interviews, a reflective diary and a home-tour. I discuss three themes about the significance of older gay men's homes that emerged from the study: the home as a 'closet' that reveals as well as conceals; household routines and ageing-in-place; and domestic belongings and attachments. These themes address this collection's subject of queer presence and absence, and moreover show the nuances shaping middle-class older gay men's relations to their homes, which both parallel but differ from heteronormative modalities of space, place and ageing.

Queering geographical gerontology

Queer is a defiant concept, as Browne and Nash (2010: 5) contend: 'Queer theory challenges the normative social ordering of identities and subjectivities along the heterosexual/homosexual binary as well as the privileging of heterosexuality as 'natural' and homosexuality as its deviant and abhorrent 'other'.' Queer theory does this by arguing that heterosexuality – particularly normative coupled and marital heterosexuality – is a social construction of normalcy, not pre-fixed, and primarily reliant on the 'absent presence' of 'abnormal' same-sex-attraction to prop up its definitive moral claim. However, as a socially-constructed moral order, the heterosexual/homosexual binary can be ruptured and subverted, enabling a range of sexual subjects to claim social validity. Given the centrality of the heterosexual nuclear family unit to the political, social and economic functioning of contemporary Western societies, contesting the heterosexual/homosexual binary is not just a challenge to the moral order of sexualities, but fundamentally anti-normative, seeking to subvert a 'host of taken-for-granted 'stabilities' in our social lives' (Browne and Nash, 2010: 7). I use queer in both senses in this chapter: as a tool for critiquing both the normative sexual order and the broader social institutions it underpins, encompassing expected norms about individual life courses, family formation and homemaking. By extension, this means queering bodies of academic knowledge constructed primarily in reference to heteronormative life courses and social worlds.

Thus, to explain middle-class older gay men's queer relations with their homes and belongings, I queer some bodies of academic knowledge to generate conceptual frames to interpret my empirical findings. I bring geographical gerontology into dialogue with queer gerontology and geographies of sexualities. All offer insights that help illuminate connections between ageing, sexuality and space. Geographical gerontology lies at the cross-section of social gerontology and areas of human geography and environmental psychology concerned with ageing populations and the experiences of older people (Wiles, 2005; Milligan, 2009). Andrews, with colleagues, has mapped this 'fuzzy' field in two papers, the first focusing on health and health care (2007) and the second on social and cultural issues (2009). The field is thus broad, taking in both medical and non-medical dimensions of ageing, but coheres around a concern 'to co-develop theories, concepts and empirical knowledge on the relationships between space, place and ageing' (Andrews et al., 2009: 1646). These spatial imperatives are varied: population ageing, distribution and movement; policy and planning for health and social services; effects of place on health outcomes; living environments, emotions and wellbeing; and social space and the ageing body. Overall, the achievement of wellbeing – the capability to live a flourishing life – is a core concern tying space, place and ageing within geographical gerontology. Wellbeing is conceived broadly, with objective (living conditions, access to resources) and subjective (individual happiness, quality of life) dimensions.

The convergence of geography and gerontology since the 1990s has been impelled by the critical/cultural turn, which advanced the relational co-constitution of place/people and space/subjectivities, and prompted conceptual and methodological alignments. There has been recognition that experiences of ageing are not only biological but also socially and culturally constructed, and thus the ageing population is not homogenous, but differentiated by gender, ethnicity, class and disability (Pain, Mowl and Talbot, 2000). Since individuals and groups don't age the same way with the same experiences, there has been a critical deconstruction of ageing and what it means to be old. An apt example is 'premature ageing' in youth-oriented gay communities, where 40 is sometimes considered old (Drummond, 2006). Moreover, the diverse social and cultural construction of ageing has encouraged closer attention to relations between ageing, the body and space: discursive expectations of ageing bodies influence older people's use of particular places, but these experiences are also affected by intersecting social positions (gender, ethnicity, class, disability, etc.) (Mowl, Pain and Talbot, 2000). Attention to everyday meanings of, and practices in, places has driven empirical and methodological changes (alongside demographic work on population ageing). To access the social and cultural construction of ageing, researchers are heeding the voices and knowledge of older people, deploying qualitative techniques such as interviews, diaries, ethnographies and visual approaches (Andrews et al., 2009). This chapter's case study aligns with these conceptual and methodological developments.

Following this critical/cultural turn, work within geographical gerontology has sought to address the relationship between emplacement, embodiment, identity and wellbeing. One of the most significant areas of interest has been the home as a physical and emotional site of identity and agency for older people. Here, older people's identities are not taken as fixed and singular. Applying insights from critical approaches, their identities are seen as changing over the life course, composite, and contingent upon intersecting experiences of gender, ethnicity, class, disability, etc. As flexible achievements, identities are understood as narrations of self to both self and others (Rubinstein and de Medeiros, 2005). There are several reasons for interest in the home as a site of identity work for older people. Increasing frailty and impaired mobility mean older people are impeded in public spaces, with their lifeworlds converging on home and neighbourhood in a process of 'environmental centralisation' (Oswald and Wahl, 2005). Ageing-in-place is a matching policy aiming to maintain older people in their own homes rather than institutional settings, prompting research on how the meaning of home changes through ageing. For instance, formal and informal home-care can blur the public/private boundary and affect feelings of belonging or place-attachment (Milligan, 2009). Ageing-in-place is not static, but a process 'whereby the older adult continually re-integrates with place (home and community) in the face of change and uncertainty through creative and social actions that foster meaning and identity' (Andrews et al., 2007: 157).

Indeed, research has affirmed the home as a fundamental site of self-recognition, identity and wellbeing for older people (Chaudhury and Rowles, 2005; Milligan, 2009). These positive connections comprise several facets. Independent living enables personal control despite decreased bodily capacity and spatial access (Percival, 2002). Moreover, domestic routines entwine body and home, creating belonging through familiar rituals, fostering home as an affective site tied to bodily reality, and enabling the self to reproduce itself through daily activities (Chaudhury and Rowles, 2005; Rubinstein and de Medeiros, 2005; Cristoforetti, Gennai and Rodeschini, 2011). Certain routines, notably housework, are used to physically, emotionally and symbolically resist the implications of ageing (Mowl, Pain and Talbot, 2000; Hecht, 2001; Percival, 2002). Belongings and objects crucially imbricate home, identity and wellbeing in older age: the different facets of one's sense of self – different fragments of one's identity – are expressed through cherished possessions arrayed at home, and these objects critically underpin the affective and personal meaning of home for older people (Percival, 2002; Sherman and Dacher, 2005; Cristoforetti, Gennai and Rodeschini, 2011).[2] In fact, Rubinstein and de Medeiros (2005) contend that the significance of objectifying self increases with age, and that such personally meaningful domestic objects link self-identity to place-identity, conjoining home and identity in the ageing process.

Issues of home and identity prompt attention to different subjectivities, intersections and their domestic inferences. Some work has addressed gendered differences. Russell (2007) finds older women more personally attached to their homes than older men due to lifelong investment of domestic and emotional labour in homemaking – place-based work which simultaneously (in)formed their identities as women over the life course. Mowl, Pain and Talbot (2000) note that differences in gendered integration with home are a legacy of the breadwinner/homemaker dyad, where older women maintain their existing connection with the home, while older men feel 'out-of-place' upon retirement, their notions of masculinity unsettled by increased time at home. Class inflects this transition, with middle-class professional men establishing 'semi-work' spaces at home (e.g. studies) enabling continuity of past routines, while working-class labourers feel more displaced (Mowl, Pain and Talbot, 2000; Percival, 2002). The balance of domestic affiliations might change with more recent generations, where both women and men undertake paid work outside home. But there are other differences, intersecting with gender, which have been largely absent from work on home, identity and ageing.

What of older gay men's meanings and experiences of home? Given 'out' gay men diverge from the conventional nuclear family household form and breadwinner/homemaker dyad, their connections to home also arguably deviate from those of heterosexual husbands (Gorman-Murray, 2007; Waitt and Gorman-Murray, 2007). Throughout their life course, gay men are homemakers as well as breadwinners, and this bears on the functional significance of home in the ageing process. But knowledge of the sexual identities of older people is largely missing within geographical gerontology; in policy and research, 'older people are frequently represented as either being sexually inactive or not having a sexual identity' (King and Cronin, 2010: 86). This lacuna can be addressed by insights from queer gerontology, which is a cross-disciplinary sub-field at the intersection of social gerontology, social work and public health studies that seeks to advance understanding of the experiences of older lesbians, gay men and sexual minorities. Queer gerontology can thus queer geographical gerontology by fundamentally contesting the heteronormative framing of 'aged care policy, research and professional practice [which] assume[s] a universal heterosexuality for older people' (Hughes, 2006: 56; Harrison, 2006). Certainly, there are similarities in ageing experiences for heterosexual and same-sex-attracted people, but there are differences that must be considered.

At the least, recognising an older lesbian or gay person's sexual identity could help their self-esteem and wellbeing, and prevent isolation from partners and friends (Hughes, 2003). Accordingly, a key research direction is tackling heterosexism in health and aged-care services, homecare, retirement villages and institutional settings, and educating staff and carers about sexual diversity in ageing (Tolley and Ranzjin, 2006; Hughes, 2007). There has been a focus on ageism in gay male communities, particularly the youth-oriented commercial scene from which older gay men are often excluded; a related concern is 'accelerated ageing', where some gay men exhibit heightened concern with body identity and 'feel old' at a younger age than heterosexual men (Jones and Pugh, 2005; Drummond, 2006; Slevin and Linneman, 2010; Robinson, 2008). Another area of work is the notable role of friendships and families-of-choice in the lives of older lesbians and gay men, providing social and emotional support (Heaphy, 2007). These insights from queer gerontology prompt geographical gerontology to be aware of the difference sexual identity makes to place-based experiences of ageing, including institutions, commercial spaces and homecare.

In addition, insights from geographies of sexualities not only complement work on home, identity and ageing, but also extend it by showing the significance of homemaking for sexual identity constitution and affirmation. Particular activities and routines help constitute sexual identities and relations; not only sex-itself, but sharing housework and homemaking practices with a same-sex partner, or hosting parties and events for lesbian and gay friends (Gorman-Murray, 2006, 2007). Objects are also crucial: the presence of belongings signifying one's sexual identity – photographs with partners or friends, paintings, books, magazines, shared beds, even household appliances purchased with a same-sex partner – write one's lesbian or gay identity into the fabric of the home, and narrate a sense of self (Johnston and Valentine, 1995; Gorman-Murray, 2006, 2007; Waitt and Gorman-Murray, 2007). This includes reconciling sexual identity with other fragments of self, juxtaposing possessions that signify familial connections, ethnic heritage, beliefs, aspirations and gender performativity (Gorman-Murray, 2008). There is a 'queer' implication here for geographical gerontology: it calls for consideration of the linkages of home, sexual identity and ageing.

Layering together geographical gerontology, queer gerontology and geographies of sexualities provides a conceptual scaffold for understanding the function of homes and domestic belongings in middle-class older gay men's lifeworlds. Geographical gerontology provides key foundational concepts about the social and cultural heterogeneity of ageing experiences, and the particular significance of home, domestic routines and cherished possessions in sustaining older people's identity, agency and wellbeing. Queer gerontology layers in the affect sexual identity has on ageing, feelings of belonging and place-attachments, and highlights the heteronormativity of much ageing research. Geographies of sexualities interlink these through conceptualising lesbians' and gay men's particular meanings and experiences of home, homemaking, belongings and public/private boundaries. I use these entwined insights to interpret a case study of middle-class older gay men's experiences of presence and absence, especially with regard to domestic environments.

Methods: *Men on the home front* and Mature Age Gays

This study is part of a project, *Men on the Home Front*, on the relations between masculinity, domesticity and urbanity in contemporary inner Sydney. This attends to men's relations to home, neighbourhood and urban public space in a context of shifting gender, employment, household, and lifestyle patterns. The focus on inner Sydney – from the east coast to Strathfield in the west, from Sydney Harbour in the north to Botany Bay in the south – provides ethnographic and socio-spatial coherence. Spaces of belonging and alienation, or presence and absence, have emerged as a key theme. Data collection occurred in 2009–10, and 52 men participated.

They represent a broad social and demographic range, and include straight and gay men of different ages, ethnicities, occupational backgrounds and household types.[3] In order to recruit a purposive sample of older gay men I approached MAG, an organisation, based in inner Sydney, providing social support and political advocacy for older gay men. MAG was established in 1991, runs twice-monthly social and educational meetings in inner Sydney, and provides informal care for men needing assistance (www.magnsw. org). A 2009 members' survey ($n = 74$) found: an average age of 64.4; 66% lived alone, 17.6% with a partner; 36.5% had chronic age-related illnesses (Wang, 2009).

Six men from MAG, aged 55–73yo, participated in an in-depth, three-stage qualitative study, offering narrative and visual information. Meth and McClymont (2009) argue that qualitative mixed-methods allow access to the complexity of lives, identities and practices. Mixed-methods enhance the credibility of qualitative data and augment the depth of insight by: layering different sets of data to build a composite picture of participants' experiences; utilising different collection techniques at various stages to enable participant reflection and revelation; and facilitating nuanced relationships between researcher and respondents via multiple meetings. The initial stage was a semi-structured interview about homelife, taking place in respondents' homes, exploring a range of themes: homemaking practices, domestic labour, leisure activities, and neighbourhood and community connections. Next, participants recorded a time-use diary of their homelife (domestic and neighbourhood activities) for one week. They documented daily activities and wrote a reflection about their significance (or not) for sense of self and wellbeing. Finally, a follow-up visit was conducted. This involved questions about the diary, a discussion about life satisfaction, and a guided home-tour. Photographs of important domestic spaces were taken with permission, providing vital visual data. Table 5.1 summarises participants' demographic information. Given the significance of class position and financial resources for housing and retirement options, it is important to note that all are retirees from middle-class professional or administrative occupations.

The data were analysed via thematic analysis, and inductively coded for key topics emerging in discussions and reflections. These topics were iteratively compared with existing literature about home, identity and ageing, discussed earlier, and further interpreted in the context of social and cultural discourses about the place of older gay men in both mainstream and gay communities.[4] In the following, I discuss three key themes about the significance of older gay men's homes: the home as a 'closet' that both conceals and reveals; home space, domestic routines and ageing-in-place; and belongings, attachments and 'passing on' (of self and possessions). These themes articulate the textured nuances shaping older gay men's relations to their homes, which are in some ways congruent with heteronormative

Table 5.1   Participant summary

Pseudonym	Age	Dwelling	Tenure	Household	Location	Ancestry	Field of Work
Harry	55	Flat	Own	Single	Inner East	Dutch	Professional
Joe	57	Flat	Private rental	Single	Inner West	Anglo-Celtic	Administrative
Neil	66	Semi	Public rental	Single	Inner South	Anglo-Celtic	Professional
Shane	68	House	Own	2 partners	Inner West	Anglo-Celtic	Professional
Doug	69	Flat	Own	Single	Inner South	Anglo-Celtic	Administrative
Tom	73	Flat	Private rental	Single	Inner East	Anglo-Celtic	Administrative

ageing and place-attachment, while diverging in subtle but important ways. The following discussion foregrounds my own interpretation of the empirical data (interviews, diaries, home-tours). Where appropriate, I give quotations from interviews and diaries. However, given the importance of 'physical' space and 'material' belonging(s), I offer photographs from the home-tours as key evidence (all taken by me, with participant direction). The juxtaposition of photographic data with interpretive discussion offers tentative but important insights into the importance of home for older gay men and their wellbeing.

Home as closet space

The first theme is foundational: I discuss and theorise the role of the home-place itself in middle-class older gay men's everyday geographies. Through my critical and inter-textual reading of the participants' interviews, reflective diaries and home-tour narratives, I contend that the meaning and function of these older gay men's homes are manifestly embedded in experiences of queer presence and absence in material and complex ways. Indeed, older gay men's lifeworlds are structured by synchronous and intersecting spaces of presence and absence. Older gay men live in two social worlds simultaneously: mainstream society and gay communities (Slevin and Linneman, 2010). But both gay and mainstream discourses about sexuality and ageing marginalise them in both social worlds, rendering them present but unwelcome, wishing them absent. In the mainstream, they face not only ageism but also its intersection with heterosexism, generating homophobic portrayals of paedophilic old gay men (Jones and Pugh, 2005). While older heterosexuals are stereotyped as sexless, older gay men are reviled as hypersexual. Gay communities are equally problematic. The valorisation of youthful bodies in gay spaces and culture, particularly the scene and the media, means older men are deemed unattractive and predatory (upon younger gay men), and marginalised in venues and cultural imaginaries (Robinson, 2008).

Present-but-absent experiences are especially so for the men in this study, who live in inner Sydney, a city with visible gay cultures. For them, the gay social world is not an imagined community of gay fraternity, but an interconnected set of commercial, residential and organisational spaces that form part of their everyday geographies and social interactions. But rather than boosting feelings of belonging, daily dealings with inner-city gay communities double their sense of alienation. Steve Ostrow, founder of MAG, has issued pointed comments about ageist exclusion in Sydney's inner-city gay spaces:

> We like to go for a drink on Oxford Street now and then, but these days not many guys seem pleased to see us. Discrimination takes many forms; a disparaging look, comments about dirty old men, even just being blanked hurts. What we have today is older gay men being a marginalised group within a minority.
>
> Attorney General's Department of NSW (2005: Appendix B)

Gay ageism, together with mainstream homophobic ageism, underpins the spatial exclusion of older gay men. As Jones and Pugh (2005: 258) put it, 'there is no public space available for older gay men'. They are liminal subjects, skirting the thresholds of two social worlds simultaneously, but not fully present, not belonging to either. They are forgotten, absent.

The men contextualised the function and place of their homes within this experience of dual marginalisation. In the face of wider erasure in both mainstream and gay social worlds, the men identified their homes as their key space of belonging. For instance, after being out one day, dealing with various public spaces and difficult interpersonal exchanges, Harry reflected in his diary: 'I return home. As always I am glad to be on my own again, but especially after the public interaction. I love the privacy, quiet and peace.' I want to reflect on how this place-attachment complicates queer presence and absence. First, it is feasible to see these men's homing desires as a form of closeting, a particular spatial response to their exclusion and absence from mainstream and gay social worlds. The closet is the spatial metaphor that describes the denial and concealment – including self-concealment – of sexual minorities within a heteronormative social order, which, as Brown (2000: 10, original italics) argues in *Closet Space*, has material implications, physically isolating and masking sexual minorities: 'The *tenor* of the closet is the concealment, erasure and denial of homosexuality in a broader punitive context of heteronormativity. The *vehicle* is a certain kind of space.' The men's homes could thus be interpreted as closet spaces, marking their erasure from not only mainstream society, but ironically from inner-city gay communities, too. Of course, in some senses this is the case: in their homes these men are hidden from both social worlds.

But simultaneously, there are other possibilities in this spatial claim: Brown (2000) argues that the closet not only conceals, but also reveals the lives of gay men: while describing their absence, it inscribes their presence. Moreover, 'it is not always a disempowered, abject artefact, but can also be the setting for creative, ingenious and transformative sexual, cultural and political resistance to heteronormativity' (Brown and Knopp, 2003: 215). Following this line of argument, if these older gay men's homes are closet spaces, they are not just zones of concealment, but also sites for resisting the erasure and/or discipline of the heteronormative gaze. Equally, given their exclusion from inner-city gay spaces, their homes are spaces that resist the expunging homonormative gaze of youth-oriented gay imaginaries. Instead of absence, in their homes these older gay men are present to themselves. Their homes facilitate senses of self-recognition, identity and wellbeing – as older persons and as gay men – largely unattainable elsewhere in their lifeworlds. Figure 5.1 is a photograph of Tom's front door, which he characterised as both the 'passage' and the 'boundary' between 'his world'

Figure 5.1 Tom's threshold to home/closet

and his experience of social sanction beyond the doorstep; it is the threshold to his 'creative closet'.

These feelings of self and wellbeing are built within the 'creative closet' through embodied routines and the presentation of meaningful belongings in a personal domestic space, both of which enable ontological security (a sense of security of being in the world) and environmental mastery (a sense of control over a defined personal space). Neil's diary entry given at the beginning of the chapter is exemplary, as is Harry's remark about the meaning of home:

Andrew: What does your home mean to you?
Harry: Security, where I can be myself. I'm always happy to be at home. Whenever I've been anywhere I think about getting home. Often I spend whole days here and I don't feel the need to go out or go away anywhere.

Figure 5.2 shows the 'heart' of Harry's home, his library/sitting room, which houses his most treasured possessions, and where he happily spends 'whole days' reading and reflecting. In the following I expand on the significance of

Figure 5.2   Harry's library/sitting room

domestic routines and belongings for these older gay men. It is also important to note that their lifelong experience of homemaking in the absence of heterosexual marriage and children contravenes and contests heteronormative expectations linking home, family and femininity. Their capacity to 'make home' – and to continue doing so through the ageing process – is an everyday form of creative resistance, and this is addressed through the following two sections.

Routines and ageing-in-place

Domestic routines are significant for these middle-class older gay men's senses of self, belonging and wellbeing. I connect these practices to work in geographical gerontology about ageing-in-place, which refers to older people living in their homes and immediate communities rather than moving to institutional settings. The reason ageing-in-place is preferred in ageing policy is that it is seen to foster wellbeing and self-recognition through place-attachment. Yet, despite the notion that older people are being maintained in a familiar environment, ageing-in-place is processual. Neither home, sense of self, nor the relationship between them, are static over the life course, and this is certainly so when homecare might be required to facilitate ageing-in-place. Consequently, ageing-in-place means a continual reintegration between an older person and their home 'through creative and social actions that foster meaning and identity' (refreshing Andrews et al.'s definition, 2007: 157). Both maintaining and developing routines are key means through which the connection between home and identity is renewed in self-affirming ways that foster belonging and wellbeing, and thus underpin self-presence. This is because the bodily performance of regular activities enables self to remake self, and to do so within a specified domestic setting that becomes an indispensable part of the self-renewal process. Sense of home and sense of self are thus entwined through performative identity work.

I suggest that ageing-in-place, and its constituent domestic routines, is differentiated by social categories like gender and sexuality, which bring into play particular expectations about home and identity. While older gay men's routine attachments certainly follow the general process of ageing-in-place, integrating older gay men with their homes and sustaining wellbeing, they are also inflected by their sexual identities and lifelong experiences of 'being different'. In fact, through work with heterosexual women and men, Russell (2007: 179) suggests that the familiarity, stability and ontological security of home 'may have comparatively less resonance in the lives of older men'. There is a gendering of processes of ageing-in-place whereby, at least in 'traditional' breadwinner/homemaker households, women's lifelong performance of domestic routines underwrites their feminine identity, and maintaining such routines through ageing bolsters their sense of self and wellbeing. Russell found that men, whose pre-retirement lifeworlds focused on work in the public sphere, conveyed less attachment to home and ageing-in-place. How do the experiences and desires of middle-class older gay men articulate with these gendered differences? Does their performance of domestic routines signify presence of self in alternative ways with different meanings?

In interviews, I asked the men about ageing-in-place: whether they intended to stay in their homes or move to a retirement or nursing home. All the men emphasised they wanted to stay at home. Shane said: 'I would like to stay at home. The thought of packing everything up fills me with despair.' This is feasible for Shane, who in fact has two co-habiting partners – an example contesting coupled heteronormative homemaking – one of whom is 15 years younger, a nurse, and able to provide homecare as Shane ages. Meanwhile, Joe felt that aged-care services don't appreciate gay men's difficulties at the intersection of age and sexuality – such as their absence in mainstream and gay social worlds – and wants to age-in-place at home. Indeed, sexuality is an important reason why all the men want to age-in-place and avoid institutional settings, eliciting a difference from heterosexual men and women. The men are concerned about heterosexist assumptions in retirement and nursing homes, where the burden falls on residents to decide whether or not to disclose their sexuality to health workers, with those who don't risking isolation from same-sex partners and friends (Harrison, 2006; Tolley and Ranzjin, 2006; Hughes, 2007). No Australian retirement or nursing homes formally cater for gay men, and the men fear that being 'out' in 'mainstream' institutions could provoke discrimination or marginalisation.

In this context, the men sought to forestall institutional living and some made changes to their routine homemaking practices to facilitate ageing-in-place. Neil said:

> I would prefer to stay here and have help come in. I really started along those lines. I have fruit and vegetables delivered to me every second week. ... I get my daily telephone call from Telecross. I have been using Telecross for a few months and it is a wonderful service by Red Cross for people like me who live alone.

Using homecare can also be a fraught experience. As Milligan (2009) argues, the presence of domestic care workers can affect privacy and belonging, and provoke a sense of alienation. For older gay men, the decision about disclosure remains. The men in this study, however, prefer homecare over institutions, as long as they sustain a sense of control over their homes and care workers coming into it.

Maintaining existing domestic routines is also important for ageing-in-place, enabling belonging, identity and wellbeing. There is a range of different homemaking practices the men felt it important to continue; some of these are informed by their sexuality. Most – Neil, Shane, Doug, Tom – entertain lesbian and gay friends through weekly or fortnightly dinner parties. This is a domestic activity that simultaneously reinforces their sexual identity, place-attachment and social and emotional wellbeing. Home-entertaining helps to sustain their friendship networks, which in turn supports their sense of self, happiness and life satisfaction. Enacting friendship networks at home, through domestic activities, boosts the significance of their homes for social and emotional support and ontological security. In fact, their homes are arranged to accommodate visitors and facilitate hospitality: none have a separate dining room but all have apportioned a section of their living space for a fixed dining setting. Figure 5.3 is a photograph of the setting in Doug's living room, which is used for weekly dinners with friends. Time alone is also necessary for wellbeing. Most of the men are religious and having time and space for meditative prayer is an important part of making self and home together. Figure 5.4 shows the terrace Harry uses for morning and afternoon prayer; he wrote: 'It means so much to me and I regard myself so fortunate to have the place and faith which has been with me all my life.'

Furthermore, housework – cooking, cleaning, tidying, washing – is one set of routines that many of the men want to keep up, and this is also inflected

Figure 5.3 Doug's dining setting

Figure 5.4　Harry's terrace

by sexuality. As gay men, they have performed their own housework throughout their adult lives, unlike similarly-aged married heterosexual men. As such, their lifelong attachment to the domestic sphere bears resemblance to the married heterosexual women discussed earlier (Russell, 2007). These older gay men, like older heterosexual women, have been considerably more involved in the lifelong domestic and affective work of making a home; homemaking is part of their embodied habits, sense of self, and feeling of belonging. Doug said: 'I do my washing, I do my laundry, I cook five days a week, and I clean – the finished product is satisfying.' Figure 5.5 is a photograph of Neil's kitchen, which is central to his domestic routine; he said: 'I cook almost every day. I always have, even when I was a manager at the bank. I've got a slow cooker, I've got a rice cooker, I've got everything I need. I find it very relaxing.' Maintaining housework patterns is thus important to their wellbeing, and moreover, is used to resist the inertia of ageing (Mowl, Pain and Talbot, 2000).

Finally, the routines of ageing-in-place extend beyond the residential dwelling to encompass the surrounding neighbourhood. All the men iterated the importance of connectivity to their local community through habitual walks and regular visits to local shops, churches and parks. Tom

Figure 5.5   Neil's kitchen

said: 'It's convenient to walk to the shopping centre, and the shop assistants are quite relaxed here, they don't get hassled.' Harry said: 'There are plenty of trees and lots of parks, and I can just walk anywhere really. There are various churches I can get to in a small walk.' In maintaining all these mul-tifaceted routines – home-entertaining, prayer, housework, neighbourhood walks – the men sought to age-in-place and sustain the various connections between home and identity that fostered their wellbeing as older people, and especially as older gay men.

Belongings and passing on

The final theme explores domestic objects – cherished possessions and mean-ingful belongings – and their role in structuring and nurturing connections between home, identity and wellbeing for these middle-class older gay men. This draws attention to the affective and symbolic materiality of domestic environments, and the significance of ongoing personal investment in sub-ject-object relations for generating a sense of belonging. Rubinstein and de Medeiros (2005) argue that domestic objects are 'expressive media' that nar-rate meanings about one's self – both to self and others – through projecting the different facets of one's identity into one's possessions, and using these belongings to represent and communicate important aspects of self. The objectification of self increases with age: as one's lifeworld converges on the space of the home, the significance of domestic objects – indeed, their signifying capacity – is amplified. Thus, Sherman and Dacher (2005) explain that cherished possessions provide a sense of self-continuity and ontological security – a mnemonic anchor (Chaudhury and Rowles, 2005) – in a continuously changing context of self and social relations over the life course (Cristoforetti, Gennai and Rodeschini, 2011). In the process, these possessions link self-identity to place-identity, refracting self through the materiality of one's home. In short, meaningful domestic objects make the self present to self.

There are also classed dimensions to these subject-object relations, which should be noted since they reveal the limitations as well as possibilities of place-attachment and sense of belonging through material possessions. A certain level of financial and material resources is needed to acquire material goods which can be later invested with personal meanings and become meaningful possessions. While these objects are not esteemed for their exchange-value – they are not valued by their owners for their capacity to be exchanged and consumed in a market system, but for the subjective meanings imputed upon them – nevertheless acquiring them in the first instance necessitates sufficient income. Obtaining possessions, and investing them with meaning, is arguably a middle-class practice. Middle-class resources, understanding and expectations enable the acquisition and holding of possessions. Classed practices also structure the divestment of such belongings: 'passing on precious things' to significant others (family, friends, charities) synchronises with the classed language of transference and inheritance. I acknowledge these dimensions since I studied middle-class men, and this classed knowledge is arguably why they raised issues of holding and divesting cherished possessions.

A crucial way in which these middle-class men are present to themselves in their homes, in the face of mainstream and gay marginalisation, is through their belongings. They do this most palpably through displaying objects symbolising their sexual identities, such as homoerotic images and rainbow flags (Reed, 1996). Their homes are often the only spaces available for such candid self-expression (Gorman-Murray, 2007). Figure 5.6 shows some of the homoerotic art and gay symbology in Neil's kitchen. But their sexuality further inflects their engagement with domestic material culture in less overt, but equally profound, ways. In each stage of the research process, the men actively drew attention to symbolic possessions arrayed around their homes and with which they engaged in visual and tactile ways on a daily basis. This elicits a homemaking activity performed by older gay men in subversion of the gender norms of heterosexual households, where interior decoration is a feminine rather than masculine responsibility (Sparke, 1995).

Figure 5.6 Queer belongings

As with housework, these men have been responsible for their own home decorating throughout their adult lives, and so arguably exhibit greater investment in the personalisation of home than married heterosexual men (cf. Sherman and Dacher, 2005 on gendered differences in older people's cherished possessions, where men identified durable items [TVs, radios], and women symbolic items [jewellery, photographs]).

Indeed, for these older gay men, their homes are personal archives of meaningful possessions which evoked memories and materialised self. Often these belongings make present what is absent – friends, relatives, past events, memories – narrating elements of a life story and its constituent relationships. They make older gay men present to themselves by accumulating and representing their personal history, and by materialising past and present interpersonal relationships with partners, friends and family. Figure 5.7 shows Shane's living room, adorned with an array of paintings, pictures, photographs, antiques, period furniture and books, which cumulatively articulate his life history and meaningful relationships. These relationships are both visually expressed (portraits and photographs of himself with partners) and symbolically embedded in the objects themselves (paintings and pictures gifted by friends, and furniture, antiques, china and silverware from parents and grandparents). The interplay of absence and presence in these belongings is complex, and it is also queer. On the

Figure 5.7   Cherished possessions/mnemonic anchors

one hand, these possessions convey a range of absent presences, such as intergenerational connections and interpersonal relationships. On the other hand, the presence of same-sex family portraits manifests his sexuality and concurrently contests normative familial ideals of homelife (Silver, 1996). Furthermore, conjoining belongings symbolically connected to family-of-origin and family-of-choice makes these inter-subjective relationships present to each other in the material fabric of the home. This is insinuated in Figure 5.8, where a same-sex family-of-choice portrait is juxtaposed with belongings inherited from Shane's family-of-origin. This suggests that collections of meaningful belongings make various intrapersonal facets of self co-present (Gorman-Murray, 2008). Different possessions can represent diverse aspects of self – ethnicity, family, religion, sexuality, etc. – and juxtaposing these at home expresses co-presence of self. Tom assembled gay movies and books, Catholic icons, Celtic memorabilia, inherited furniture, investment art and mementos from world travel, intersecting his 'whole self' through domestic material culture.[5]

While domestic belongings most meaningfully narrate a sense of self to oneself, they also convey our identities to others as well. Leach (2002) describes the home as a gallery or museum in which we curate our domestic

Figure 5.8   Materialising family-of-choice and family-of-origin

material culture. For me, this prompts the question of who these men's belongings will speak to in the absence of their owners; that is, who will they be passed on to when the men 'pass on', and what will they say? These belongings – and their domestic settings – are the material artefacts of these men's life histories. They are deeply personal, but they also represent lives lived in connection with others – partners, friends, families, social networks. Each biography is embedded in and conveys wider social history (Hecht, 2001). In a very real sense, the men's belongings are archival records of a collective gay history, a narrative of coming out in, and living through, the post-war era. As well as making personal histories, they can be seen as custodians of the collective history of gay domestic life. Fellows (2004) argues that gay men often have a passion to preserve domestic material culture.

The findings of this study suggest this preservation imperative might have something to do with older gay men's lifelong need to undertake their own homemaking, rather than any essential connection between gay men and domestic desires. Irrespective, older gay men's domestic geographies constitute an important contribution to collective gay history, including the sexual politics of the domestic sphere (Oram, 2011). Through these material legacies older gay men become present to contemporary gay cultures and mainstream society.

Conclusion

This chapter has explored the belonging and exclusion of middle-class older gay men in mainstream and gay social worlds. Using a case study from inner-city Sydney, I analysed the interplay of presence and absence woven through their homes. I suggest that domestic spaces, routines and belongings facilitate creative place-based resistance to heterosexist and ageist marginalisation in mainstream and gay communities. Configured as a productive closet, home inscribes feelings of belonging – senses of presence – through homemaking practices that constitute, perform and express self. Homes cannot be simply interpreted as marginal spaces of absence, but as places where these men are present to themselves. They also become present to others through their domestic material culture, curating social as well as personal stories that convey collective gay histories, especially insights into everyday life.

This analysis queered geographical gerontology via dialogue with queer gerontology and geographies of sexualities. This has theoretical and practical implications which are more-than-academic, prompting a rethink of policy work: it calls for queering ageing policy and its implementation. Queer contests the (hetero)norms of home-and-family; including diverse households in ageing policy means building queer frameworks recognising sexual difference. As preferred policy, ageing-in-place must address the heterogeneity of ageing and meanings of home, accounting for gay men's homemaking that subverts heterosexual ideologies of home. The challenge is not only policy inclusion but implementation by service providers. Housing agencies must be sensitive to different clientele; home-carers must be educated about sexual diversity and its habitual and material expression at home, which supports senses of self and wellbeing. Another challenge is inclusion of diversity within the older gay male demographic, such as class and ethnic differences, rarely explicit in gay-inclusive policies. The men in this study were white and middle-class, but non-white and working-class gay men face further difficulties in accessing housing and homecare due to resource and cultural constraints. Attending to their experiences is vital for advancing policy and scholarship on ageing, sexuality and space.

Notes

1. Ageing is not only biological, but a socio-cultural construct differing between individuals and groups. 'Older' is used here to signify gay men who subjectively identify as 'older' or 'mature', and objectively have a biological age of 55 and over.
2. While I utilise approaches to subject-object relations from gerontology and environmental psychology, the relation between the ageing self and objects also speaks to discussions of reflexive self in sociology.
3. Sample characteristics: 39 heterosexual, 13 gay; 46 of European heritage, six of Asian heritage; 42 working, ten retirees; 44 middle-class professionals (inc. retirees), eight labourers or retail assistants; 32 living with partners or family, 15 single-occupiers, five in group households.
4. In Gorman-Murray, Johnston and Waitt (2010), I discuss the problems and possibilities experienced as a 'younger' gay man from a white, working-class family, in interviewing 'older' lesbian and gay respondents.
5. See Gorman-Murray (2008), which analyses the co-presence of the lesbian or gay self in domestic materiality at length.

Bibliography

Andrews, G., Cutchin, M., McCracken, K., Phillips, D. and Wiles, J. (2007) 'Geographical gerontology: The constitution of a discipline', *Social Science and Medicine*, 65(1): 151–68.

Andrews, G., Milligan, C., Phillips, D. and Skinner, M. (2009) 'Geographical gerontology: Mapping a disciplinary intersection', *Geography Compass*, 3(5): 1641–59.

Attorney General's Department of NSW (2005) *GLBTI Ageing and Discrimination Forum*, 24 March 2005, Anti-Discrimination Board, NSW Government, Sydney, http://www.lawlink.nsw.gov.au/lawlink/adb/ll_adb.nsf/pages/adb_glbti_consultation, accessed on 6 February 2012.

Brown, M. (2000) *Closet space: Geographies of metaphor from the body to the globe*. London: Routledge.

Brown, M. and Knopp, L. (2003) 'Queer cultural geographies – We're here! We're Queer! We're over there, too!' in K. Anderson, M. Domosh, S. Pile and N. Thrift (eds) *Handbook of cultural geography*. London: Sage, pp. 313–24.

Browne, K. and Nash, C. (2010) 'Queer methods and methodologies: An introduction' in K. Browne and C. Nash (eds) *Queering methods and methodologies: Queer theory in social science research*. Farnham: Ashgate, pp. 1–23.

Chaudhury, H. and Rowles, G. (2005) 'Between the shores of recollection and imagination: Self, aging, and home' in G. Rowles and H. Chaudhury (eds) *Home and identity in late life: International perspectives*. New York: Springer, pp. 3–18.

Cristoforetti, A., Gennai, F. and Rodeschini, G. (2011) 'Home sweet home: The emotional construction of places', *Journal of Aging Studies*, 25(3): 225–32.

Drummond, M. (2006) 'Ageing gay men's bodies', *Gay and Lesbian Issues and Psychology Review*, 2(2): 60–6.

Fellows, W. (2004) *A passion to preserve: Gay men as keepers of culture*. Madison: University of Wisconsin Press.

Gorman-Murray, A. (2006) 'Gay and lesbian couples at home: Identity work in domestic space', *Home Cultures*, 3(2): 145–68.

Gorman-Murray, A. (2007) 'Reconfiguring domestic values: Meanings of home for gay men and lesbians', *Housing, Theory and Society*, 24(3): 229–46.

Gorman-Murray, A. (2008) 'Reconciling self: Gay men and lesbians using domestic materiality for identity management', *Social and Cultural Geography*, 9(3): 283–301.

Gorman-Murray, A., Johnston, L. and Waitt, G. (2010) 'Queer(ing) communication in research relationships: A conversation about subjectivities, methodologies and ethics' in K. Browne and C. Nash (eds) *Queering methods and methodologies: Queer theory in social science research*. Farnham: Ashgate, pp. 97–112.

Harrison, J. (2006) 'Coming out ready or not! Gay, lesbian, bisexual, transgender and intersex ageing and aged care in Australia: Reflections, contemporary developments and the road ahead', *Gay and Lesbian Issues and Psychology Review*, 2(2): 44–53.

Heaphy, B. (2007) 'Sexualities, gender and ageing: Resources and social change', *Current Sociology*, 55(2): 193–210.

Hecht, A. (2001) 'Home sweet home: Tangible memories of an uprooted childhood' in D. Miller (ed.) *Home possessions: Material culture behind closed doors*. Oxford: Berg, pp. 123–45.

Hughes, M. (2003) 'Talking about sexual identity with older men', *Australian Social Work*, 56(3): 258–66.

Hughes, M. (2006) 'Queer ageing', *Gay and Lesbian Issues and Psychology Review*, 2(2): 54–9.

Hughes, M. (2007) 'Older lesbians and gays accessing health and aged-care services', *Australian Social Work*, 60(2): 197–209.

Johnston, L. and Valentine, G. (1995) 'Wherever I lay my girlfriend, that's my home: The performance and surveillance of lesbian identities in domestic environments' in D. Bell and G. Valentine (eds) *Mapping desire: Geographies of sexualities*. London: Routledge, pp. 99–113.

Jones, J. and Pugh, S. (2005) 'Ageing gay men: Lessons from the sociology of embodiment', *Men and Masculinities*, 7(3): 248–60.

King, A. and Cronin, A. (2010) 'Queer methods and queer practices: Re-examining the identities of older lesbian, gay, bisexual adults' in K. Browne and C. Nash (eds) *Queering methods and methodologies: Queer theory in social science research*. Farnham: Ashgate, pp. 85–96.

Leach, R. (2002) 'What happened at home with art: Tracing the experience of consumers' in C. Painter (ed.) *Contemporary art and the home*. Oxford: Berg, pp. 153–80.

Meth, P. and McClymont, K. (2009) 'Researching men: The politics and possibilities of a qualitative mixed-method approach', *Social and Cultural Geography*, 10(8): 909–25.

Milligan, C. (2009) *There's no place like home: Place and care in an ageing society*. Farnham: Ashgate.

Mowl, G., Pain, R. and Talbot, C. (2000) 'The ageing body and the homespace', *Area*, 32(2): 189–97.

Oram, A. (2011) 'Going on an outing: The historic house and queer public history', *Rethinking History*, 15(2): 189–207.

Oswald, F. and Wahl, H. (2005) 'Dimensions of the meaning of home in later life' in G. Rowles and H. Chaudhury (eds) *Home and identity in late life: International perspectives*. New York: Springer, pp. 21–45.

Pain, R., Mowl, G. and Talbot, C. (2000) 'Difference and the negotiation of "old age"', *Environment and Planning D*, 18(3): 377–93.

Percival, J. (2002) 'Domestic spaces: Uses and meanings in the daily lives of older people', *Ageing and Society*, 22(6): 729–49.

Reed, C. (1996) '"A room of one's own": The Bloomsbury Group's creation of a modernist domesticity' in C. Reed (ed.) *Not at home: The suppression of domesticity in modern art and architecture*. London: Thames and Hudson, pp. 147–60.

Robinson, P. (2008) *The changing world of gay men*. Basingstoke: Palgrave Macmillan.

Rubinstein, R. and de Medeiros, K. (2005) 'Home, self, and identity' in G. Rowles and H. Chaudhury (eds) *Home and identity in late life: International perspectives*. New York: Springer, pp. 47–62.

Russell, C. (2007) 'What do older women and men want? Gender differences in the "lived experience" of ageing', *Current Sociology*, 55(2): 173–92.

Sherman, E. and Dacher, J. (2005) 'Cherished objects and the home: Their meaning and roles in late life' in G. Rowles and H. Chaudhury (eds) *Home and identity in late life: International perspectives*. New York: Springer, pp. 63–79.

Silver, K. (1996) 'Master bedrooms, master narratives: Home, homosexuality and post-war art' in C. Reed (ed.) *Not at home: The suppression of domesticity in modern art and architecture*. London: Thames and Hudson, pp. 206–21.

Slevin, K. and Linneman, T. (2010) 'Old gay men's bodies and masculinities', *Men and Masculinities*, 12(4): 483–507.

Sparke, P. (1995) *As long as it's pink: The sexual politics of taste*. Hammersmith: Harper Collins.

Tolley, C. and Ranzjin, E. (2006) 'Heteronormativity amongst staff of residential aged care facilities', *Gay and Lesbian Issues and Psychology Review*, 2(2): 78–86.

Waitt, G. and Gorman-Murray, A. (2007) 'Homemaking and mature-age gay men "down under": Paradox, intimacy, subjectivities, spatialities, and scale', *Gender, Place and Culture*, 14(5): 569–84.

Wang, T. (2009) 2009 MAG Survey, *MAGazine*, April–June 2009, pp. 13–14.

Wiles, J. (2005) 'Conceptualising place in the care of older people: The contributions of geographical gerontology', *International Journal of Older People Nursing*, 14(8b): 121–9.

6
The Meaning of Home for Transgendered People

Youngsook Choi

Introduction: Queering geographies of transgendered people

This chapter explores the practices of gender policing in domestic spaces and evaluates the impact that such practices have on transgendered people's everyday subjectivities, social interactions and embodiments. These realities call for constant negotiations with and a battling against the gender binary system inscribed in the space called 'home'. With a focus on domestic settings and the social relations within them, this chapter attempts to position a home as an ambivalent closet space by depicting it not only as a space of relentless gender policing and the re-enforcer of heteronormative gender binarism but also as a space for the queering of these conventions adopted in the home. The empirical data used in this chapter has been derived from the outcome of research on 'gender policing and transgendered people's everyday spaces', conducted between 2008 and 2010.

Moss (2002: 7) argues that 'geography as a discipline has privileged a masculine subject position and produced binaries such as male/female, culture/nature, and object/subject where more value has been placed on the first part of the dichotomy.' Feminist geographers have tried to overcome such dichotomies by (re)politicising traditional ways of framing and conducting research and relating the geographical scales of trans-locality to the body and domestic spaces in a way which questions the division between private and public as well as local and global (Fincher, 2007; Hayden, 1980; Massey, 1994, 2005; McDowell, 1999, 2002). For instance, the home has been reinvestigated as a place of disciplining and reproducing social norms and patriarchal power relations rather than a private space separated from the outer world. In this respect, Hayden's (1980) analysis of the design of homes suggests that the physical arrangements for domestic environments are based on gender divisions and patriarchal values.

While feminist geographers' debates have sought to uncover the power relations and social hierarchies naturalised by male dominance and, simultaneously, to develop new epistemologies of and for those who are marginalised by their genders and sexualities, these debates have not yet heralded a departure from the fundamental ways of categorising gender. The gendered border between men and women, and the imbalance between the two, has been recognised, but the border itself has been profoundly questioned in the field of geography in only a few works (Browne, 2004; Browne, Nash and Hines, 2010; Doan, 2007, 2010). As most studies of inequality and marginalisation relating to gender and sexuality are still based upon the binary system, those whose genders do not fit into the male or female categories are often excluded from these debates. With the emphasis upon the safe access to physical spaces in terms of empowering transgender subjectivities, Doan (2007) contends that the significant effect of physical spaces for gender variant people is rarely researched, in comparison with the attention paid to spaces utilised by gay/lesbian and women. While geographical studies regarding transgendered subjects remain marginal, one of exceptions is the geography journal, *Gender, Place and Culture* that dedicated a special issue to the study of transgender geographies (Browne, Nash and Hines, 2010). In that issue, Browne, Nash and Hines (2010: 573) state that 'geographical enquiry has yet to explore the lives and experiences of people, including trans people, that trouble and call into question these hegemonic, normative, binaries. Such omissions (in the literature) mean that assumptions predicated on a straightforward gender mapping onto biological sex organs and gender roles and relations grounded in male/female and man/woman separations, are often uncritically reproduced.' It is not only transgendered subjects whose embodied experiences have not been sufficiently explored in the field of geography, but also the space called 'home' by those marginalised subjects. As Sibley (1995) asserts in his work 'Geographies of Exclusion':

> The 'house as a haven' is a much more common theme than 'the house as a source of conflict' [...] In human geography, the home as a locus of power relations has been neglected almost entirely, but this is more a problem of recognizing legitimate systems of interest than a failure to see the home environment as one affected by territorial disputes. In geography, interest in residential patterns wanes at the garden gate, as if the private province of the home, as distinct from the larger public spaces constituting residential areas, were beyond the scope of a subject concerned with maps of places. If we are to understand the constitution of social space, the neglect of private space does not make sense.
>
> Sibley (1995: 91–2)

More than a decade after Sibley's criticism, Fincher (2007: 14) suggests that there is still a lack of concern about domestic settings in Western feminist geography and calls for the investigation of the family as 'a moral frame of reference'. The home needs to be explored as a microcosm of the power structure, which conveys and reproduces social norms and conventions within the institutional matrix of power and knowledge, in particular, imposing gender binarism and oppression upon those who fall outside the accepted binary system. My research sets out to fill the gap in gender and sexuality geography, where there is still a relative absence of questioning of the boundaries of gender binarism, by exploring transgendered people's everyday realities and investigating domestic settings as a source of conflict as well as contestation for those who transgress, and hence *problematise*, the naturalised borders between men and women.

More crucially, problematisation of gendered borders and, therefore, of everyday spaces inscribed by gender divisions and hierarchies within transgendered people's experiences, has the 'queering' power that calls into question the conventions and norms charged in them, regardless of whether this problematisation is the involuntary result of gender transitioning or the intentional acts of gender transgression. Here, the term 'queer' is interpreted as the embodied critique of transgendered subjects and its deconstructive power against heteronormativity. Hence, the ontology of queer is made more meaningful not by the identification of non-heterosexual subjectivities, although these are significant, but by the constant questioning and resistance to normativity through embodied experiences (Brown, 2007; Butler, 1993, 2004, 2006; Fuss, 1991; Sanger, 2008; Sedgwick, 1990). There is also a methodological gap, leading to the identification of transgender subjects as queer merely because their gendered acts do not comply with accepted gender norms and conventions. Many transgendered people are often more comfortable when defining their gender identity within the framework of the gender binary system, using accepted terms such as 'man' or 'woman' rather than as queer, mainly due to its connotation with non-heterosexual identities and practices. In the case of my research, all key participants considered that their gender identities result from a gender disorder or they simply disagree with gender binaried conformity. The issues of sexual orientation are generally considered to be a separate matter from their gender identities; although it is often true that gender crossing/transitioning complicates identifications with sexuality (Hines and Sanger, 2009; Monro, 2007; Sanger, 2007, 2008).

Despite the aforesaid, the term 'queer' still remains a useful epithet with which to characterise transgendered people's embodied experiences, regardless of how they define their genders. The subversive power they exert against the conventional context of the gender binary system is often inevitably embraced in their bodily engagement of transgender subjectivities. As McDowell (1999: 21) claims, 'there are many different ways of doing gender, of being a man and a woman', and these different ways are enabled by challenges to heteronormativity. Browne and Lim's (2009) work on transgendered people's perception of their gender identities and its impact upon their embodiment suggest that transgendered people's subjective ways of sensing their genders calls for a reconceptualisation of the very meaning of gender. By locating subjective narratives of transgendered informants at the forefront of their investigation and avoiding theoretical generalisation, Browne and Lim conclude that the wide array of transgendered people's gender identities is beyond the intelligibility of existing discourses and social systems. As a result of this, the meaning of transgender is utilised not only to refer to a state of gender identity but also to an embodied phenomenon, responsively or resultantly linked to the acts of contesting these existing discourses and systems. Challenging the existing moral ethics and conventions is the core essence of the performative effect that the term 'queer' conveys, and this chapter applies the meaning of queer in this interpretation to the analysis of transgendered people's lived experiences within domestic spaces. The following sections discuss the methodological concerns arising from transgender subjectivities with an introduction on how the research was conducted, and how the home is depicted as an ambivalent, or limited, closet space which is not only a site of oppression but also one of constant negotiation and challenge by transgendered people in their effort to queer the space, if not merely to survive.

Presenting transgender voices and methodological concerns

This research is based upon a qualitative ethnographic approach with feminist critiques on the recovery of subjective voices, emphasising reflexive and intersubjective relationships between researchers and respondents (Hollway and Jefferson, 2000; Letherby, 2003; Moss, 2002; Sandercock, 2003; Skeggs, 1994; Smith, 2005). In conducting the research as a non-transgender person, ethical challenges were recognised in terms of understanding transgendered people's standpoints and delivering their subjective voices. Research methods were developed to respond to these challenges, and therefore the process of research was subjected to constant adjustments of, and negotiations with, the views of research participants and transgender communities. Hence, the goal of the research was not to produce a conclusion in a form of generalisation but rather to lead an open-ended discussion driven by transgendered people's narratives in their own terms and to present the outcome of the research not as a finished product but as a part of ongoing struggle.

One of the challenging aspects of transgender-related research is that the understanding of transgender subjectivities cannot be fully covered within existing discourses and theories (Browne and Lim, 2009) as pointed out earlier. In a similar account, Butler (2004: 73–4) recognises the 'ineffability' of transgender subjectivity and suggests the empowerment of a discourse of self-reporting and self-understanding. However, Butler is also concerned about how far self-reporting and self-understanding can go beyond the existing knowledge framework since it is almost impossible to explain the nature of transgender identity when working with pre-existing terminology and within current norms.

Butler's argument poses a dilemma but, at the same time, identifies a great challenge for researchers. Her recognition of subjects who are unrecognisable within the existing discourses brings us back to the beginning point about what subjectivism is really about, and it inspires us to pursue inexplicable voices which evokes Stryker's (2006: 248) subverting metaphor for transsexuality, Frankenstein's monster: '[T]he newly enlivened body of creature attests to its maker's failure to attain the mastery he sought. Frankenstein cannot control the mind and feelings of the monster he makes. It exceeds and refutes his purposes'. The problem is that Frankenstein's monster does not possess an adequate language. The tragic fate of Frankenstein's monster is that explaining the self is only possible through use of the inventor's language and this will never fully deliver what Frankenstein's monster subjectively wants to relate. The crisis of language is a critical issue in terms of recovering subjective voices, and hence producing knowledge based upon them.

Another challenging aspect of the research is situated in my subjective position and its relation to transgendered people and their communities. Even though I have full respect for gender variant people and their lived experiences, my own experience is limited to being a heterosexual woman from a different cultural background This position not only limits me to a role of outsider observer, but it also encourages me to position myself as an active learner and to recognise that the research is inevitably contingent upon research participants' trust and collaborations. In that regard, the methodology was designed in a flexible way to allow for the adoption and embracing of participants' views and application of their individual situations and perceptions to the research process. To meet the challenging aspects regarding the nature of transgender subjectivities, described previously, and to capture and situate transgendered people's everyday experiences of domestic spaces within the power relations and social system, research methods were adapted to link three major resources: the community knowledge, documentary resources, and the life stories from and interviews with research participants. However, the research was mainly conducted in London, which means that community knowledge, institutional resources and research participants' experiences, adopted in the research, were derived solely from a UK context. Transgendered people form a very small part of the population and are geographically sporadic which makes it difficult to observe and categorise the diverse situations that relate to different locales (Reed et al., 2009). London was a strategic choice for the access to prevailing transgender community activities and political consensus around that city.

The first resource is the community knowledge of transgendered people, which provides the basic knowledge of how they view their situations in their own terms, and leads to an understanding of the subcultural substances of transgender communities. Respecting community knowledge is the very starting point for learning how to engage in actual talk with transgendered people. This is also the reason why I included one year of volunteer work for a transgender-related organisation as part of the research programme. Understanding basic terms and conditions related to various transgendered subjects, and their community culture, is the first step which needs to be taken when conducting research in this field and must be done before looking for participants and approaching communities. In addition, exploring community knowledge is essential if one is to understand the minor politics constructed by community members. As Bauer (1996: 3) maintains 'Members of social groups or subcultures tell stories with words and meanings specific to certain social groups. The lexicon of a social group constitutes its perspective of the world.' Every subcultural and minority-related term has its own history and this history contains a politics of oppression and resistance. While it is impossible to introduce all transgender-related terms, a few key terms, which have informed the research, should be defined.

Even the most-basic of terms 'transgender', carries a huge weight: Transgender is commonly used as an umbrella term to cover all gender variant individuals and phenomena, such as transsexual, transvestite, cross-dresser, gender-neutral, non-gendered, and so on. The term 'transgender' should be understood as a political consensus among all gender variant people rather than a fixed description of one's gender identity. The concern with the use of this term arises from the question whether it is possible to define transgender within a gender-binary linguistic system since the language tends to resort to the use of a definitive gender direction that refers to whether an individual is male-to-female or female-to-male. In reality, the attributes of the two, or more, genders coexist in many cases, and the gender direction does not necessarily manifest itself one way or the other, constant crossing-over being possible. This is the queerness that many transgendered people cannot explain by using the existing language. Relatively speaking, 'transsexual' is a definitive term regarding its gender direction. Transsexual people are a particular group of people who believe that their gender is different from the one to which they were assigned at birth. Often being diagnosed as gender dysphoric, transsexual people may seek medical treatment, such as hormone therapies or surgical procedures to align their psychological gender with their physicality. However, in reality, not all transsexual people undergo medical transitioning. Some transsexual people exist as closet cross-dressers, while they strongly identify themselves as female inside their bodies. This is often because, apart from the sense of gender, there are other social factors such as family and employment, which limit the person's ability to present their genders they aspire to. One other crucial community term to be understood is the prefix 'cis'. Cis is normally used in chemistry and biology for meaning 'on the same side', as in its Latin origin, while the contrary prefix 'trans' means 'on the other side' or 'across'. Transgendered people use the term 'cisgender' for non-transgendered people as a counter to non-transgendered people's objectification of transgendered people, revealing how labelling is involved in empowerment as well as othering.

The second method used in the research is documentary analysis to understand textual realities and institutional relationship in which transgendered people are engaged. Smith (2005: 101) argues that the overall aim of collecting documentary resources is to create 'maps of ruling relations'. In this respect, the life conditions of transgendered people are closely related to their legal and medical situations such as whether they have had medical transitioning and the subsequent legal adjustment to their official gender. Recent UK legislation regarding transgender human rights such as The Gender Recognition Act (2004) and The Equality Act (2010), as well as a series of consultation documents for transsexual people published by the Department of Health in the UK government, were reviewed. In addition, the media resources including television documentaries, soaps, advertisement and news articles, dealing with transgendered subjects, were reviewed to observe how the media articulates and reflects public perception of transgender subjectivities, which, in turn, affects transgendered people's social engagements and access to physical spaces.

Thirdly, the core of the research was based upon my involvement and interaction with seven key participants who contributed their life stories. These stories were collated through the context, primarily, of 43 narrative interviews but also by spending time with them in various social settings over a period of 18 months. All seven key participants were assigned male at birth. Two identify themselves as transsexual women, two as transgendered women, and one as a transvestite, another as a cross-dresser and another as a woman. The common factor between all participants is that they desire femininity and femaleness, whether it is for gender identity or sexual stimulus. Despite considerable variety in the self-identification and lived experiences of these seven transgendered female subjects, the research does not include transgendered men's perspectives. This is the decision made from the preliminary observation on the transgender community. There are distinct differences between trans men and trans women in terms of gender crossing experiences. The transitioning from (inferior) female to (superior) male is often socially more acceptable than the other way around, and this may influence the social responses to those subjects differently, as one of key participants calls transgendered women 'second class women'. The act of gender crossing from male to female challenges the gender hierarchy between male and female and is seen by some men as an insult or a betrayal of male superiority. Effeminacy, or the desire to be female, had been criminalised and treated as a major target of gender surveillance in modern history (Cook, 2003; Houlbrook, 2005). The research limits the participants' profile to transgendered women who identify themselves female regardless of their experience of medical transitioning. In addition, the research is necessarily limited in terms of generalising the broadcloth of transgender experiences regarding key participants' ethnicities, ages and cultural identities. Since all participants are white English, educated, and professionals, this research does not encompass other intersectional issues, such as different ethnic backgrounds and non-professional class. The age profile of the key participants span from the late 40s to early 80s, and their view may be inconsistent with younger generations who have benefited from being part of the transgender community and accessing the community knowledge in their early years through emerging network technologies.

However, the type of interview utilised in this research was not restricted to a narrative approach with key participants. Further interviews were conducted to find out how transgender subjectivities are restricted, and have evolved in response to family perspectives and community relationships. Two of the key participants' partners agreed to be interviewed. The semi-structured interviews with them focused on their management and negotiation with transgendered partners within domestic spaces and related social situations. In-depth interviews were carried out with community players in various social domains such as a self-help group, a social enterprise, an activist group and a club events community. The questions posed to them were focused on safety concerns for transgendered people and the meanings of community space for them. The data for the roles of community spaces was elaborated by a questionnaire distributed through the small trans youth club of Gendered Intelligence, a social enterprise for LGBT youth in London. Six young people responded, returning the completed questionnaires. To prevent unwanted coming-out situations, and a potential threat to research respondents' safety, all names used for key participants, their partners, and other interviewees are pseudonyms, excepting those who are representatives of organisations and are publicly out as a transgendered person. Drawn upon the data from various resources and interviews, the following two sections identify the home as a site of disciplining of the gender binary system and of transgendered people's negotiations with as well as their contestations against its constraints, and more importantly how their acts of gender crossing have a subversive (queering) effect upon conventional domestic settings.

Home as a site of gender binary disciplines

The home is perhaps the most intimate unit where the disciplining of gender norms begins. Under pressure from the conventions and moral ethics around gender roles and sexuality, the general perception of home as a haven, and the only place to be a real self, is often not consistent with the domestic situation of those who have gender identities and sexual preferences, which are not compliant with the heteronormative gender binary system. In fact, a home can be a place of oppression for them. For instance, a home can be a place of concealment of the self and a site of alienation to some gay men and lesbian women (Taylor, 2004; Valentine, 1993, 1995, 2008; Valentine and Skelton, 2003).

Sexual minority people often feel out of place in their own home as the result of a family member's inconsiderate and, at worse, violent response to their sexuality. In the case of gender variant people, the situation can be worse. Many are estranged from family members after gender transitioning and end up having to go through a divorce when they come out to their partners. The Equality Review in UK (Whittle, Turner and Al-Alami, 2007), where more than 800 transgendered people participated in the survey, reveals that 45% of the respondents experienced family breakdown due to their transgender identity, 37% are excluded from family events and lost their links to family members due to their transitioning. Two out of three transsexual participants in my own research also experienced divorce and estrangement from family members. Jenny, who maintains her family, is however a different case from the other two because she started her transitioning only when she was in her late 70s, and her transitioning programme did not include a surgical procedure due to her age and a health condition. This means that she is still able to manage her dual gendered roles on different social occasions such as disguising herself as a father in family events. If transitioning is definitive like the other two cases, family breakdown is often the case as Holly expressed her resentment towards her family:

> They [family] can't or won't accept the changes. Now they're shutting Holly out, it's kind of funny really. But people deal with it or they don't. The choice is that they would have Holly or a graveyard visit and I wasn't going to give them the graveyard option and they wouldn't take Holly. So … I will say they pushed me away, they will say I pushed them away. Maybe it's both, I don't know but the end result as far as I'm concerned I'm now estranged from my family. My niece will email, just a short email every month or so … That is the only point of contact I have with my family.
>
> Holly, 53

Holly's family sees her transgender identity as a life choice and maintains their attitude that her selfish choice discounts how other family members feel, and, thus she no longer deserves familial attachment. There is no account taken of Holly's 50 years of painful resistance against her sense of gender as a woman before her first attempt to commit suicide and finally making the decision to transition to a woman. Estrangement from family hurt Holly most when her father was critically ill and eventually passed away. None of family members wanted her to visit him including her father himself while he was in hospital, and Holly was implicitly refused attendance at the funeral by being given no information about where and when it happened. She had to endure her sorrow in isolation. Foreseeing that she was not going to be invited to her father's funeral, Holly spoke to me about her anxiety a few days before her father passed away:

> I am a bit numb and distracted. I'm taking a couple of days off work to try and get my head together. No idea when the funeral will be or whether I will be allowed to go. It is like my life will never be completed in a way because such as important part of a memory like loss of family will be blanked out. This is very sad and strange.
>
> Holly, 53

Being deprived of the right of mourning for her father, this incident left Holly with no hope of reuniting with her family. The case of family break-down is not limited to only those who have gone through medical transitioning. The possibility of maintaining family relationships after coming out as a transgendered person is not merely up to whether transitioning takes place or not. It is more up to the degree of family understanding and acceptance, based upon their moral values. In those moral frames, transgendered people's existence is often interpreted as a threat to the maintenance of a heteronormative family structure and becomes subject to oppression and marginalisation. For one of my key participants, Gina, who identifies her a transvestite, dressing up as a woman with no intention of transitioning, the situation was equally traumatic, ending in a divorce:

> We went for marriage guidance counselling. I shared it [female side] with her [Gina's wife] but she couldn't turn on with it or allow me to be it so we tried to bury it with marriage guidance counselling, which had nothing to do with helping me sort myself out … I wanted it to be real and again I swallowed it so I went to red dwarf [with a reference to a British comedy series, meaning 'being trapped while disliking each other'] on that for a while. As soon as I did separate with her, I couldn't wait to get into it and started to wear makeup and a wig and go to the TV/TS [Transvestite/Transsexual] group in Shoreditch as it was then.
>
> Gina, 55

However, moral codes in domestic settings come not only with certain disciplines but also with punishment (Foucault, 1977). Other family members' feelings of frustration or shame not only confine a transgendered member of the family but also may turn into a form of violence. The recent community-based reports in the UK call for actions and policies preventing domestic violence against transgendered people. For instance, Browne and Lim's work (2008) on discrimination against transgendered people in the Brighton and Hove area, which is known to be a gay-friendly neighbourhood in the UK, reveals that 64% of survey respondents experienced domestic violence. In one other paper, released from the Scotland LGBT Domestic Abuse Project and the Scottish Transgender Alliance (Morton et al., 2010), 80% of transgendered respondents suffer abuse at home and 45% of them had experienced physical abuse from a partner or ex-partner.

A home as a moral entity can be a safe haven for the members who conform to that morality, but may be a place of exclusion for those who do not. There is a constitutive relationship between a home and an occupant where the moral frame drawn upon heteronormative familial values within domestic settings plays a significant role in defining the limits of the body, therefore gendered and sexual subjectivities. The question here is, in that constitutive relationship, who creates, manages and regulates a space, the home in this case? Massey (1994: 167) states that there is an issue of 'whose identity we are referring to when we talk of a place called home and of the supports it may provide, of stability, openness and security'. This issue becomes more evident in young transgendered people's situations. For young people, home is the place regulated by their parents' ethics and socio-cultural identities, and it is often based upon heteronormative values. Young people who identify themselves as not conforming to these values can feel not only out of place at home but also vulnerable to the resulting enforcement of discipline and punishment. Their sense of gender often becomes a secret, as Dorothy as a young transgendered person reflected:

> I am only out to one of my sisters who is accepting, but not out to any parents, more siblings or extended family, as they are what I perceive to be non-accepting. I would like to be out to my mum, but I don't think this is the right time.
>
> Dorothy, 19

As Dorothy implies, the moral frames of family operate not only as a criterion of judgment from other family members but also as a barometer of the acceptance, or exclusion, which might be expected from them. When a home is considered to be a non-accepting environment and not expected to provide appropriate support from other family members, community spaces become a significant platform for developing and enjoying transgender subjectivities. Hine's (2007) work on transgender-specific communities in the UK suggests that care and support through communities and friendship within them is crucial in terms of transgender movements and the construction of discursive spaces for transgender identity while criticising a lack of institutional assistance for those communities. However, care and support from communities cannot be achieved if safety is not first guaranteed. Four of the six young transgendered people I interviewed stated that a safe environment is the most necessary service or support they would expect from transgender communities:

> Safe environments to be themselves ... just more organised meets in a relaxed, informal atmosphere ... even a kind person's front room would be great setting!
>
> Kye, 18

> A safe space where they can openly be themselves and not have to worry about the people around them, not understanding.
>
> Josie, 21

Non-judgmental acceptance of diverse genders is a benefit of community, which has an impact on other social relations as Jamie attested:

> Being in an environment where you are accepted for who you are and not judged or looked at in a weird way, knowing that you're in the company of people who understand you and that you can relate to is comforting. I don't feel so alone anymore ... Those closest to me have said that I seem happier and more confident in myself.
>
> Jamie, 22

The positive experiences of community spaces pave the way for dealing with other social relations but, as Jamie reflected, a new concern arises when attending these, that of how to travel there from their home space. Gendered disciplining and confinement of transgender identities within the home continue to spread to spaces beyond the home such as neighbourhoods (Moran, 2007; Moran and Sharpe, 2004; Morton, 2008; Taylor, 2004). One of the most cautionary spaces mentioned by all of key participants is their locale and neighbourhood, partly because of the concern for their family reputation and partly of the fear of violence by local people as Natalie asserted:

> One thing every trans person I think is always worried about is the brick through the window. The one I am most careful about is the area 100 yards from my house ... I don't generally go out locally ... I mean pubs and things you have to be careful with these outside the centre, 'cos they have a sort of regular crowd and everybody know everybody else and they could gang up on you a bit, so you've gotta be a bit careful. But I'm sure I wouldn't have trouble in most, but I don't wanna find out.
>
> Natalie, 48

This concern with the prying eyes of neighbours affects local boundaries of transgender subjectivities, such as making a decision about where to go and not to go, and necessitates the development of tactics for moving around from place to place in the local area, without being exposed to the neighbours' eyes. Jenny explained her complicated process of going out such as approaching her car while being dressed as a man, driving up to the quiet corner of the public park and changing into a female attire to go to community meetings, and the other way around on the way back home. Her major concern is to avoid the exposure of her transgender identity and recognition from neighbours:

> I usually get the car out in drab and then pop into it. We fortunately have a drive as you noticed, so I can get the car up the drive where I would be unfortunate if anyone saw me ... I certainly very rarely go to Muswell Broadway dressed because I'm too likely to meet neighbours and so on, and the wife would have kittens if the neighbours knew.
>
> Jenny, 84

As Jenny testifies, even if there is the acknowledgement and acceptance of one's transgender identity from family members to a certain degree, home cannot stand alone as a safe space. As home and neighbourhood are parts of the extension of moral frame of the society, exposure of transgender identity to neighbours can have an impact upon the safety of home and family members within it. Rene, as a closet cross-dresser, lives with her partner who has gone through a hard time to understand and eventually accept Rene's desire for cross-dressing. While Rene is appreciating her partner's acceptance, she is also aware of the possibility of her partner being on the receiving end of negative responses from neighbours and the impact this could have upon their marital relationship as well as her hard-won acceptance from her partner:

> I am mindful of possible repercussions for Francesca [Rene's partner]. They may say to her what sort of bloke have you married? I don't want to upset her. It's a concern for Francesca. I'm not really bothered what neighbours say but I don't want to cause any embarrassment reflected into Francesca. She's gone so far with this. I respect her the way she has assisted me and accepted up to a point ... The last thing I want to do is to cause her any unnecessary embarrassment.
>
> Rene, 69

In an account of home and neighbourhood as sites of negative responses towards gendered and sexual minorities and social marginalisation, Moran (2007: 425–7) warns about 'the privileged positions of stranger-danger model of violence' by insisting that the preoccupied perception of stranger-danger model marginalises 'the importance of *low-level* incidents and the messiness of violence that occurs in the context of physically and socially proximate and enduring relationships (original emphasis)'. More crucially, the violent responses from family members and neighbours, whether it is symbolic or physical, can precipitate a housing crisis and lead to homelessness. Namaste's (2000) empirical research, based in the US, reveals that domestic violence and school bullying of young transgendered people often force them into homelessness, and prostitution becomes the only option for earning a living, since shelters providing overnight stays are also segregated by the gender-binary system and the managers of these are often reluctant to accommodate transgendered people in order to avoid possible violence by other shelter residents. In Morton's (2008) work, based in the UK, more than a quarter of research respondents reported that they had to move out of their home due to transphobic reactions and harassment by family members and neighbours. One of my research participants, Gina also experienced such problems. She had to move to another place as a result of a physical attack in her previous area:

> I've been living here since the year 2000. We're close to our neighbours but we're not out to them. We fled to here as a result of a homophobic and racist siege that we underwent living a few miles further east. That included having the local kids throw rocks through our windows on more than one occasion, being physically assaulted in the street so we just fled from there and of course as soon as we arrived here it was comparatively a sanctuary and somewhere to start again. We very much since landing here have kept ourselves to ourselves.
>
> Gina, 55

Gina calls her new home a sanctuary but it is a limited one as her transgender identity is imprisoned, not to be exposed at all outside the boundaries of her own space. However, this imprisonment of a transgendered body within a home does not mean necessarily that a home is merely a space of confinement. But it also means that, as Gina implies, a home can be a closet space for expressing and liberating transgender subjectivities under certain conditions. The next section attempts to position home as a site of queering the gender binary system by transgendered subjects' gender-crossing acts and explains the limitations and restrictions for this transgression.

Home as an ambivalent closet space

While many transgendered people are subjected to gender policing in domestic spaces and their subjectivities are limited in various ways by it, a home, as a private space, provides a closet space for many transgendered people as well. Even so, the use of this space calls for constant negotiation with and the development of a sensitive awareness of social relations with other members who share this space, such as family. Home can be a place for heteronormative disciplining through gender division and prescribed roles for men and women but these social and cultural conventions can be also transcended by private practices of gender transgression, as Rene recollected:

> I would like to be dressed at home. I feel personally changes when I'm dressed. It does. My feminine side comes out. I feel happier.
>
> Rene, 69

However, the level of privacy available is conditioned by other family members' understanding or acceptance of transgender identities, where space is conceptualised as a 'socially produced set of manifold', requiring relational understanding (Crang and Thrift, 2002). In her auto-ethnographic work, Doan (2010: 647), as a transsexual scholar, suggests that 'private spaces can be places of refuge or exclusion' for many transgendered people on account of the different conditions developed through 'co-constructed' events. Different conditions are built upon as a result of how social relations between family members and domestic settings are negotiated to handle transgender subjectivities. For instance, Gina, a transvestite and pansexual, has lived with her gender variant friend for more than 20 years. They live together as partners but they are not tied to each other as a couple in their open relationship. With a great degree of understanding about each other's gendered and sexual needs, they take care of each other like family. The family relationship that they have mutually developed allows them to maintain a respectful atmosphere for gender-crossing acts and queer sexualities. Crucially, this respectful atmosphere is possible through spatial settings. Gina's home is like a dark cave since thick fabrics cover all the windows day and night so that no one can see inside the house from outside and interfere with her when she is dressed as a woman. Gina's home manifests her reluctance to be seen in the public eye by virtue of the dark interior of her house. This is mainly because of her experience of violence in her previous residence, and, hence, it is important for her to be able to hide, or protect, her transgender identity from external eyes. The dark fabrics covering the windows are the demarcation between the private and the public, as well as transgender space and gender binary spaces, and the spatial materialisation of Gina's safety concerns.

Grosz (1994: 80) calls this 'incorporated spatiality' by suggesting that space is a significant factor in defining 'the limits and shape of the body' and, therefore gendered and sexual behaviours, in the constitutive relationship between the body and its surroundings. However, spatial arrangement for transgender subjectivities may not grant freedom of gendered expressions if a transgendered person lives in conventional familial settings. The domestic space cannot be fully free from the gaze of gender policing. Rene remembers how she managed to keep her cross-dressing secret from her parents when she lived with them:

> I hide items in the shed, the bottom of the garden. Obviously my parents didn't know ... My parents never found out my interest in feminine clothing.
>
> Rene, 69

This secrecy often continues after marriage, having children and becoming a parent until it reaches the moment when transgendered subjects want to come out to their partners. It can be a shock for most partners, and lead to anxiety and suspicion about their relationship. Many instances end with breakdown of relationships especially when a person decides to undergo medical transitioning. In this research, four of seven key participants maintained their marriage relationship, and none of them underwent medical transitioning whether they define themselves transsexual or not. However, knowing and acknowledging a partner's secret, and the acceptance of a partner's transgender identity are different matters. Acceptance is an enduring and gradual process that takes time and efforts between family members, as a partner of one of key participants, Friede remembers:

> When he [Pat, also known as Paul to her family] told me, that was quite a shock to me. Because until then I didn't know such a thing existed ... There was a time, I felt, 'what is this? I married a man not a woman' ... Gradually over the time, 'yes, he is a man and he just dresses as a woman.
>
> Friede, 69

Interestingly, the way to overcome shock and anxiety, and to accept a partner's transgender identity, is developed by gaining knowledge of, and increasing one's understanding of what transgender means. This involves sharing written resources and discussions between partners, as two of key participants' partners experienced:

> He gave me books and other information about it then I found out more about it. It is quite a common thing but it's not talked about that much, maybe not that much at that time, and we talked about it for different lengths of time, sometimes short conversation, sometimes long talk ... Once I know about it, that's the time process [of acceptance] started.
>
> Friede, 69

> Just living with it, and talking about it all the time ... We've just talked and talked and talked.
>
> Francesca, 64

As knowledge about transgender subjectivities is developed, the level of acceptance is increased. And the acceptance of family members affects a transgendered family member's gender-crossing practices in domestic spaces. As many queer and feminist theorists remark (Fuss, 1991; Grosz, 1994; Halberstam, 2005; Sedgwick, 1990), in the development of the inter-relationship between power, knowledge and space, acquired knowledge of transgender subjectivity empowers a transgendered person and this empowerment enables spatial practices of transgender identities. The knowledge becomes real and powerful when the visibility of a new body is *in* space as Friede recollects when she saw Pat, Paul's other side, for the first time:

> I would know that he would be upstairs changing to Pat. And I would be probably downstairs and he would not want me to see him. At that point, I don't know whether he was even Pat ... He just didn't want to be disturbed when he was dressing up. Then gradually, he said, 'do you like to see me?' then I said, 'okay'. After a while, he came downstairs and was still there for me to look, and I said 'wow' which was very strange because to me he was always Paul ... I guess that, although I by that time accepted him having two sides, it was also how to come to terms again to see visual aspect of it from just knowing there is something about him to actually see him changed.
>
> Friede, 69

A home is a space where there is a constant challenge and negotiation between family members in order to define the acceptable boundaries for the emergence and presence of transgender identity and this was reflected in the account Pat gave of the gradual expansion of her transgender territory within home from her study upstairs to the lounge downstairs. However, it appears to be important to retain these boundaries if the relationship is to continue. Natalie, who is known to be proactive in transgender communities and 'out' to her work colleagues as a transgendered woman, explains her struggle to maintain these boundaries with her partner:

> Yeah, it's difficult to make out sometimes but I know where her [Natalie's partner] boundaries are. It's worked out as an arrangement. She sees me as one particular identity, maybe she has difficulty conceiving of me with a different identity.
>
> Natalie, 48

A home is, however, the place not only for immediate family members but also for the extended family. Extended family members' visits can change the condition of home as a closet space and the boundaries of transgender practices previously agreed between partners. It also affects the level of security that a transgendered family member feels within domestic settings.

A partner's understanding and acceptance of transgender identity can be regressed and this changes the boundary of transgender subjectivities within home as Pat experienced:

> We've got my wife's nephew, Thomas, staying from Germany ... Pat is not allowed out tomorrow as Thomas doesn't know about her. So, it's Paul going to the rehearsal ... It is really annoying. You know, the house is not a safe space.
>
> Pat, 71

While the acceptable boundaries of transgender subjectivities are in a state of constant change, as demanded by different social settings such as family acceptance and visitors, the negotiation of boundaries is not only the matter of territorial practices within domestic spaces, but also of bodily presentations. Davy (2011: 57) suggests 'the aesthetics of gender – femininities and masculinities – as central to trans people's "habitus" and "fields" and as a form of generative cultural capital.' A home as a private space is often a site of practices of femininity for male-to-female transgendered people and the level of these practices of bodily aesthetics is developed, as well as limited, through the process of constant negotiation between family members. Jenny explains how she changes her gendered presentation as a response to her partner's reaction to it:

> I first agreed I would just dress upstairs [the study] and not come down so she [Jenny's partner] wouldn't have to see me but because my wife is almost deaf if she's sitting in here she can't see the phone outside so I had to come down and tell her. I couldn't undress before people rang off the phone so she had to accept seeing me occasionally dressed. At first she used to burst into tears when she saw me fully dressed with a wig on so I think I used to come down minus a wig.
>
> Jenny, 84

One other aspect of the practices of gender aesthetics for transgendered women within domestic settings is that their practices often start from their study rooms (men's rooms) as Pat and Jenny attested earlier. Men's study rooms used to be a sacred space for a father to keep all the family documents such as financial and genealogical records. Wigley (1992: 347) argues that 'the first truly private space was the man's study, a small locked room off his bedroom which no-one else ever enters'. While the wife was given a dressing room, which was open to young children, girls and a nurse, the husband was given this private space to keep his knowledge, and his power, in safety. Transgendered women's practicing of femininity in the study deconstructs not only the binary order of gender but also subverts the gendered context inscribed onto the space, which is the queering effect of transgender subjectivities.

Distribution of time is also an important dimension influencing the fluidity and changing nature of spaces, and temporality becomes the object of negotiation between occupants (Halberstam, 2005; Taylor, 2012). While the home is a perfect closet space for Rene when she is dressed as a woman, this same space is also a perfect home for the heteronormative couple when Rene is in men's attire. For Rene, keeping the balance between her male and female sides is crucial to maintaining her relationship with her partner, Francesca. To facilitate this, Rene draws an imaginary line between male and female part of her life at home:

> There are times she [Francesca] feels that Rene takes over and Roy [Rene's male side] is not a person she has married. Francesca might say, from time to time, 'I'd rather see Roy a little more often than Rene.' And I think I mustn't cross. I feel I have to respect Francesca. I shouldn't cross that line ... I don't want to destroy this acceptance Francesca has got and what she allows me ... She is a great guiding light for what I'm doing. Her acceptance of that, you can't measure it, I can't measure it.
>
> Rene, 69

'Acceptance' is a conditional and relational term in respect of the boundaries of what can and cannot be crossed; and these boundaries are constantly negotiated through different social relations, presentations of bodily aesthetics and temporal sensitivity. However, this complicated articulation of transgender identity within the domestic settings not only affects transgendered subjects' gender-crossing practices but also extends the boundary of a closet space through the relationships with their loved ones. In this regard, Sedgwick (1990: 80) maintains that circulating the secret creates someone else's closet space:

> Living in and hence coming out of the closet are never matters of the purely hermetic; the personal and political geographies to be surveyed here are instead the more imponderable and conclusive ones of the open secret ... The pathogenic secret itself, even, can circulate contagiously *as* a secret: a mother with her says that her adult child's coming out of the closet with her has plunged her, in turn, into the closet in her conservative community.
>
> (original emphasis)

This was the case for Francesca. She thinks that revealing her partner's cross-dressing secret may make her lose her social capital accumulated as a heteronormative couple over the years. It is a fear of being marked out and isolated. Coming out with her partner's secret can damage her sense of belonging to the place where she is socially located and maintaining heteronormative performativity as a couple is important her, to avoid herself being classified as an outsider as Francesca recounted:

> I can guarantee you, if we walk up to the road, we'll see at least one of our friends or maybe two or maybe three, and some of them are elderly, we think, quite prudish. People don't need to know. I personally would rather they didn't know. But he couldn't care less of things … They might shun us, we don't know … I would fee hurt if that happens. We've got friends for 40, 50 years. I would hate to lose those friends. Not everybody understands. They think this is something that could hurt them.
>
> Francesca, 64

Francesca's concern transcends the relationship between herself and her partner, Rene. It goes beyond their domestic spaces and into the neighbourhoods, local communities and circle of friends. In addition, exposure of her partner's transgender identity to those who are close, but may not have a sympathetic understanding, could threaten the security of their domestic space and their relationship. However, this posits contesting practices of gender and sexuality within domestic settings as a significant starting point of changes regarding gender diversity and queer subjectivities. While a home is considered to be a confinement of transgender subjectivities in a secretive way, there is always a possibility of breaking out of this confinement by further challenges. And this possibility carries a subversive power to problematise gender norms and conventions that people have never questioned. This is the reason why some people think 'this is something that could hurt them' as Francesca expresses in the previous extract. Here, hurting means questioning of the belief that is supposed to be firm and unbreakable for the majority of people, and therefore the sheer presence of queerness.

Conclusion

The home, as an intimate unit of society and, as one of the basic elements of a social system, plays the role of moral frame catering for heteronormative familial structures and, within this moral frame, the gender binary system often prescribes and enforces certain behaviours for men and women creating a hierarchy between them which gives rise to oppression of transgendered people within domestic settings. Resulting from this, there are prevailing issues of domestic violence against transgendered people whether it is physical/verbal attack or symbolic exclusion. However, the private characteristics of domestic spaces simultaneously allow for transgendered subjects to transgress this moral frame by individual performances of crossing, or blurring, conventional gender categories, which are not often possible in public spaces.

More crucially, the presence of transgender subjectivities facilitates a *queering* impact on heteronormatively – prescribed domestic environments, which questions gender divisions and patriarchal orders. Although this presence is still limited, as it is the subject of negotiations and sometimes has to be turned off by other family members' requirements to maintain heteronormative environments such as in Jenny, Pat and Rene's cases, the possibilities of articulating presence and absence of transgender subjectivities in responses to different social dynamics, is subversive enough to challenge the gender binary system inscribed in domestic spaces.

In addition, the possibility of protesting and challenging the heteronormative gender binary system in domestic settings can have a further impact upon other interrelated social territories such as friends, neighbours and local communities since the strategies developed to deal with these call for the adoption of different degrees of openness about transgender identity. In turn, this posits the idea of a home, not only as a confinement of transgender subjectivities, but also as a significant social space from which to start making changes to gender diversity and queering practices which challenge unquestioned norms and conventions regarding gender.

Bibliography

Bauer, M. (1996) 'The narrative interview: Comments on a technique for qualitative data collection', *Papers in Social Research Methods Qualitative Series*, 1, Methodology Institute, London School of Economics and Political Science.

Brown, G. (2007) 'Mutinous eruptions: Autonomous spaces of radical queer activism', *Environment and Planning A*, 39(11): 2685–98.

Browne, K. (2004) 'Genderism and the bathroom problem: (Re)materialising sexed sites, (re)creating sexed bodies', *Gender, Place and Culture*, 11(3): 331–46.

Browne, K. and Lim J. (2008) *Count me in too – Trans people: Additional findings report*, Spectrum and the University of Brighton, http://www.spectrum-lgbt.org/frames/researchA.htm, accessed in August 2010.

Browne, K. and Lim J. (2009) 'Senses of gender', *Sociological Research Online*, 14(1), http://www.socresonline.org.uk/14/1/6.html, accessed in November 2010.

Browne, K., Nash, K. and Hines, S (2010) 'Introduction: Towards trans geographies', *Gender, Place and Culture*, 17(5): 573–7.

Butler, J. (1993) *Bodies that matter: On the discursive limits of 'sex'*. New York and London: Routledge.

Butler, J. (2004) *Undoing gender*. New York and London: Routledge.

Butler, J. (2006) 'Doing justice to someone: Sex reassignment and allegories of transsexuality' in S. Stryker and S. Whittle (ed.) *The transgender studies reader*, New York and London: Routledge, pp. 183–93.

Cook. M. (2003) *London and the culture of homosexuality, 1885–1914*. Cambridge: Cambridge University Press.

Crang, M. and Thrift, N. (eds) (2000) *Thinking space*. London and New York: Routledge.

Davy, Z. (2011) *Recognizing transsexuals: Personal, political and medicolegal embodiment*. Farnham and Burlington: Ashgate.

Doan, P. (2007) 'Queers in the American city: Transgendered perceptions of urban spaces', *Gender, Place, and Culture*, 14(1): 57–74.

Doan, P. (2010) 'The tyranny of gendered spaces: Reflection from beyond the gender dichotomy', *Gender, Place and Culture*, 17(5): 635–54.

Fincher, R. (2007) 'Space, gender and institutions in processes creating difference', *Gender, Place and Culture*, 14(1): 5–27.

Foucault, M. (1977) *Discipline and Punish: The Birth of the Prison*, translated by A. Sheridan, Harmonsworth: Penguin Books.

Fuss, D. (ed.) (1991) '*Inside/Out: Lesbian theories, gay theories*. New York and London: Routledge.

Grosz, E. (1994) *Volatile bodies: Toward a corporeal feminism*. Bloomington and Indianapolis: Indiana University Press.

Halberstam, J. (2005) *In a queer time and place: Transgender bodies, subcultural lives*. New York and London: New York University Press.

Hayden, D. (1980) 'What would a non-sexist city be like? Speculations on housing, urban design, and human work', *Women and the American City*, 5(3): 170–87.

Hines, S. (2007) 'Transgendering care: Practices of care within transgender communities', *Critical Social Policy*, 27(4): 462–86.

Hines, S. and Sanger, T. (eds) (2009) *Transgender identities: Towards a social analysis of gender diversity*. New York and London: Routledge.

Hollway, W. and Jefferson, T. (2000) *Doing qualitative research differently: Free association, narrative and the interview method*. London, Thousand Oaks and New Delhi: Sage.

Houlbrook, M. (2005) *Queer London*. Chicago and London: The University of Chicago Press.

Letherby, G. (2003) *Feminist research in theory and practice*. Buckingham and Philadelphia: Open University Press.

Massey, D. (1994) *Space, place and gender*. Cambridge: Polity Press.

Massey, D. (2005) *For space*. London: Sage.

McDowell, L. (1999) *Gender, identity and place: Understanding feminist geographies*. Cambridge: Polity Press.

McDowell, L. (2002) 'Unsettling naturalisms', *Signs*, 27(3): 815–22.

Monro, S. (2007) 'Transmuting gender binaries: The theoretical challenge', *Sociological Research Online*, 12(1), http://www.socresonline.org.uk/12/1/monro.html, accessed in August 2010.

Moran, L. J. (2007) '"Invisible minorities": Challenging community and neighbourhood models of policing', *Criminology and Criminal Justice*, 7(4): 417–41.

Moran, L. J. and Sharpe, A. N. (2004) 'Violence, identity and policing: The case of violence against transgender people', *Criminal Justice*, 4(4): 395–417.

Morton, J. (2008) *Transgender experience in Scotland: Research summary*, Scottish Transgender Alliance, http://www.scottishtrans.org/, accessed in August 2010.

Morton, J., Richie, G., Roch, A. and Equality Network and LGBT Youth Scotland (2010) *Out of sight, out of mind? Transgender people's experiences of domestic abuse*, Scottish Transgender Alliance and Scottish LGBT Domestic Abuse Project, http://www.scottishtrans.org/Uploads/Resources/trans_domestic_abuse.pdf, accessed in November 2010.

Moss, P. (ed.) (2002) *Feminist geography in practice: Research and methods*. Oxford: Blackwell Publishers.

Namaste, V. K. (2000) *Invisible lives: The erasure of transsexual and transgender people*. Chicago and London: The University of Chicago Press.

Reed, B., Rhodes, S., Schofield, P. and Wiley, K. (2009) *Gender variance in the UK: Prevalence, incidence, growth and geographic distribution*. London: GIRES.

Sandercock, L. (2003) 'Out of the closet: The importance of stories and storytelling in planning practice', *Planning Theory & Practice*, 4(1): 11–28.

Sanger, T. (2007) 'Queer(y)ing gender and sexuality: Transpeople's lived experiences and intimate partnerships' in L. Moon (ed.) *Feeling queer or queer feelings? Radical approaches to counselling sex, sexualities and gender.* Oxford: Routledge, pp. 72–88.

Sanger, T. (2008) 'Transpeople's intimate partnerships and the limits of identity politics' in Z. Davy, J. Downes, L. Eckert, N. Gerodetti, D. Llinares and A. C. Santos (eds) *Bound and unbound: Interdisciplinary approaches to genders and sexualities.* Cambridge: Cambridge Scholars Publishing, pp. 58–75.

Sedgwick, E. K. (1990) *Epistemology of the closet.* Berkeley and Los Angeles: University of California Press.

Sibley, D. (1995) *Geographies of exclusion: Society and difference in the West.* London and New York: Routledge.

Skeggs, B. (1994) 'Situating the production of feminist ethnography in M. Maynard and J. Purvis (eds) *Researching women's lives from a feminist perspective.* London: Taylor & Francis, pp. 72–92.

Smith, D. (2005) *Institutional ethnography.* Lanham, New York, Toronto and Oxford: Altamira Press.

Stryker, S. (2006) 'My words to Victor Frankenstein above the village of Chamounix: Performing transgender rage' in S. Stryker and S. Whittle (eds) *The transgender studies reader.* New York and London: Routledge, pp. 244–56.

Taylor, Y. (2004) 'Negotiation and navigation: An exploration of the spaces/places of working-class lesbians', *Sociological Research Online*, 9(1), http://www.socres online.org.uk/9/1/taylor.html, accessed in March 2011.

Taylor, Y. (2012) *Fitting into place? Class and gender geographies and temporalities.* Farnham and Surrey: Ashgate.

Valentine, G. (1993) '(Hetero)sexing space: Lesbian perceptions and experiences of everyday spaces', *Environments and Planning D: Society and Space*, 11(4): 395–413.

Valentine, G. (1995) 'Out and about: Geographies of lesbian landscapes', *International Journal of Urban and Regional Research*, 19(1): 96–111.

Valentine, G. (2008) 'The ties that bind: Towards geographies of intimacy', *Geography Compass*, 2(6): 2097–110.

Valentine, G. and Skelton, T. (2003) 'Coming out and out-comes: Negotiating lesbian and gay identities with/in the family', *Environment and Planning D: Society and Space*, 21(4): 479–99.

Whittle, S., Turner, L. and Al-Alami, M. (2007) *Engendered penalties: Transgender and transsexual people's experiences of inequality and discrimination*, The Equality Review, http://www.pfc.org.uk/files/EngenderedPenalties.pdf, accessed in August 2010.

Wigley, M. (1992) 'Untitled: The housing of gender', in B. Colomina (ed.) *Sexuality & space.* New York: Princeton Architectural Press, pp. 327–89.

7
Belonging: Lesbians and Gay Men's Claims to Material Spaces

Mark Casey

This chapter examines feelings of belonging of lesbians and gay men in the UK city of Newcastle upon Tyne.[1] In examining the experiences of lesbians and gay men of everyday spaces in Newcastle, the chapter is responding to calls made by Jackson (2008) to give a greater priority to 'mundane everyday' sexual lives. She argues there is a need to understand more about ordinary day-to-day patterns of sexual relations in which most people live their lives (2008: 34). Such an investigation allows understandings of why some sexual identities and practices are accepted, taken as a norm, where others are positioned as the 'extraordinary other'. Similarly, Scott (2009: 1) states that 'everyday spaces' share the trait that they represent sites in which people do (perform, reproduce and occasionally challenge) social life, day to day. In looking at two key spaces in the city of Newcastle – the home and everyday spaces (e.g. the street, work, leisure spaces), I am trying to move beyond earlier work that has positioned spaces within a fixed framework of 'the mundane'/'extraordinary'.[2]

This chapter draws on the idea that spaces are not fixed or distinctly separate from one another, where feelings and emotions attached to one place can and do inform feelings and experiences of other places, spaces and experiences. In utilising the ideas of Browne (2007: 996) space can be understood as performative, in that it is always 'in the process of becoming and is produced between actors and actants', informing how everyday space is re-worked and re-made. As Johnston and Longhurst (2010: 16) add, 'space is complex, changeable, discursively produced and imbued with power relations'. Place is used to refer to specific places, in so doing it highlights the materiality of spaces, reminding the reader that real people live in real places that offer real experiences (Johnston and Longhurst, 2010: 16).

Gorman-Murray's (2010: 2) framework of 'belonging' is utilised in this chapter. For him, people are placed in grids of social power through dualistic norms of gender (man/woman), sexuality (heterosexual/homosexual), race (white/black) and so on. He positions 'belonging as a form of boundary maintenance that articulates which categories of people – or embodied social locations, should be included in a given place and scale' (2010: 2). Although this chapter is solely concerned with lesbians and gay men, it is not intended to support a dualistic norm between lesbians and gay men and other sexual minorities. Lesbians and gay men are the sole focus of this chapter due to the limits and strengths of the research that this chapter is based. Following on from this the chapter asks how are feelings of belonging experienced? How do such feelings change in different spatial sites across the city and life course? What local knowledges are needed and how can the right local knowledge be accessed? And, who decides what knowledge(s) are worth knowing? As lesbians and gay men go through their lives, it is likely that their relationships with space and place change. Some lesbians and gay men can make claims to identities that 'normalise' their sexual identity and allow them wider and more secure claims to varied sites, utilising diverse resources in doing so. For other lesbians and gay men the ability to access or utilise spaces can at best be hindered or at worst denied through identities they posses, or a lack of empowerment or knowledge.

In drawing on data from interviews with lesbians and gay men in the city of Newcastle, I analyse feelings of belonging, inclusion, exclusion and emotional attachment to space(s) (see Brown and Pickerill, 2009). In particular this chapter captures a key moment in the history of Newcastle, one in which it witnessed significant gentrification, before the current global economic downturn that has changed individual's attachments to and understandings of space and place (Gorman-Murray, 2010). In the early twentieth century gentrification became established as a significant urban phenomenon in reshaping many cities (Bridge, 2006). Gentrification impacts feelings of belonging and displacement, where attachment to place can be changed and displacement may arise. Both Taylor (2009) and Casey (2004, 2007) have shown that gentrification has winners and losers, and is not beneficial to all. Through gentrification certain identities and bodies become valued above others, where 'undesirable' otherness is excluded. For example, the large-scale gentrification of Newcastle city centre has created new economies that increasingly exclude undesirable bodies and flawed consumers who are unable to buy into neoliberal times (Chatterton and Hollands, 2001; Kitchen and Lysaght, 2003; Nayak, 2006).

The research was undertaken during a time when the then Labour Government, (often under the direction of the EU), introduced large sweeping changes to the citizenship rights of lesbians and gay men. These new laws and civil rights have repositioned lesbians and gay men within the UK (see Casey, 2011). This repositioning has been theorised as a threat to earlier queer activism that challenged normalisation discourses held around sexual identities and practices, and has positioned the queered body as the 'other', out of time and place in an age of growing homonormalisation. Identities and practices that disrupt become problematic in city centres which are increasingly owned and semi-privatised by global corporations, where private security firms are employed to police the behaviour of those present. During a time of economic boom and large-scale gentrification across many cities, tied with a new and positive visibility and place for (some) lesbians and gay men in the UK, (safe) diversity has been positioned as a 'sophisticated allure' (Rushbrook, 2002: 184). The non-threatening lesbian or gay body and the spaces and venues they attend, have provided a cultural capital for the cosmopolitan city dweller, where 'cool places' become those frequented by lesbians, gay men and their friends (Johnston and Longhurst, 2010: 87).

By focusing on everyday 'mundane' spatial realities of lesbians and gay men and their feelings of belonging and comfort, this chapter seeks to contribute to a broader knowledge around quotidian lives in the cityscape. Rather than those elements of lesbian and gay male culture that are increasingly visible, I am concerned with those lives and spatial realities that are not understood as 'cool' or 'cosmopolitan'. In looking at experiences and feelings of belonging within a number of varied spatial sites across the city of Newcastle, the complex process of gentrification and the fluidity of spatial sites can be examined alongside the identities people posses and the demands of everyday life worlds. The chapter now moves to outline some of the previous work upon the lesbian and gay home and everyday spaces, followed by a discussion of research methods utilised in this study. I pay attention to how the data was produced and how the everyday realities of those involved in the research can inform the way that the city and the complex place of those who live within it are theorised.

Days of our lives

Representations of 'home' as a built dwelling are common, however the work of feminists and those concerned with the lesbian and gay home space has problematised this assumption. For Blunt and Dowling (2006: 10) 'one can live in a house and yet not feel at home'. Access to a physical shelter does not necessarily allow feelings of 'being at home' or belonging to be experienced. Privacy, control, safety and support are all closely related in experiences and meanings of home (see Veness, 1994; Young, 2005). That said, home is also a site of surveillance and intrusion by other occupants and 'outsiders', where safety and support may have to be sought elsewhere. Violence, power and control all intersect in the lesbian and gay home, policing the identities and daily lives of residents. As Stella (2010) found in her research on lesbian identity in Russia, everyday categories of identification intersect with the everyday setting of the cityscape, it's public site(s) or the home. Privacy is 'closely linked to enabling control over one's home and the activities that take place therein, thus creating a safe and secure place' (Gorman-Murray, 2007a: 239).[3]

It was not until the 1990s that those such as Gill Valentine (1993) and Julia Smailes (1994) offered insights into the home lives of non-heterosexual women. Valentine (1993, 1996) positioned the lesbian home space as providing a dual reality – a site for identity development and fulfilment, while also placing limits on lesbian lives and visibility. In Elwood's (2000) study of wealthy upper middle class lesbians in Minneapolis home spaces were used to assert identity. 'Normative bodies', a successful career and home ownership in middle class suburbs, allow some degree for home to become a site of safety, allowing (homonormative) identity development (Lynch, 1987). The more recent work of Taylor (2007, 2009) has shown the clear intersections of class and sexuality within the home for working-class and middle-class lesbians. Her work problematises claims by Kitchen and Lysaght (2003) who argue that low-income areas are more likely to be homophobic. However, Taylor did find that socio-economic position does have consequences for emotional comfort within the home. Many lesbians in her study discussed unease about their housing presentations and the judgements and gaze of middle class visitors upon their 'distasteful' interiors and furniture (2007: 128). As Browne (2011: 110) argues, 'acceptance can [...] be classed'.

The work of Weinberg and Williams (1974) and Lynch (1987) are two of the earliest studies to look at gay male[4] home spaces. Although Weinberg and Williams produced some important findings on gay men's lives in the suburbs, it was the work of Lynch that was the first to examine the home and feelings of belonging. Soaring rents and growing crime rates in inner city America during the 1970s and 1980s, not only drove heterosexuals into the suburbs, but also gay men who possessed sufficient economic and cultural capitals to migrate to 'better areas'. Such areas reinforced a powerful middle class heteronormative ideal – with demands of successful careers, maintaining the home and good neighbourly relationships, leaving little time to 'engage in the commercial gay community' (Lynch, 1987: 31). Although a number of his interviewees valued homes that allowed them to 'escape' from both work and the scene, life in the suburbs came at a cost. As one noted, 'look, the suburbs are different. It's more conservative out here. People can't flaunt their gayness' (Lynch, 1987: 33). Inclusion and belonging was accessed through adhering to middle class heteronormative norms, in a country reeling from the AIDS pandemic and the growing conservative backlash against 'sexual others'.

Nearly two decades after the work of Lynch (1987) Gorman-Murray (2006a/b, 2007a/b) has shown that although the home is still predominantly associated with the heterosexual nuclear family and the domestic sphere (see Hockey, Meah and Robinson, 2007), a new lesbian and gay visibility in and around home is emerging. In some urban centres the lesbian or gay man is no longer the 'threatening other'. New levels of 'acceptance' held around the homonormative ideal are allowing some lesbian and gay visibility to be tolerated in limited suburban streets (Browne, 2011). However this is often a 'sanitised' or limited visibility, where calculated decisions about neighbours and the passing and the intrusive gaze inform decisions about visibility as *lesbians* or *gay men*. 'Mundane realities', such as a heteronormative suburban street can hide extraordinary sexualities and acts that may challenge oppressive norms and realities. For example, Gorman-Murray outlines how one gay man in his research uses his garage as a sex room – sling, condoms and lubricant abound. Yet, the requirement to perform acceptable gender norms and dress appropriately marks spaces and places from the work environment, the dropping off of children at the school gates, to the shopping mall, as sites where the assumption of heterosexuality is ever present (Moran and Skeggs, 2004; Hockey, Meah and Robinson, 2007).

Methods

This chapter developed from my ESRC funded Ph.D. that was concerned with the experiences of lesbians and gay men of everyday city spaces in Newcastle.[5] Through including both men and women in my study insights concerning the intersecting of gender with sexuality are offered (see Casey, 2007 for a further discussion). The age of the research sample was given considerable thought. Identity development across the life course can change an individual's relationship with space, with this relationship needing to be understood as shifting and evolving (see Hunter et al., 1998; Varley and Blasco, 2001; Gorman-Murray, 2008). Three age bands were created placing eight people in each (four men, four women, with a total of 23 participants).[6] The age groups were 18–25, 26–40 and 41+. These groups were chosen as they were felt to reflect three key life stages of 'youth', 'middle adulthood' and 'the older years'.[7] The placing of sample members into groups was based exclusively on their age, not through how they self defined or understood their current life stage(s). It is acknowledged that the creating and placing of individuals into such age specific groups can be problematic (see Weeks, 1981).

Social class of participants was an important factor in the development of the research sample. Social class has a significant role in the types of spaces people can access and make claims to. In each of the three age groups half self-identified as 'working class', with the other half identifying as 'middle class'. Understandings offered around class identity are complex, reflected through the massive decline of traditional industries associated with the 'working classes' and the growth of new technologies that have little association with traditional class groupings (Reay, 2001; Taylor, 2007). Consequently, understandings of 'working class' and 'middle class' in the research project were to be self-defined by respondents, with most respondents citing occupational background(s) as the reason for the claiming of a specific class position. Data produced has even allowed an engagement with not only the impact of economic but also cultural and social capitals in respondent's ability to access or claim belonging to specific spaces (see Skeggs, 1999; Taylor, 2009).

The research sample was accessed in a number of ways – from contacts made on the commercial lesbian and gay scene, non-commercial social groups, advertisements in local press and through snowballing (Casey, 2004). Those who participated in the research lived within the city's suburbs of Jesmond and Heaton in the East of the city and Fenham in the West of the city. Jesmond is characterised through its affluence, close proximity to the city centre and a mix of middle class residents and wealthy students. Heaton is less affluent, attracting a mix of middle income young professionals, young families, students and local working class life-long residents of the area, and may be characterised by liberal attitudes. Fenham, the most ethnically diverse of the three neighbourhoods is characterised through a mix of low to mid income residents comprising students, young professionals and families. Respondents were interviewed using qualitative semi-structured interviews. A number of key themes were used to structure the interviews, such as 'leisure spaces', 'the street', 'work' and 'the home', as developed from existing literature upon spatial experiences of lesbians and gay men (e.g. Bell and Valentine, 1995; Moran and Skeggs, 2004), and were also informed through gaps in current work. Interviews lasted between one to three hours, most averaging 1½ hours. The quotes and excerpts that are drawn upon in this chapter reflect the complex intersecting of sexuality, social class and age with and within the spaces of the city (Silverman, 2006; Taylor, Hines and Casey, 2010).

Home

The ability to establish a home of one's own has been found to be a key goal for many lesbians and gay men (see Kirkey and Forsyth, 2001; Moran and Skeggs, 2004; Gorman-Murray, 2006, 2007a; Taylor, 2007). A 'home of one's own' can become a crucial socialising and identity-affirming site. The ability to be out in the home was found to be important for lesbians and gay men in affirming identities and facilitating wider acceptance in their neighbourhoods (see Kirkey and Forsyth, 2001). Sue Kentlyn's (2008) study of lesbian and gay home spaces found that 'the queer home provides a safe space where people can cast off the constraints of heteronormativity and do varieties of sexuality and gender that would be sanctioned in other contexts' (p. 327). These findings have been echoed by both gay men and lesbians within this research.

> [I]t was so important for me to make sure everyone in my house totally knew and were ok about it … I couldn't call it home if everyone in my house didn't know … 'cos it's important. If I want to bring someone back.
>
> Glen, 20, middle class

> I think just little things that I kind of take for granted. Like just being able to sit with my girlfriend and hold hands if we want, or she can just like

fall asleep on my shoulder. Bring gay friends back and not having to worry about what people are going to say … And I think that's why I consider here home now rather than back in Manchester … up here I can say I am going to 'The Powerhouse'[8] and it's not a problem.

Sandra, 20, middle class

In conversation with Sandra it became clear that her parents now accept her lesbian identity, but previously she was expected to police her behaviour in the family home, so as not to disrupt its heteronormativity. Before moving out of the family home to come to university, Sandra could only find comfort and the ability to 'be herself' within the lesbian and gay scene of Manchester. Her experience draws attention to the limits of portraying meanings of home and commercial scene spaces as distinct and separate from one another, or positioning the scene as solely a site of 'the extraordinary'. Glen experiences his house as a place in which to relax and perform his gay male identity, through bringing back men for sexual encounters. But Glen is in a favourable position in owning the house he lives in. If flatmates were to react negatively to his coming out, he can terminate their residence 're-making' his home as gay friendly in finding new flatmates. As an affluent young gay man, he has access to a neighbourhood (Jesmond), where other young 'cool' people want to live, surrounded by a safe and commercially attractive diversity.

Lower income lesbians and gay men who rent may not have the luxury in securing 'accepting' flat mates or 'tolerant' landlords (Smailes, 1994; Gorman-Murray, 2007a). These claims were echoed by another interviewee, Owen, (41, working class) who claimed 'where I live, it's about the most secure property I can afford'. We must be careful not to associate low income lesbians and gay men and/or low income areas as automatically indicative of powerlessness. Living in low income areas, both Sarah and Pauline engage and work with other residents to create a safe(r) lesbian (in)visibility. Their claims echo arguments by Taylor (2004) that homophobic or threatening neighbourhoods can provide feelings of home and belonging for lesbian or gay residents:

Well it has always been women only flats, but fortunately the top three are lesbian … Not having men who are strangers around and talking to each other and that. And there is a pin board up in the hallway and if … my brother in law is coming, even if it's for half an hour, just to let people know. There is a lot of care.

Pauline, 35, working class

I have lived for years in Hardwich, which is somewhere you will not feel safe as a lesbian, but always surrounded by other lesbians. I lived in a street before … and there was a lot of lesbians living there at the time, it was a bit famous in lesbian folklore.

Sarah, 35, working class

Pauline lives in Hardwich which Sarah once called home, and although the area 'may not be the safest place to be a lesbian', the presence of other lesbians, community action and sociability allow feelings of safety. Unlike private blocks of apartments where security is often provided at a premium cost (see Blunt, 2005: 507), Pauline and her co-tenants are pro-active in ensuring the safety of each other. Male visitors are marked out as the 'other', temporary guests in a female only space. A lack of safe public spaces and an increasing exclusion of lesbians from the Newcastle 'gay scene' (see Casey, 2004), adds emphasis to the importance of the 'lesbian home' as social, political and identity affirming space (as found by Taylor, 2007). The loss of lesbian space through gentrification reflects 'how the ability to enact some identities or realities rather than others is highly contingent on the power laden spaces in and through which our experiences are lived' (Valentine, 2007: 19). Although the lesbian home may provide a social setting away from the scene, a number of the women in the research reflected earlier concerns that the home is anything but 'private':

I would like to sit in the garden a little more ... the only difficulty that I do have if friends come, they might be louder than Kate and I are. And well some ... talk very differently to what we do. But I am getting better at not caring if the next-door neighbours hear.

Holly, 58, middle class

[I]n the summer when you are in the house and you have windows open and you have conversations that revolve around being lesbian then I do feel a little nervous about what the neighbours are over-hearing ... and I am a little nervous about what the neighbours can see, but I try not to let that be too much of an overriding thing.

Margaret, 46, middle class

I have had quite explicit conversations about donor insemination and then thought, oh the neighbours are on their balcony.

Lisa, 36, working class

These conversations with Holly, Margaret and Lisa reflect how everyday actions, conversations or relationships can become sites of regulation by the self or outsiders. Even if restricted to the inside spaces of the home, the opening of windows may bring its 'private' spaces into the surveillance of the wider public (see Bailey, 2000). Experiences of sitting in gardens or balconies reflect the contradictory experiences offered within the many spaces of the home (Andrews, 2011). What is to be private in the home can only be those things that cannot be overheard or witnessed by outsiders, which in itself is affected through home size, location and setting. All three women discuss how they try to not let the concern of what 'others hear' restrict their own or guests' conversations and actions, they still play out their lesbian lives. Holly later discusses that as she is getting older she desires a 'quiet life' with 'few problems'. Her want reflects how individual's relationships with the home, space and comfort change as people age, and of course this intersects with gender, social class and sexuality (see Lynch, 1987; Kirkey and Forsyth, 2001).

Yet, not all lesbians can make claims to comfortable or tolerant areas, where the lesbian home becomes 'hyper-visible' through the potential or reality of homophobic violence:

> We behave as friends, 'cos everyone can see into the garden you know? Because people can see you, especially where I live in the West End, and I'm surrounded by ... families who are kind of very West End Newcastle.
>
> Lauren, 23, working class

> There are people who keep trashing my car and the police think it is because I am a lesbian. Well it's just a natural reaction now, I get up and make sure me car is alright and then I get ready ... Otherwise I have got to get me car sorted as I work freelance ... it usually happens around winter time, sort of every week, sometimes two or three times a week ... it's a window being put through here, somebody has shit on my windscreen. One time it happened 29 times within 31 days and every window day by day had been broken and every tyre had been slashed.
>
> Eileen, 41, working class

Lauren's experiences of living in the West End of Newcastle, a low-income area, reflect the interplay of other identities. Sexuality, gender and social class have very real consequences for access to and experiences of residential space. Low-income West End families are positioned as the threatening other for Lauren. 'Home' and the experiences if offers, needs to be addressed as a multi-layered phenomena that intersect with the identities of its inhabitants (and I would argue, with the identities and lives of neighbours as well). The violent punishment of Eileen for not conforming to the heterosexual 'norms' of her neighbourhood becomes part of her daily routine (echoing findings by Moran and Skeggs, 2004). In further discussions around the attacks, Eileen strongly believes her lack of a 'feminine appearance' instigated the homophobic violence, where her lack of performing an appropriate gender identity is understood as indicating that she is a lesbian and does not belong. The homes of lesbians and gay men come under heteronormative regulation from surrounding communities (Gorman-Murray, 2007b: 198). However, although Eileen has the resources to move, she will not – she likes her neighbours. Her stance echoes arguments made by Taylor (2004) that some lesbians and gay men can and will fight to claim belonging where emotional attachment to neighbours and friends act as support networks in challenging homophobia that tries to re-make spaces and places as heterosexual.

The everyday

M: How would you define heterosexual space?
Eileen (41, working class):   Oh, the world.

The urban landscape, although undoubtedly heterosexualised, is also a gendered landscape in which performances of heterosexual masculinised identities have the strongest claims.[9] The embodied experience of space is underpinned through both 'commonly held assumptions' and expectations reiterated within laws about the place of men and women in spaces. The coding of the city landscape as belonging to certain groups who have greater or weaker claims is historically produced through struggles of legitimation (see Taylor, Hines and Casey, 2010). However, the performance of a heterosexual identity alone does not create or maintain belonging in space, it is the performance of a male, white and heterosexual identity that affects access, safety and claims to urban spaces, as Ali reflected:

> A lot of gay men I speak to feel more comfortable than I do walking around on their own and I don't know if that is instilled in you as a woman that you should be completely careful as you are vulnerable.
>
> Ali, 25, working class

Ali's experience exemplifies how certain identities intersect with the material spaces of the urban landscape. It is not enough to be careful, but one has to be 'completely careful' as a woman. Women have to work hard to ensure they do not provide the 'opportunity' for a perpetrator to commit an offence against them, to avoid being blamed as a 'careless' victim (Moran and Skeggs, 2004). What Ali discusses here echo comments made by lesbians and gay men in the work of Kitchen and Lysaght (2003) in Northern Ireland. For many of their research sample when abuse or violence was experienced the victim was blamed for not 'taking enough care' or 'being in the wrong place' and 'provoking people' (p. 505). Ali's embodied experiences as a female and not being able to claim the same level of comfort or belonging when walking alone as her male friends, positions her as 'vulnerable'. As she goes on to argue, 'It's that male attitude that a woman's sexuality in particular is their business. And even lesbians, it has still got something to do with them, it's that invasion of privacy'. Unfortunately, Ali's experiences were not unique in the research:

> It's large groups of heterosexual men that I find threatening and I think any woman will find that threatening, but then I think as a lesbian, well if they knew I was a lesbian I would be in serious trouble.
>
> Margaret, 46, working class

[T]here are some key safety issues about being a woman ... I went into a kebab shop and this bloke came in really pissed ... and he was like talking to me in a way that he wouldn't have if I was a bloke, so that was about being a woman. And he then started saying stuff about KD Lang, which I am sure was about me being a dyke, but it was really hard to separate off you know?

Sarah, 35, middle class

Both Margaret and Sarah reflect upon the intersecting of their gender and sexual identities within unsafe spaces and how these are perceived by heterosexual men. Their claims to safety and the right to belong in space(s) are problematised by others. Margaret understands the threats she feels when near groups of heterosexual men as an experience shared by all women. Sarah's comments reflect the value of intersectionality in theorising the everyday lives of lesbians and gay men (Taylor, Hines and Casey, 2010). In her encounter she experiences both sexism and homophobia; Sarah finds it difficult to separate her abusers responses to her identity as a woman and as a lesbian – they are interconnected. The discussion by Margaret and Sarah show how women's lives are differentiated by their membership of different categories of inequality (e.g. sexuality, class, ethnicity, etc.), with this informing their daily lived realities (McDermott, 2010). In the research it was not only lesbians who experienced threats to their visibility, many of the gay men in the research did too. The following quotes from Gavin and Colly show that although men can make claims to spaces in a way that is denied to women, many gay men are unable or do not wish to do so:

I probably wouldn't feel as safe going from bar to bar if there was big gangs of lads hanging around.

Gavin, 36, working class

Safety issues? Well obviously heterosexual men think that they completely own the streets and they can shout abuse and be as threatening as they like.

Colly, 39, middle class

Colly went onto explain:

I think that most space is owned by heterosexual men from the street upwards ... it's like straight men own all the office space, and everywhere that I have worked ... it doesn't matter if a woman is in charge, like in an overall environment straight men rule the space. I worked in an organisation that was mostly staffed by women and the only extra day

we got off was for the World Cup, and I think that makes is a heterosexual men's place.

Heterosexual boys and men are socialised into gender roles where they
learn to be, or learn that it is acceptable to be, aggressive and dominating
in public spaces. Heterosexual masculinity is presented as the dominant
identity, where heterosexual men position themselves as the 'gatekeepers'
in deciding which other identities are allowed visibility and at what cost.
Lesbian and gay identities are stigmatised, problematised and policed,
marked through silences, repressions and exclusions (Corber and Valocchi,
2003). As heterosexual men encounter sexual others and make claims to
spaces through violence and abuse the heterosexual/homosexual, pub-
lic/private binaries are re-made, where dominant cultures are reproduced
(Browne, 2007). Echoing findings by Johnston and Valentine (1995), Colly
positions the workplace as a place dominated by heterosexual men. The
day off for the World Cup, the sport that is often most associated with
heterosexual men in the UK, reflects the worth given over to male dominated activities in British society. Although women may be in charge in
the work environment, it is heterosexual men who 'rule' the space, where
the women are 'out of place' in the arena of work. Both Colly and Gavin
echo Ali's concerns around safety in the street when heterosexual men are
present. Unlike Ali they do not understand it as necessarily restricting their
movements in public sites, where as men they are 'in place'. Both these men
presented themselves in the interviews through gender normative clothing
and hair, and I would argue that this allows them to pass through spaces as
the 'anonymous other' as outlined by Turner (2003).

Threats of homophobic violence were a real concern for a number of
those in the research, this was particularly intensified when encountering
groups of heterosexual men:

> I think alcohol and being in a gang of friends, when they sort of want
> to look good.
>
> > Neil, 36, middle class

> I find them really threatening at St James Park when there is a match day
> on. But that is just groups of loads and loads of blokes, but I do find large
> groups of men, wearing the strip intimidating.
>
> > Lisa, 36, working class

> I would specifically say on match days, kind of things, massive crowds of
> drunk, testosterone fuelled men is not like the safest thing in the world
> for me.
>
> > Sandra, 20, middle class

[I]t is always men who say something ... they are usually in a group and you see them whispering and looking at each other ... and I find it quite difficult to know how to react as you feel quite threatened and they ask you "are you a lesbian?" and I don't want to say yes in that situation, but I don't want to say no neither.

Ali, 25, working class

Acts of verbal or physical violence within male group settings can be identified as individual heterosexual men attempting to affirm their status within their peer group. This behaviour reaffirms their heterosexual identity. As Kitchen and Lysaght (2003: 494) suggest, homophobic violence reproduces heterosexual hegemony and can have 'severe consequences for the everyday lives' of lesbians and gay men. Similar to the experiences of Colly, Sandra and Lisa understand a strong relationship between football and potential homophobia from heterosexual men. Newcastle is quite unique in that the city's football stadium is located in the heart of the city, allowing the tens of thousands of football fans to mingle with shoppers, diners and tourists. As residents of the city, Lisa and Sandra possess the knowledge concerning the potential threats to safety that can exist around 'match days' for them as women and lesbians (see Valentine, 1996). What is interesting about both Lisa and Sandra is that they employed a form of 'compartmentalisation' where they positioned match days and the spaces where fans were likely to be encountered as unsafe and threatening (Kitchen and Lysaght, 2003: 495). In doing this they have drawn from their knowledges concerning wider societal homophobia, the geographies of Newcastle and the associations they attach to football and heterosexual men to create a mental map of where to avoid in the city. As I have shown in other work (see Casey, 2004) and as the work of Erel et al. (2010) has shown sexuality and gender become inseparable, intersecting with space and oppression, and conflating to inform views of who belongs and who can make safe claims to space(s).

Conclusion

In this chapter I have attempted to utilise more subtle understandings of space to move beyond the marking of sites as being understood as simply either spaces of 'the ordinary' or 'spectacle'. In drawing on experiences of 'mundane everyday life' that are played out in the streets of Newcastle I have illustrated the complex claims lesbians and gay men make to spaces. Building on the work of Gorman-Murray (2008) I have sought to engage with the diverse realities of the lesbian and gay home. Within this study home has been understood as a site of belonging, where a lesbian and gay visibility can be claimed. As new normative ways of 'doing' sexuality are culturally and legally encouraged, the lesbian and gay home can make claims to sit alongside the heterosexual home as just another mundane site. For others in this research the home is fragile, dependent on a neighbour's tolerance, the ability or desire to 'fit into' an area, or having sufficient economic or cultural capitals to claim safe and secure sites. This new normative home life is not available to all (nor do all desire it), where the continued threat of homophobic violence polices who or what belongs in space, where violence in itself becomes an extraordinary threatening part of everyday reality. By examining the subtle processes of power that heterosexualises everyday spaces, these can be understood as sitting alongside the extraordinary and violent methods deployed to privilege male heterosexuality. Some heterosexual men are the gatekeepers in policing which bodies and identities belong, where the complex intersecting of multiple identities with sexuality and space, along with varied power struggles to claim space, have consequences for marking out those who belong in space and those who are out of place and time. I would like to conclude by suggesting that although the 'in your face' queer politics as witnessed in the 1990s may have given way to normalisation discourses and practices, lesbians and gay men can still utilise subtle methods to fracture heterosexual spatial privilege. The diverse daily realities offered in the home, street or commercial scene present contradictory realities for lesbians and gay men, where they are at once visible/invisible, present/absent and belong/out of place and time.

Notes

1. Newcastle upon Tyne will be referred to as 'Newcastle'.
2. In some work the lesbian and gay scene has been positioned as the extraordinary, part of a unique 'queer time' (Taylor, 2010), positioned as separate and distinct to everyday life worlds of work, home or family. The commercial scene is not positioned in this chapter as separate to 'everyday spaces', instead it is understood in a framework as developed by Moran (2005). The spaces of the scene are sites of leisure consumption, a place in which mundane, everyday experiences are offered (alongside the extraordinary or unique), and one in which feelings of belonging or exclusion often depend on experiences provided through other spaces and sites.
3. The experiences of marginal populations, such as homeless people who live in public housing are useful in examining the limits of privacy, control and safety within understandings of home. Veness (1994) found that controls imposed in homeless shelters removed feelings of privacy and comfort and reinforced the very public and controlled environment of the shelter.
4. Both Weinberg and Williams (1974) and Lynch (1987) use the term 'homosexual male' in their studies. For this chapter I utilise the more contemporary identity label 'gay'.
5. Lewis (1994) positioned Newcastle as being characteristically homophobic, rendering any lesbian or gay cultures 'invisible'. Since his work Newcastle has undergone significant cultural, social and economic transformations and has witnessed the

emergence of one of the largest commercial gay scenes in the UK (see Chatterton and Hollands, 2001; Casey, 2004, 2007).

6. Both the lesbian and gay male 18–25 age group had three lesbians and three gay men in each and the lesbian group aged 26–40 had five women within it.

7. Through the selecting of these age bands it was felt the groups would reflect the cultural and social changes within the UK such as British culture pre-1967 Sexual Offences Act, experiences of the gay liberation movement and lesbian feminism in the 1970s, the AIDS crisis in the 1980s and recent shifts which have affected lesbian and gay visibility and the place of sexual others in UK society.

8. The Powerhouse is the main lesbian and gay nightclub in Newcastle.

9. Heterosexual women rarely claim city spaces in the same way as heterosexual men do (Hird, 2002). The recent 'SlutWalks' that have spread across the Western world in response to Toronto Police claims that women should not dress 'as sluts' to avoid sexual assault, is a clear example of the different embodied experiences of space for men and women. Street space is gendered, and to avoid being victims of crime heterosexual women, some heterosexual men, lesbians and gay men are expected to dress appropriately for their gender – in a manner that does not 'provoke' heterosexual men's violence or sexual assault.

Bibliography

Andrews, H. (2011) *The British on holiday: Charter tourism, identity and consumption.* Bristol: Channel View Publications.

Bailey, J. (2000) 'Some meanings of the private in sociological thought', *Sociology*, 34(3): 381–401.

Bell, D. and Valentine, G. (eds) (1995) *Mapping desire*. London: Routledge.

Blunt, A. (2005) 'Cultural geography: Cultural geographies of home', *Progress in Human Geography*, 29(4): 505–15.

Blunt, A. and Dowling, R. (2006) *Home*. London: Routledge.

Bridge, G. (2006) 'It's not just a question of taste: Gentrification, the neighbourhood, and cultural capital', *Environment and Planning A*, 38(10): 1965–78.

Brown, G. and Pickerill, J. (2009) 'Space for emotion in the spaces of activism', *Emotion, Space and Society*, 2(1): 24–35.

Browne, K. (2007) '(Re)making the other: Heterosexualising everyday space', *Environment and Planning A*, 39(4): 996–1014.

Browne, K. (2011) 'By partner we mean' ... Alternative geographies to "gay marriage"', *Sexualities*, 14(1): 100–22.

Casey, M. (2004) 'De-dyking queer spaces: Heterosexual female visibility in gay and lesbian spaces', *Sexualities*, 7(4): 446–61.

Casey, M. (2007) 'The queer unwanted and their undesirable otherness' in K. Brown, J. Lim and G. Browne (eds) *Geographies of sexualities: Theory, practice and politics.* Aldershot: Ashgate, pp. 125–36.

Casey, M. (2011) 'Sexual identity politics: Activism from gay to queer and beyond' in A. Elliott (ed.) *Routledge Handbook of Identity Studies*. London: Routledge, pp. 275–90.

Chatterton, P. and Hollands, R. (2001) *Changing our toon: Youth nightlife and urban change in Newcastle*. Newcastle: Newcastle University Press.

Corber, R. J. and Valocchi, S. (eds) (2003) *Queer Studies: An Interdisciplinary Reader.* London: Blackwell.

Elwood, S. A. (2000) 'Lesbian living spaces: Multiple meanings of home' in G. Valentine (ed.) *From nowhere to everywhere: Lesbian geographies*. London: Harrington Park, pp. 11–27.

Erel, U., Haritaworn, J., Rodriguez, E. G. and Kleese, C. (2010) 'On the depoliticisation of intersectionality talk: Conceptualising multiple oppressions in critical sexuality studies' in Y. Taylor, S. Hines and M. Casey (eds) *Theorizing intersectionality and sexuality*. Basingstoke: Palgrave Macmillan, pp. 56–77.

Gorman-Murray, A. (2006a) 'Gay and lesbian couples at home: Identity work in the domestic sphere', *Home Cultures*, 3(2): 146–68.

Gorman-Murray, A. (2006b) 'Homeboys: Uses of home by gay Australian men', *Social and Cultural Geography*, 7(1): 53–69.

Gorman-Murray, A. (2007a) 'Reconfiguring domestic values: Meanings of home for gay men and lesbians', *Housing Theory and Society*, 24(3): 229–46.

Gorman-Murray, A. (2007b) 'Contesting domestic ideals: Queering the Australian home', *Australian Geographer*, 38(2): 195–213.

Gorman-Murray, A. (2008) 'Reconciling self: Gay men and lesbians using domestic materiality for identity management', *Social and Cultural Geography*, 9(3): 283–301.

Gorman-Murray, A. (2010) 'Economic crisis and the emotional fallout: Work, home and men's sense of belonging in post-GFC Sydney', *Emotion, Space and Society*, 4(4): 211–20.

Hird, M. (2002) *Engendering violence: Heterosexual interpersonal violence from childhood to adulthood*. Aldershot: Ashgate.

Hockey, J., Meah, A. and Robinson, V. (2007) *Mundane heterosexualities: From theory to practices*. Basingstoke: Palgrave Macmillan.

Hunter, S., Shannon, C., Knox, C. and Martin, J. I. (eds) (1998) *Lesbian, gay and bisexual youths and adults: Knowledge for human service practice*. London: Sage.

Jackson, S. (2008) 'Ordinary sex', *Sexualities*, 11(1/2): 33–7.

Johnson, L. and Longhurst, R. (eds) (2010) *Space, place and sex*. Plymouth: Rowman and Littlefield Publishers.

Johnson, L. and Valentine, G. (1995) 'Whereever I Lay my Girlfriend that's my Home: The Performance and Surveillance of Lesbian Identities in Domestic Environments', in D. Bell and G. Valentine, (eds) *Mapping Desire*. London: Routledge, pp. 88–103.

Kentlyn, S. (2008) *The Radically Subversive Space of the Queer Home: 'Safety House' 1 and 'Neighbourhood Watch*, in Australian Geographer, 39(3): 327–37.

Kirkey, K. and Forsyth, A. (2001) 'Men in the valley: Gay male life on the suburban-rural fringe', *Journal of Rural Studies*, 17(4): 421–41.

Kitchen, R. and Lysaght, K. (2003) 'Heterosexism and the geographies of everyday life in Belfast, Northern Ireland', *Environment and Planning A*, 35(3): 489–510.

Lewis, M. (1994) 'A sociological pub crawl around gay Newcastle' in S. Whittle (ed.) *The margins of the city: Gay men's urban lives*. Aldershot: Arena-Ashgate Publishing, pp. 85–100.

Lynch, F. R. (1987) 'Non-ghetto gays: A sociological study of suburban homosexuals', *Journal of Homosexuality*, 13(4): 13–42.

McDermott, L. (2010) 'Multiple methodologies: Researching young people's well-being at the intersections of class, sexuality, gender and age' in Y. Taylor, S. Hines and M. Casey (eds) *Theorizing intersectionality and sexuality*. Basingstoke: Palgrave Macmillan, pp. 235–55.

Moran, L. and Skeggs, B. (2004) *Sexuality and the politics of violence and safety*. London: Routledge.

Moran, J. (2005) *Reading the everyday*. London: Routledge.

Nayak, A. (2006) 'Displaced masculinities: Chavs, youth and class in the post-industrial city', *Sociology*, 40(5): 813–31.

Reay, D. (2001) 'The double-bind of the "working class" feminist academic: The success of failure or the failure of success?' in B. A. Arrighi (ed.) *Understanding inequality: The intersection of race/ethnicity, class and gender*. Oxford, Rowman and Littlefield Publishers Inc., pp. 72–82.

Rushbrook, D. (2002) 'Cities, queer spaces and the cosmopolitan tourist', *GLQ: A Journal of Lesbian and Gay Studies*, 8(1–2): 183–206.

Scott, S. (2009) *Making sense of everyday life*. Cambridge: Polity.

Skeggs, B. (1999) 'Matter out of place: Visibility and sexuality in leisure spaces', *Leisure Studies*, 18(3): 213–32.

Silverman, D. (2006) *Interpreting qualitative data: Methods of analyzing talk, text and interaction*. London: Sage.

Smailes, J. (1994) 'The struggle has never been simply about bricks and mortar: Lesbian's experiences of housing' in R. Gilroy and R. Woods (eds) *Housing women*. London: Routledge, pp. 152–72.

Stella, F. (2010) The language of intersectionality: Researching "lesbian" identity in Russia' in Y. Taylor, S. Hines and M. Casey (eds) *Theorizing intersectionality and sexuality*. Basingstoke: Palgrave Macmillan, pp. 212–34.

Taylor, J. (2010) 'Queer temporalities and the significance of music scene participation in the social identities of middle aged queers', *Sociology*, 44(5): 893–902.

Taylor, Y. (2004) 'Hidden in the small ads: Researching working class lesbians', *Graduate Journal of Social Science*, 1(2): 253–77.

Taylor, Y. (2007) *Working class lesbian life: Classed outsiders*. Basingstoke: Palgrave Macmillan.

Taylor, Y. (2009) *Lesbian and gay parenting: Securing social and educational capital*. Basingstoke: Palgrave Macmillan.

Taylor, Y., Hines, S. and Casey, M. (eds) (2010) *Theorizing intersectionality and sexuality*. Basingstoke: Palgrave Macmillan.

Turner, M. (2003) *Backward glances: Cruising the queer streets of New Work and London*. London: Reaktion Books.

Valentine, G. (1993) '(Hetero)sexing space: Lesbian perceptions and experiences of everyday spaces', *Environment and Planning D: Society and Space*, 11(4): 395–413.

Valentine, G. (1996) '(Re)negotiating the heterosexual street: Lesbian productions of space' in N. Duncan (ed.) *Body space*. London: Routledge, pp. 146–55.

Valentine, G. (2007) 'Theorizing and researching intersectionality: A challenge for feminist geography', *The Professional Geographer*, 59(1): 10–21.

Varley, A. R. and Blasco, M. (2001) 'Exiled to the home: Masculinity and ageing in urban Mexico', *European Journal of Development Research*, 12(4): 115–38.

Veness, A. R. (1994) 'Design shelters as models and makers of home: New responses to homelessness in urban America', *Urban Geography*, 15(2): 150–67.

Weeks, J. (1981) 'The problem of older homosexuals' in J. Hart and D. Richardson (eds) *The theory and practice of homosexuality*. London: Routledge and Kegan Paul Ltd., pp. 177–84.

Weinberg, M. S. and Williams, C. (1974) *Male homosexuals: Their problems and adaptations*. Oxford: Oxford University Press.

Young, I. M. (2005) 'House and home: Feminist variations on a theme' in I. M. Young (ed.) *On female body experience: Throwing like a girl and other essays*. New York: Oxford University Press, pp. 123–54.

8
'That's Not Really My Scene': Working-Class Lesbians In (and Out of) Place

Yvette Taylor

Introduction

This chapter reflects on LGBT scene space in the UK as shaped by changing economies of place and personhood, which re-produce class as a central point of exclusion, even as inclusion is celebrated, visible and announced (Hines and Taylor, 2012). The re-production of such space via city regeneration, as newly carved out and promoted terrains indicative of city sophistication (the 'pink triangle'; the 'merchant quarter'), mediates both place and people and often queerly so. The felt experience that such places were 'not really their scene' is suggestive of varied queer (working-class) absences within a limited queer-present. Working-class lesbians both participated in and felt excluded from scene spaces, often criticising them as 'pretentious' and 'unreal' for their superficiality and cosmopolitan gloss. This fractures the celebration of queer visibility and a commercial viability based on a regenerated 'coming-forward' of queer consumer-citizens in 'global gay' cities (Binnie, 2000; Stella, 2010; Bassi, 2012). In the aesthetic upgrading of LGBT scenes, a politicised perspective was often believed to have been sacrificed and jeopardised by gendered and classed based inhabitations which interviewees themselves were part of.

Encounters in – and away from – LGBT spaces are troubling and sometimes uneasy to describe based on a *desire* for affirmation and belonging and a *disappointment* in going through the pub-door into the lesbian ('once a month') venue and finding no points of connection or community (see Gieseking, this volume). Queer venues both demand and offer identity premiums but the cost of not 'fitting in' is often felt as failure, embodied as lack and derided too as pointless partying. The promise of access fails to deliver as described in felt pains and embodied exclusions, with social value 'read on the body', and setting 'limits on who can be known and how' (Skeggs, 2004: 26). Demarcations of lesbian styles, tastes and appearances are loaded with meanings of identity, value and distinction, renewing the (in)accessibility of changing scenes and feelings of being in (and out of) place.

Economies of place map onto meanings of personhood (Skeggs, 2004; Gidley and Rooke, 2010; Wilson-Kovacs, 2010). Interviewees spoke of changing scenes with a sense of loss and nostalgia as a better 'fit' to place was positioned in the past and now out of reach. A future 'fit', as an increasing trend, was located in often derogatory terms and landscapes of 'pretension' and 'unreality'. Descriptions from interviewees across the age range frequently conjured up binaries of now/then, political/apolitical, marginal/mainstream, metropolitan/ provincial, highlighting persisting measures of value which often produced an uneasy situation in and out of place (Binnie, 2000; Hines and Taylor, 2012). Positionings in social space involve more than individual choices to access and enter and are enabled and constrained by classed inflected 'plausibility structures' embedded in senses of what is (not) 'for the likes of us' (Skeggs, 2004). There are distinct conditions structuring dispositions and practices as space is negotiated. These pressing classed intersections, spaces and knowledges (Armstrong, 2010; Evans, 2010; Taylor, 2010) reside in and reproduce even queer maps of place and personhood.

This chapter echoes many researchers in calling for a greater attentiveness towards spatialities of class as multiple and various, rather than condensed as 'essentialist' and fixed in time and place (embodied in the wrong efforts of the wrong academic). In aiming to be attentive to queer presences and absences, an effort is made towards a more intersectional politics of class, and a more materially located sense of 'queer'. Vivid examples exist on the historical and contemporary productions and parallels between class, sexual and gender classifications (Skeggs, 2004), which nonetheless variously slip off the map, even as McDowell warns that any new focus on class must not marginalise gender, or sexuality; it must not make claim to a simple return-to-class as abandonment of intersectionality and other lines of difference (see Binnie, 2011; Taylor, 2012). Yet, as with Brown's (2011) 'anxious' commentary on the potentiality of 'intersectionality' I often feel painfully 'failed' by even (traditional) class theorists, where LGBT/class constitutes a dividing rather than contour line between projects, traditions and trajectories, where class and sexuality seems a particularly awkward dis-connection (Taylor, Hines and Casey, 2010). What if our own disciplinary placements fail? And what to do if there is only space for one (my work, and perhaps myself, have been pointed to as I've asked questions on class, to sexualities scholars, and questions on sexualities, to class scholars: 'that's what *you* do'. I know that already).

Knowing already? Working-class lesbian life

Here I draw upon 53 interviews undertaken with self-defined working-class lesbians in the UK, as part of a broader Economic and Social Research Council funded project: *Working-Class Lesbian Life: Classed Outsiders* (2007a). The fieldwork began in 2002 and so my distance and proximity (geographical, temporal, emotional) has changed since being present in this place (as researcher, resident, 'native'). In returning to this project, I feel the mis-fits in academic and non-academic space have travelled with me: I'm speaking about 'them' 'then', while I re-engage now and envisage future conversation, subjects and spaces. My efforts (then and now) are in locat-ing 'scene' spaces and 'queer lives' within a wider conceptualisation of respondents' experiences, considering childhood and schooling, the tran-sition to employment, scene spaces and relationships and intimacy (Taylor, 2004a, 2005a,b,c). Class affects childhood memories of not having and wanting, the meaning of family, educational experiences, work opportuni-ties, dating, desire, sex, ethical values, and friendships. Participants speak in detail about not only the *struggle* of being working-class, but also the *pleasures* – including a sense of working-class communities as more friendly, comfortable, politicised, decent and real than middle-class communities, which are, in contrast, positioned as embarrassingly normative and preten-tious (see also Taylor, 2012). Here I examine the (dis)satisfaction voiced by interviewees in different scene spaces.

For many interviewees, 'buying into' commercial venues was achieved at much expense and often at an articulated cost of 'selling out', in the felt necessity of emulating middle-class lesbian and gay male appearances in order to fit in. The compulsion to upgrade your style, to work on your self-presentation, to 'come out' in the right, recognisable ways, can be uneasy. Yet interviewees also spoke of their dissatisfaction with different, more 'real', working-class venues. Again, ambivalence and unease underscored accounts, where the 'reality' of working-class space was sometimes too real, excessive and hedonistic, thereby failing to constitute a pleasing presence or an agreeable aesthetic. In negotiations of commercialised scene spaces, named as middle-class *and* working-class, interviewees experienced material and embodied intersections of class, gender, sexuality and age, shaping a sense of being in and out of place.

Within the literature on lesbian and gay urban spaces, different scenes have been positioned as places of refuge and tolerance – and spaces of con-suming and consumable (dis)identifications (Skeggs, 1999, 2001; Hennessey, 2000; Binnie, 2004; Casey, 2010; Richardson, 2005). Increasingly such spaces are valued as niche markets for development and exploitation, as part of the 'global gay' capital-making provided by the cosmopolitan 'mixed' city, which houses a good balance of varied venues and a liberal tolerance of (commodity) difference. The pleasures and problems of scene spaces are sharply highlighted in the idea of 'buying into' commercialised leisure space and therefore, by choice or by default, ultimately 'selling out' politicised identity credentials for market based, purchasable ones (Chasin, 2000). Chasin links the development of the US lesbian and gay movement and the growth of 'niche markets' which promise inclusion at a price. Within her account, social recognition is dependent on ability to consume as identity becomes branded, commodified, consumed and, it would seem, depoliticised. The scepticism aired regarding the price of inclusion resonates with many other accounts (Casey, 2010; Hennessy, 2000; Evans, 1993; Warner, 1993; Taylor, 2009). The acceptance offered to the consumer is rather precarious: not only do you have to 'fit in' but you have to stay in and this perhaps consolidates some spaces while preventing and eroding the creation of other scene spaces not dependent upon cash, consumption and credit (Binnie, 1995; Field, 1997). Alongside branding, niche marketing and the 'commercial hijacking of gayness', it is important to remember that 'not everyone is invited to the party' (Simpson, 1999: 213).

The increasing existence of 'pink triangles' in city centres across the UK has come to symbolise cultural ascendancy, regeneration and gentrification as they are actively promoted as indictors of city cosmopolitanism and development (Binnie, 2004; Casey, 2010; Taylor, 2007). Such mainstreaming processes may be seen to produce a new homonormativity, whereby non-threatening, spending lesbians and gay men are afforded a certain visibility, acceptability and a route into the city (Bell and Binnie, 2000; Duggan, 2002; Taylor, 2009). Here the 'queer unwanted' encompass those excluded and disqualified from sophisticated homonormative status, for whom movement into lesbian and gay commercial spaces is becoming more restricted (Binnie, 2004; Bassi, 2012).

In re-locating scene space within a class framework, Binnie (2000) speaks of 'queer cosmopolitanism' as involving a distinction between cosmopolitanism and provincialism, articulated through discourses of 'sophistication' and a certain knowingness 'about the hippest destinations and urban sites for queer consumption' which then becomes 'a self-reflective marker of their own sophistication' (p. 173). In contrast, working-class and provincial sexualities are marked as being unsophisticated and 'less developed', where class 'sticks' (as waste, as wrong, unworthy) in words, subjects and spaces (Skeggs, 2004; Taylor, 2010). Weston (1995) describes the connection between 'coming-out', developing a gay identity and becoming a 'sophisticated' city dweller, which ultimately requires access both culturally and economically to these spaces and positions. As such, 'not having the financial capability seriously compromises one's attempts to lead a 'modern gay lifestyle'. It directly impacts upon one's ability to take up space within the city' (Binnie, 2000: 171).

Many women in this research did indeed know of gay spaces, including 'trendy' and 'cosmopolitan' ones, but this knowledge was often unsupported by economic know how. The emphasis on consumption renders scene space inaccessible to many working-class lesbians and while window-shopping may indeed be safe, it is not very satisfying. Similarly, they were often critical of commercialised scene spaces and unlikely to describe the space itself, or its inhabitants, as sophisticated. Instead, typical and much repeated descriptors pointed to the 'pretentiousness' and 'unreality' of scene space, even as these locations were spatially and materially bound up in sexual identity negotiation. Alongside a critique of the pretentiousness of middle-class scene space, there exists a realisation that an alternate working-class space is often not a viable substitute (Kennedy and Davis, 1993). It seems that the dichotomy Binnie (2000) invokes is embodied in the women's choices of where to go and what to do.

This question of 'what to do?' extends to the critique of queer scenes, which may be read as a 'manoeuvre which individualizes sexual subjects and divides queer community' (Holliday, 1999: 483). But to sideline already existing divisions, as class in particular is effaced in accounts of sexual lives, is to be seduced into a too easy account of the 'world we have won', while collapsing different 'worlds' within the 'global gay city' (Weeks, 2007; McDermott, 2011; Stella, 2010). Criticism of scene spaces are made with an awareness of the multiple meanings these have for many different occupants with a desire to class, rather than castigate, these spaces and their occupants, while paying attention to intersecting identities, inclusions and exclusions (Taylor, 2007; Taylor, Hines and Casey, 2010). Interviewees expressed a desire to become part of such (commercialised) communities – as well as the limitations upon, rejection of, and impossibilities of doing so; the frustrations of never quite getting what was expected.

The following section will give an account of research methods before exploring changes to lesbian and gay leisure spaces in the areas where respondents came from, as areas often off-the-map of *the* 'queer presence'. In the move from and persistence of 'grubby wee pubs', to celebrity 'places to be' (gay), interviewees articulated a tension between simply having more space versus more diverse and equalised space: inequalities based on class and gender were seen as continuously relevant within changing scenes. I focus on shifting boundaries of inclusion/exclusion, operating beyond financial barriers to encompass styles, appearance, ways of being and values. Interviewees engage in re-circulations of value and distinction, as mapped on to place and people, as the 'queer unwanted', lacking a homonormative classed status. It is hoped that the data presented here will give a more embodied account of negotiating LGBT scene spaces and the complexities of (dis)identifying with such spaces in being queerly present and absent, in occupying, embracing and challenging constructions of now/then, apolitical/political, marginal/mainstream, metropolitan/provincial.

Not all bright light and big city? (Dis)Locatedness

Fifty-three women, who identified themselves as working-class and lesbian, from Scotland (the Highlands, Glasgow and Edinburgh) and England (Yorkshire and Manchester) took part in this research, through a combination of one-to-one interviews, paired and group interviews. Elsewhere I have discussed the (in)effectiveness and (dis)comfort of my own repeated visits to commercialised and community scene spaces to elicit interview respondents, as I too negotiated urban trendiness, front and backstreet locations and, even, 'dirty wee dives' (Taylor 2005a,b,c): I did so in a particular time and in particular places, and also felt many of the presences and absences reported here. Lesbians are a 'hard to reach' group and working-class lesbians may be even harder to locate, given their marginality if not absence from academic agendas and from typical, commercial scene spaces (Taylor, 2004b). As such, it is inevitable that the women I interviewed are not representative of all who may fit this categorisation, nor are they one internally cohesive group. Respondents ranged from 16–64 years. Notably all, except one British Asian interviewee, were white. Lesbian accounts are 'subjected to a severe process of selection from homosexual identification to the particularities of the research projects sample criteria' (Kitzinger, 1987: 66), a sentiment echoed by John and Patrick (1999) who, in attempting to measure the extent of poverty and social exclusion of lesbians and gay men in Glasgow, also note the difficulties in researching lesbian lives, compounded by combined exclusions (see also Held, 2009).

Research on scene spaces in the UK has mostly concentrated upon 'Big cities' of London (Binnie, 1995; McDowell, 1995), Manchester (Skeggs, 1999, 2001; Moran and Skeggs, 2004) and Brighton (but see Casey, 2010 who looks at the 'Pink Triangle' in Newcastle) so there is an enduring need to chart differently (dis)located economies of place and personhood (Binnie, 2000). Manchester, as one fieldwork location, has been rebuilt and rebranded as an entrepreneurial city with a range of new developments, businesses and commercial centres. This regeneration marks a continuation of the transformation of Manchester from a Northern city of urban decline and de-industrialisation, to a vibrant cultural and economic centre. Manchester's 'gay village', a clearly defined space covering Canal street and reaching back into Blossom Street, has experienced a cultural ascendancy in the last six or seven years, popularised by the British TV programme *Queer as Folk*, which used Manchester's gay village as its central focus. Post-gentrification, Canal Street is now the focus for open entertainment, for both the straight and gay tourist (Skeggs, 2001). The village is highly commercialised; venues take the form of cafes, pubs and clubs, which are surrounded by a range of businesses and upmarket residential units. Yet, Manchester's gay space extends outwards geographically and politically to include community groups such as the Lesbian and Gay Foundation and the Lesbian Community Project. There is a women's bar situated (unsurprisingly behind the central focal point of Canal Street) on Blossom Street, which is not exclusively female in its clientele. In a stable gay space, lesbians still have limited choices and, it seems, cannot fully 'buy into' such sophisticated, upgraded territory (Binnie and Valentine, 1999; Valentine, 2000). Cathy (37, Manchester) situates her own desire for a separate women's space as something belonging in the past, now gone and impossible, and therefore an 'old fashioned' sentiment; 'I'm a bit of an old fashioned separatist, I like going to where it's just women but there aren't that many places that do that, you've only got Vanilla'. 'Old fashioned separatist spaces' are held up as allowing for more possibility, more visibility. While it is likely that even within such venues, divisions and demarcations were also reproduced, albeit in different ways, what is important for Cathy is the way that previous possibilities are eroded in gendered exclusions. Nonetheless, women from Manchester and Yorkshire were particularly familiar with this space (in terms of recognising its meanings and knowing of it, if not fully or even partially accessing it), although it featured in the 'imagination' of most interviewees – given its celebrity status as the 'place to be'.

May (23, Yorkshire) speaks of the financial restrictions even in 'grubby pubs', while noting that Manchester and Leeds attract more middle-class lesbians, a simple matter of bigger choices and bigger places: 'you tend to get more of the middle-class, what I'd call middle-class lesbians, in Leeds or Manchester. I think that's purely because they are bigger places'. Leeds, like Manchester is successfully reworking its image from de-industrial 'grim and grit' to urban glam, gaining recognition as one of the fastest growing cities in the UK and as Yorkshire's commercial capital. Speaking of the climate within gay and lesbian venues in Leeds, Kim relates her frustration in the polarisation between 'normal pubs', 'old men's pubs' and those places for 'pretty little boys', conveying a sense of not belonging anywhere, of having no accessible 'niche' within revamped leisure venues:

> I think it depresses me really because you have the old men's pubs ... then you have the, like totally teeny, what's the word, like poptastic-esque[1] thing. What's wrong with having just a normal pub? Why do you have to go to a bar where you can't hear anything and all the pretty little boys are on the stage dancing? There's no need for it really.
>
> Kim, 22, Yorkshire

Kim's sentiments relate the prevailing aesthetic, encompassing visual and musical styles and features, to her own discomfort pointing to the gendering of such space and to the relevance of age within this.

In Scotland, accessing scene spaces tended to be a matter of choosing which city, Glasgow or Edinburgh, to go to – women from the Highlands particularly lacked this kind of social space although monthly discos in temporary accommodation were sometimes hosted by the Rural Lesbian Group. Notably there was an assertion that this was 'real' working-class space, rather different from the 'posh' venue where the group organisers and established members (named as 'middle-class') met. This group provided one of the only support mechanisms to women in the vast and isolated Highlands region, making clear that the urban/rural divide also served as another axis of difference (Valentine, 1993). While isolation and poverty may be easier to imagine in such a rural landscape, the capital status of Edinburgh and its recent property boom masks extremes of poverty and affluence: its well planned and central residential, leisure and business complexes discord with peripheral housing estates and involve a geographical exclusion at first out of sight.

Edinburgh's gay space merges with (and is contained by) upmarket space – similar to but smaller than Manchester. Broughton Street, situated in the expensive New Town area, houses two lesbian and gay cafes, marketed as 'versatile', 'eclectic' and 'vegetarian', descriptors generally absent from venues appealing to a more working-class clientele. At the top of the street there are two more glitzy gay pubs, sitting alongside a newly built cinema complex. Like Manchester, these spaces are relatively open, both in their design (e.g. large windows declaring a presence) and in their locations – this is central Edinburgh, but a bit off centre for the traditional tourist and in this respect the problem of 'straight intrusion' may be less severe than in Manchester but the respective gender compositions, and the flow of 'pink pounds' probably match up (Skeggs, 1999, 2001).

Glasgow's lesbian and gay venues are somehow more diffused. Although still in the centre of town they crop up in different ways at different times, perhaps representing the city's dual processes of attempted 'regenerations' sitting alongside its working-class images and connotations. Despite these cultural claims, wholesale regeneration has not occurred and several of Glasgow's most deprived areas continue to rank at the top of UK wide poverty scales (Paton, 2010). Yet the re-development of scene space is bound up with the city's claims for cultural pre-eminence. More traditional pubs have recently been redesigned to project a more upmarket, expensive and 'classy' feel – cappuccinos rather than pints, mirroring those venues in the Merchant quarter of the city. This contrasts with the less exclusive venue opposite Queen Street train station, which is straight during the day and gay in the evening, women's space sometimes, discos and quiz nights other times. This mixture, which works through specific time/space allocations, features in community venues, a case of doubling up and making do (Valentine, 1995). For Sharon, such a 'mix 'n match' does not constitute variety, nor is re-development and change necessarily improvement or expansion (Taylor, 2012). The regeneration of scene space seems not to have adhered to the idiom that the 'customer knows best', certainly not this customer at least, and Sharon is left to pay the price of having nowhere suitable to go:

> There isn't any nice places to go really, the Tron used to be quite gay friendly, it's no really the scene, Palladium is just a bogin wee pub, Roxy's, you know, their toilets are badly needin' done. The Acid Lounge is about

the best of them and Bennets is just [sigh]. There used to be this place called Club X that I'd go to in the Royal Exchange Square but it was like ten years ago.

Sharon, 47, Glasgow

Sharon expresses a sense of loss, something given up 'ten years ago', being replaced with what seems like less than sophisticated places and more 'bogin wee pubs'; she would like to go to 'nice' places but, for her, things are not getting any better even though she can now name many more venues. Here the desire for the 'sophisticated' and the 'cosmopolitan' are never actualised and instead contradictory (dis)investments mark out her choices and hopes amidst the changes. Such sentiments of wanting somewhere to go to but being disappointed with the offerings also applied to the Glasgow Gay and Lesbian Centre, which is hidden behind a discount supermarket, still managing to fly its rainbow flag upon an otherwise gloomy landscape. Down another dark alley is Glasgow Women's Library, which houses a lesbian youth group. It is a hidden and rather precarious venue: out of sight out of mind. As 'respectable' scene spaces became firmly established on city maps, a process experienced differently across various locations, less commercialised spaces, with different participants were rendered more vulnerable, existing further off the map, becoming physically and economically marginal to and distant from *the* scene (Binnie, 2000).

Access into the scene necessitated physical, geographical travel but it also represented a movement between classed localities (Valentine, 1993; Taylor, 2004a). Most, if not all, interviewees had to negotiate physical and emotional journeys when attempting to enter scene space, to gain recognition and affirmation of identity, and that was often just to get through the front door. Lamenting the expense incurred when first 'coming out' and then going out in Glasgow, Tracey (23, Glasgow) states that she just 'couldn't have gone out' in her home town as there was 'no gay clubs or pubs or anything like that, the only place is Glasgow so I needed to come through here ... I was 16 or 17 when I first came through to go out, under age drinking!' Tracey's journey into and experience of lesbian and gay urban space changed across time, from initial 'coming out' into a new space, to a gradual sense of knowingness, if not complete comfort. Going out to be 'out' does mean something rather different if it involves a bus journey across town rather than a stroll to the corner: these distances from – and desired proximities to – scene spaces where made more complex but a lamentation of what was but now was now. Past scenes were re-imagined and filled with value, situated against a future 'fit' in unreal, apolitical landscapes of 'pretension' and 'unreality'. Being in and out of place 'then' and 'now' was powerfully linked to embodied appearances, actively classing enduring senses of discomfort and disappointment.

All pop and little politics? Change, comfort and disappointment

Interviewees spoke of proliferating scenes often with a sense of longing and nostalgia, as if something had been given up rather than gained. In describing the changes to scene spaces across the different locations, respondents often contrasted what had been against what currently was, constructing previous times as more political and less consumerist. Mavis tells of many positive changes in the scene, even if these still remain unequally available. Mavis' account of the changes within scene spaces is underpinned by a dissatisfaction with that which is on offer; even though things have got better they are still not that good. The changes she narrates are physical ones, from the back alley to the open plan, where imaginings, memories and materialities all intersect:

> Oh well, the first time I went out into the gay scene was in London and that was very freaky, that was very freaky because at that time, that would have been in the '70s and at that time they were dirty wee dives really, up wee backstreets where you knocked the door and they let you in and it was all very furtive ... I remember going to this place down a wee dark alley ... Nah, I didn't like it but it had changed by the 1980s and there were a lot more places, I mean it's an absolute fact that gay men are still, economically, have the power that gay women don't have. There's probably more available for men than women.
>
> Mavis, 52, Edinburgh

Despite improvements across time, the choice to occupy a 'dirty wee dive' as opposed to a large, legitimate and open space perhaps remains a gendered one, certainly still affected by spending power. However, the changes from 'seedy' 'dives' to cosmopolitan venues, are seen to echo broader changes: the trade off between politicised occupation of bad space, or apolitical consumption within 'trendy' places. Reflecting on this uneasy paradox, Jeannette relates a tale of loss and contradiction:

> Has anybody been telling you about the Arena and the women's dances at the Arena? Well, over where the Sheriff Court is, there was a club, it's still there. It was the Star Club and Lesbian Line used to have monthly women's discos there and it was like a community hall almost. It was like a social club, it was like a wee social club and it held probably about 200 people and it was a fairly non threatening environment to go into because it didn't take you long before you felt like you knew about 90% of the 200 women that went there. I'm not idealising it because it was quite boring and the music was terrible [laughs], some day I'm gonna do a compilation of Arena records [laughs].
>
> Jeannette, 39, Glasgow

Often 'boring' times were nonetheless positioned as more political even if in community halls with bad music: 'good' and 'bad' times were signified by changing appearances displayed by those in place. Jill speaks of furtively sneaking into venues frequented mostly by gay men 'which then was a slimy wee pub, wet walls, a crap karaoke singer, a wee hole', but she relates changes in upgraded space to renewed tensions rather than a comfortably visibility:

> It was before all these fucking lipstick dykes, do you know what I mean. I remember when all that kicked off and there was all these good looking lassies and I was like 'Ah, they must be straight'.
>
> Jill, 28, Edinburgh

Jill's presence and appearance once positioned her out of place, yet in describing new appearances and a new presence, Jill arguably re-invokes such (mis)recognition. The commercialisation and branding of lesbian identity ('lipstick lesbians') is highlighted but Jill's own response and place-ment within this remains ambivalent and fraught, with the move from an almost absent past to a commercialised, popularised present fractured by feelings of loss and gain. In 'old' and 'new' times leisure space mediates the construction of lesbian styles, appearances and identities, demarcating boundaries of inclusion; where once Jill's long hair cast her as an outsider in the mostly gay male 'slimy wee pub', now it may be cast simply as another style. However, the existence of different 'styles' doesn't necessarily equate to equal access or entitlement to lesbian territories and it seems that this sense of being in and out of place is what carries across time.

Differences between working-class and middle-class lesbians appearing in place were often strikingly noted. Ali suggests that middle-class lesbians are less 'trendy' and outlines the various styles and wardrobe possibilities of middle-class lesbians, arguing that working-class lesbians dress straighter:

> Class is connected to clothes, there is a difference between working-class and middle-class people in terms of clothes, and working-class and middle-class lesbians. They're less trendy in terms of you get more kinda walking gear type of casual clothes, the walking gear and fleeces, things like that, although if they're dressing they wear nice blouses and suits and things like that. Working-class lesbians they wear more straight fashion.
>
> Ali, 42, Manchester

Ali describes the different ways she perceives middle-class and working-class to embody class position and sexuality: in investing, signifying, even capitalising upon these bodily appearances women are differently able to lay entitlement claims to different settings, a correlation, or opposition, between looking and being 'in place' (Skeggs, 1999, 2001). The desire and (in)ability to be 'fashion conscious' is such that feelings of not quite meeting the required standard were common place, even as such standards were ridiculed and challenged. Many interviewees question, redefine and resist proper taste, or 'gay taste' but their re-evaluations are not always self-empowering or authoritative, rather they are often disappointed and frustrated utterances and ambivalences – rather than refusals. Across the different UK locales, scene spaces were often simultaneously portrayed as 'tacky' and 'pretentious', of being too overt and 'abnormal', evident in Jill's (28, Edinburgh) comment that 'Heart Break has got fucking leopard skin walls, you know big pink fluffy seats in it and it's like I just want to go to the pub'.

In going to the pub the sentiment that this was never just a simple journey, was repeated. Gay men were often understood to inhabit gay spaces more easily and comfortably, embodying a masculine aesthetic (Binnie, 1995; Casey, 2010), which women were seem to be 'emulating' to fit into place. For several interviewees this process of emulation was simultaneously interpreted as an erasure of politicised values and as a continuation of designer display and pretence:

> [A] lot of gay women now seem to be acting like gay men, they seem to be wearing the same clothes, getting the same hairstyles, doing the same things and not following their own path.
>
> Liz, 23, Manchester

Liz's comments echo voiced resentments about the negation and refusal of separate lesbian space; even if its previous existence may well be somewhat romanticised in past recollections, the present sense of loss and disappointment still illuminates the desire for something different. Within a space that effectuates a commonality of appearance, the consequence for working-class lesbians often manifests in resentment; a feeling of not wanting and not being able to 'buy into' commercialised scene spaces. Lacking the means and motivation for incorporation, Sukhjit risks being an outsider; hers is an 'opting out' of sorts but the reported commonalities in interviewees' accounts is suggestive of a more general restriction in liberal times:

> I perceive gay men's scene to be much more individualistic and it's much more hedonistic. It's more about body beautiful than the lesbian scene but I see the lesbian scene as emulating it, I've never liked that and I don't want it. I don't like the fact that the politics have been rubbed out of it in the same way, everybody's becoming very liberal and very individualistic ... The internalised sexism within the scene about how women are viewed and objectified and also about how you have to look as well 'cause it's really easy for me to chop my hair off and I had

short hair for ages but it's also really hard for me to grow it. But it's really difficult when you go out and people just assume you're straight.

Sukhjit, 29, Manchester

Sukhjit implies there are different users within the same space but is not willing to take the 'easy' move of chopping her hair off in order to make herself more or less readable.

The shifting critique of contemporary scene spaces as 'pretentious', where the 'politics have been rubbed out' was, like that of middle-class spaces and identities more generally, made within certain limits and constraints. In this case there were few alternatives to commercial scene space. Faye (45, Manchester) describes her complex feelings about scene spaces – her desire for identification is not fulfilled but there is also a sense of resignation, expressed by many other respondents, that something is better than nothing. Her account is littered with reservations and justifications and her feelings of discomfort are tangible as the 'place of business' is also as a place of leisure: Faye's conveys a certain desire to still be there, to get a drink, if not affirmation. Such views indicate more about the lack of choice, rather than the suitability of current scene spaces as comfortable and validating places for working-class lesbians, where the notion of scene space as a 'sanctuary' sits rather uncomfortably with its other purpose as a 'business'. It would seem to be a case of 'any port in a storm' as opposed to a genuine choice based on where one feels at home. The financial restrictions are very pressing and real, nicely summed up by Amy (29, Edinburgh) in asserting that 'they rip the arse out, especially when like CC's is charging you £2 for a bottle of water'.

The commercial nature of many venues and events, such as Manchester Pride discussed by Liz (23, Manchester) inevitably exclude many groups and many felt that a lack of political direction or purpose made such events 'pointless' (Chasin, 2000; Hennessy, 2000), instead being just another expensive excursion into another man's land. Although such comments may be similarly voiced via a anti-consumerist, feminist ethic, Liz observes the coercive nature of being forced out, 'if you didn't have the money', as opposed to an opting out. Liz's comments about the rather depoliticised T-shirt wearing event ('If you're politicised in any way, it's a bag of shit') links to Holliday's (1999) claims that that the acceptance and 'comfort' of scene space produces an easy 'unthinking' state: 'The comfort gained through many uncomfortable years of political struggle, the comfort of a revamped scene, the comfort of a more liberal state and some protection from discrimination in the workplace have all produced a more comfortable (lesbian and gay) identity politics' (Holliday, 1999: 489). Sonia's (32, Yorkshire) forthright assertion conveys this (dis)comfort, stating that 'The only value you've got is the value of the pink pound, isn't it?'

Sonia's response is suggestive of an enduring, even painful, political consciousness, pitted again the (un)comfortable drive to consume. The evident (dis)satisfactions expressed by working-class lesbians in resisting as well as 'fitting into' scene space, and the (dis)comforts experienced therein, illustrate these intimate and awkward inhabitations, recollections and refusals on an everyday level, where many have pointed to the structural classed and gendered dimensions (Binnie, 1995, 2000; Holliday, 1999; Chasin, 2000; Hennessy, 2000). For interviewees, negotiations of marginal/mainstream and apolitical/political space are local and immediate, where even working-class venues do not constitute viable alternatives.

See you down the local? Excessive presences

In highlighting different scenes, groups and networks available for working-class and middle-class lesbians, Kelly suggests not simply a benign existence of 'different types of lesbians', but implicates social and sexual transactions as reliant upon occupational and friendship networks:

> I know in London they have professional lesbian groups … Dining groups or whatever, networks where all the ladies go out and shag each other afterwards. There are certain cliques of lesbians, like in Hebden[2] there's a lot of hippy lesbians or alternative lesbians or there's more working-class lesbians going out, getting pissed. There are different types of lesbians.
>
> Kelly, 23, Yorkshire

Kelly is imagining what such professional lesbian groups get up to, confident of the different 'cliques' of lesbians in different places, while situating working-class lesbians very much within the pub, 'getting pissed' (presumably not being 'properly political'). Moral and material value is loaded onto metropolitan/provincial locales and bodies in comparing urban, professional London with rural, drinking Yorkshire.

Professional or otherwise, venues that aim to attract alternative audiences, or 'different types of lesbians', are very vulnerable as Amy describes:

> The one I used to work in was really, really working-class, like really down to earth, spit 'n sawdust down to earth. Em, Habana's more bright, more music, where I used to work it was a lot darker, it was a lot of older poofs and lesbians that came in because it was much more of a family feel pub 'cause you knew everybody … it's got new management … she more or less barred people, anybody who she didn't like she just barred them. So I left and everybody scattered.
>
> Amy, 29, Edinburgh

The pub, which Amy describes as a working-class venue, where everyone knew each other, is transformed into a flasher, brighter one and its previous clientele, with no clear viability also come to lack queer visibility – something which maybe was always hidden in this darker space. Scene spaces that can be named as both 'working-class' and 'lesbian' would appear to be particularly vulnerable to re-branding and upmarketing, marking the apparent upgrading and transformation of city space, leaving behind spatial scattering of disparate others.

Some women did say that lesbian and gay pubs existed within their working-class localities but, unlike Amy, they were mostly dissatisfied with these. Often these places were 'too real' and the harsh realities within (working-class) communities could not always be glossed over through consumption. Kelly is disappointed with the local lesbian pub in her area and discusses the classed aspects of this with Lisa, portraying working-class spaces, and working-class lesbians in particular, as hedonistic. It seems that Kelly is also disappointed by the lack of community resources, other than pubs and clubs and the limitations this produces:

L: *They're* all drunk and they've all got alcohol problems and they're all on happy pills.

K: Psychological problems.

L: They have, they really have. It's so fucked up here in terms of the dyke community, it's *really* depressing. You just, we know a hell of a lot of lesbians in Hull who go out on the scene and how many of them could you form a relationship with?

K: None.

[...]

L: Well basically the only gay things in Hull are The Mall, which is a gay friendly pub and not a gay pub.

K: It's so working-class.

L: It is, yeah. Oh I don't know.

K: It is Lisa, it's very hedonistic.

L: Yeah but so what you're having a good time there, having a laugh.

K: It's alright doing it occasionally but to do it every evening.

L: I've got no problem with that, I normally do it about three or four times a week! I never drink, I only drink on a Friday.

K: I do have a problem with that, I get quite depressed by it.

L: I get quite high off it 'cause I can go in there and do whatever I want.

Kelly, 23 and Lisa, 23, Yorkshire

Scene spaces are often portrayed and criticised as excessive and hedonistic, where sexuality is overtly displayed in a 'over-the-top' manner (Binnie, 2000; Skeggs, 2004). With the addition of working-class bodies, this apparent 'excess' becomes too much; the overload, for Kelly at least, being depressing rather than pleasurable. Working-class gay friendly culture is pathologised through the positioning of all occupants as having alcohol and mental health problems, a positioning regularly attached to working-class places and people, making clear Kelly and Lisa's own boundaries, disinvestments and distinctions. So while the 'pretence' of middle-class scene space was often criticised in comparison to more 'real' working-class pubs and clubs, Kelly and Lisa's account also renders more working-class places problematic, although through quite different criteria. Rather than being 'pretentious', they are 'hedonistic', conveying the temporary (and unjustified) pleasure within otherwise depressing places. There seems also to be a suggestion that while things are superficially fine, underneath this there exist deeper problems, adding to the sense of 'unreality' even in more working-class venues. There does not appear to be a middle ground, somewhere to go for a drink without either taking out a bank loan and wearing a feather boa or drinking orange squash out of plastic cups:

> I don't want to buy the whole Fibre/Crush bar type of scene 'cause that's not me and I think that's the problem with Manchester is that it's so expensive and I don't want that. But at the same time, I don't want a disco in a school hall either.
>
> Kim, 22, Yorkshire

Kim's own description vividly highlights the unsatisfactory binary between 'queer cosmopolitanism' and working-class 'provincialism' (Binnie, 2000) and the discomfort in rejecting the expensive option and being left with something a bit sparse and marginal, or simply a 'bit boring'. Comments highlight unease and ambivalence experienced when negotiating, contesting and even rejecting changes to scene space. From regretful sighs to allegations of pretence and excess, via 'pointless' consumption and 'boring' alternatives, many working-class lesbians who I spoke to expressed significant discontent with commercialised scene spaces and ultimately a sense that it was not *their* space.

Conclusion

In this chapter I considered working-class lesbians' experiences of commercialised scene spaces as shaped by economies of place and personhood, which re-produce class as a central point of exclusion, even as inclusion is celebrated, visible and announced. Much of the literature on lesbian and gay urban spaces has pointed to commercialisation and niche branding as processes which differently though increasingly apply across the cities and regions of Manchester, Yorkshire, Glasgow and Edinburgh. Despite previous attempts to class scene spaces by drawing attention to structural socio-economic inequalities (Warner, 1993; Chasin, 2000; Hennessy, 2000), there has been a lack of attention into classed individuals' experiences of and responses to different scenes (Binnie, 2011; Seidman, 2011). It is hoped that the data presented here gives a more embodied account of the social and economic changes to scene spaces and the complexities experienced by those (dis)identifying with and against such spaces.

Interviewee accounts demonstrate the intersections of gender and class in generating inclusions and exclusions. Interviewees frequently mobilise binaries in describing their experience of and existence in lesbians and gay urban spaces, demonstrating fraught investments, claims and disappointments. Ideas and discussions of changes across time and place (as 'then' and 'now', 'metropolitan' or 'provincial') are apparent throughout interview account and can be understood as capturing their own changing placements in and out of *the* scene. Points of exclusion operate as (in)visible signifiers, written on and recognised from and through the bodies of interviewees and other inhabitants of scene space. While the production of such space, via regeneration and sophistication, mediates the construction of visible and legitimate lesbian styles, appearances and identities, individuals themselves also negotiate, refuse and reproduce such dynamics. Interviewees were *critical of* and *threatened by* gendered and classed consumer based expectations and inhabitations, generating a sense of loss that some limited space and entitlement had been given up; many named this as a political and well as personal loss.

Binnie's (2004) useful distinction between (un)sophisticated places nonetheless elides the multiple ambivalences and intersections felt and reproduced within 'cosmopolitan' and 'provincial' spaces: it would seem that the conflict faced by interviewees between the two ends of the spectrum is a battle for the creation of a more comfortable middle ground. Neither working-class lesbian venues, nor their inhabitants, were recuperated as properly political, as outside the dynamics of sophistication, regeneration, cosmopolitanism and consumerism. Scene spaces are variously and vividly classed spaces, apparent in the location of such venues, the marketing of these as upmarket venues and in the (classed) individuals who occupy, critique and depart from these places. The inclusion of the voices of working-class lesbians allows classed (dis)comfort with contemporary queer scene space to be charted, even if this is not a straightforward or easy connection.

Notes

1. 'Poptastic' is an event within Leeds pub 'The Cockpit'.
2. Hebden Bridge, Yorkshire.

Bibliography

Armstrong, J. (2010) 'Class and Gender and the intersection: Working-Class Women's Dispositions Towards Employment and Motherhood' in Y. Taylor (ed.) *Classed Intersections: Spaces, Selves, Knowledges*. Farnham: Ashgate, pp. 235–54.
Bassi, C. (2012) 'Shanghai Goes West: A Story of the Development of a Commercial Gay Scene in China' in S. Hines and Y. Taylor (eds) *Sexualities: Past Reflections, Future Directions*. Basingstoke: Palgrave. pp. 226–45.
Bell, D. and Binnie, J. (2000) *The sexual citizens*. Cambridge: Polity Press.

Binnie, J. (1995) 'Trading places: Consumption, sexuality and the production of queer space' in D. Bell and G. Valentine (eds) *Mapping desire*. London: Routledge, pp. 53–74.

Binnie, J. (2000) 'Cosmopolitanism and the sexed city' in D. Bell and A. Haddour (eds) *City visions*. Harlow: Prentice Hall, pp. 29–48.

Binnie, J. (2004) *The globalization of sexuality*. London: Sage.

Binnie, J. (2011) 'Class, sexuality and space: A comment' in Y. Taylor (ed.) Special Issue 'Sexuality and Class', *Sexualities*, 14(1): 21–6.

Binnie, J. and Valentine, G. (1999) 'Geographies of sexuality – review of progress', *Progress in Human Geography*, 23(2): 175–87.

Brown, M. (2011) 'Gender and sexuality I: Intersectional anxieties', *Progress in Human Geography*, pp. 1–10.

Casey, M. (2010) 'Even poor gays travel: Excluding low income gay men from understandings of gay tourism' in Y. Taylor (ed.) *Classed intersections: Spaces, selves, knowledges*. Farnham: Ashgate, pp. 181–98.

Chasin, A. (2000) *Selling out: The gay and lesbian movement goes to market*. Basingstoke: Palgrave Macmillan.

Duggan, L. (2002) 'The new homonormativity: The sexual politics of neoliberalism' in R. Castonovo and D. Nelson (eds) *Materializing democracy: Towards a revitalized cultural politics*. Durham: Duke University Press, pp. 35–46.

Evans, D. (1993) *Sexual citizenship: The material construction of sexualities*. London: Routledge.

Evans, S. (2010) 'Becoming "Somebody": Examining Class and Gender Through Higher Education' in Y. Taylor (ed) *Classed Intersections: Spaces, Selves, Knowledges*. Farnham: Ashgate, pp. 53–72.

Field, N. (1997) 'Identity and lifestyle market' in R. Hennessy and C. Ingraham (eds) *Materialist feminism: A reader in class, difference, and women's lives*. London: Routledge, pp. 137–58.

Gidley, B. and Rooke, A. (2010) 'Asdatown: The Intersections of Classed Places and Identities' in Y. Taylor (ed) *Classed Intersections: Spaces, Selves, Knowledges*. Farnham: Ashgate, pp. 95–116.

Held, N. (2009) 'Researching "Race" in Lesbian Space: A Critical Reflection', *Journal of Lesbian Studies*. 13(2): 204–15.

Hennessy, R. (2000) *Profit and pleasure: Sexual identities in late capitalism*. London: Taylor & Francis.

Hines, S. and Taylor, Y. (eds) (2012) *Sexualities: Reflections and futures*. London: Palgrave Macmillan.

Holliday, R. (1999) 'The comfort of identity', *Sexualities*, 2(4): 475–91.

John, S. and Patrick, A. (1999) 'Poverty and social exclusion of lesbians and gay men in Glasgow', Glasgow Women's Library, unpublished.

Kennedy, E. L. and Davis, M. D. (1993) *Boots of leather, slippers of gold: The history of a lesbian community*. New York: Routledge.

Kitzinger, C. (1987) *The social construction of lesbianism*. London: Sage.

McDermott, L. (2011) 'The world some have won: Sexuality, class and inequality' in Y. Taylor (ed.) Special Issue 'Sexuality and Class', *Sexualities*, 14(1): 63–78.

McDowell, L. (1995) 'Body work: Heterosexual gender performances in city workplaces' in D. Bell and G. Valentine (eds) *Mapping desire: Geographies of sexualities*. London: Routledge.

Moran, L. and Skeggs, B. (2001) 'Property, boundary, exclusion: Making sense of hetero-violence in safer spaces', *Social and Cultural Geography*, 2(4): 407–20.

Paton, K. (2010) 'Making Working-Class Neighbourhoods Posh? Exploring the Effects of Gentrification Strategies on Working-Class Communities', in Y. Taylor (ed.) *Classed Intersections: Spaces, Selves, Knowledges*. Farnham: Ashgate, pp. 137–58.

Richardson, D. (2005) 'Desiring sameness? The rise of a neo-liberal politics of normalisation', *Antipode*, 37(3): 515–35.

Seidman, S. (2011) 'Class matters ... but how much? Class, nation, and queer life' in Y. Taylor (ed.) Special Issue 'Sexuality and Class', *Sexualities*, 14(1): 36–41.

Simpson, M. (1999) *It's a queer world: Deviant adventures in pop culture*. New York: Harrington Park Press.

Skeggs, B. (1999) 'Matter out of place: Visibility and sexualities in leisure spaces', *Leisure Studies*, 18(3): 213–32.

Skeggs, B. (2001) 'The toilet paper: Femininity, class and mis-recognition', *Women's Studies International Forum*, 24(3/4): 295–307.

Skeggs, B. (2004) *Class, Self, Culture*. London: Routledge.

Stella, F. (2010) 'The language of intersectionality: Researching 'lesbian' identity in urban Russia' in Y. Taylor, S. Hines and M. Casey (eds) *Theorizing intersectionality and sexuality*. Basingstoke: Palgrave Macmillan, pp. 212–34.

Taylor, Y. (2004a) 'Negotiation and navigation: An exploration of the spaces/places of working-class lesbians', *Sociological Research Online*, 9(1), http://www.socresonline.org.uk/9/1/taylor.html, accessed on 1 October 2012.

Taylor, Y. (2004b) 'Hidden in the small ads: Researching working-class lesbians', *Graduate Journal of Social Science*, 1(2): 253–77.

Taylor, Y. (2005a) 'Classed in a classless climate: Me and my associates...', *Feminism and Psychology*, 15(4): 491–500.

Taylor, Y. (2005b) 'Real politik or real politics? Working-class lesbians' political "awareness" and activism', *Women's Studies International Forum*, 28(6): 484–94.

Taylor, Y. (2005c) 'What now? Working-class lesbians' post-school transitions', *Youth and Policy*, 87: 29–43.

Taylor, Y. (2007) *Working-class lesbian life: Classed outsiders*. London: Palgrave Macmillan.

Taylor, Y. (2009) *Lesbian and Gay Parenting: Securing Social and Educational Capital*. London: Palgrave Macmillan.

Taylor, Y. (2010) 'Not all Bright Lights, Big City' in B. Pini and B. Leach (eds) *Gender, Rurality and Class*. Farnham: Ashgate, pp. 179–199.

Taylor, Y. (2012) *Fitting into place? Class and gender geographies and temporalities*. Farnham: Ashgate.

Taylor, Y., Hines, S. and Casey, M. (eds) (2010) *Theorizing intersectionality and sexuality*. Basingstoke: Palgrave Macmillan.

Valentine, G. (1993) 'Hetero-sexing space: Lesbian perceptions and experiences of everyday spaces', *Environment and Planning D – Society and Space*, 9(3): 395–413.

Valentine, G. (1995) 'Out and about: Geographies of lesbian landscapes', *International Journal of Urban and Regional Research*, 19(1): 96–111.

Valentine, G. (2000) *From nowhere to everywhere: Lesbian geographies*. Cambridge: Polity Press.

Warner, M. (1993) *Fear of a queer planet: Queer politics and social theory*. London: University of Minnesota Press.

Weston, K. (1995) 'Get thee to a big city: Sexual imaginary and the great gay migration', *GLQ: A Journal of Lesbian and Gay Studies*, 2(3): 253–77.

Wilson-Kovacs, D. (2010) 'Class and Sexual Intimacy: An Everyday Perspective' in Y. Taylor (ed.) *Classed Intersections: Spaces, Selves, Knowledges*. Farnham: Ashgate, pp. 217–35.

9
Queering the Meaning of 'Neighbourhood': Reinterpreting the Lesbian-Queer Experience of Park Slope, Brooklyn, 1983–2008

Jen Jack Gieseking

> Still, all of the women I talked to affirmed the spatial significance of the lesbian 'community' of Park Slope.
>
> Rothenberg (1995: 173)

> But it's interesting because we [lesbians and queer women] all talk about Park Slope as this sort of Shangri-La of lesbian safety. ... I guess it doesn't really matter, I suppose, because if people feel like something's a lesbian neighbourhood, than by dint of their believing it, it is.
>
> Sarah '85 (age 41)

The lesbian or lesbian-queer neighbourhood is a slippery idea, and for many women throughout the world it is an elusive ideal, even in LGBTQ meccas such as San Francisco, London, Berlin, and New York City. Renowned enclaves such as the Castro district, Soho, Schöneberg, West Village, Lower East Side, and Chelsea developed as cities within cities, where LGBTQ people could safely find one another and build communities together. But practices of territory-making and place-claiming are antithetical to women's economic and social abilities in the urban sphere, and the urban is a historically unwelcoming environment for women. I suggest, then, that lesbian-queer neighbourhoods, then, do not work in ways identical to gay and queer men's neighbourhoods, but, as Tamar Rothenberg's quote reveals, they are still spatialised 'communities'. As Sarah, a participant from my research, describes in the quote above, the Park Slope neighbourhood in Brooklyn is produced as lesbian-queer in the way it affords these women safety and refuge. So what then is a lesbian-queer neighbourhood to lesbians and queer women? What does it afford them in their everyday lives? Dynamics of gender, race, and class have not been fully accounted for in studies of LGBTQ neighbourhoods; however, recent work has begun to confront assumptions that all LBGTQ people will be granted equal access and can politically and economically maintain such properties over time (Manalansan, 2005; Taylor, 2008; Moore, 2011). This chapter attends to these absences and differences by showing not how these groups have failed to make successful neighbourhoods, but how our imagining and understanding neighbourhoods in new ways affords possibilities for connection, self-understanding, and work towards justice.

Queer theory affords ways of understanding practices, processes, and ways of being that refuse the normative. The work of 'queering' heralds and makes room for difference, questions the powers behind the purported 'normal', and situates pleasure and politics side-by-side. My deployment of queer theory in this chapter is in step with the idea that queering reveals 'inconsistencies of social boundaries and their discourse' (Elder, 1999: 89). In turn, queer theory provides recognition and consideration for alternative perspectives that break from norms. Adding another interpretation, the feminist concept of 'intersectionality' is a core organising principle to confront supposed normativities by describing the complicatedness of everyday life. The examination of intersectionalities helps to illuminate how people (and spaces) are co-produced through our multiple subjectivities of gender and sexuality and race and class and age and generation and so on (Crenshaw, 1996; Taylor, 2007). Together this feminist-queer frame uses the standpoint of experience to unpack not only normative values but limiting and unjust spatial models as well.

Drawing from inter-generational group interviews with 47 lesbians and queer women who came out between 1983 and 2008 with mental mapping and artefact sharing exercises, as well as archival research, I examine and reinterpret the ways these women experience and find meaning in the space of the lesbian-queer neighbourhood. Participants were attached to the idea of neighbourhoods as important lesbian-queer spaces even when their lived experience often did not match the 'typical' idea of neighbourhood. I was curious to understand what spoke to participants in their experiences and ideas of this type of space. As such, I pay special attention to what the lesbian-queer neighbourhood affords participants over time. In this chapter I focus on Park Slope, the LGBTQ mecca of New York City's only lesbian neighbourhood is not the only one in the U.S. I suggest that the meaning and survival of Park Slope is not predicated on retaining physical territory. Rather, I propose it is derived from the mobile, fragmented, fleeting social, cultural, historic, economic, and political elements of a neighbourhood. Lesbians and queer women continually piece together these elements to claim not only a politics of visibility but also a politics of and space for recognition. I argue that the model of the LGBTQ neighbourhood must be queered, that is, rethought against the grain of normative paradigms of property ownership-as-success, in order to address the experiences and concerns of women, working class people, and people of colour. Rather than refuse these women's experiences and ideas of Park Slope as a lesbian-queer neighbourhood, lesbians and queer women instead queer the meaning of neighbourhood itself by enacting a fleeting and fragmented spatialised community that does not adhere to the concept of a neighbourhood as a fixed, physical, and visible territory. I use the term 'lesbian-queer neighbourhood' to encompass the identities participants used in this project, while the actual analysis is an act of queering.

What's in a neighbourhood?

A neighbourhood is understood as being 'dominated by residential uses,' 'walkable' in scale, and a (physical) territory (Gregory et al., 2009). The concept of the neighbourhood retains a pleasant image in the geographical imagination. Neighbourhoods represent American nineteenth and twentieth century urban life at their best, in that they supposedly mimic small town life. However, it is important to note that producing neighbourhoods depended upon the making of territory and claiming of place, whether by force, coercion, or choice. For example, the production of poor neighbourhoods of colour across the U.S. was a process dependent upon excluding these groups from access to jobs, loans, equal education, and sufficient housing through practices of redlining (see Fine et al., 2004). These idealisations of neighbourhood give a historical background as to why some urban studies scholars are frustrated that the physical territory of a neighbourhood is often conflated with social communities that live within those territories (Colombo, Mosso and De Piccoli, 2001). Still, the concept of the physical-social neighbourhood persists.

While LGBTQ people have always existed in urban areas (Aldrich, 2004), LGBTQ spaces were most clearly articulated in neighbourhoods (Chauncey, 1995; Weston, 1995). LGBTQ people in the 1970s formed spatial concentrations in urban residential areas which, over time, became more visible and fixed as 'gay ghettos'. Those who lived in or used these spaces experienced more segregation, a reprieve from isolation, and a community from which to develop social and political gains (Knopp, 1997; Enke, 2007). By 1983, Manuel Castells argued that gay men in San Francisco's Castro district were living not in a ghetto but in a 'neighbourhood' based on the confluence of their unique production of culture, economy, and physical spaces (see Castells, 1983). Furthermore, the difference between marginalised ghetto space and gay space was one of agency:

> While [...] others used the term 'ghetto', gay militants speak of 'liberated zones': and there is indeed a major difference between ghettos and gay areas since the latter are usually deliberately constructed by gay people to create their own city, in the framework of the broader urban society.
>
> (p. 272)

Castells went on to claim men's 'territorial aspirations' as the galvanising inspiration for these new spaces. He wrote that while women's more ethereal worlds were unspatialised in 'relationships and [...] networks [...] of solidarity and affection' (140), so that only men possessed agency to produce such physical spaces. Such a viewpoint extols the privileged patriarchal arguments of elite capitalist society, wherein property ownership indicates maturity of both individuals and groups.

In my reading, the majority of research on LGBTQ spaces continues to expand on Castells's understanding of cultural and economic territorialisation in the form of physical, geographical neighbourhoods. Even popular representations of gay male neighbourhoods depict a world in which 'gay male sexuality becomes mature through spatial claiming and territorialization' (Skeggs et al., 2004: 1846). In actuality, gay and queer working class men and men of colour have found their neighbourhoods to be more cyclical as their bars and cruising areas are often dissolved and reconstituted through intermittent practices of cruising and instances of homophobia (Manalansan, 2005). The (supposed) LGBTQ neighbourhood is still the most often referenced LGBTQ space in both academic and popular literature. Through its popularity, idealisation, and role in producing a 'safe space' for LGBTQ people (see Elwood, 2000), the LGBTQ neighbourhood has been read a space of liberation, community, and possibility, particularly through the lens of American ideals of ethnic success via territorialisation. Richard Florida's (2012) marketing of 'creative class' that brings and adds wealth, innovation, and cosmopolitanism to the city via processes identical to gentrification has extended this idealisation of LGBTQ neighbourhoods into the heterosexual public sphere, and perhaps led to their demise (see Ghaziani, 2010).

Scholars of lesbian and queer spaces have sought to respond to this fixation on neighbourhoods, including Castells's arguments that infused them by identifying 'spatial concentrations' of lesbians in various U.S. cities, residential, commercial, or a combination thereof (Wolf, 1979; Adler and Brenner, 1992; Kennedy and Davis, 1994; Kenney, 1998). Yet each of these studies, in the end, relays a concept of 'concentrations' rather than neighbourhoods in that these women do not visibly occupy and control these areas.[1] Unlike gay men's neighbourhoods or cruising grounds, lesbians and queer women are rarely known to possess and retain actual territories within urban areas via mass property ownership (Rothenberg, 1995; Podmore, 2006). Lesbian commercial spaces such as travel agencies, sex toy stores, hair salons, and are sometimes not as present or commercially successful as gay men's commercial spaces, and therefore make these areas less visible (Podmore, 2001), and early waves of gentrifiers who possess less wealth – namely women – are eventually economically displaced by later waves of gentrification (Doan, 2010). Studies in the 1990s found middle-class lesbians to be more educated but make less money than their straight female counterparts (Baker, 1997; Kenney, 2001). Still the continuing debate over lesbian neighbourhoods' existence is most often attributed to women having less access to capital (Adler and Brenner, 1992; Rothenberg, 1995). Yet as Rachel Pain (2001) has suggested, public space continues to evoke feelings of fear in women rather than security, even as such public urban spaces are usually envisioned as the locations of diversity and difference (see Young, 1990). It is unsurprising then that throughout the literature on lesbian and queer spaces, lesbians and queer women are marked and understood as 'invisible'. This invisibility derives from in comparison to the patriarchal and heteronormative social, political, and economic landscape, as well as to heterosexuals; gay, bisexual, and queer men; trans persons; and even among lesbians, bisexuals, and queer women (Wolfe, 1997; Eng, Halberstam, and Muñoz, 2005).

Overall these historic dynamics and overarching structural oppressions make it difficult for lesbians and queer women to produce, let alone sustain, a physical neighbourhood with economic, social, historic, and political ties among its residents and users. The only 'lesbian neighbourhood' mentioned as such in the literature is Brooklyn, New York's Park Slope and is most likely the only lesbian urban neighbourhood in the U.S. Historian Robert Aldrich has suggested that 'New York offered a prototype for American gay cultures' (2004: 1727). Home not only to the beginning of the LGBTQ movement in the 1969 Stonewall riot, the city spawned the three most prominent radical LGBTQ activist groups in recent history including ACT-UP, Lesbian Avengers, and Queer Nation, and its prominent 'gaybourhoods' such as the West Village, Chelsea, and Park Slope inform and propagate U.S. and global LGBTQ geographic imaginaries. While LGBTQ studies have begun to extend to prioritising the rural and other non-urban environments (Knopp and Brown, 2003; Halberstam, 2005; Gray, 2009), studies of the urban are still necessary, especially as only one study of lesbian experience in Park Slope exists. Tamar Rothenberg's (1995) interviews with lesbians about their experiences of Park Slope in the early 1990s found that a 'spatial concentration' of lesbians developed and sustained itself through a spatialised community of social networks and word-of-mouth, as well as the lesbian-queer and lesbian-queer friendly places that put down roots in Park Slope. The neighbourhood's loose spatial community was 'related to the timing of early gentrification and the particular politically-oriented population who moved in' (175). But is Park Slope or was it ever a lesbian or lesbian-queer neighbourhood? This chapter reconnoitres the literature on lesbian-queer neighbourhoods, women's urban spaces, and general LGBTQ neighbourhoods. Drawing upon inter-generational group interviews with lesbians and queer women, and other mixed methods, I reply to Rothenberg's work from a cross-generational, -race, and –class perspective. I suggest that a queering of the concept of neighbourhoods is in order to reveal the fleeting and fragmented qualities of these spaces.

Participatory methods for a participatory understanding of self and space

In order to find a way to talk through and at times against the framework of invisibility, my research made use of participatory qualitative methodologies that connect individual and collective experiences, and bridge the shifts of history with everyday memories. This chapter draws from a larger historical geography of contemporary lesbian and queer society, culture, and economies in New York City. The overall study addresses the shifts in lesbians' and queer women's spaces in New York City from 1983 to 2008 – that is, from the AIDS epidemic to the rise of internationally syndicated television drama 'The L Word' – in order to understand the associated shifts in these women's experiences of justice and oppression over time. I chose a 25 year period in order to address multiple generations of these women's experiences, including the under-examined experiences of lesbians and queer women in the 1980s whose history is often eclipsed by the tragic loss of a generation of mostly gay men dying in the HIV/AIDS epidemic.[2]

Queer theorist Ann Pellegrini's (2004) feminist-queer theorisation of the terminology for gay women's identities implies that 'lesbian' is used by older women more closely identified with second-wave feminism, while 'queer' would apply to younger, third-wave individuals. However, this is not always the case as these identities may be complicated by personal and/or political factors (see also Browne, 2006). I use 'lesbians and queer women' to reference my participants' own naming of their identities, and 'lesbian-queer' as an adjective throughout to describe the experiences of this group of women. I refer to each participant population with the identity and/or term used by that author.

While I highlight many the intersectional identities of participants throughout this chapter, it is also important to situate them as a group for the general arguments of this work. Participants came out (broadly and self-defined) between 1983 and 2008; spent the majority of that time in New York City; and primarily identified as middle or working-middle class, White, and had attended some college.[3] In order to queer notions of community and connection, this study does not use age alone as a marker of generation but foregrounds the year in which participants 'came out'. I theorised that the coming out moment/period often provides a profound shift in consciousness in the years that follow, and my participants agreed. All participants were between the age of 12 and 29 when they came out to follow similar trends in the life course.

The project included within and across generation group interviews with 47 self-identified lesbians and queer women, including mental mapping and artefact-sharing components. Participants took part in three kinds of group interviews: those comprising women within a generational cohort spanning five year periods (1983–1987, 1988–1992, etc.); across generational cohorts from women of different generational cohorts; and a follow-up, private online participatory group interview.[4] A total of 22 group interviews were accompanied by mental mapping exercises whereby participants drew individual maps of places in the city important to them around the time of their coming out, and combined these maps across generations to see trends over time (see Figures 9.2 and 9.3). Participants also took part in artefact sharing exercises which involved presenting an object or memento important to the participant at her time of coming out and explaining its meaning. These conversations and exercises addressed the women's disparate and overlapping experiences while keeping them focused on the spatial qualities of their experiences during and since their coming out. I presented the first draft of summary findings to participants via a private, online blog so that my arguments could be critiqued and formed in a participatory manner, and these responses were incorporated into final arguments.

As this data collection with participants was on-going, I examined records from the Lesbian Herstory Archives in Brooklyn, New York, the largest collection of materials by, for, and about lesbians in the world. This two-pronged approach of collecting primary and secondary research provides a more vivid political and socioeconomic backdrop for the group conversations, maps, and artefacts than previously afforded (cf. e.g. Faderman, 1992; Chauncey, 1995; Nash, 2005; Podmore, 2006). I foremost draw on themes I developed from group interview conversations in this chapter, using archival materials as a lens through which to read the changing geographies of these women's everyday lives.

So what's a lesbian-queer neighbourhood? The special case of Park Slope, Brooklyn

When I asked participants what type of lesbian and/or queer space was most important to their everyday lives in NYC, they consistently chose neighbourhoods, even over more oft-mentioned bars, parties, and the city itself. New York City, like most global cities, operates as a series of characteristic neighbourhoods that afford distinct identities, economies, and politics. Therefore it makes sense that the word 'neighbourhood' was used 186 times in participants' conversations, and 34 neighbourhoods were mentioned by name a total of 695 times. Naming each of these neighbourhoods relayed a sense of what these spaces afforded lesbians and queers. The dramatically large number of neighbourhoods mentioned by name indicates that the concept and experience of the neighbourhood is perhaps less important than the lived experience of these neighbourhoods as residential zones.

The neighbourhood of Park Slope, Brooklyn, was the most often referenced neighbourhood with 201 mentions and therefore the topic of nearly one-quarter of all neighbourhood conversations. As a striking indication of Park Slope's importance to lesbian-queer everyday life in the city, the internationally renowned LGBTQ neighbourhoods of NYC trailed far behind: Greenwich Village, aka West Village (84 mentions); Chelsea (41); East Village (37); and hipster Williamsburg (39) in Brooklyn (see Figure 9.1). While not every participant had interest in or could afford to live there,

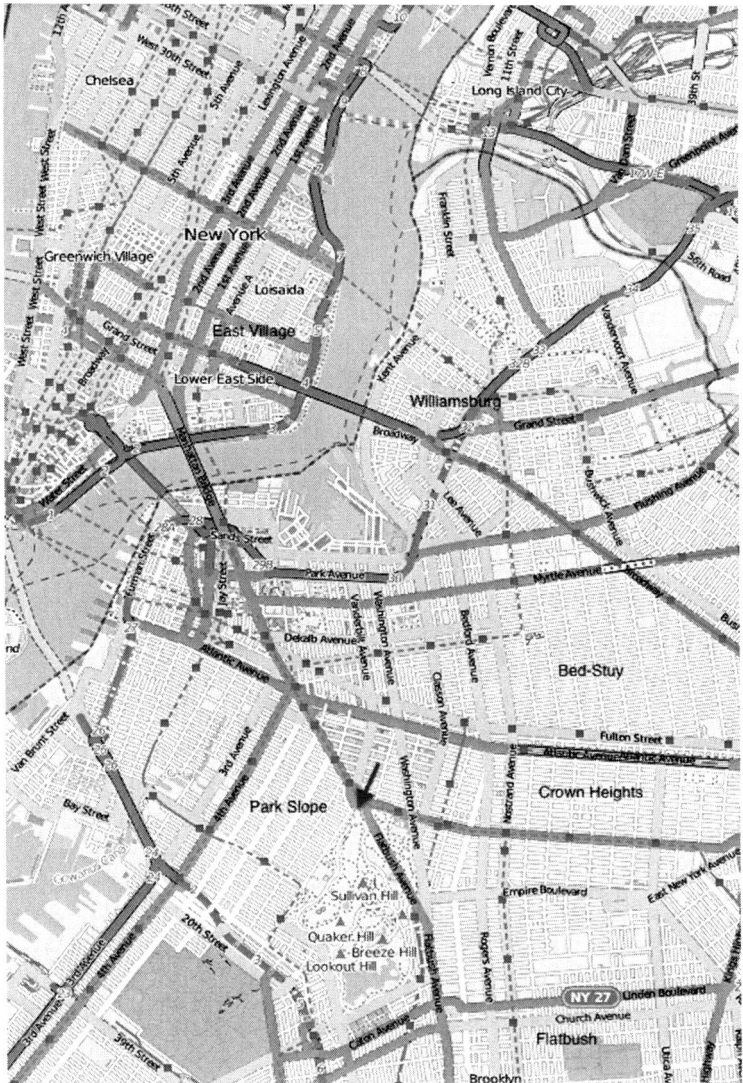

Figure 9.1 Map of Brooklyn and lower Manhattan indicating neighbourhoods; Grand Army Plaza is marked with an arrow. ©OpenStreetMap contributors, CC BY-SA

every participant had been to Park Slope and everyone knew another lesbian and/or queer who lives there or who had lived there.

In order to understand what a lesbian-queer neighbourhood is to participants, I focus on Park Slope, one of if not *the* most well-known, lesbian spatial concentrations in the U.S. (see Figure 9.1). Situated next to prominent Prospect Park in north-central Brooklyn, the boundary of Park Slope has grown in recent years due to ever-present gentrification in New York City. In the 1970s and 1980s, the neighbourhood was predominantly home to working class Blacks and Puerto Ricans, as well as a small population of working class and middle class Whites, many of whom were lesbian. By the 1990s, Park Slope was and continues to be referenced in LGBTQ movies, publications, and websites as a sort of lesbian mecca. Brooklyn Pride, founded in 1996, marches only in Park Slope since its inception. Yet since the early 2000s, Park Slope has been portrayed as a bastion for upper-middle class New York City parenting, namely among the large population of Whites who now reside there, whereby sexualities go unnoticed or unrecognised. As such, over time, the ways in which lesbians fit and feel at home in any space based on class and race has shifted dramatically (Taylor, 2007, 2009), even while the idea of the space as the only lesbian-queer NYC neighbourhood persists. The idea of the lesbian-ness of Park Slope is predicated on few materialities afforded these women, which are far greater in number than the general absence to which they are accustomed. For example, at most, there have been two or three bars at any given time, a women-only gym, a lesbian/women's bookstore, and, most importantly, the Lesbian Herstory Archives.

Producing a territory called Park Slope, generation by generation

Participants shared similar experiences of the neighbourhood, which many referred affectionately to as 'Dyke Slope'. Across races and classes, women who came out in the 1980s and 1990s had more attachments and experiences in living there than those who came out in the 2000s, that is, before the housing process had doubled in the area. Birtha '84 (age 50) who identified as White and her class as 'cultural worker' had lived in Park Slope in the 1980s. She remembered how crack dens dotted the area since the financial crisis in the late 1970s and worsened as a result of the crack epidemic of the 1980s. During this period, participants remembered taking cabs home to Park Slope from workplaces in Manhattan because of the discomfort of being a woman in an urban public sphere, particularly a lesbian who was the target of homophobic attacks. Even in such a seemingly unsafe environment for Birtha, Park Slope offered the promise of a lesbian community she could not find elsewhere. In retrospect, the lesbian spaces and events held there and places that developed there were unaffordable to produce and support over such a long period and on such a large scale in other neighbourhoods.

Gentrifiers – middle class and often White, with many lesbians along them – remodelled crack dens into their former 'brownstone' (a colloquial term for elegant Brooklyn town homes) glory throughout the 1990s. Black, middle class Desi '89 (age 35) was 15 when, following her weekly youth group at The LGBT Community Center of New York, she would eagerly make the 30 minute train ride to Park Slope. Once there, she would sit at a coffee shop, do her homework, and, as she described it, see what she was supposed to look like when she 'grew up'. Radical and stand out lesbian-queer styles of the 1980s (such as the power dyke or activist aesthetic) and 1990s (that blended both looks into even more radical styles with mohawks, piercings, and tattoos) dominated the streets and denoted a lesbian-queer presence (see Valentine, 1996). The burgeoning LGBTQ market stood out in the Pride flags that dotted the region and the rainbow bracelets and activist shirts that were sold more and more widely then denoted a sign of resistance. These better futures were not only embodied in the lesbian-queer bodies she saw, but in an entire territory that supported such embodiments during periods of heightened homophobia.

Even in 2008, White, working-middle class Lisa '97 (age 39) shared how she and her partner travel from their more affordable apartment in a less tolerant, White-ethnic neighbourhood deeper into in Brooklyn back to Park Slope every couple of weeks: 'We get out of the subway, and suddenly you can breathe and hold hands.' Safety and comfort became more certain as time progressed due to waves of gentrification into Park Slope through the 1990s. However, participants made clear that this sense of justice was almost exclusively for White women and for middle and upper class women of colour. These trends made spaces popular while still affordable, and, subsequently, a highly social atmosphere. The ability for lesbians and queer women to outright claim Park Slope as a lesbian-queer neighbourhood evolved in these interdependent processes and practices. And, as soon as some headway was made for some, that sense of community and connectivity, both social and spatial, became less palpable.

By the turn of the century, Park Slope was more and more composed of now elegant, renovated brownstones, tree-lined streets, and throngs of small, welcoming shops which erase and price out much of the lesbian-queer presence. Through the eyes of those women who came out in the 2000s, one may not be sure what is 'so gay' about Park Slope. Participants were unlikely to live in or spend the majority of their time in Park Slope unless they had purchased their apartment in the 1990s, so much so that no one who had come out in the 2000s mentioning residing there. However, all participants frequented Park Slope's bars, restaurants, events, or merely to walk around in a LGBTQ space for women, especially when coming out. The neighbourhood housed one lesbian bar as of 2008 (which still stands in

2012), and parties are thrown in lesbian-queer friendly spaces. At the same time, more wild styles, looks, and appearances have been absorbed by hipster chic while Pride flags have become passé. What is LGBTQ is now often illegible in the White, middle class rhetoric of politically correct liberalism. Participants described how lesbians and queer women are less recognisable to one another on the streets of NYC, and became less visible as a population to heteronormative, mainstream society.

Still, the spatial evidence of 'Dyke Slope' remains. While Rothenberg (1995) argued that Park Slope lacked 'distinct' lesbian places in the early 1990s, participants in this study felt much more comfortable in the 2000s marking spaces as their own based on their safety and comfort in and access to such spaces, even if they could not claim them outright. A number of places such as the Brooklyn Women's Martial Arts Center and the Park Slope Food Co-op read more so as lesbian-queer-friendly spaces than actual spaces of their own. These places persist and their continued importance to lesbians and queer women continues. In so doing, Park Slope retains its place in the lesbian-queer geographical imagination as a lesbian-queer neighbourhood even though it does not offer all lesbians and queer women equal refuge or promise.

Race and class: Claiming space and/or gentrification

White, upper middle class Sarah '85 (age 41) recalled how safety as a claim to the neighbourhood had to always be reproduced in the act of claiming and being there:

> But, you know, there's been a number of times I've walked down the street holding hands with my girlfriend in Park Slope in the '80s and we'd get yelled at. Some old, Irish guys shouted at us, 'Go back to San Francisco!' … Like, 'I live on St Mark's Place [a street in the heart of Park Slope]! I don't know what to tell you.' That was pretty hilarious.

Sarah's residence on St. Mark's Place, a core artery of Park Slope, refigures the neighbourhood as lesbian-queer against the 'old, Irish guy'. It is a space where Sarah's White, upper-middle class body belongs and his body, presumably working class, aged, and White, fits alongside her in a way, implying also that needs to catch up to what is modern (Binnie and Skeggs, 2004). She uses her St. Mark's Place address in the heart of Park Slope to both laugh off a verbal assault and to legitimate and claim a place for her body and identity in the heart of the neighbourhood and its meaning. Mixed-race, working-middle class Bailey '95 (age 29) described how that Fifth Avenue in Park Slope 'used to be largely Puerto Rican and so I'm sure that there were Puerto Rican lesbians there who didn't get fucked with' but gentrification had forced almost all of these women out by 2008. It is at the intersection of

Sarah's laughter and Bailey's anger that how *unsafe* the economic land grab of gentrification is. Not only does it produce negative images of mostly White and mostly middle class LGBTQ people in the midst of poor neighbourhoods of colour which then inflicts more homophobia with those communities, such gentrification is clearly not a sustainable tactic of these women's resilience or resistance to homophobia and sexism because it eventually moves them out of those spaces they increased in value as well. Castells (1983) painted this shift towards the neighbourhood as a path to better tomorrows for gay men, but this trend continues to leave women, people of colour, and the poor forced to out further environs from the city centre.

White participants of varying classes sometimes felt unsafe in Park Slope, like Birtha, but often felt free to occupy the neighbourhood's venues and streets, even during the 1980s and 1990s when the neighbourhood was less moneyed and still home to a large Black and Puerto Rican population. Black-Caribbean, working class Tre '03 (age 21) had grown up in the nearby working class, Caribbean neighbourhood of Crown Heights, northeast of Park Slope (see Figure 9.1). She described how her patterns of access to neighbourhoods were regulated by her skin colour and class, as well as the homophobia that surrounded her:

> But spaces in between there was – access? It was just, like, you don't go there. We did not go to Park Slope. Park Slope felt – you – you knew you weren't – it was just like – mmmm. You shouldn't belong here. Shouldn't belong here. ... And that's not sexuality, that's blackness. ... I don't fuck around in my neighbourhood. Like I don't hold my girlfriend's hand, like if you see that – I'm whatever – I don't play. I do after the Grand Army Plaza stop. Then I'm fucking with it. So Park Slope. [Sarcastically] Yay. ... Um, and then skip over to Manhattan.

Many women of colour referenced the Grand Army Plaza as drawn in Tre's map (see Figure 9.2; also see Figure 9.1, Grand Army Plaza is the arrow at the northeast point of Park Slope) as the absolute borderland between predominantly African-Caribbean-American and working class Crown Heights and Flatbush neighbourhoods, both as the subway underground and the memorial statue on the site above dividing Park Slope from Crown Heights. It makes sense that many participants of colour marked a shared boundary at Grand Army Plaza about where they could express their lesbian-ness and/or queerness regardless of race and class more easily within Park Slope, but still did not feel they belonged. Above or below, there is no escaping the literal and figurative intersection of these oppressions. At the same time, while Tre does not feel welcome in Park Slope because of her Blackness, she uses Park Slope as the borderland of where she *can* be publicly gay, like sliding on a suit of White, middle class privilege as armour. Participants of colour discussed the struggles they experienced about finding a neighbourhood

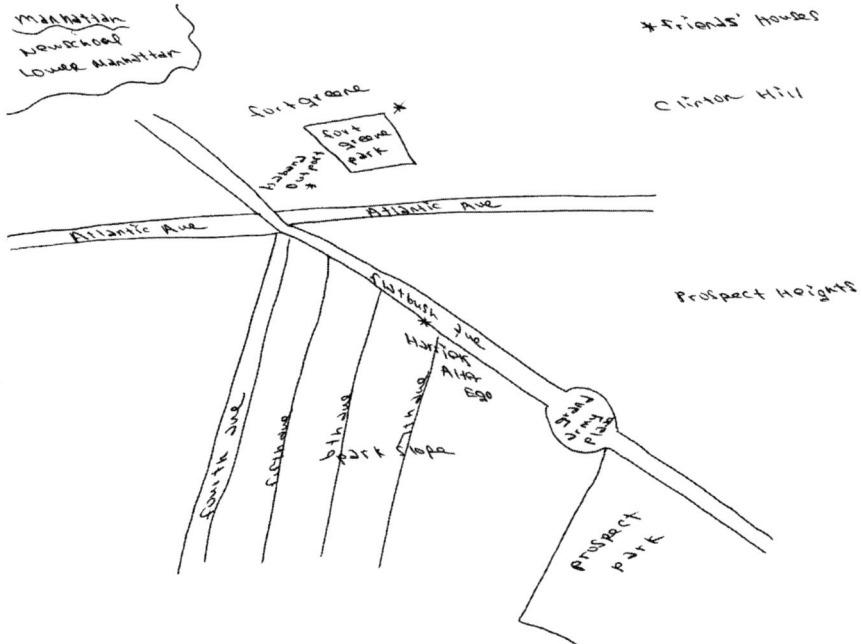

Figure 9.2   Tre '03's mental map of important lesbian-queer spaces in NYC

where they felt understood about their race as well as their sexuality, especially Black participants. Latina participants found that Latina/o neighbourhoods varied in levels of acceptance of lesbians. The history of the pricing out of poor lesbians of colour is always overlooked for the sake of claiming an LGBTQ haven. This denial allows lesbians and queer women to live in the projection of the imagined Park Slope while recognition, representation, and redistribution are so vastly lacking.

In her research on the neighbourhood, Rothenberg (1995) discussed how the Park Slope boundary remained unfixed and continued to spill into – that is, claim space from – other neighbourhoods in the early 1990s. By 2008 when I conducted my research, that spillage had stopped. Later waves of gentrification more forcefully demarcated different neighbourhoods from one another, and producing a hard boundary of Park Slope, for now. Mixed race, working-middle class Bailey '95 identified participants remarked that she knew how to 'talk' White and 'wear Whiteness' in her gestures and voice in order to camouflage herself into belonging or a state of power, even if the affect was not as secure. It is unsurprising then that many women of colour participants marked a shared boundary at Grand Army Plaza about where they could express their lesbian-ness and/or queerness more easily within Park Slope regardless of race and class, but still did not feel they truly belonged. Participants recalled how affective needs for safety and comfort shifted over time in response to varying levels and types of homophobia, sexism, racism, and classism. I suggest then that a neighbourhood was more often a territory to navigate those oppressions rather than an absolute, material refuge for these women. These findings illuminate how the concept of the lesbian-queer neighbourhood not only legitimates lesbian-queer presences but points out their absences in and refusals to these spaces.

Fleeting and fragmented, that is, the queered notion of neighbourhood

Participants clearly demonstrated a need for and an idea of a territory, but the patterns of gentrification show that their place in it is unsteady and not wholly welcoming. Regardless, across generations, all participants agreed Park Slope was a core, if not the core, anchor of the lesbian-queer world in New York City. Yet White, upper-middle class Sarah '85 (age 41) who moved there soon after coming out in its 1990s lesbian-queer heyday shared:

> I almost never go to Park Slope. I feel like it's not a lesbian neighbourhood [now]. … [M]y girlfriend's aunt lived there in the '70s and when we moved there in 1989 she was like, 'Oh! It's not a lesbian neighbourhood anymore! All of the Columbus Avenue [wealthy, predominantly White elites] people have moved in.' … like all of the … institutions, like, The Rising [Café and Bar].

In fact, almost all participants noted there was often something missing about their experience of Park Slope, as if they had just missed it, or were at the apex or tail end of it. Rothenberg's participants in her 1995 study of Park Slope also recognised their spaces bore a 'loose configuration'. What is most important about this looseness is recognising how the sense of the lesbian-queer neighbourhood assumes an eternally fleeting or devolving dynamic. Even as New York City itself is constantly changing, participants reiterated how the loss of the few places they had to call their own was profound. Together with oppressions of homophobia and patriarchy, as well as racism and classism, the precarity of everyday lesbian-queer life results in few places and territories these women can lay claim to and sustain.

As the boundaries of Park Slope have grown over time due to gentrification, these places grow less and less clustered, which leaves a sense of increasing fragmentation in participants' experiences of the neighbourhood. Lesbian-queer spaces and places in the city are often fragmented as, for example, in Brenda '95's (age 40) map (Figure 9.3). Brenda's spaces and places dot the landscape spanning multiple boroughs (i.e. NYC counties) and even draw in

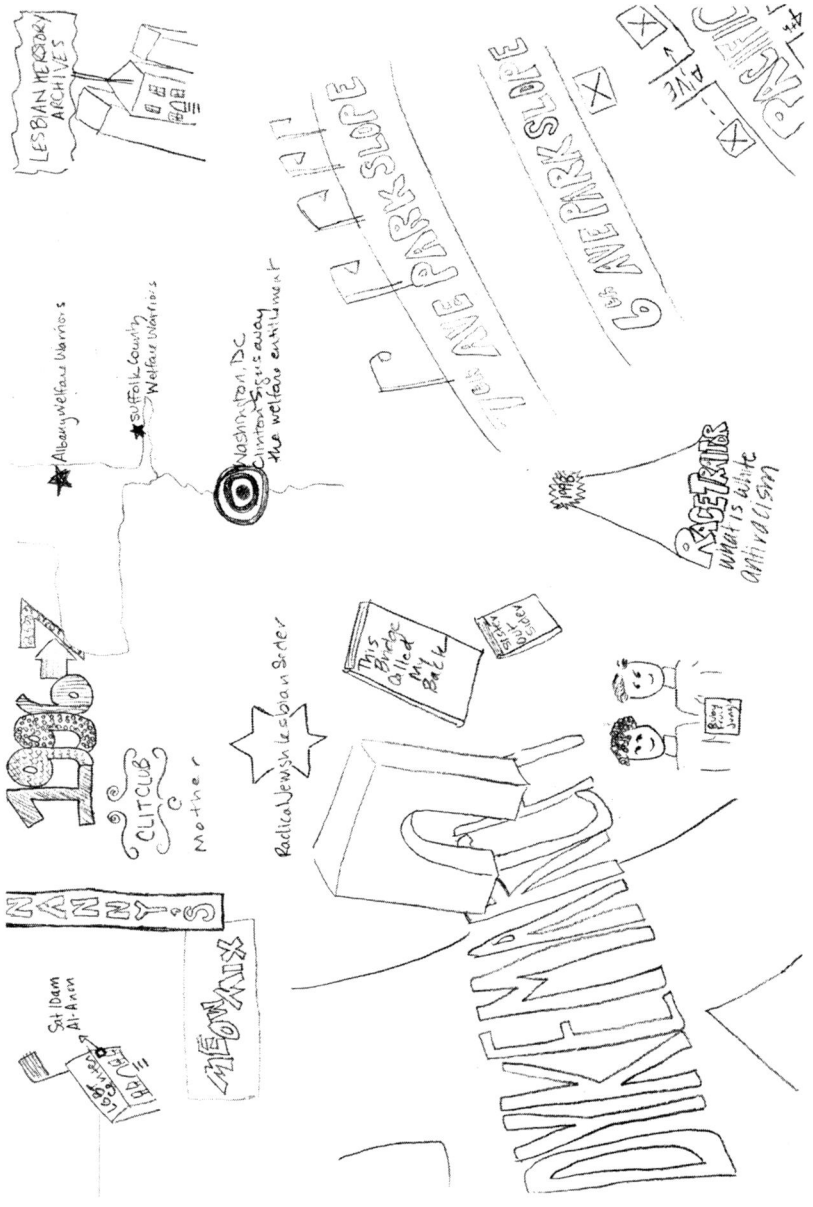

Figure 9.3 Brenda '95's mental map of important lesbian-queer spaces in NYC

connections to experiences in other cities, towns, and the State of New York which is drawn in the top centre of the map. On the right-hand side of the map a series of streets and the Lesbian Herstory Archives congeal the space of Park Slope in the late 1990s, while the bars in the top left corner (Crazy Nanny's, Meow Mix, Clit Club), the LGBT Center of New York, and Dyke March were/are scattered through a number of neighbourhoods.

In many of our conversations, participants debated whether practices of claiming and sustenance supported lesbian feminist and/or queer politics. A core characteristic of neighbourhoods is their physical territoriality, but this is less evident for lesbians and queer women in both Rothenberg's and my own research. While Rothenberg illuminated the importance of spatial clustering of lesbians queer women, and their places and events around similar social, cultural, economic, and political values, my participants described less interest or ability in such outright, permanent spatial clustering. Rather, participants suggested that although they desired places and spaces to call their own, the very nature of territory-making and -claiming was politically and economically questionable to many. When I asked participants about the possibility of lesbian-queer territories to which White, middle class Sally '96 (age 30) responded:

> I think there's something a little insidious about colonising a patch of land and calling it your own and taking out everything else and owning everything. It's just not – it doesn't quite appeal to me, but on the other hand sometimes it does because you see what men have and ... yeah [sighs].

The likening of territorialisation to a practice of physical, patriarchal colonisation repeated many participants' desires to not produce the kind of exclusive spaces from which they themselves had been rejected. In so doing, participants expressed how they saw themselves defying processes of oppression that served to deny their equality. In another expression of this tendency, I suggest that gay and queer men's practices of cruising for anonymous sex in areas of public parks or pornographic movie theatres is erroneously labelled as a timeless, radical use of public space for all LGBTQ people without taking account of gender (see Chisholm, 2005); such publics are not accessible in everyday life or even in the geographical imaginations of most lesbian-queer participants. While Harvey (1973) once sought to articulate an idea of 'territorial justice,' the uneven development under capitalism necessarily makes territories unequal. Seeking to territorialise then is no solution or politic to support the recognition and safety lesbians and queer women seek.

Podmore suggests lesbian urban territorialities in Toronto are 'invisible' since their communities are constituted through social networks rather than commercial sites' (Podmore, 2006: 595). However, my participants felt little allegiance to the notion of 'territory' at all, and did feel that place and space and social networks served a role in formulating a sense of connection and community. Physical territories were seen as somewhat distinct from lesbian-queer neighbourhoods more as a practice of long-term place claiming and property ownership and play less of a role in the lesbian-queer production of neighbourhoods. The meaning and survival of Park Slope and its existence as a LGBTQ mecca of New York City and its role as its only lesbian-queer neighbourhood is not determined by claiming and defending a physical territory. This way of identifying became clear since the take-off of the LGBTQ marker became more a tool to commodify, sexualise, and fetishise LGBTQ people and their interests rather than support social change for LGBTQ people. Many participants were distressed that most LGBTQ social interactions seemed to involve costly cover fees, especially when younger and/or first coming out. For example, the Starbucks-ification of urban landscapes erased the small, specific LGBTQ-friendly coffee shops so popular in the 1990s that felt more safe and welcoming than generic coffee places. As small increases in acceptance towards lesbians and gay were notable during my period of study (1983–2008) (see Yang, 1997), the desire for a place of their own to buffer against the vast levels of non-acceptance still remains. This sentiment expounded especially by women who came out in the 1980s and 1990s, working class women, and women of colour.

Discussion: So what's a lesbian-queer neighbourhood?

> The very concentration of lesbians [in Park Slope] has created a recognisable social space – recognisable most importantly to each other.
>
> Rothenberg (1995: 180)

Park Slope is a paradox. Since the 1970s, lesbians and queer women constituted a neighbourhood in Park Slope, but processes of sexism, homophobia, racism, and classism, as well as the gentrification that binds all of them, show how unstable this space is. In recent years, LGBTQ identity has become increasingly bound to these 'neighbourhoods and territories in which material and symbolic expressions of homosexuality are clearly visible and, increasingly, the status of these cities as destinations in the global gay and lesbian travel marketplace' (Markwell, 2002: 87). From my participants' conversations and maps, it is clear that lesbians and queer women do not produce neighbourhoods like gay men or in any traditional sense of the neighbourhood. The precarious political and economic position of women, LGBTQ people, and the double jeopardy of being lesbians and queer women make these women's spaces fleeting and fragmented. Participants who had come out in the 2000s often felt they could not 'find' or 'see' Park Slope when they visited, especially that same generation of women who wore less lesbian- and/or queer-specific styles with which to produce recognisably lesbian-queer streets. The lesbian-queer market was once a social, political, and economic form of solidarity (Chasin, 2001), but some LGBTQ people repurposed the LGBTQ market as a way to homonormalise and absent their difference, and others had the market commodified out from under them. Duggan's homonormativity necessitates that the LGBTQ people uphold 'a privatized, depoliticized gay culture anchored in domesticity and consumption' (2002: 197). Quite differently, my participants sought not to homonormalise through their attachment to the space of the LGBTQ neighbourhood, but rather they sought to find one another, and hold on to the idea if not the experience a place for themselves. While fragmented places are a common phenomenon of lesbians-queer spaces (Podmore, 2001), I want to emphasise how important it is that 47 women with such disparate backgrounds consistently framed the Park Slope neighbourhood as affording them with historic, social, and political recognition and connection in the form of a neighbourhood they were unable to produce elsewhere.

Those spaces and experiences that were specifically lesbian-queer were often piecemeal and vanishing, but congealed into a space with boundaries, institutions, and thoroughfares. This thickening into a neighbourhood keeps its hold through these women's reiterated experiences of recognition and expectations of safety, access, and comfort. While Park Slope is experienced as a neighbourhood for lesbians and queer women, particularly compared to other LGBTQ spaces often dominated by gay and queer men, Park Slope also exists as this bastion of possibility and security because so many other neighbourhoods limit and threaten lesbians' and queer women's everyday lives. For working class women and women of colour, Park Slope increasingly feels like a foreign, rich, White, gentrified environment for normative models of families – both homo and hetero. Still it continues to provide a form of cover if not recognition for them in findings acceptance for their sexuality if not their skin colour, income, and education level.

The supposition that lesbian-queer neighbourhoods do not exist because they do not support the model of physical and commercial territoriality core to traditional models of neighbourhoods is faulty. I take a different route, following the possibilities of resistance afforded by queer theory to claim these women are illegitimate in their claims is to make lesbians and queer women fit the traditional models of the neighbourhood, which reproduces the limited spatial models of queer subjectivities and weakens the power of queer agency. Lesbians and queer women experience and produce the neighbourhood of Park Slope, in many ways, as their own. The necessary course of action is to queer the meaning and definition of neighbourhoods themselves.

Reading the lesbian-queer neighbourhood against the solid, fixed, visible Castro district examined by Castells, a new way of thinking and understanding space emerges. It is not lesbians and queer women who needs to change their practices or understandings of their space to 'claim' it, but that the definition of neighbourhoods must be queered to account for these women's experiences. The lesbian-queer neighbourhood is produced in the specific, temporal, fragmented, fleeting, and unstable elements of a comparatively invisible neighbourhood. Lesbians and queer women fit together these social, cultural, historic, economic, and political dynamics to claim not only a politic of visibility but a space and politics of recognition in contemporary New York City. It is this recognition that Rothenberg's previous quote attests to, that is the driving force of the Park Slope as a persistent lesbian-queer neighbourhood, and a space that queers the meaning of neighbourhood. Like Deborah Martin's approach to neighbourhoods, the 'enacted neighbourhood' of Park Slope as it is produced by lesbians and queer women is produced by the practices of everyday life rather than mere structural forces and, as such, is a territory of 'intangible and imagined product of action rather than a fixed space' (2003: 377). From its embedded position in New York City history, women's history, and LGBTQ history, Park Slope affords lesbians and queer women support for political action to continually improve their lives.

What the lesbian-queer neighbourhood, then, affords not only lesbians, queer women, and others is the malleability to spatialise their sense of community, imagined and otherwise, and to do so to promote social and spatial justice. The colonising physical territory can be redrawn for those who get by or prefer other more fleeting and fragmented spaces. Such a queering of the meaning and affordances of neighbourhoods also makes way for more types of 'scenes' (see Taylor, 2008), producing spaces of difference and for difference, in terms of race and class especially. More recent scholarship has pointed out how notions of neighbourhood and community are not synonymous, nor are they ever homogenous (Colombo, Mosso and De Piccoli, 2001). This type of fixed thinking between the meaning of space and society must be queered and altered too in order to afford these women the right to the city on their own terms.

Acknowledgements

I am forever thankful to Joana Coppi, as well as Desiree M. Fields, Rachel Goffe, Elizabeth R. Johnson, and the editors of this volume for their comments on this chapter and their incredible support; all mistakes are my own. This research was supported by the following fellowships and awards: Joan Heller – Diane Bernard Fellowship in Lesbian and Gay Studies from the Center for Lesbian and Gay Studies; Woodrow Wilson Dissertation Fellowship in Women's Studies; Center for Place, Culture, and Politics; and the CUNY Graduate Center Proshansky Dissertation Award and Doctoral Students Research Grant. I dedicate this chapter to Tamar Rothenberg in thanks for her work.

Notes

1. This focus on urban environments does not take up lesbian-identified towns such as Northampton, Massachusetts (Forsyth, 1997) or Asheville, North Carolina (Doan,

2007). Similarly, UK gay villages such as Brighton and Manchester have become increasingly LGBTQ identified during the study period so that, today, most if not all of the towns are assumed to be LGBTQ-welcoming if not LGBTQ-friendly.

2. Rather than begin this study based upon an important moment for gay and queer men's experiences or a dominant narrative of LGBTQ people in general, 1983 was selected to queer the focus of passing time on the everyday lives of lesbian-queer participants and to locate their knowledge in their own time and space (see Inckle, 2010). Furthermore, the year 1983 was also chosen as the starting point because three influential texts on LGBTQ spaces and their associated economies appeared (Anderson, 1983; Castells, 1983; D'Emilio, 1983). Selecting 2008 as the endpoint afforded participants the opportunity to compare their past to the present, in the year the study was conducted, which in retrospect stops as the credit and fore-closure crisis and recession began in the U.S. and became clear and rooted at an international level. This project seeks to confront and queer the spatial and temporal invisibilisation of lesbian-queer spaces, bodies, and experiences of injustice through the choice of site and period.

3. Participants ranged in age from 18 to 57, with a median age of 32. Extra efforts were made to recruit women of colour and working class and upper class women by attending bars, parties, and events that these women frequent; however, a large number of self-identified women of colour dropped out due to time constraints. It is of note that the histories of upper class lesbians are notoriously absent from the bar- and neighbourhood-based studies to date, as these women often socialise in private parties in their homes or elite locales (see Moore, 2006). No one identified as upper class, which may be linked to lesbian-feminist politics in the 1970s to seek downward mobility (Enke, 2007). Like many American study groups, participants were likely to not identify their social class or identify as middle class (27 total), but 13 women identified as working or working-middle class, and 10 as upper-middle class, often claiming multiple class identities which they linked to their education levels and these high levels of education are common among middle class U.S. lesbians and queer women. I had hoped that frequenting venues and events in working class neighbourhoods or popular among this social class would secure the participation of those who had not finished college or high school but this was unsuccessful. Only one participant had not yet finish high school and the remaining had some college. A total of 37 participants identified as White or White-Jewish, six women identified as mixed race, and two women, each, identified as Black and Latina. One participant chose not to identify her gender, and all others identified their gender as female, woman, femme, or butch.

4. Mannheim's (1972) concept of 'political generations' became useful when grouping lesbians' and queer women's shared and unique geographies into eras specific to their political experience and range of action. With an eye to determining lesbian-queer 'political generations' in this study, I broke participants into what I call 'generational cohorts' of five-year blocks (1983–7, 1988–92, etc.) (see Gieseking, 2007). I also use this idea to theorise the generational breakdowns further.

Bibliography

Adler, S. Y. and Brenner, J. (1992) 'Gender and space: Lesbian and gay men in the city', *International Journal of Urban & Regional Research*, 16(1): 24–34.

Aldrich, R. (2004) 'Homosexuality and the city: An historical overview', *Urban Studies*, 41(9): 1719–37.

Anderson, B. (1983) *Imagined communities: Reflections on the origin and spread of nationalism*. New York: Verso.

Baker, D. (1997) 'A history in ads: The growth of the gay and lesbian market' in A. Gluckman and B. Reed (eds) *Homo economics: Capitalism, community, and lesbian and gay life*. New York: Routledge, pp. 11–20.

Binnie, J. and Skeggs, B. (2004) 'Cosmopolitan knowledge and the production and consumption of sexualized space: Manchester's gay village', *The Sociological Review*, 52(1): 39–61.

Browne, K. (2006) 'Challenging queer geographies', *Antipode: A Radical Journal of Geography*, 38(5): 885–93.

Castells, M. (1983) 'Cultural identity, sexual liberation and urban structure: The gay community in San Francisco' in *The city and the grassroots: A cross-cultural theory of urban social movements*. Berkeley, CA: University of California Press, pp. 138–72.

Chasin, A. (2001) *Selling out: The gay and lesbian movement goes to market*. New York: Palgrave Macmillan.

Chauncey, G. (1995) *Gay New York: Gender, urban culture, and the making of the gay male world, 1890–1940*. New York: Basic Books.

Chisholm, D. (2005) *Queer constellations: Subcultural space in the wake of the city*. Minneapolis, MN: University of Minnesota Press.

Colombo, M., Mosso, C. and De Piccoli, N. (2001) 'Sense of community and participation in urban contexts', *Journal of Community & Applied Social Psychology*, 11(6): 457–64.

Crenshaw, K. (1996) 'Mapping the margins: Intersectionality, identity politics, and violence against women of color' in K. Crenshaw, N. Gotanda and G. Peller (eds) *Critical race theory: The key writings that formed the movement*. New York: The New Press, pp. 357–83.

D'Emilio, J. (1983) *Sexual politics, sexual communities*. Chicago: University Of Chicago Press.

Doan, P. L. (2007) 'Queers in the American city: Transgendered perceptions of urban space', *Gender, Place & Culture: A Journal of Feminist Geography*, 14(1): 57–74.

Doan, P. L. (2010) 'The tyranny of gendered spaces – Reflections from beyond the gender dichotomy', *Gender, Place & Culture: A Journal of Feminist Geography*, 17(5): 635–54.

Duggan, L. (2002) 'The new homonormativity: The sexual politics of neoliberalism' in R. Castronovo and D. D. Nelson (eds) *Materializing democracy: Toward a revitalized cultural politics*. Durham, NC: Duke University Press, pp. 175–94.

Elder, G. S. (1999) '"Queerying" boundaries in the geography classroom', *Journal of Geography in Higher Education*, 23(1): 86–93.

Elwood, S. (2000) 'Lesbian living spaces: Multiple meanings of home' in G. Valentine (ed.) *From nowhere to everywhere: Lesbian geographies*. Binghamton, NY: Harrington Park Press, pp. 11–28.

Eng, D. L., Halberstam, J. and Muñoz, J. E. (2005) 'What's queer about queer studies now?' *Social Text*, 23(3/4): 1–17.

Enke, A. (2007) *Finding the movement: Sexuality, contested space, and feminist activism*. Durham, NC: Duke University Press.

Faderman, L. (1992) *Odd girls and twilight lovers: A history of lesbian life in twentieth-century America*. New York: Penguin.

Fine, M., Weis, L., Powell Pruitt, L. and Burns, A. (eds) (2004) *Off white: Readings on race, power, and society*, Second edition. New York: Routledge.

Florida, R. (2012) *The rise of the creative class – Revisited: 10th Anniversary Edition – Revised and Expanded*. New York: Basic Books.

Forsyth, A. (1997) '"Out" in the valley', *International Journal of Urban and Regional Research*, 21(1): 38–62.

Ghaziani, A. (2010) 'There goes the gayborhood?' *Contexts*, 9(4): 64–6.

Gieseking, J. (2007) '(Re)Constructing women: Scaled portrayals of privilege and gender norms on campus', *Area*, 39(3): 278–86.

Gray, M. (2009) *Out in the country: Youth, media, and queer visibility in rural America*. New York: NYU Press.

Gregory, D., Johnston, R., Pratt, G., Watts, M. and Whatmore, S. (eds) (2009) *The dictionary of human geography*, Fifth edition. Malden, MA: Wiley-Blackwell.

Halberstam, J. (2005) *In a queer time and place: Transgender bodies, subcultural lives*. New York: NYU Press.

Harvey, D. (1973) *Social justice and the city*. Baltimore, MD: The Johns Hopkins University Press.

Inckle, K. (2010) 'Bent: Non-normative embodiment as lived intersectionality' in Y. Taylor, S. Hines and M. E. Casey (eds) *Theorizing intersectionality and sexuality*. New York: Palgrave Macmillan, pp. 255–73.

Kennedy, E. and Davis, M. (1994) *Boots of leather, slippers of gold: The history of a lesbian community*. New York: Penguin.

Kenney, M. R. (1998) 'Remember, Stonewall was a riot: Understanding gay and lesbian experience in the city' in L. Sandercock (ed.) *Making the invisible visible: A multicultural planning history*. Berkeley, CA: University of California Press, pp. 120–32.

Kenney, M. R. (2001) *Mapping gay L.A.: The intersection of place and politics*. Philadelphia, PA: Temple University Press.

Knopp, L. (1997) 'Gentrification and gay neighborhood formation in New Orleans: A case study' in A. Gluckman and B. Reed (eds) *Homo economics: Capitalism, community, and lesbian and gay life*. New York: Routledge, pp. 45–64.

Knopp, L. and Brown, M. (2003) 'Queer diffusions', *Environment and Planning D: Society and Space*, 21(4): 409–24.

Manalansan, IV, M. (2005) 'Race, violence, and neoliberal spatial politics in the global city', *Social Text*, 23(3/4): 141–55.

Markwell, K. (2002) 'Mardi Gras tourism and the construction of Sydney as an international gay and lesbian city.' *GLQ: A Journal of Lesbian and Gay Studies*, 8(1): 81–99.

Mannheim, K. (1972) 'The problem of generations' in P. G. Altbach and R. S. Laufer (eds) *The new pilgrims: Youth protest in transition*. New York: David McKay, pp. 101–38.

Moore, M. R. (2006) 'Lipstick or timberlands? Meanings of gender presentation in black lesbian communities', *Signs: Journal of Women in Culture and Society*, 32(1): 113–39.

Moore, M. R. (2011) *Invisible families: Gay identities, relationships, and motherhood among black women*. Berkeley: University of California Press.

Nash, C. J. (2005) 'Contesting identity: Politics of gays and lesbians in Toronto in the 1970s', *Gender, Place & Culture: A Journal of Feminist Geography*, 12(1): 113–35.

Pain, R. (2001) 'Gender, race, age and fear in the city', *Urban Studies*, 38(5–6): 899–913.

Pellegrini, A. (2004) 'Mind the gap?' *GLQ: A Journal of Lesbian and Gay Studies*, 10(4): 637–9.

Podmore, J. A. (2001) 'Lesbians in the crowd: Gender, sexuality and visibility along Montréal's Boul. St-Laurent', *Gender, Place & Culture: A Journal of Feminist Geography*, 8(4): 333–55.

Podmore, J. A. (2006) 'Gone "underground"? Lesbian visibility and the consolidation of queer space in Montréal', *Social & Cultural Geography*, 7(4): 595–625.

Rothenberg, T. Y. (1995) '"And she told two friends": Lesbians creating urban social space' in D. J. Bell and G. Valentine (eds) *Mapping desire: Geographies of sexualities.* New York: Routledge, pp. 165–81.

Skeggs, B., Moran, L., Tyrer, P. and Binnie, J. (2004) 'Queer as folk: Producing the real of urban space', *Urban Studies*, 41(9): 1839–56.

Taylor, Y. (2007) *Working class lesbian life: Classed outsiders.* New York: Palgrave Macmillan.

Taylor, Y. (2008) '"That's not really my scene": Working-class lesbians in (and out of) place', *Sexualities*, 11(5): 523–46.

Taylor, Y. (2009) *Lesbian and gay parenting: Securing social and educational capital.* New York: Palgrave Macmillan.

Valentine, G. (1996) '(Re)Negotiating the "heterosexual street"' in N. Duncan (ed.) *BodySpace: Destabilizing geographies of gender and sexuality.* New York: Routledge, pp. 155–69.

Weston, K. (1995) 'Get thee to a big city: Sexual imaginary and the great gay migration', *GLQ: A Journal of Lesbian and Gay Studies*, 2(3): 253–77.

Wolf, D. G. (1979) *The lesbian community.* Berkeley, CA: University of California Press.

Wolfe, M. (1997) 'Invisible women in invisible places: The production of social space in lesbian bars' in A. Bouthillette and Y. Retter (eds) *Queers in space: Communities, public places, sites of resistance.* Seattle, WA: Bay Press, pp. 301–24.

Yang, A. S. (1997) 'Trends: Attitudes toward homosexuality', *The Public Opinion Quarterly*, 61(3): 477–507.

Young, I. M. (1990) *Justice and the politics of difference.* Princeton, NJ: Princeton University Press.

Part III
'Queer Presences and Absences: Everyday and Everywhere?'

10
Present Absences: Hidden Geographies of Lesbian Parenting

Karina Luzia

Introduction

Recent geographical scholarship emerging from the UK and the US on the diverse queer/questioning, undecided, intersex, lesbian, transgender/transsexual, bisexual, asexual and gay, or 'quiltbag'[1] identities and communities has drawn attention, both to the theoretical perspectives that ignore lived experiences of certain sexual subjects, and to the invisibilities in empirical research into the everyday realities of identifying as queer[2] (Brown, 2008; Gabb, 2005; Taylor, 2008, Valentine, 2008). This body of work intersects with another within the social sciences, that argues that the complexities and diversity of 'queer' life – that is, other than urban, white, middle-class and able-bodied gay men and lesbians in Western, neoliberal, industrialised societies – are under-represented (Bell and Binnie, 2004; Duggan, 2002; Puar, 2006; Taylor, 2008, 2009). This chapter draws on this knowledge work around sexuality, everyday life and space to highlight some 'queer absences' that become apparent at such junctions; namely, knowledge of everyday 'quiltbag' family[3] life outside the UK, European and US context, and specifically, the everyday socio-spatialities of women parenting together[4] in Australia.

In one sense, this focus on the social geographies of Australian lesbian mothers who are more-or-less comfortably situated within the intersections of professional, educated, employed, white, Western and middle-class identities, situates this chapter within the active discussion around relatively privileged forms of queer life that in many ways 'replicate(s) aspects of state-endorsed heterosexual primacy and prestige located in the home and related practices' (Brown, 2009: 1499). However, this analysis, based on Australian case-studies and taking into account local Australian cultures and practices, also reveals very localised instances and geographically-specific experiences of what Elizabeth Peel (2001) has called 'mundane heterosexism', and in doing so, underscores those everyday experiences that do not fit so neatly into those 'homonormative' representations of lesbian home and family life that have been largely constructed and debated within other national contexts. This explication of the socio-spatial specificities of same-sex parenting is thus aimed beyond (pointing to) *who* and *what* regularly takes centre stage in the discussions around queer lives and identities, to concentrate instead on the important *where/s* of queer family life. Using a geographical lens that focuses on some of the physical, symbolic, official, and informal sites of same-sex parenting in and around one Australian metropolitan centre, I reveal part of the quiltbag quotidian from 'down-under' (Gorman-Murray, Waitt and Johnston, 2008) and in doing so, draw attention to the material and experiential difference that the local 'politics of location' (Rich, 1986) make to parenting, family, and 'queer' life.

A geographical perspective of family

This discussion is part of ongoing work that explores the diverse, local/ised, intimate geographies that are emerging in the everyday intersections of Australasian[5] urban, sexual, familial, ethnic and parental identities (Gorman-Murray, Waitt and Johnston, 2008). Here, I draw on findings from my research that examined the spatialities at work in contemporary Australian family life, and how such geographical understandings of what it is to 'be' and 'do' family are reshaped and recast through incorporating the spatial materialities and imaginaries of individuals and familial groups who do not operate within heteronormative parameters (Luzia, 2008, 2010, 2011a). This geography of same-sex parented family life also brings together what have been until now relatively separate bodies of geographic work on sexuality and family in acknowledgement of the complex spatial grammar around our most intimate relationships that incorporates what Adrienne Rich (1986) calls the geographies 'closest in': the sites, networks, spaces and places into which we are born; grow; live; and die; and that therefore play decisive and enduring roles in our experience in and of cultural and social life.

Exploring everyday geographies of intimacy is complicated. On one level, it means contending with The Family, one of the oldest social institutions; the bedrock of modern society, the cornerstone of contemporary culture. On another level, the family is also shifting terrain; the locus of social changes in the industrialised world where 'new' modes of family configuration and intimacy are emerging – or at least, becoming more visible (Weeks, Heaphy and Donovan, 2001; Stacey and Davenport, 2002). Family can no longer be defined as any specific form or structure or model, but is instead increasingly understood in terms of diverse and divergent forms, processes and practices that have only one thing in common: the formation and maintenance of interpersonal and intimate (including sexual) relationships that are based in – but are by no means limited to – the home and related domestic spheres.

To date however, many socio-spatial analyses on family have neither reflected these dimensions nor acknowledged that the everyday geographies of family are multi-scalar, straddling the intimate, domestic, civic, state and national spheres, sometimes simultaneously (Luzia, 2011b). Instead geographical work on families have kept to the scale of the domestic: the home; the street; the local neighbourhood, and strictly to the heteronormative: 'family' as the heterosexual, nuclear couple with (presumably) biologically related offspring. At the other end of the spectrum, there are significant gaps in much work around sexuality and space around familial relationships. Instead, sexual geographies have been constructed mainly from the point of view of the single lesbian or gay man, (although for exceptions see Gorman-Murray, 2006a,b; Gabb, 2005; Taylor, 2009), and without (explicit reference to) children or other dependants, or indeed, any other intimate familial or extra-familial relationships (Valentine, 2008). Combined, these gaps have contributed to a rather 'straight and narrow' (Luzia, 2011b) perspective of the geographies of everyday family life.

The conceptual framework for this discussion of local spaces of same-sex parenting is therefore based on two key ideas: first, that the geographies of intimacy include those of sexuality and of family, and that these are produced by and products of interpersonal relations including and beyond the hetero/sexual dyad and offspring; and second, that intimate geographies are produced in and by interactions in a variety of settings, including and beyond the intimate and private domestic, and public and commercial 'scene' spaces such as bars (Gilmartin, 1996), bathhouses (Nash and Bain, 2007), and 'beats'[6]. The accompanying empirical analysis is also set within a specific national context and against a broad background of broad federal and state legal and policy reforms with many of these directly impacting or indeed, specifically directed at same-sex couples with children. Changes to the processes of birth registration and certification; revisions to the national health scheme; opening access to assisted reproductive technology (ART) services – these and other changes and the inevitable 'flow-on' effects to other organisations and networks, have already been extensively documented and analysed in terms of what they might mean for Australian same-sex parented families (see Millbank, 2002, 2006). How such changes are transforming the spatial materialities and imaginaries of Australian family life, however, is yet to be fully examined. This chapter begins to fill in this lacuna through examining some of the ways that Australian same-sex parenting geographies are being reshaped.

A methodology for researching the geographies of women parenting together

Working with 38 Australian women, the specific research focus of the *Women Parenting Together* project was on the spaces, places and networks currently inhabited, navigated and avoided by women parenting children-under-five with other women. To recruit participant couples, I both advertised in, and was interviewed for a free nationally distributed magazine for lesbians;[7] I directly approached potential participants at the 2007 Sydney Gay and Lesbian Mardi Gras Fair Day, which is always attended by numerous same-sex parented families with children; and I used personal networks to connect with a key Sydney lesbian parenting group. As I am not a parent, this last approach heavily relied on 'credentials' provided by friends who are parents. After an initial interview, each parent-couple were issued with a disposable camera and instructions to take photos of their 'parenting places'; in other words, anywhere they considered an important site for their everyday parenting practice, with details noted in an accompanying 'parenting diary'. Follow-up interviews with couples were conducted in order to clarify and elaborate upon results, and give participants an opportunity for further reflection on their experience. Used together, the interviews, photographs and diaries offered a way to capture diverse parenting experiences, particularly the everyday experiences often elided in contemporary accounts (see Browne and Nash, 2010 on methods for representing queer lives, and Luzia, 2011b for extended discussion of the usefulness of photography and diaries in empirical research with same-sex families).

Participants were self-selecting, thus all data and analysis are specific to a small, relatively affluent and educated sector of both the non-heterosexual identifying communities and the broader 'middle-class' population; a sector that already figures heavily in academic and mainstream representations of same-sex parented families (Brown, 2009; Taylor, 2009). However I contend that the research benefitted from this cultural specificity in three ways. First, the mixed use of oral, written and photographic methods supplied participants with a range of media with which to represent their experiences. Second, the assumptions within the project methodology regarding participant facility (or familiarity) with at least one of these methods, be it writing regularly in a diary, talking about one's parenting experiences, taking photos, or any combination of these, were borne out with the majority of participants in professions based on developing oral, visual and written communication techniques. This meant a particularly detailed body of multi-media material to draw on. Third, the methodological triangulation proved useful in providing participants a broad and active role in establishing the themes of the project; and in directing early analysis, familiar terrain for the many respondents based in academia. These factors were instrumental in providing particularly detailed representations, not only of the significant spaces and places for parenting in one of Australia's major metropolitan centres, but also of the rights and responsibilities afforded (or not) to women parenting with other women, and how these vary geographically, even within the national context.

In Australia, for example, certain rights as a same-sex parent and as a person in a same-sex relationship will differ according to which state or territory[8] one resides in, while others are entrenched at the national or federal level. For example, the Miscellaneous Acts Amendment (Same Sex Relationships) Act 2008 NSW means that children born to female same sex couples in the state of New South Wales (NSW), through assisted reproductive technologies (ART) including donor insemination have two legally-recognised mothers with regard to state-governed and state-regulated agencies. This differs to laws in other Australian states, such as Victoria, South Australia and Western Australia single women and same-sex couples are excluded from accessing or using ART (Victorian Gay and Lesbian Rights Lobby, 2011). However, at the national level (also in 2008) a suite of major reforms was passed in the Australian federal parliament and also aimed at same-sex relationships. Among these changes was the inclusion of same-sex couples within the category of 'de facto relationship' in all federal laws (previously restricted to unmarried heterosexual couples). The definition of 'parent' and 'child' was extended to include non-biological same sex co-parents who have children through assisted reproductive means (Millbank, 2006), and in more limited cases, co-parents who have children born through surrogacy arrangements (Millbank, 2009). As these and other legislative changes at the national and (individual) state level reset official definitions of families as too did they recast 'local' understandings of both 'queer' and 'family' space by opening up particular sites of legitimatisation and recognition previously denied to certain types of families.

Such changes and their effects are not of course, exclusive to Australia. Recent developments around the formal recognition of same-sex family relationships in North America, Canada, Europe, and the UK including the introduction of same-sex marriages in some countries; the recognition of co-habitant same-sex couples as *de facto* in others, only further emphasise the need to consider how other 'relational' spaces of sexual identity are being reshaped. The discussion thus expands on those analyses on less tangible, and/or more ephemeral spaces of sexuality, such as lesbian friendship networks (Valentine, 1993); lesbian cultural spaces (Gilmartin, 1996); and extends work on particular neighbourhoods, streets and venues (Podmore, 2001, 2006; Nash and Bain, 2007) to the everyday spaces where sexual identities intersect with parental and other familial identities, including some apparently mundane spaces of reproduction, recognition, and support, without which Australian same-sex family life would be quite different.

Spaces of reproduction: The fertility clinic

One issue common to same-sex couples is that they must, in one way or another, go 'outside' the couple to conceive. In Australia, women who want to parent with other women have several options. 'Official' routes to same-sex parenting vary according to the state or territory of residency. Living in NSW, for example, women may access a limited range of fertility services, mostly based in inner-city clinics and/or linked to some of the major Sydney city hospitals. Living in the state of Victoria or South Australia, however, means crossing state borders to NSW, where providing assisted reproductive services including use of national donor banks to unmarried 'socially-infertile' women is legal. Other routes to conception for lesbians and single women include private arrangements with 'known' donors – often family friends or relatives – through home insemination; and others yet employ a combination of these methods – private 'known' donors and insemination at clinics. Out of the 19 families participating in the *Women Parenting Together* (WPT) project, 17 had 'planned' pregnancies. Table 10.1 shows the various methods of conception as well as sites of conception, indicating that the majority of participants accessed commercial fertility services before or at conception:

While the NSW Anti-Discrimination Act 1977 has made it unlawful to discriminate against people on the basis of sexuality in the areas of employment, public education, accommodation, and the provision of goods and services, with regard to providing fertility services, it has been left up to the operators of individual clinics – and more recently, through the Assisted Reproductive Technology Act 2007 NSW left up to individual donors – to decide to whom they will provide their services[9]. Thus, since NSW-based reproductive services do not have to accept lesbian couples (or single heterosexual women) for treatment, some do not, citing the reasons that participant Stacey outlines next:

> I rang up lots of other clinics– dozens, it felt like. And they were so rude! Telling me that they didn't treat 'socially infertile' women. I'm not socially infertile! I've had a child!
>
> Interview with community nurse

Table 10.1 The 'how' and 'where' of conception for participants in the *Women Parenting Together* project

Method of conception	Conceptions (n=23)	Comment
Accessed formal ART services at clinic	17 [–14 (donor unknown to couple) –3 (donor known to couple)]	All accessed at least one out of three Sydney-based fertility services/clinics
'Private arrangements' including 'known' donors with at-home insemination	4	Two conceptions – inner city Two conceptions – rural NSW
Unplanned pregnancies	2	Two conceptions taking place 'outside' the home (one inner-city Sydney, one in outer Sydney suburbs)

Source: Luzia (2011b).

Other Sydney clinics are more indirect in indicating their treatment 'preferences', as parents Sam and Jen explain next:

Sam: I think I must have called up at least half a dozen clinics. Some sounded great, others were really rude ... we ended up choosing two and visited both of them. We made our decision on how they responded to us, I mean, they basically provide the same services. So we went with the one that we both liked.

Karina: Why did you like this particular clinic?

Jen: They treated our relationship better.

Interview with Sam, 32, solicitor and
Jen, 36, doctoral researcher

Therefore, as these couples go outside the couple dyad to 'make' family, their access to reproductive technologies is dependent on a number of socio-spatial factors, including the state they reside in (and the facility with which they can cross state borders, if need be); their proximity to amenable' fertility services including potential donors, 'known' and 'unknown' (see Taylor, 2009 for a detailed discussion of social factors enabling and inhibiting mobilities and access, with regard to conception and fertility).

I also want to emphasise how local politics of location enlist NSW-based fertility services as 'lesbian space'. With their services theoretically available to all women, regardless of sexuality or marital status, or indeed, state of residency, NSW fertility clinics are places that women can access and develop important relationships specifically *as* lesbians, and/or because they are lesbian. This view of the clinic as a key lesbian space is evoked in the following parenting diary excerpt from the *Women Parenting Together* project:

'Sacred place' – We took this photo to mark a most important place for our family. This is the front of RPA [Royal Prince Alfred] hospital,[10] which is where Joely was conceived and born! The process of conception was very involved and sometimes quite emotional. One wonderful aspect was how close we lived to the hospital where the fertility clinic and the birth centre / labour ward are based. During the process of donor insemination, we would travel to RPA each morning between 7 and 8am for blood tests around the time of Carly's ovulation each month. Then on the 'right' day we would for in for inseminations. Being only 8 minutes away by car made this feasible before work, and it was wonderful to go back there for Joely's birth

Diary entry by Carly, 32, academic, and Jess, 37, IT manager

As the previous excerpt indicates, the fertility clinic can play a very important role for lesbian families, both as an actual site of conception – and in this case, a birth site – and also for (self-)conceptions *as* family. For this family, the clinic is a 'sacred place' – a space that has enabled their family and is therefore an extension of the spaces of familial intimacy that in (homo/hetero-)normative discourse is typically reserved by, and confined to, the home. The Sydney clinic, although not a typical site for the expression and enactment of desire between women, is a 'lesbian' space in that women access it because they are lesbians; as lesbians; and/or to extend a lesbian relationship.

Of course, clinics were not used by all couples to expand upon their relationship. While the majority of participants were in a position to access official assisted reproductive technologies (ART), a few couples in the *Women Parenting Together* project opted for making private arrangements with family friends, citing clinic location, distance, convenience and cost as factors that influenced their choices. Willa and Kim living in the Blue Mountains on the outer fringes of the greater metropolitan area of Sydney chose to home-inseminate. Having access to sperm via Kim's (male) ex-partner (with the reportedly enthusiastic agreement of his wife), Kim conceived two children via this route. The couple's reasons for choosing this particular route were simple:

> It costs a bundle to access fertility services – at least it did for us when we investigated. Not just money but time; I mean you have to travel to the clinic every morning for weeks; you have to pay for the donor – all that stuff. It was easier for us to do it at home with my ex – I mean we know him really well and his wife, they're among our best friends and they've got kids of their own.
>
> Interview with Kim, 35, ex-public servant

Willa and Kim therefore have used the 'normative' setting of the home space to extend their family but in an arguably 'queer' way. Moreover, their access to a 'suitable' known donor secures their choice with their personal networks enabling them to bypass use of a donor bank and associated services, and the inconvenience (at best) of travelling to and from the clinic each morning.

Spaces of recognition – from consent orders to birth certificates

Before September 2008, the options for the legal recognition of family created outside a heterosexual dyad in Australia were limited. Some participants chose to apply to the Family Court for consent (parenting) orders that ascribe parental status to non-biological mothers (Millbank, 2006). In a May 2008 interview, co-parents Jess and Carly spoke about obtaining consent orders for six-month old baby Joely sometime after her birth:

> Jess: We got parenting orders for Joely pretty much, what? Straight away? How old was she?

Carly: She was only three or four months old, when we did that, it was pretty early on, we met the lawyer at Fair Day ... they had a stall ... It was a fantastic experience, actually going to the court and the judge was really great in saying how wonderful it was that we were doing it and how important that we were looking at the interest of Joely and you know, making sure everything was covered ... but for the first time, we've actually used [the orders], 'cos we went to the Redfern Occasional Child Care Centre to sign up in case we needed to go there while our nanny is sick, and for anybody else who has a parenting role, you have to, it says [...] you have to provide a birth certificate but you also have to provide any consent orders as well.

Without the option of having both their names on the birth certificate as parents, Carly and Jess felt it necessary to have their family formally recognised via parenting orders almost immediately after becoming parents. Obtaining the 'protection' represented by parenting orders, however, required a relatively involved series of manoeuvres and the mobilisation of resources that would not have been necessary if they had been a heterosexual-parented family. Carly and Jess did not receive a birth certificate citing them as both Joely's parents, and that was more or less 'automatically' generated and available almost immediately after the birth of their child. Instead the route to official recognition of their family was more circuitous – visiting the Mardi Gras Fair Day to obtain 'queer family-friendly' legal advice; seeking out and paying for legal assistance in obtaining, completing and submitting the actual applications; attending court and filing the orders – all to obtain formal documentation that confirmed Jess's rights and responsibilities as (the non-birth) co-mother, and thus her very identity as a lesbian parent.

They also had to rely on finding 'lesbian – or at least, 'lesbian-friendly' – space in the form of a non-homophobic Family Court; in legal firms familiar with the legal options for queer families; and a child-care centre directorship that understood family diversity, allowing them to bypass certain requirements for registering children for child-care:

[I did] a tour (of the child care centre) and ended up doing up a lot of paper work and stuff and said, oh by the way, we're actually a lesbian couple ... we have a parenting order for Jess's role as a parent and, you know, the woman just didn't blink she said, no worries, fantastic, photocopy [the parenting order], and I thought that's cool, it was kind of nice, you know, it was something different but she would see all kinds of difference, particularly with consent orders.

Carly

Parenting orders, however, were not an option available to all families interviewed: as co-parents Cate (48, ex-librarian, now stay-at-home mother) and Leah (29, teacher) stated in their March 2008 interview, obtaining these parenting orders could be an expensive process requiring not insignificant resources of time, money and energy. Similar claims were made by Marie (37, nurse) and Laura (29, nurse), who met at a Sydney fertility clinic, which they were accessing as single women. Marie and Laura ended up using the same donor; becoming pregnant; and giving birth within three weeks of each other. At the time of interview, both were on maternity leave, with Laura mostly confined to bed, having suffered a number of complications, during and after the birth. Neither had the financial, emotional, or physical resources at that stage, to organise parenting orders, however, both affirmed their intention to have their family legally recognised as soon as possible.

In September 2008, birth certificates carrying the names of two female parents became available. These 'two-mother certificates' were a critical part of a package of amendments to existing NSW state legislation that was aimed at bestowing 'equal rights' on the children of female de-facto couples (NSW Attorney-General's Department 2008). Under the Miscellaneous Acts Amendment (Same Sex Relationships) Act 2008 (NSW), children with two mothers now had equal rights, compared to children of heterosexual married and unmarried couples. Along with the inclusion of their female non-biological mothers on their birth certificates, these entitlements included access to workers compensation and victim compensation payments where one or both co-parents are killed or injured; inheritance of both of their parents' assets; recognition of both parents by school authorities; improving access to guardianship orders for elderly co-parents. This brought NSW into line with the other Australian states and territories of Western Australia, the Australian Capital Territory and the Northern Territory, and resonates with similar laws in other countries, such as New Zealand and Canada.

However, the new laws only apply to children of *female* same-sex de facto relationship, and also only to those children conceived through ART. Previously, under the Status of Children Act 1996, parental presumption applied only to married and unmarried heterosexual couples; now they also applied to only those female same-sex couples who had accessed IVF; donor insemination, or 'home insemination' (which is apparently presumed to be legally different to (hetero)sexual intercourse).

Talking to participants after the Bill was passed demonstrated some of the bureaucratic issues dealing with the agencies and organisations that were the instruments for implementing and enforcing the new laws:

Delia: Well I went to get my name put on Logan's birth certificate 'cos you, know it's retrospective and all that. What a schmozzle that was!

Karina: How so?

Delia: Well because it's retrospective, I had to go back to the hospital to get the forms and because the law is so new, you know, they haven't worked out what they're doing yet – the hospitals, I mean, with regard to adding co-parents.

The 'schmozzle' that Delia refers to here is perhaps nothing more than indication of the necessary 'adjustment' period for organisations and agencies to catch up to the requirements of the new laws. However Delia's own extensive background in public hospitals and her current role in executive management team of a Sydney health district, gives her further insight into the ramifications of making space for lesbian mothers on a birth certificate:

Delia: I mean it's not just popping two names on a piece of paper. Usually there's a 60 day cut off after the birth to register your child and you know, your own names as parents and that, but of course in this case I'd missed that cut off point, I mean Logan's nine now! (laughter) So you have to produce these other forms of identification both for yourself as a parent and for your child as your child, you know. But of course did I have anything that would show that I was Logan's parent? No marriage certificate, no immigration papers, no letters or emails from Stacey (birth mother and partner) talking about our shared parenting. So not only did they not have proper forms for two mothers to fill out they also had no guidelines for legitimate forms of identification of a same-sex relationship because we haven't been allowed to register as a de facto couple until now.

Karina: So what did you do?

Delia: Well thank god before Logan was born, Stacey and I changed to a hyphenated version of both our surnames. We've only used it once, when we changed electricity providers and Stacey put our new name on the electricity bill. That and the change-of-name certificates with our new names got us through.

Accessing the space of family relatedness that is the birth certificate is therefore still not a straightforward process, even after the issue of allowing space for two mothers' names on a certificate is addressed. Delia's account reveals yet another aspect to the heteronormativity embedded in bureaucracy that demands extra effort – or just effort – on the part of some families to prove that they *are* family, in order to receive recognition that they are entitled to. It also points to the intractability of systems and how this so often manifests at best in small (but significant) inconveniences, and at worst, major disruptions.

Lesbian family space: The lesbian mothers' group

Once the *Women Parenting Together* participants became pregnant, most reported entering a process, that is impartial and relentless in its bureaucratic efficiency – as new parents Sallie and Jen stated in an interview: 'you just go into the system of being pregnant, go in one end and then you're sort of spat out the other side'. Part of this bureaucracy of pregnancy is linking new parents to mothers' groups, organised through hospital and early childhood centre networks and linking mothers from the same birth centre and/or within the local area who have given birth at around the same time.

Most participants referenced attending mothers' groups very soon after the birth of their babies – see Table 10.2. While most participants cited visiting mother's groups at least once after giving birth, attendance rates after the first weeks varied enormously (see Table 10.2).

The WPT participants gave various reasons for not attending: 'not our scene'; 'the other mothers – I felt like I had nothing in common with them'; 'as the kids got older, we saw them less and less'. Not one participant explicitly cited sexuality as a crucial point of difference in these groups.

One mothers' group cited by all parent-participants and accessed at least once by most, was the lesbian mothers' group *Rainbow Babies*. This is perhaps the most well-known and certainly the longest running lesbian mothers group in Australia (*Rainbow Babies*, 2011a). Founded by one inner-city Sydney-based lesbian-parented family in 1998, and receiving no outside funding, the organisation has over 1000 email list members including individual families as well as government and non-government organisations. Regular events held under the *Rainbow Babies* banner include weekly mothers' groups, playgroups supported by the state-government-funded *Playgroups NSW* and monthly picnics, to biannual camping trips, and annual discos. With up to 50 families regularly attending the monthly picnics in an inner-city park, and up to 30 families regularly attending bi-annual camping trips on the south coast of NSW (Hunt, 2007), the group's objective is explicitly focused on the children of lesbian mothers – 'giving them a peer group in which to identify as children of lesbian parents' (*Rainbow Babies*, 2011a).

At the same time, the website and the regular newsletters describe the organisation as a social group that is open to all same-sex parents, while the *Rainbow Babies* playgroups are for all children from birth to school age but the organisation also has a mission to provide parents and carers with an opportunity to meet other parents, make friends and share experiences

Table 10.2   WPT participants attending organised mothers' groups after giving birth

Mothers' group attendance/regular contact	Number of participants
WPT participants attending mother's groups regularly for up to 8 weeks after the birth.	19
After 8 weeks after the birth.	11
After 1 year.	2

and ideas (*Rainbow Babies*, 2011b). It is this potential as a strong support network for lesbian parents that is of interest here, in terms of the different kind of community space now available for lesbians (and more recently, gay men) who also happen to be parents. Again however, regularly accessing this particular cultural space depends on geographical factors. While smaller *Rainbow Babies* sub-groups have recently emerged throughout greater metropolitan Sydney, it remains very much an inner-city Sydney-based organisation and therefore sometimes difficult for non-inner-city residents to access. As one of the founders stated, 'we try to include everyone from all over Sydney but it is often very unwieldy; people who live further away [outside the inner-city] always say they feel left out, or that the park is too far away for them, or [they] ask why we can't have the picnics further out' (Hunt, 2007). In other words, geography plays a role in accessing this network regularly; those based in the queer-friendly neighbourhoods (Gorman-Murray and Waitt, 2009) of inner-city Sydney are physically better placed to access and occupy this particular lesbian family space.

This is not to say that those based outside inner Sydney do not benefit. Suburban-based parents who regularly attended *Rainbow Babies* events cited the valuable community connection afforded by the regular get-togethers. For these parents, events such as the monthly picnics provided much valued connection to 'child-friendly' but still 'lesbian' scene. As 'suburban' parent Sabrina states:

> We don't live in town and there's not many lesbian families out here. So we go to the picnics and we go on all the camping trips. It's a way of staying in touch.
>
> Interview with Sabrina, 41, corporate accountant

Here, however, the interdependence between certain forms of social and economic capital, geography and accessing support networks (see also Taylor, 2009) is also evident. For example, in Sabrina and Faye's case, their physical distance from inner-city 'lesbian family space' is ameliorated by other forms of economic and cultural capital. With a vehicle, camping equipment; and a budget that is flexible enough to accommodate regular picnics, these parents are equipped, physically and financially, to access this site of support for their same-sex parented family, despite being 'inconveniently' located outside the inner-city.

Symbolic spaces of family: The Medicare card

The material and imagined spaces associated with a national health care system would not usually figure prominently in any analysis of same-sex family life. As outlined earlier, however, the material spaces of Australia's relatively well-resourced public health care system that includes comprehensive reproductive and fertility services can play a large role, not only in supporting, but in creating same-sex parented family. In this section, I consider a more intangible but still health–related 'space' that is taken for granted by many Australian families, but one that is particularly significant for families living outside the heteronormative: the Australian Medicare card. Through the inscription of the names of children and their parents – different-sex *and* same-sex – on a plastic card that allows those on the card to access 'free' healthcare together, and as family, this apparently mundane feature of contemporary Australian life has become a symbolic space that enshrines family – all configurations of family – *as* family.

Australia's health care system did not always function as a beacon of equality. Certainly, the issuing body Medicare Australia was originally established in the 1970s to 'ensure [...] that all Australians have access to free or low-cost medical [...] care' (Medicare 2010) with the system including a 'family safety net'[11] and a Pharmaceutical Benefits Scheme (PBS) if a person or their family need a lot of medicines. However, until 2009, for the purposes of use of Medicare benefits, a family was defined only as a (heterosexual) couple that was legally married[12] and not separated; or a man and a woman in a de-facto relationship with or without dependent children (under 16 years or a full time student under 25 years under parental support); or a single person with dependent children.

The pre-2009 arrangement made it difficult for those families who did not fit this definition. For same-sex parents, it meant among other things, additional complications to their day-to-day childcare arrangements and mobility through having to anticipate and prepare for various emergencies; that, no matter how seemingly mundane, could be very serious if one's paperwork was not in order. Sick children might not be able to be picked up from day-care by non-birth mothers (or gay dads) without parenting orders, for example, and in theory at least, accessing free medical care could be delayed, even denied without the appropriate medical care. While the denial of medical care to children is fortunately an unlikely scenario, the rule nonetheless further complicated things for families operating outside the heterosexual normative, as Carly states here in a 2008 interview:

Carly: Let's hope that we never have to really use [the parenting orders] but there's other things, like Joely's on my Medicare card with me so I was thinking the other day if something happened to me suddenly and Jess has to suddenly take over, she'd have to apply for another Medicare card and get Joely on that Medicare card and that could be complicated but yeah. So every now and then I'll think of some other little scenario.

Karina: Can you all be on a Medicare card – a family Medicare card?

Jess: We can't be on the same Medicare card because Medicare doesn't acknowledge [us as family] 'cos they're part of the

Federal laws so they don't recognise us as spouses and you have to have a spousal relationship so we can't have the safety net as a family so that's one of the areas of discrimination I think where they're trying to get rid of. It's probably one of the few areas that really worries me.

After 1 January 2009, the Medicare safety net definition of family was widened to include same-sex couples and their dependants on the one card. As such it provided the same access to benefits to all families, regardless of marital status of the parents. Furthermore, and unlike the Miscellaneous Acts Amendment (Same Sex Relationships) Act 2008 (NSW), this extended benefits to *all* same-sex families, regardless of parental gender or whether they had dependants through ART. Kim and Willa commented on the seemingly small but significant difference that the Medicare change meant for their family:

I had to go into hospital for a couple of nights and Willa had to take time off work and look after the kids. Well Sari got sick, I mean, it wasn't major or anything – just a cold but we were already a bit stressed and you know, you tend to make mountains out of molehills – anyway, Willa was able to take her to the doctors and there was no problem. Not that they wouldn't have treated her of course, but it just made things easier all being on one card. A year ago it wouldn't have been so straightforward if Geordie had gotten sick, 'cos Willa wasn't on our [Medicare family] card.

Kim

While this has obvious consequences for individual lesbian families as the previous excerpt suggests, the broader ramifications for conceptualisations not only of family in Australia, but of sexual identity are also significant. Unlike fertility clinics run by faith-based organisations, or NSW birth registrations available only to heterosexuals and female same-sex couples, the lack of exceptions to the 2009 Medicare ruling means no possible prevarications on the part of individual health providers and operators – no legal basis to refuse treatment or services to or require payment by any Australian citizen or their dependents, regardless of sexual identity and/or familial configuration. In other words, the Australian Medicare card is one of the few national symbols that fills a little of the 'queer absences' left around recognition of quiltbag families *as* families in Australia.

Conclusion – On the everyday spaces of queer

The spaces and places explored here are only a starting point for what is a much-needed in-depth consideration of quiltbag 'family spaces' that include but are not limited to the 'homonormative' home, the 'queer-friendly' neighbourhood, or the urban social and commercial 'scene'. Examining these everyday sites and processes are a useful contribution to any discussion on 'lesbian' or 'queer' space, as it is at this level that the inherent contradictions embedded in such constructs become apparent, showing how such spaces are framed and buttressed by 'local' legislation and policy, and are reliant on processes, perceptions and attitudes enacted and embedded at other similarly local and apparently mundane scales. They also reveal the disparities and discriminatory processes that remain even in the face of radical change – the queer absences that are enacted at the everyday level of the family. These accounts by parents in same-sex relationships show, for example, how being 'granted' recognition and access to space at one scale (e.g. through apparently 'sweeping' changes to national law) does not entail recognition at other more immediately crucial scale (e.g. a faith-based fertility service) nor does it necessarily assist with access to existing local 'community-based' support networks, such as lesbian parenting groups, that have long been working towards ameliorating the small but significant stresses of mundane heterosexism.

Despite then, the (needed and welcomed) changes in federal and state laws, queer Australian families – *all* queer families– must still negotiate; remain subject to; and be constrained by, factors that do not affect heterosexual parented families. There is not much one can do, for example, about being denied access to an individual faith-based service, for example, if such refusals are accommodated for within existing law, however comprehensive changes to other laws might be. Access to certain forms of social and financial capital here becomes even more critical during times of reform where full equality is still not available; raising the possibility that this will the generation of Australian 'rainbow babies' whose parents were those socially and financially positioned to access (and persist with) assisted reproduction. Furthermore, we are still to see the effect of other 'local' specificities and idiosyncrasies, for example, the amendments made to NSW birth registrations that separate same-sex family rights and responsibilities according to gender and that therefore operate to introduce new types of segregation, according to parents' sexuality and gender; in essence, placing other families (those with two dads, for example) at the bottom of a hierarchy of 'legitimate' family.

While the analysis here has only addressed some of the 'queer absences' around family, its geographical perspective serves as a reminder of how queer 'ways of being' intersect with other ways of identifying and relating – including through family and parenting and other forms of intimacy – in and through everyday space. Empirical analyses that are geographically specific and that incorporate local politics of location are also particularly useful for showing the material realities of quiltbag family life as very much a patching-together; a shifting and mobile fusion of conventional and non-conventional, mainstream and queer interactions with regard to becoming, and doing, parenting and family. For all that certain types of families are considered in academic spheres, prototypical of the 'homonormative', in the mainstream, quiltbag families can still be, and indeed are, understood as part of the 'exceptional everyday'.

Notes

1. See http://www.urbandictionary.com/define.php?term=QUILTBAG.
2. Here I use Larry Knopp's (2007) explanation of 'queer' as based on a 'family' of intellectual and political developments emerging from the academy and radical sexual politics, that is characterised by anti-essentialism and inclusivity – ideas that (like members of most families) are sometimes in tension.
3. Here I define a family as two or more co-habitants in an intimate relationship that may or may not involve parenting.
4. My thanks to Kathryn Almack for letting me use her project title.
5. Following on from Gorman-Murray, Waitt and Johnston (2008) I use 'Australasia' here to refer specifically to Australia and New Zealand, rather than use terms with wider geographical connotations such as 'Asia Pacific' or 'Oceania'
6. An Australian colloquial term for gay cruising spots; known as 'cottages' (UK) or 'tea-rooms' (US).
7. A free monthly publication *LOTL* (*Lesbians on the Loose*) produced in Sydney and distributed throughout selected venues in some Australian cities.
8. The Commonwealth of Australia comprises six states and two territories: New South Wales, Victoria, Queensland, South Australia, Western Australia, Tasmania, the Northern Territory, and the Australian Capital Territory.
9. Clause 17 in the *Assisted Reproductive Technology Act 2007* allows donors to nominate classes of people to whom their sperm or eggs may not be given.
10. Royal Prince Alfred Hospital is based in inner-city Sydney.
11. This mechanism ensures that once a family reaches a threshold in terms of medical costs, further doctors' visits and medical tests cost less.
12. This option is still not available to same-sex couples in Australia.

Bibliography

Bell, D. and Binnie, J. (2004) 'Authenticating queer space: Citizenship, urbanism and governance', *Urban Studies*, 41(9): 1807–20.
Brown, G. (2008) 'Urban (homo)sexualities: Ordinary cities and ordinary sexualities', *Geography Compass*, 2(4): 1215–31.
Brown, G. (2009) 'Thinking beyond homonormativity: Performative explorations of diverse gay economies', *Environment and Planning A*, 41(6): 1496–510.
Browne, K. and Nash, C. J. (2010) *Queer methods and methodologies: Intersecting queer theories and social science research*. London: Ashgate.
Duggan, L. (2002) 'The new homonormativity: The sexual politics of neoliberalism' in R. Castronovo and D. D. Nelson (eds) *Materializing democracy: Towards a revitalised cultural politics*. Durham and London: Duke University Press, pp. 175–94.
Gabb, J. (2005) 'Locating lesbian parent families', *Gender, Place and Culture: A Journal of Feminist Geography*, 12(4): 419–32.
Gilmartin, K. (1996) '"We weren't bar people": Middle-class lesbian identities and cultural spaces', *GLQ: A Journal of Lesbian and Gay Studies*, 3(1): 1–51.
Gorman-Murray, A. (2006a) 'Imagining King Street in the gay/lesbian media', *M/C Journal*, 9(3), http://journal.media-culture.org.au/0607/04-gorman-murray.php, accessed on 4 September 2011.
Gorman-Murray, A. (2006b) 'Gay and lesbian couples at home: Identity work in domestic space', *Home Cultures*, 3(2): 145–67.

Gorman-Murray, A., Waitt, G. and Johnston, L. (2008) 'Guest editorial–geographies of sexuality and gender "down under"', *Australian Geographer*, 39(3): 235–46.

Gorman-Murray, A. and Waitt, G. (2009) 'Queer-friendly neighbourhoods: Interrogating social cohesion across sexual difference in two Australian neighbourhoods', *Environment and Planning A*, 41(12): 2855–873.

Hunt, K. (2007) '*Rainbow Babies* and Kids', personal communication with Karina Luzia. Sydney 15 April 2007.

Knopp, L. (2007) 'From lesbian and gay to queer geographies: Pasts, prospects and possibilities' in K. Browne, J. Lim and G. Brown (eds) *Geographies of sexualities: Theory practices and politics*. Farnham: Ashgate, pp. 21–8.

Luzia, K. (2008) 'Day care as battleground: Using moral panic to locate the front lines', *Australian Geographer*, 39(3): 315–26.

Luzia, K. (2010) 'Travelling in your backyard: The unfamiliar places of parenting', *Social and Cultural Geography*, 11(4): 359–75.

Luzia, K. (2011a) 'Growing home: Reordering the domestic geographies of "thrown-togetherness"', *Home Cultures*, 8(3): 297–316.

Luzia, K. (2011b) *Beyond the straight and narrow: Geographies of same-sex parenting*, Thesis submitted: Department of Environment and Geography, Macquarie University, Sydney.

Millbank, J. (2002) *Meet the parents: A review of the research on lesbian and gay families*. Sydney: The Gay and Lesbian Rights Lobby (NSW) Inc.

Millbank, J. (2006) 'Parental status for lesbian mothers having children through assisted conception', *Australian Family Lawyer*, 19(1): 6–11.

Millbank, J. (2009) 'De facto relationships, same-sex and surrogate parents: Exploring the scope and effects of the 2008 federal relationship reforms', *Australian Journal of Family Law*, 23(3): 1–42.

Nash, C. and Bain, A. (2007) '"Reclaiming raunch"? Spatializing queer identities at Toronto women's bathhouse events', *Social and Cultural Geography*, 8(1): 47–62.

Peel, E. (2001) 'Mundane heterosexism: Understanding incidents of the everyday', *Women's Studies International Forum*, 24(5): 541–54.

Podmore, J. A. (2001) 'Lesbians in the crowd: Gender, sexuality and visibility along Montréal's Boul. St-Laurent', *Gender, Place and Culture: A Journal of Feminist Geography*, 8(4): 333–55.

Podmore, J. A. (2006) 'Gone 'underground'? Lesbian visibility and the consolidation of queer space in Montréal', *Social and Cultural Geography*, 7(4): 595–625.

Puar, J. K. (2006) 'Mapping US homonormativities', *Gender, Place and Culture*, 13(1): 67–88.

Rainbow Babies (2011a) http://www.rainbowbabiesandkids.com.au, accessed on 4 September 2011.

Rainbow Babies (2011b) *Rainbow Babies Newsletter*, First edition, Sydney, December 2011.

Rich, A. (1986) 'Notes towards a politics of location' in A. Rich (ed.) *Blood, Bread, and Poetry: Selected prose*. New York and London: W. W. Norton and Company.

Stacey, J. and Davenport, E. (2002) 'Queer families quack back' in D. Richardson and S. Seidman (eds) *Handbook of lesbian and gay studies*. London: Sage, pp. 355–74.

Taylor, Y. (2008) '"That's not really my scene": Working-class lesbians in (and out of) place', *Sexualities*, 11(5): 523–46.

Taylor, Y. (2009) *Lesbian and gay parenting: Securing social and educational capital*. Basingstoke: Palgrave Macmillan.

Valentine, G. (1993) 'Desperately seeking Susan: A geography of lesbian friendships', *Area*, 25(2): 109–16.

Valentine, G. (2008) 'The ties that bind: Towards geographies of intimacy', *Geography Compass*, 2(6): 2097–110.

Victorian Gay and Lesbian Rights Lobby (2011) *Becoming a parent*, http://www.vglrl.org.au/the-law-and-you/parents-and-children.php, accessed on 1 August 2011.

Weeks, J., Heaphy, B. and Donovan, C. (2001) *Same sex intimacies: Families of choice and other life experiments*. New York: Routledge.

11
'Queer' and 'Teacher' as Symbiosis? Exploring Absence and Presence in Discursive Space

Max Biddulph

Introduction

This chapter explores absences and presences in the narratives of queer men who work in the UK as educators in the 11–18 secondary phase of education. Implicit in the role of educator are professional skills enabling teachers to not merely be coaches or imparters of knowledge, but to be intimately involved in professional relationships with students and colleagues. Thus educational communities consist of a complex web of social relations in which individuals are profoundly exposed and implicated on a daily basis. This intense environment is a rich territory for considering queer absences and presences, particularly in terms of the discourses that enable and disable their expression.

Foucault (1981) foregrounds the role of discourse in institutions and social relations as the primary means by which human values are communicated, 'naturalised' and reproduced. In the UK context, discourses relating to sexuality in school environments are clearly in evidence, Epstein, O' Flynn and Telford (2002), Renold (2005), Taylor (2007), DePalma and Atkinson (2009), noting that the ethos in these spaces is strongly heteronormative. Browne and Nash (2010) argue that implicit in this term, is the hegemonic privileging of a certain type of sexual relationship – for example, monogamous, heterosexual, married, which carries particular currency in school environments where protective discourses of sexuality assert that 'vulnerable young people' should receive clear messages about moral behaviour and viable relationships (DfEE, 2000). Casey (2007) acknowledges the recent extension of these 'officially approved of' relationships, to certain types of homosexual relationships, also. Hence the emergence of 'homonormativity', which Browne and Nash (2010) attribute to the political and social assimilation of some lesbians and gay men through legislative 'gains' made in the UK and other Western countries.

'Queer' however, lies outside of these normative structures and for men who identify as queer, the lifestyle of these homo/heteronormative relationships can sit in stark contrast to their private 'worlds', which are characterised by behaviours and practices influenced by markedly different sexual cultures (Brown, 2008). Rofes (2005: 101) questions why gay male educator's performance of queerness – for example, hypermasculinity, kink/BDSM, drag and non-monogamy is so invisible in their professional personae? The notion of 'intersecting identities' has been the focus of scrutiny elsewhere (Puar, 2007; Taylor, 2010; Dean, 2011), although as Taylor, Hines and Casey (2011) observe, less attention has been given to identity intersections with sexuality. In this instance, research into the experience of secondary teachers intersectionality with (homo)sexuality and professional identity in the USA and the UK over the last two decades (Griffin, 1991; Sparkes, 1996; Kissen, 1996; Biddulph, 2005a; Barnfield and Humberstone, 2008) indicates a number of 'splitting strategies' used to strictly delineate the public-professional from the private aspects of identity. Acknowledging this and the slow recognition of non-heterosexual teachers, Rofes (2005:119) issued a call for a more radical, integrated queer teacher presence in school classrooms and other educational spaces. He observes that:

> All too often, as we've made these efforts, we've made compromises and sacrifices that have gone unspoken and unacknowledged. We've gained limited entry into the classroom by denying authentic differences between many gay men's relationships to gender roles, sexual cultures and kinship arrangements compared to those of the heteronormative hegemony.
>
> Rofes (2005: 119)

Rofes (ibid.) questions why he edits out his queerness in classroom settings, asserting that he feels 'bound and gagged', the implication being that whilst the normative construction of 'gay' is now just about acceptable in some education environments, 'queer' is not. In presenting the intervention that follows, my aim is to gain a more detailed understanding the relationship between spaces, the discourses present within them and the social and cultural capitals that individuals can import (Bourdieu, 1990; McNay, 2004). What is new is that I consider identity deployment in two contrasting locales, extending my analysis beyond the classroom into a wider definition of space traversed by queer educators, to include sexual spaces. I do this via the use of two ethnographic narratives (Inckle, 2011) constructed from data collected in research with educators in the UK, the detail of which is expanded later in the chapter in the methodology section. Binnie (2001) argues that ethically, whenever texts containing 'sexual data' are presented, it is important to ask who are these texts being produced for and what is their purpose? This brings into focus a second claim to originality.

Piper and Sikes (2010) note that the pressure to disassociate non-normative sexualities from education apparent in the practice domain is now being felt by educational researchers, hence the presentation of these narratives is an attempt to reveal queer experience, to not collude with the historical position of silence. In identifying absences and presences, I will argue that whilst the discourses within educational spaces are specifically configured, the individuals under investigation are neither neutral nor stable in the ways they are (in)visible. McNay (2004) argues that personal agency enacted by individuals in social relations is a significant influence in determining their response and this has direct implications for understanding queer absences and presences. I begin by reviewing theoretical perspectives on this from the work of Pierre Bourdieu.

Mobility, spaces and 'cultural capitals'

In her review of the contribution of Bourdieu to feminism, Adkins (2004a: 3) acknowledges his theoretical contribution to the theorisation of social agency and the politics of cultural authorisation. Skeggs (2004: 19) notes that what Bourdieu offers is 'explanatory power' in terms of linking objective structures in the environment to subjective experience. She notes the significance of the metamorphic structure of social space in which human beings embody and carry with them different 'capitals' thus enabling the consideration of the different types of and value of social mobility. Central to the understanding of this process are the Bourdieusian concepts of 'field' and 'habitus'. Bourdieu and Wacquant (2002: 97) define field as 'a network, or a configuration, of objective relations between positions', hence as McNay (2004) notes, space can be conceptualised not just in terms of being a physical entity, but in terms of the symbolism that it holds for individuals in terms of social relations. This is significant in the understanding of 'habitus', which Lawler (2004: 111) notes is the way in which 'the social' is incorporated into the phenomenological frame of reference of the individual. Bourdieu (1990: 56) argues that 'habitus is embodied history, internalised as a second nature and so forgotten as history'. Drawing on the work of Johnson (1993), Lawler (2004) goes on to argue that this internalised knowledge operates as a 'second sense', 'practical sense' or 'second nature' that equips social actors with practical 'know-how'. In summary, Adkins (2004b: 193–4) usefully defines field as 'the game (of social relations) itself' and habitus as the 'feel for the game'.

Research methods: Generating ethnographic fiction from researcher and participant accounts

The primary data that informs the basis of the ethnographic fictions that follow originates from a doctoral research project that investigated the identity management strategies of 14 gay and bisexual men who are educators (Biddulph, 2005a). Within this cohort, ten of the participants worked in the secondary and tertiary phases of education, working with young people aged 11–18. In depth semi-structured interviews generated transcripts in which all participants talked extensively about their classroom experiences; most also talked about the deployment of their teacher identities in their personal lives, including the sexual spaces they traverse. For the purposes of this account, the data from three participants, 'Lee', 'Seb' and 'Tom' (pseudonyms) are drawn upon. Browne and Nash (2010: 4) note that queer developments in the academy also have implications for the process of researching in that the notion of the 'unassailable, 'objective' researcher inexorably uncovering a knowable reality through relational reality of truth' has been questioned, hence researching 'queerly' is now cognisant of the positionalities of researchers as well as those being researched. Britzman (1998) argues that researchers are inevitably caught in the 'tangles of implication' of their work and Gemignani (2011) observes that this includes affective as well as cognitive engagements. My sense of being personally involved in this work was confirmed when I explored my own researcher positionality using visual methods (Biddulph, 2005b), which revealed not just my own subjective frame of reference in analysing the data, but my 'political' positioning as a queer, gay activist researcher.

Gemignani (2011) argues that politics and issues of researcher positionality are connected to the representational practices we employ in constructing the images of our research subjects and I am acutely aware that I am working with highly complex accounts, containing sensitive data. Piper and Sikes (2010: 568) argue that by integrating data into fictionalised composites, greater anonymity may be assured and, as Inckle (2011: 265) suggests, there are a number of epistemological as well as methodological advantages in transforming such data into ethnographic fiction. The genre is well placed for exploring the complex and multi-faceted nature of intersectionality and this fosters an 'intersubjective connection with the reader' through which events and contexts can receive 'another level of attention'.

The narratives that follow are constructed as a 'patchwork text' (Winter, Buck and Sobiechowska, 1999), using an amalgam of voices, locations and sources of data. Clough (2002) offers a technique for giving transparency to the process of narrative composition by offering a model for a schematisation in which units of meaning, data sources and data methods are outlined for characters, environments and events, and I will indicate this in my commentary. The narrative contains two episodes of the same story linked by a central character, queer teacher Andy, the sources for who are a composite of the research participants and myself. The character of Sean, was developed by drawing on the research of Keogh, Dodds and Henderson (2004) into the experiences of working class gay and bisexual men. The sequence and structuring of the narratives is steered by a number of considerations. The texts themselves are interspersed by two commentaries in which I attempt to use a more reflective voice to 'queer' the stories, locating points of 'instability and messiness' (Browne and Nash, 2010: 5) together with 'disjunctures, fractures and contradictions' (Miller, 1998: 370). I also offer insights into my researcher subjectivity and identify a series of emergent themes that form the basis of the subsequent discussion later in the chapter.

Preamble

Andy Jeffers is three years into his career working as a Physical Education (PE) teacher in an 11–18 year old secondary school. Whilst most of his timetable is dedicated to the teaching of PE, Andy also teaches Personal, Social, Health Education (PSHE). The school is located in an outer city council estate in the fictional English city of 'Brockhampton' where Andy also resides, living close to an inner city park, fringed by an urban walk way alongside a canal.

End of Term

The final ascent of the year, up the wearying stairs. Andy braced himself ... on the timetable, it was his weekly venture indoors into the classroom to teach Year 9 PSHE. The usual scenario, 'less conventional' teachers and those with a gap on their timetable were put down to teach PSHE. Andy wondered which category he fitted into – perhaps it was the PE tracksuit that gave him an entrée. Funny that, the messages a tracksuit can give; a cover for 'a multitude of sins'.

Today, it could hardly be called a lesson. More of a holding operation, a whole Friday afternoon reduced to 45 minutes before the kids could go home. He could hear them long before he got to the classroom door, shouting, chasing around desks and knocking over chairs. On entering the room, the surprise was that those who turned up constituted a depleted group of six – all lads. The rest had not come back after lunch or had not bothered coming at all that day and those that remained were either too conscientious or too disorganised or just plain barmy, individuals who, for whatever reason, had nothing else better to do but to stay until the bitter end. They draped themselves over every corner of the room, disparate and dissolute.

So how to fill 45 minutes with something meaningful?

'We not doin' no work you know.'

They were obviously not in the mood for working – and yet Andy knew intuitively that they would not be able to handle 45 minutes with no structure. He swept them up and sat them down. They quietened and fell into a kind of relaxed and easy conversation with each other. One of the individuals in the group was Daniel. Andy realised, somewhat guiltily, that this was the first time that he had had an opportunity to really sit down and spend some time in his company – the previous ten weeks having been dominated by more vocal and outgoing individuals who were now very conspicuous by their absence.

Daniel sat there quiet, neat, looking older than his years, his cheeks already showing the downy presence of a future beard. He held himself well – his clothes had that 'I've got a good frame underneath' look. To look at him you would say he was not a troublemaker – he would be the kind of kid who could easily go by unnoticed. The kind of kid that teachers would have to trot out a standard phrase for when writing his report … 'satisfactory progress' because he kept his head down.

The kids in the group also noticed Daniel's neat appearance.

'That's not school uniform', one of them remarked, referring to his black polo shirt.

Daniel grinned and said 'So?'.

'It's the logo', one of them explained, 'you're not supposed to come to school wearing polo shirts that have a logo'.

'What is the logo?'

'It's a City top', Daniel replied.

This was PSHE and Andy saw his way into a conversation with Daniel.

'So you like football then, Daniel?'

Daniel also saw his cue and replied at length. He told about the season ticket he always gets for his birthday (it costs hundreds, you know), about the new stadium, the most recent signings and his hopes for the forthcoming season.

'So what do you get out of it?'

'It's a buzz', he replied.

'Say some more …'

'It's being close to the crew, you know, the firm … the lads who are the hard nuts, the real men amongst the supporters. They are the guys who sort out the opposition fans; we beat the shit out of them queer bastards. We're not disorganised yobos, you know … These guys in the crew are in a different league, they are in their 20s and 30s. They have proper jobs, wear designer labels. I've got my place you know …'

He meant literally 'his place'.

'There's this bridge on the way up to the ground. I stand at the edge to get a really good view of the action – the other fans don't stand a chance – they get ambushed – and the coppers don't have a clue – they just pick up the pieces afterwards. That's the bruders for you.'

Something inside Andy stirred, a kind of sinking feeling that, left to its own devices, could easily turn into panic. Every time this happened it felt harder and harder. Why the reference in German when most lads of Daniel's age seem to run a million miles from the idea of foreign languages? The other kids seemed not to have noticed. Andy retreated from the conversation into an inner world made fuzzy by the need to sleep. In some ways this was the best but also the hardest day of the year. Just get through, get to the end, see it out … and then sleep.

A bell rang and Andy knew he had been spared. No more of this for six weeks. Everyone was released, including him.

He gathered his stuff in his bag and took one last look around the room. The dust was drifting on top of the cupboards and the faded sugar paper hung off the wall. He gazed down three storeys to see that, on the field, preparations were well in hand for the staff barbecue. Leaving speeches, a glass of wine; the camaraderie of 'the best afternoon of the year'. Soon, a fleet of four-wheel drives would be under starter's orders to make a dash home where caravans would be hooked, wife and kids collected before making for the channel ports by midnight.

'We'll be in Cherbourg by 5am – it's the only way …'

And Andy knew he couldn't face it. He slipped away. He was owed it, having played tennis with the kids till six most nights of late.

Reflections on 'End of Term'

On reading this narrative I am aware of just how present I am as a researcher-writer. Caulley (2008: 430) notes that the selection and sketching of descriptive material demands detail, and I have drawn extensively on my past professional experience as a secondary school teacher to describe this environment and these interactions. The fatigue felt in the final lesson of the year was a very familiar feeling to me. I'm struck by how the depleted nature of these teaching groups and the removal of structured classroom activity opens up the possibility for new, more direct personal encounters that can reveal things about social relations in the classroom, exposing subtle, previously unseen presences in the group. Embodiment is a strong theme in the narrative. The portrayal of Daniel as being a potent presence is noticeable, not just in terms of his physical presence and its homo-erotic qualities, but in terms of his clothing also. The non-standard polo shirt that deviates from school uniform mirrors the non-standard garb worn by Andy, PE teachers often being visibly different to classroom teachers in secondary schools. The reference to 'hiding a multitude of sins' is significant in that it resonates with a number of participants in my research who referred to the 'wearing of a costume' that is part of the role of being a teacher, literally covering the more personal dimensions of their identity. What is significant about Andy's PE teacher garb is that, like Daniels city top, there is a connection with sport. The discussion of sport becomes the vehicle for the expression of a significant theme in the narrative, namely the discourse of hegemonic masculinity. Daniel's reference to his older affiliates that he refers to as 'bruders', introduces a more sinister turn. Despite the overt credentials of respectability visible in the wearing of designer clothing, the reference to bruders (German for 'brothers') could indicate the presence of neo-Nazi sympathisers within groups of football fans. The experience of football on Saturday afternoons therefore, is not merely a spectator sport but a vehicle for the expression of masculinities and political positions.

A significant schism opens up at this point. For Andy, hearing the word queer and references to violence articulated in Daniel's conversation is the moment when he disconnects and retreats to a more marginal position in the group. An interesting question is to what extent this reflects a more general pattern in his relationship with the school. His work as a PE teacher takes him away physically from the more central spaces of the school to pitches, gyms and sports halls more likely to be on the fringes of the school site. Withdrawal is also his response to the prospects of the end of term barbecue where the heteronormative discourses inherent in the staff group are revealed in the discussion of plans for the holidays.

Sleeping Bream

Tonight, darkness had been slow in coming and the twilight cast long shadows over the vast green expanse of the park, the last of the Asian families, footballers, dads and kids slowly drifting away to the nearby streets of terraced houses for baths and then bed. Now night came – by the time Andy got there a warm, still Mediterranean-like balminess hung over the tree-lined walk alongside the canal.

He scanned the length of the walkway, which extended into the distant gloom as far as he could see. Great shafts of neon light emanated from the factory windows on the other side of the water. A huge moon rose over the skyline, bathing the bushes and shrubbery in a silvery sheen – the stillness was only punctuated by the background hum of the city and the occasional plop from the canal, as some creature moved around. The activity was underway, the towpath busy with men cruising up and down, some disappearing into the bushes, others focussed in a kind of silent, determined searching.

Andy leaned back against a tree trunk. Hours could pass at this game, it was a complete lottery. Some nights there was just too much attitude and nobody wanted to know him. On others, he was fighting them off. He glanced down at his mobile, and noticed the 'message received' icon flashing. He listened against the earpiece:
'Message received today, at 11:14 pm …
Andy?
It's Jo.
Where were you at the barbecue today?
Are you ok? Just thought I'd give you a call.
Actually babes, I'm worried about you … where are you?
Will you give me a call … oh just had a thought … perhaps you've met Mr. Right or Mr. Right-Now [giggle].
Anyway, give me a call, come round … love you loads.'
Jo. She was a star. Some days she was his guardian angel, a sister … always his confidante. What was it about that woman that he ended telling her stuff? She was the only person at school he had told … on a staff night out and after way too many beers. It kind of just happened. She had

been honest in her reply. 'I had wondered ... people are talking about you Andy. They're putting two and two together. Good-looking bloke, not married and no girlfriend. And the kids reckon you must be too, though God knows, nobody I know has said anything to them.'

Andy sighed. Just thinking about it instigated a downer.

Tonight, in another universe, he would be with the four-wheel drive brigade heading for Portsmouth ... instead, life had dealt him this card.

'All right, mate?'

Andy was snapped back to the present.

'Got the time mate? Fancy a beer?'

A young guy stared out of the darkness, his face tinted by the cigarette lodged in the corner of his mouth. Under his arm he carried a clutch of lager cans, swinging and tenuously held together by a plastic top. His smile revealed teeth that shone out like some kind of beacon. Andy realised that this was an entrée, an invitation and yes, tonight he had all the time in the world.

'Been waitin' for my mate ... been stood up'. He laughed.

Andy checked out the newcomer. Nineteen? Twenty at a push? Outwardly cocky, confident ... and such a townie, such a scally. The apparent informality of dress was carefully sculpted: Adidas trackies, Fred Perry top ... and a lithe, muscled physique. Despite the outward appearance, there was something about this kid (and that's the word that sprung to mind), there was something about him that was unsure, unconfident, not definite. Andy knew intuitively, that there was more to him than met the eye.

The cans were cracked open.

'Sean'.

A hand reached out to shake hands. He squinted through a spiral of cigarette smoke.

'Steve', Andy replied.

'What do you do for a living, Steve?'

'I work in an office'. Andy's second lie.

'Couldn't stand it, mate. I work in a factory yard driving a fork lift truck ... fucking office, no thanks.'

They sat down on the bank.

'I used to come down here with my Dad and brother, fishing all day. See that pool over there?' Andy stared at the inky blackness of the canal.

'Bream mate, that's where they lie on the bottom – sleeping'. He laughed again at his own joke.

There was a pause.

'So, how do you know if you are, then? How do you know if you've turned?'

Andy realised that this conversation was about deduction, a kind of exercise in 'filling in the gaps'.

'Go down the Kiwi Bar and you'll soon know right enough'

'Been fucking banned, mate.'

An alarm bell rang, and Andy wanted to know more but stepped back from asking.

Forty minutes passed. His story unfolds: his relationship with his girl-friend ended six months ago ... he has slept rough ... had to deal with multiple losses ... friend was killed, problems at work ... all this hit him a week after they split ... he was being used ...

The detail is interspersed with the same question.

'So do you think you can turn?'

Another pause. The alcohol began to assert itself. Andy felt its warm ambience and his eyes averted to the lad's crotch.

The scally caught his gaze and acted on his cue. 'Fancy some cock, mate?'

'Not here ... it's too open. Through the railings, in the park'.

Andy knew the drill. The rhododendron bushes in the park provided the cover for sexual intimacy, away from dog walkers and the other cruis-ers. He began to lighten up so that by the time they reached the grassy space in the park, he could hold back no longer. He pressed his lips against the kid, forcing his mouth in response. The lad seemed to be in some sort of trance. He slowly undressed until he stood before Andy totally naked.

'You can do anything you like to me ...'

Andy was so caught up by the beauty, and make no mistake – he was classically beautiful, tattooed, firm and sculpted – that it took a couple of seconds for the headlights to register. Two hundred yards away a police car swept around the corner from behind a band stand, the beam from a powerful hand-held light probing the undergrowth.

Andy ordered 'Get in the fucking bushes now!' The lad obeyed in an instant. The car was upon them in seconds and the beam changed sides to probe the opposite side. It followed the path and then was gone, almost as quickly as it had appeared. Andy parted the branches, sighed and realised that he was shaking.

The lad began 'Do you want to ...'

'Get dressed, just get dressed'.

The tone of Andy's order had shocked both of them. They fell silent as they walked back to the towpath. It was as though the inci-dent had momentarily revealed, an aspect of their relatedness. It was embarrassing.

'Here's my number. Will you phone me?'

'Sure' Andy replied.

The lad looked him in the eye and decided to make his final bid of the night.

'There's something else I need to tell you. I'm into cross dressing and I want you to fuck me.'

Just for once, Andy was at a loss for words.

Reflections on 'Sleeping Bream'

The environment described in 'Sleeping Bream' is an amalgam of my obser-vations of a cruising area for which I recorded written (fieldwork notes) and photographic data as well as the public sex environment research of (Coxon, 1996; Flowers, Marriott and Hart, 2000). A striking thing about this setting is its daytime transformation from an inner city park to a nighttime cruis-ing area. Although living locally and being familiar with this location, what he cannot contemplate are dealings with police that he risks in undertaking this non-normative sexual activity. The message left on his mobile from his colleague Jo provides not just a verbal connection to the professional domain but reveals further information about the portrayal of Andy as an isolate in the social system of the school. A rupture appears here in that this is not strictly true, as evidenced by the closeness he obviously has with her

The appearance of Sean introduces a theme of instability and unpredict-ability. Everything about Sean is open to question and repeated questioning is one of his main modes of communication. To be asking 'how do you know if you are?' could indicate that here is a person who is fluid, in a state of becom-ing, unsure. There is a striking dissonance between his outward machismo as expressed by his physicality, clothing, manual job and the threat of violence (he's been banned by the Kiwi Bar) and his less obvious preference for cross dressing activity and his submissive role as a bottom in sexual interactions. There is also a suggestion of emotional vulnerability in the life story nar-rated to Andy and then in his sexual submission to Andy in their clandestine encounter. He is willing to be literally and metaphorically naked, whereas Andy is not. Unsurprisingly as far as Andy is concerned, the theme of control emerges in a number of ways. Although he lies and hides his professional self, I think this surfaces in the form of a subtext in the tense moments between Sean and himself following the incident with the police car. As the author of the text, I find this an uncomfortable moment because although both par-ties are in a position to consent to sexual activity, there is a proximity and resonance with Andy in his professional setting. It does not take too much imagination to see Andy in teacher mode when he barks the instructions to Sean. On the face of it this appears to be an encounter between an older (professional, middle class?) man and a younger working class man. Such an interpretation would seem to advantage Andy in terms of power relations. Ultimately though, it is Sean who seems to be in control as the instigator of moments in their encounter.

Considering the discursive properties of 'field' and its impact on habitus

So what messages are contained in discourses present in the respective spaces of the narratives and what is their influence on personal agency?

Skeggs (2004) argues that messages understood and internalised by the individual has a direct bearing on the perceptions of the social capital they feel they can bring to the respective spaces. In terms of queer identity, there is a strong theme of absence in the school environment and it is pertinent to question the reasons for this. Donnelly (2000) notes that the ethos of any educational institution is not just composed of the official, formal discourses contained in statements it makes about itself but, of the more elusive messages received about 'atmosphere' and unspoken norms derived from individual interactions between members of the school community during a school day. An insight into the complexity of this can be gleaned from the fact that in any secondary school classroom, its discursive properties may change hourly, with every movement of the timetable. This has significance for queer educator's conceptualisation of field, in that many risk assessment decisions have to be made in such a dynamic environment, in terms of which identities are revealed, and which are kept hidden.

Skeggs (2004: 22) notes that the volume of embodied capital brought to any situation is directly correlated to entitlement to social relations and both Andy and Daniel bring significant embodied capitals in relation to masculinity, presented via their affiliation with sport (Wellard, 2009). It is unsurprising that football becomes a strong theme in the classroom conversation, Anderson (2011) arguing that sport has historically been a vehicle for expressions of hegemonic masculinities, sexist and homophobic discourses producing a hierarchy of men, queer masculinities being relegated to the bottom of the pile. So in Andy's case any capital accrued via his physicality and professional role has the potential to be erased because of his queer identity. It is not coincidental that the reference to violence injects a more sinister tone in the first narrative, changing the atmosphere at which point Andy withdraws from his interaction with Daniel.

Even where classroom and staffroom atmosphere is more open and liberal, the 'official' discourses relating to the definition and scope of secondary teachers role are major inhibitors to the expression of queer identities. Implicit in the new teacher professionalism is a growing weight of responsibility in that the role demands a strict maintenance of boundaries, being proactive as a moral/spiritual arbiter of society and communicating knowledge about sexuality in careful terms (GTCE, 2009a; DfEE, 2000). Significantly, the discourses contained in Sex and Relationships Education (SRE) guidance has been identified as a revealing indicator of norms and discourses within school settings (Epstein and Johnson, 1998; Atkinson, 2002). The current guidance makes explicit references to the position of separation expected in the teachers role via statements such as 'parents and pupils may need to be reassured that the personal beliefs and attitudes of teachers will not influence the teaching of sex and relationship education within the PSHE framework' (DfEE, 2000: 14) and 'teachers can avoid embarrassment and protect pupils' privacy by always depersonalising discussions'

(DfEE, 2000: 22). Similarly, heteronormativity is strongly in evidence when emphasis is placed on:

> the importance of marriage for family life, stable and loving relationships, respect, love and care. It is also about the teaching of sex, sexuality, and sexual health. It is not about the promotion of sexual orientation or sexual activity – this would be inappropriate teaching.
>
> DfEE (2000: 5)

Following the establishment of the General Council for Teaching in England (GTCE) in the last decade, guidance now exists to 'maintain and improve standards of professional conduct' (GTCE, 2009a: 3) in 'strengthening teacher professionalism' both inside and for the first time, outside the school classroom in the public arena away from school. As an agency independent from government, the potency of GTCE authority extends to both regulatory powers as the awarding body for qualified teacher status (QTS) in England and to compliances required in professional discourses identified by practising teachers and others in society involved in teaching and learning. As far as queer teachers are concerned it could be said to have contradictory influence, on the one hand being supportive via the demonstration of 'respect for diversity in learning communities' (including sexual orientation) (GTCE, 2009a: 11), but then being far less supportive with regard to any potential non-normative sexual activity practiced by teachers in their personal lives. The GTCE makes both implicit and explicit statements about this, requiring teachers to 'maintain reasonable standards in their own behaviour that enable them to maintain an effective learning environment and also to uphold public trust and confidence in the profession' GTCE (2009a: 15). More explicitly, they observe that 'it's exceedingly rare for us to take action against non-criminal behaviour outside of school. We reprimanded just two teachers for this in 2009, both already sacked by their schools: one for promoting unsafe sex on TV, the other for appearing in a pornographic film' (GTCE, 2009b).

Away from school, discourse also seems to have a potent impact on Andy's approach to managing his professional identity when he is cruising. Flowers, Marriott and Hart (2000) and Jeyasingham (2002) acknowledge the motivations for cruising are highly complex and these environments are characterised by particular codes of behaviour in which communication is kept to a minimum. Brown (2008: 916) notes that men remake these spaces in ways that are 'representational, haptic, performative, embodied, material and affectual', arguing that media (including Internet) discourses are significant in communicating the unspoken rules of cruising and public sex. Drawing on Deluze's notion of 'affect', Brown (ibid.) argues that the identity of a cruiser does not neatly map onto existing identity categories. In these spaces an exploration of 'what a body can do, how it can give and experience pleasure is of more importance than the adoption of neat identity categories.' Whilst embodiment is also a significant theme in this environment also, the physical and discursive presence of unspoken authorities is a major inhibitor for Andy. The GTCE teachers code of conduct presumably extends its reach to this space also, reinforced by the presence and authority of the local constabulary. So teacher identity is hidden, lied about, avoided in this context.

If habitus, as Lawler (2004) suggests, is intuitive knowledge assimilated over a period of time about 'the rules of the game', it is important to question the historical influences that have shaped perceptions of this. Greenland and Nunney (2008) note that as recently as 2008, and in spite of its repeal in 2003, the sleeper effect of Section 28 of the Local Government Act 1988, was still being felt in English secondary school spaces, contributing to confusion and ambivalence towards homosexuality's relationship with education. In the twenty-first century, queer educators are caught in the dilemma of wanting to be out as role models for young people whilst needing to be cautious and protective of their identity in the normative gaze. Participants in this research reported vulnerability to old stereotypes such as being 'irresponsible' and 'corrupters of youth', although interview data showed them to be exactly the opposite, being highly responsible, talented, dedicated teachers who were very conscious of the need to maintain boundaries. Skeggs (2004: 26) reminds us that in his consideration of 'Sexuality after Foucault', David Halperin (2003) asserts that lesbians and gay men have learned to not just occupy positions of ambiguity in social spaces but to deploy ambiguity to resist forces of power and violence, making themselves 'unrecognizable, difficult to read or appearing abject in a non-pathological way'. Taylor (2009) observes that such silences and articulations, tensions and contradictions, claims and denials, are all part of the intersectional slippages which happen when professional identities are negotiated in education spaces. Arguably 'the novelty of queerness is a consolation for the awkwardness of it' or in the case of Andy, the use of extended working hours is a method of appeasing the guilt, of 'settling the account'.

Reviewing agency: Critiquing field and habitus

So to what extent have recent perspectives on field, habitus and their relationship with personal agency fixed possibilities of who can be present and absent? In her consideration of gender as 'a lived relation', McNay (2000; 2004: 179) points out that personal agency 'cannot simply be understood as a property of unstable discursive structures', opening up the possibility that social contexts and individuals are dynamic and subject to change. Reviewing the concept of 'performative agency' in the exchange between Judith Butler and Pierre Bourdieu, McNay (2004: 180) argues that both offer an incomplete account of agency. She critiques Butler's account of in that it falls short due to the limited existence of certain linguistic preconditions than need to exist for certain types of linguistic innovation to be possible. Similarly, in her view Bourdieu's perspective is also lacking in that it fails to take into account the possibility of linguistic innovation, assuming instead that social relations are predetermined and static. Dean (2011) points to the construction of masculinities as an example of how the (re)constitution of subjects in social relations is subject to change.

Although earlier literature points to the presence of hegemonic masculinities in many school classrooms (Mac an Ghaill, 1994; Renold, 2005), Dean critiques hegemonic, essentialist perspectives on masculinity, noting the new complexities of intersectionality which is generating non-homophobic heterosexualites and masculinities, opening up the possibility for greater expression of queer subjects. There is also evidence that the field is also shifting in English secondary schools in that previous guidance issued by the then DCSF into homophobic bullying (DCSF, 2007) and transphobic bullying (DCSF, 2009) is now reinforced by the new Office for Standards in Education (OFSTED) inspection framework (OFSTED, 2012), constructed in response to the Equality Act 2010. For the first time, school inspectors will grade schools according to their record on tackling homophobia and transphobia and on creating an inclusive, accepting environment for LGBT people in terms of pupils' behaviour towards other young people and adults.

So against this changing, more inclusive backdrop who can be present? McNinch (2007: 211) implies that homonormative men who fit the stereotype of the 'happily together couple' are now being made visible, even though the role of queer teacher remains conflicted. In the past this was by the burden of the closet and Socratic dualism whereby the mind is strictly delineated from the body and now 'by the burden of modelling health and openness beyond stereotypes promulgated in popular cultures obsession, like gay culture itself, with youth'. Such modelling comes with 'strings attached' and whilst there is a new homonormative presence there is also a re-production of an 'absent other', queer seemingly out of the frame having no discursive capital in professional/social terms. Despite this, McNay (2000; 2004: 179) points out that acts of resistance and subversion *are* mechanisms for displaying visibility and the fact that queer men who are educators traverse queer spaces and perform queer acts *is* a kind of presence in itself. This raises the possibility that the experiences individuals have in each space might leak into the other, resulting in the potential for a symbiotic as well as an adversarial relationship. My participants confirm this when they note the transferability to the classroom of intuitive skills related to non-verbal communication honed through cruising and when they reflect on cruising activity as something central to the project of 'finding oneself', mirrored in the experience of becoming a teacher. McNinch (2007: 210) argues that it is naive to assume that the erotic lies outside the construction of queer teacher identity, the very act of teaching always involving an element of seduction, requiring teachers to walk 'the tightrope stretching between eros and the erotic, between innocence and wisdom, between the young and the old'.

So how realistic and appropriate is it to enact Rofes' vision of a more visible queer educator identity? In his career Rofes worked as an educator with both children in schools and adults in a university setting and it can be argued that it might be easier to make queer visible in educational spaces with adults than those involving children and young people. The discursive practices relating to educational space is key here, secondary schools in England having specific discursive conditions that bring a strong influence to bear. Cress (2009) and Sand (2009) both note that irrespective of context, the act of coming out and sharing 'the personal' remains a tension, constituting a complex process requiring negotiation, disentangling and a skilled understanding of professional relationship. I have proposed elsewhere (Biddulph, 2012), a view of how teachers can engender compassionate, insightful citizenship in relation to sexualities in all their students, that goes beyond a position of mere tolerance, echoing Tatchell's (2012) vision of life 'beyond equality'. In considering what queer culture can offer the mainstream, perhaps the way forward in school classrooms is neither to deprive students of a queer-teacher role model nor to edit out the discussion of theoretical perspectives on sexualities at an age appropriate level.

Bibliography

Adkins, L. (2004a) 'Introduction' in L. Adkins and B. Skeggs (eds) *Feminism after Bourdieu*. London: Blackwell, pp. 3–18.

Adkins, L. (2004b) 'Reflexivity: Freedom or habit of gender?' in L. Adkins and B. Skeggs (eds) *Feminism after Bourdieu*. London: Blackwell, pp. 191–209.

Atkinson, E. (2002) 'Education for diversity in a multi-sexual society: Negotiating the contradictions of contemporary discourse', *Sex Education*, 2(2): 119–32.

Anderson, E. (2011) 'Masculinities in sport and physical culture: Three decades of evolving research', *Journal of Homosexuality*, 58(5): 565–78.

Barnfield, D. and Humberstone, B. (2008) 'Speaking out: Perspectives of gay and lesbian practitioners in outdoor education in the UK', *Journal of Adventure Education and Outdoor learning*, 8(1): 31–42.

Biddulph, M. (2005a) *Gay and bisexual men who are educators: A narrative analysis of space, identity and deployment*, Unpublished doctoral thesis, Nottingham Trent University, Nottingham.

Biddulph, M. (2005b) 'The monochrome frame, mural-making as a methodology for understanding self' in C. Mitchell, S. Weber and K. O'Reilly-Scanlon (eds) *Just who do we think we are? Autobiography and self-study in teaching*. London: Routledge-Falmer, pp. 49–57.

Biddulph, M. (2012) 'Sexualities and citizenship education' in J. Arthur and H. Cremin (eds) *Debates in citizenship education*. London: Routledge, pp. 100–14.

Binnie, J. (2001) 'The erotic possibilities of the city' in D. Bell, J. Binnie, R. Holliday, R. Longhurst and R. Peace (eds) *Pleasure zones: Bodies, cities, spaces*. Syracuse, NY: Syracuse University Press, pp. 103–30.

Bourdieu, P. (1990) *The logic of practice*. Cambridge: Polity Press.

Bourdieu, P. and Wacquant, L. J. D. (2002) *An invitation to reflexive sociology*. Chicago: University of Chicago Press.

Brown, G. (2008) 'Ceramics, clothing and other bodies: Affective geographies of homoerotic cruising encounters', *Social & Cultural Geography*, 9(8): 915–32.

Browne, K. and Nash, C. (2010) *Queer methods and methodologies: Intersecting queer theories and social science research*. Farnham: Ashgate.

Britzman, D. (1997) 'The tangles of implication', *International Journal of Qualitative Studies in Education*, 10(1): 31–7.

Casey, M. (2007) 'The queer unwanted and their undesirable "otherness"' in K. Browne, J. Lim and G. Brown (eds) *Geographies of sexualities: Theory, Practice and Politics*. Aldershot: Ashgate, pp. 125–35.

Caulley, D. (2008) 'Making qualitative research reports less boring: The techniques of writing creative nonfiction', *Qualitative Inquiry*, 14(3): 424–49.

Clough, P. (2002) *Narratives and fictions in educational research*. Buckingham: Open University Press.

Coxon, A. (1996) *Between the sheets: Sexual diaries and gay men's sex in the era of AIDS*. London: Cassell.

Cress, C. (2009) 'Pride and prejudice in the classroom: Navigating boundaries of personal and professional', *Lesbian and Gay Psychology Review*, 10(1): 13–17.

Dean, J. (2011) 'Thinking intersectionality: Sexualities and the politics of multiple identities' in Y. Taylor, S. Hines and M. Casey (eds) *Theorizing intersectionality and sexuality*. London: Palgrave Macmillan, pp. 119–39.

DePalma, R. and Atkinson, E. (2009) *Interrogating heteronormativity in primary schools: The no outsiders project*. Stoke on Trent: Trentham Books.

Department for Children, Schools and Families (DCSF) (2007) *Homophobic bullying. Safe to learn: Embedding antibullying work into schools*. London: DCSF.

Department for Children, Schools and Families (DCSF) (2009) *Guidance for schools on preventing and responding to sexist, sexual and transphobic bullying. Safe to learn: Embedding antibullying work into schools*. London: DCSF.

Department for Education and Employment (DfEE) (2000) *Sex and Relationships Education Guidance*. London: DfEE.

Donnelly, C. (2000) 'In pursuit of school ethos', *British Journal of Educational Studies*, 48(2): 134–54.

Epstein, D. and Johnson, R. (1998) *Schooling sexualities*. Buckingham: Open University Press.

Epstein, D., O' Flynn, S. and Telford, D. (2002) 'Innocence and experience: Paradoxes in sexuality and education' in D. Richardson and D. Seidman (eds) *Handbook for lesbian and gay studies*. London: Sage, pp. 271–90.

Flowers, P., Marriott, C. and Hart, G. (2000) 'The bars, the bogs and the bushes: The impact of locale on sexual cultures', *Culture, Health and Sexuality*, 2(1): 69–86.

Foucault, M. (1981) 'The order of discourse' in R. Young (ed.) *Untying the text: A post-structuralist reader*. London: Routledge, pp. 48–78.

Gemignani, M. (2011) 'Between researcher and researched: An introduction to countertransference in qualitative inquiry', *Qualitative Inquiry*, 17(8): 701–8.

Greenland, K. and Nunney, R. (2008) 'Section 28: It ain't over till it's over', *Pastoral Care in Education*, 26(4): 243–51.

Griffin, P. (1991) 'Identity management strategies among lesbian and gay educators', *Qualitative Studies in Education*, 4(3): 189–202.

General Teaching Council for England (GTCE) (2009a) *Code of conduct and practice effective from 1 October 2009*. London: GTCE.

General Teaching Council for England (GTCE) (2009b) *Code of conduct and practice for registered teachers: Outside the classroom* [online] (updated 16 September 2009), http://www.gtce.org.uk/teachers/thecode/outside_class/, accessed on 18 February 2012.

Halperin, D. (2003) 'Sexuality after Foucault', Plenary address Sexuality after Foucault Conference, University of Manchester, UK, 28–30 November 2003.

Inckle, K. (2011) 'Bent: Non-normative embodiment as lived intersectionality' in Y. Taylor, S. Hines and M. Casey (eds) *Theorizing intersectionality and sexuality.* London: Palgrave Macmillan, pp. 255–73.

Jeyasingham, D. (2002) 'Ladies and "gentlemen": location, gender and the dynamics of public sex, in K. Chedgzoy, M. Francis and M. Pratt (eds) *In a queer space, sexuality and belonging in British and European contexts.* Aldershot: Ashgate, pp. 73–81.

Johnson, R. (1993) 'Editor's introduction' in P. Bourdieu *The Field of Cultural Production: Essays on Art and Literature.* Cambridge: Polity Press.

Keogh, P., Dodds, C. and Henderson, L. (2004) *Working class gay men: Redefining community, restoring identity.* London: Sigma Research.

Kissen, R. (1996) *The last closet: The real lives of lesbian and gay teachers.* Portsmouth, NH: Heinemann.

Lawler. S. (2004) 'Rules of engagement: Habitus, power and resistance' in L. Adkins and B. Skeggs (eds) *Feminism after Bourdieu.* Oxford: Blackwell, pp. 110–28.

Mac an Ghaill, M. (1994) *The making of men: Masculinities, sexualities and schooling.* Buckingham: Open University Press.

McNay, L. (2000) *Gender and Agency: Reconfiguring the Subject in Feminist and Social Theory.* Cambridge: Polity Press.

McNay, L. (2004) 'Agency and experience: Gender as a lived relation' in L. Adkins and B. Skeggs (eds) *Feminism after Bourdieu.* Oxford: Blackwell, pp. 175–90.

McNinch, J. (2007) 'Queering seduction: Eros and erotic in the construction of gay teacher identity', *Journal of Men's Studies*, 15(2): 197–215.

Miller, J. (1998) 'Autobiography as a queer curriculum practice' in W. Pinar (ed.) *Queer theory in education*, Mahwah, NJ: Lawrence Erlbaum, pp. 365–74.

Office for Standards in Education (OFSTED) (2012) *The framework for school inspection. guidance and grade descriptors for inspecting schools in England under section 5 of the Education Act 2005, from January 2012.* Manchester: OFSTED.

Piper, H. and Sikes, P. (2010) 'All teachers are vulnerable but especially gay teachers: Using composite fictions to protect research participants in pupil–teacher sex-related research', *Qualitative Inquiry*, 16(7): 566–74.

Puar, J. (2007) *Terrorist assemblages: Homonationalism in queer times.* Durham: Duke University Press.

Renold, E. (2005) *Girls, boys and junior sexualities: Exploring children's gender and sexual relations in the primary school.* London: Routledge Falmer.

Rofes, E. (2005) *A radical rethinking of sexuality and schooling: Status quo or status queer?* Oxford: Rowman and Littlefield.

Sand, S. (2009) 'To reveal or not to reveal, that is the question', *Lesbian and Gay Psychology Review*, 10(1): 23–6.

Skeggs, B. (2004) 'Context and background: Pierre Bourdieu's analysis of class, gender and sexuality' in L. Adkins and B. Skeggs (eds) *Feminism after Bourdieu.* Oxford: Blackwell, pp. 19–33.

Sparkes, A. (1996) 'Teachers and the search for self: Two cases of structured denial' in N. Armstrong (ed.) *New directions in physical education, Volume 3: Change and innovation.* London: Cassell, pp. 157–78.

Tatchell, P. (2012) *Beyond equality*, Keynote address, Nottingham City Joint Partnership Conference, March 2012.

Taylor, Y. (2007) 'Brushed behind the bike shed: Working class lesbians' experiences of school', *British Journal of Sociology of Education*, 28(3): 349–62.

Taylor, Y. (2009) 'Facts, fictions, identity constrictions: Sexuality, gender and class in higher education', *Lesbian and Gay Psychology Review*, 10(1): 38–41.

Taylor, Y. (ed.) (2010) *Classed intersections: Spaces, selves, knowledges*. Farnham: Ashgate.

Taylor, Y., Hines, S. and Casey, M. (eds) (2011) *Theorizing intersectionality and sexuality*. London: Palgrave Macmillan.

Wellard, I. (2009) *Sport, masculinities and the body*. London: Routledge.

Winter, R., Buck, A. and Sobiechowska, P. (1999) *Professional experience and the investigative imagination The ART of reflective writing*. London: Routledge.

12
Organisation Studies: Not Nearly 'Queer Enough'

Nick Rumens

Introduction

In 2005, Stephen Valocchi's article 'Not yet queer enough' (2005) argued for a theoretically 'queerer' sociology of gender and sexuality, characterised by its anchoring of discursive power arrangements within economic and political intuitional processes. This is a welcome reassertion of the same plea made by Seidman (1996) some years previously, intended to encourage sociologists to build inroads in conjoining queer theory with sociological analysis. While promising work has been undertaken by queer theorists and sociologists in that respect, much the same cannot be said for the state of queer theory's progress in crossing disciplinary boundaries in areas such as law, technology and organisation studies (Halley and Parker, 2011; Landström, 2007; Parker, 2001). This might be a self-evident point to make but we should not overlook the difficulties experienced by scholars in some disciplines in even raising the subject of queer theory, let alone addressing pressing issues such as developing a queerer sociology, the possibilities of queer futures, whether particular theories are 'queer enough' or, as others have speculated, whether the intellectual and political power of queer theory is bankrupt (Edelman, 2004; Freeman, 2010; Halley and Parker, 2011). Such questions are more likely to be broached and addressed in disciplines within the humanities, arts and education and some parts of the social sciences. Elsewhere, scholarly debates on queer theory have yet to reach the maturity displayed within sociology, let alone the humanities and arts where queer theory has established deep roots. The field of organisation studies is one such example and is the central concern of this chapter.

You will be hard pressed to find references to queer theory in management and organisation studies textbooks. Organisation studies has not warmly embraced queer theory, despite a history of drawing widely from other disciplines including anthropology, sociology, economics, cultural studies and psychology, in order to understand organisation, work and its effects on individuals. For the most part, organisational theory has been drafted into the service of improving business performance. In that respect, queer theory appears to have little relevance or 'value' as a key component in the toolkit of managers and organisations committed to the maximisation of efficiency and productivity. Equally, not many queer theorists have shown sustained interest in the study of organisations and contemporary work life. As Borgerson (2005: 64) remarks of Judith Butler, although critical of the organisational arrangements implicated in the process of becoming gendered, 'Butler rarely discusses business or management and organizational issues *per se*'. Nonetheless, Borgerson and others (Parker, 2002a) suggest that theorists synonymous with queer, like Butler and Sedgwick, offer valuable conceptual resources for those scholars wishing to examine the gendered and sexual dynamics of work, organisation and economy. One notable example is Lisa Adkins who examines issues of gender and sexuality in the workplace and asks who can move through identity categories (as a 'queer' mobility) within cultural economies where gender and sexuality have become 'mobile, fluid and indeterminate' labour market resources (2002: 6). For Adkins, one immediate issue is who might be 'stuck' in certain identities (e.g. women/lesbian) that become fixed, and not seen as a new capital/ resource or a 'diversity dividend' within the workplace. Crucially, Adkin's analysis sounds a cautionary note about the 'risk' in assuming gender and sexual categories are easily 'undone' by mobility.

This chapter gauges the progress that scholars have made in mobilising queer theory within the field of organisation studies. One aim of this chapter is to reassert earlier academic appraisals of queer theory as a destabilising mode of organisational analysis (Parker, 2002a). Of course, it is possible that some readers might point out that I, like other organisation studies scholars, have come to the table too late, only to find the appetite for queer theory greatly diminished in others. Put differently, hailed as a whirlwind within academic circles during the 1990s, the queer theory hurricane finally spent itself. However, for the sake of organisation studies scholars new to queer theory, or queer theorists new to organisation studies, I turn to Valerie Rohy (2011), who offers a way forward. Rohy suggests that we need not 'resist the death of queer theory, or not in the way one might think', as she goes on to say:

> While it is ironic that queer theory should also be enlivened by prophecies of its death [...] there is no reason why that conversation should not continue. If we choose to accept the humanizing trope that gives life to queer theory, it must therefore be dying, like all of us: after all, the condition of life is its ending. And if so, the question becomes how long and how richly queer theory can live that dying, busy with the work of its time.
>
> (p. 219)

Indeed, this chapter reviews queer theory at 'work' within organisation studies, its reception and its contemporary relevance for studying organisation and organisational life. To begin, I discuss the presence of queer theory within university business schools, revealing its uneasy position and its slow uptake among organisation studies scholars, even among those who inhabit its critical margins. Next, I argue that queer theory is vital to problematising the heteronormativity of organisational life. This issue scythes straight to the heart of discussions about the many purposes of queer theory, particularly within a discipline that is dominated by a managerially biased approach to the study of organisation. Without a doubt, the most illuminating work so far has provided queer readings of some of the concepts at the core of organisation studies such as 'management', revealing how they reproduce heteronormative discourse and gender binaries. What is more, queering 'management' and 'organisation' encourages us to stray from the more trampled paths of queering such things as identity, and into relatively unexplored terrain of queering forms of organising and relating in the workplace. Here I draw upon my research on gay men's workplace friendships to illustrate the potential of queer theory in that endeavour, before concluding with some remarks on why organisation studies ought to be queerer.

Queer theory and university business schools

While queer theory has long been a resident of cultural studies and humanities departments in many universities, its presence within UK and North American university business schools is barely detectable. This is not altogether surprising. Arguably, the 'business' of business schools is to generate practitioner-based research, endorse the career-improving, salary-increasing benefits of business education and to educate the managers and business people of the future. While academic debates on the purpose of business schools are heated and contested (Starkey and Tempest, 2008), for many, a business school orthodoxy is apparent, promulgating managerially biased understandings of organisation, employees and work (Parker, 2002b). From one angle, queer theory seems out of place in debates on improving organisational performance. Indeed, from personal experience, bringing queer theory into the management classroom is no small matter, generally understood by business students as an intrusion into learning how to 'do' management, generating bewilderment, discomfort or derision. Such reactions are, in part, 'reasonable'. From a management perspective, queer theory has no obvious utility for improving the bottom line, although 'queers' and sexualities most certainly do when they are constructed as commodities, lucrative niche markets or affluent consumers.

What is more, in business schools, as in some other higher education environments, the discussion of queer theory can reinforce the common diagnosis of academics as theoretical acrobats; too busy being 'clever' by discussing things nobody else understands. Organisation studies scholars who identify as queer theorists might expect to come under fire for not taking seriously the matter of how theory can be used to improve organisational performance. Even when queer theory has been initially received by business school students with interest and curiosity, it can easily provoke the types of complaints voiced by its most outspoken critics elsewhere (Jeffreys, 2003), as being theoretically opaque, neglectful of the materiality of everyday life and the esoteric plaything of the cognoscenti. Of course no one ever said teaching queer theory is easy, but within many business schools introducing a theory that, for some, appears to liquidate the materiality of organisations, brick by brick, is particularly challenging.

Another way of understanding the controversial presence of queer theory within university business schools is to ask the question: why wouldn't business schools tend to be focused on improving organisational performance? Indeed, business schools are more likely to garner reputations as excellent incubators of managers, especially those with MBAs, than as hotbeds of radical deconstructionism and subversion. However, on closer inspection there is much activity within university business schools to be critical of. As Parker (2002b) notes, in frustration, the orthodoxy of business schools, many of which (particularly those in North America) attach high value to positivistic analyses of organisation, is characterised by a propensity to reduce organisation and organising to managerialism. In other words, when many of us think about organising in the workplace, we tend to think of managers as being a prerequisite. Yet, historically, people have organised remarkably well without the need for individuals to be designated 'managers' and slotted into managerial roles. In business schools where orthodox organisation theory is taught sympathetically and in a non-reflexive fashion, the interests of managers, employers and organisations are frequently privileged. This has been roundly criticised by some scholars as a narrow way of understanding organisational worlds, one that ignores or marginalises the perspectives and experiences of other stakeholders, such as employees. In that regard, what is 'good' for the organisation is not necessarily 'good' for employees, a unitarist assumption that underpins much management scholarship (Delbridge and Keenoy, 2010). For example, managerialist approaches to understanding how people organise at work, illustrated nicely in the breathless debates about how to best motivate employees, typically focus on such things as what compels individuals to work at certain levels and to specified standards. Approached in this way, employees' motives and interests are neatly and conveniently aligned with organisational priorities and managerial values, with the aim of improving business performance.

Crucially, however, critical management studies (CMS) scholars have provided alternative 'critical' ways of understanding, among other things, human organising. Here being 'critical' often means generating radical critique, which Adler, Forbes and Willmott (2007: 120) argue involves directing attention towards exploitative and destructive structures (e.g. capitalism) that 'condition local action and conventional wisdom'. As such, some CMS research on the various techniques for motivating employees, which countless employers have found attractive over the decades, reveal how traditional beliefs and practices about motivation have negative effects, by sustaining larger divisive and potentially inimical structures and forms of organising (Brewis et al., 2006: 15). From a CMS point of view, the limitations of what has been branded as 'mainstream' approaches for motivating individuals at work are understood in terms of how they are enmeshed within relations of power and domination, which squash alternative ways of understanding how employees may organise, such as those that make work more satisfying for employees than employers.

It is not altogether surprising, then, that queer theory occupies the critical fringes of organisation studies. Emerging in the UK during the 1990s as an assortment of critical responses and debates, CMS has embraced different research methods, been animated by an array of critical theories (e.g. Marxism, poststructuralism, feminism, post-colonialism) and focused on diverse subject matter (e.g. identity, power, hierarchy, gender, race). As such, CMS is usefully understood as a loosely connected set of critical debates rather than a unified mass of knowledge (Parker, 2002b), and it is here where queer theory has managed to secure a toehold. While debates on the purpose and future of CMS fall outside the scope of this chapter (see Grey and Willmott, 2005 for discussion), an important point to make here is that, some years on from the birth of CMS, queer theory resides only in its outer critical edges. Although CMS has been and continues to be shaped by the conceptual resources that have helped to constitute queer theories (e.g. poststructuralism, postmodernism, feminism), it is lamentable that queer theories have not gained ground to the extent that some other critical theories have within CMS, most notably poststructuralism and labour process theory. Discussion and references to queer theory in CMS texts is uncommon and, when found, tends to be cursory. For Tatli (2011), while CMS scholars have been busy attacking the 'mainstream' for endorsing a non-reflexive, managerially biased approach to understanding management, they have largely failed to reflect on the mechanisms of hierarchy and exclusion that operate within the CMS. As Tatli goes on to argue, if CMS was to hold a mirror to its face, it will find a 'white, heterosexual, most probably Western, able-bodied man staring back'. Tatli's observation about the narrow demographic make-up of the CMS community is pertinent and alerts us to a problem. It might be that some CMS scholars are non-reflexive about the reproduction of relations of domination, such as those which are marked by heteronormativity, within their own camp. This can hinder the development of much needed scholarly efforts to denaturalise organisational heterosexualities as much as lesbian, gay, bi and trans (LGBT) sexualities. Queer theory, although overlooked by many CMS academics, is potentially helpful in that endeavour, since it maintains a crisp analytical focus on sexualities and genders, moving from examining these only in relation to homosexualities to a focus on the operation of the heterosexual/ homosexual binary as an organising principle in everyday life (Seidman, 1996). As such, many CMS scholars may be as guilty as their imagined counterparts whom occupy the 'mainstream', for not interrogating more closely how a politics of knowledge and difference helps us to mark the 'normal' from the 'abnormal' and the 'acceptable' from the 'unacceptable', whether that be within academic ranks or in the workplace. In that regard, different avenues of inquiry for interrogating what is currently regarded as axiomatic about the world of work remain hidden.

From the previous, necessarily brief, outline of organisation studies and CMS, there is still good reason to be optimistic. A small and important body of literature, emerging over the last decade or so, has acted in a corrective fashion by drawing on queer theory to challenge what is taken-for-granted or 'naturalised' about organisation (Bendl, Fleischmann and Walenta, 2008; Bendl, Fleischmann and Hofmann, 2009; Bowring, 2004; Tyler and Cohen, 2008; Gibson-Graham, 1996; Harding, Ford and Gough, 2010; Harding et al., 2011; Lee, Learmonth and Harding, 2008; Parker, 2002a; Williams, Giuffre and Dellinger, 2009; Williams and Giuffre, 2011). While queer theory is a famously difficult concept to define and employed by academics in different ways, those organisation studies scholars inspired by queer theory have tended to use it in a similar manner. Adopting queer theory to expose a queer presence inside and outside of normality, organisation studies scholars have sought to reveal signs of 'queerness' where we least expect to find it. Put differently, much organisational research animated by queer theories engages in a process of queering, a process where queer existences and possibilities are exposed, with the view to disrupting, denaturalising and transgressing heteronormative structures and practices. For example, queer readings of notions such as 'management' (Parker, 2001, 2002b; Tyler and Cohen, 2008), and 'leadership' (Bowring, 2004; Harding et al., 2011) challenge the multiple binaries that underpin both terms, limiting extant knowledge about how management and leadership can be studied and practiced. In a similar vein, other commentators have developed queer readings of 'public administration' (Lee, Learmonth and Harding, 2008), 'capitalism' (Gibson-Graham, 1996) and diversity management discourse (Bendl, Fleischmann and Walenta, 2008; Bendl, Fleischmann and Hofmann, 2009). Harding, Ford and Gough (2010) also use queer theory as one of several conceptual resources to show how accounting and management academics are susceptible to control and exploitation through the norm of the 'ideal academic'. At the same time, although attracting less scholarly attention so far, queer theory has been used to destabilise heterosexuality and homosexuality as a fixed signifier for particular groups of men and women, noting the possibilities for how relations between and among men and women can be structured in ways beyond the grip of heteronormativity (Rumens, 2011).

As the remainder of this chapter demonstrates, the recent rash of organisation studies publications that embrace queer theory are beginning to chart a wider horizon of possibilities for queering the world of work and its effects on individuals. Put differently, such a project is not confined to specific matters of sexuality and gender in terms of LGBT identity politics, although this subject has not always received the sustained scholarly attention it deserves. Crucially, queering organisation and organisational life can involve disrupting workplace forms of heteronormativity, supplanting dominant ideas about human organising in the workplace and make queer organisation studies theory.

Queer theory and the heteronormativity of organisational life

Queer theorists have consistently raised concerns about the heteronormativity of everyday life (Warner, 1993, 1999); concerns rarely voiced by many but crucially not all organisation studies scholars. Insights into the habitual (re)production of heteronormativity in organisation and its effects on members are derived from a body of research on the sexuality of organisation (Adkins, 2002; Brewis and Linstead, 2000; Hearn et al., 1989; Schilt and Westbrook, 2009; Skidmore, 2004). Much of the scholarship in this area points to how heteronormativity, understood in this chapter as the norms related to gender and sexuality that (re)produce power relations of compulsory heterosexuality, operates within and shapes the sexual and gendered dynamics of organisational environments. Although heteronormativity takes culturally and historically specific forms, previous research reveals the different ways heteronormativity ascribes heterosexuality a normative and privileged status by reinforcing a heterosexual/homosexual binary. The relevance of Adkins' (2002) research is worth noting here, not least because it (dis)engages different queer/materialist frames and utilises Bourdieu's framework to discuss the re-production of the workplace, examining the conditions of possibility this gives rise to for rearticulating organisational genders and sexualities. Viewed as a regulatory regime that structures many facets of everyday organisational life, some queer analyses have shown how the heterosexual/homosexual binary supports the institutionalisation of heterosexual norms that risks excluding, stigmatising and marginalising individuals whose sexualities do not conform to these norms (Ward and Winstanley, 2003). Of course, this includes heterosexuals as much as it does LGBT people, who struggle to realise ideal norms of heterosexuality. However, three decades of organisational scholarship on LGBT sexualities reveals how heteronormativity can breed organisational animosity towards LGBT employees, with particularly damaging outcomes for those who seek to openly participate in work life. Recent research conducted in Canada (Bowring and Brewis, 2009), Australia (Burnett, 2010) and Turkey (Ozturk, 2011), to mention just a few, reminds us that these gains are contextually contingent and not enjoyed by all. As these studies show, employment discrimination based on sexual orientation is still reported in many occupational domains, with some LGBT employees experiencing the same types of negative outcomes reported decades earlier, such as job loss, truncated career trajectories and persecution after coming out at work. At the same time it would be wrong to deny that LGBT people are making important and positive choices about how they want to work on a daily basis. There have been significant equality gains for LGBT people in the workplace. But, through a queer lens, an important issue comes into focus about whether equality gains undermine the power relations which continue to reproduce heteronormativity in the workplace. On this matter, much remains empirically open within the field of organisation studies.

New possibilities for living sexual diversity in specific cultural contexts have been documented and celebrated (Weeks, 2007), allowing us to bear witness to how homosexuality is 'tolerated' or 'accepted' at and outside work. Indeed, more apparent in some quarters are 'new' forms of homosexuality considered to be 'culturally acceptable', recognised largely by their capacity to demonstrate enough synchronicity with hetero-norms on gender, class and race (Seidman, 2002). This is not to say that an 'anything goes' approach currently prevails, where lesbians and gay men might be seen to select and discard 'normal' identities and lives at will. For example, in a special issue of the journal *Sexualities* (February, 2011), dedicated to opening debates on class and sexuality, the optimistic tone of Seidman's perspective is tempered. McDermott (2011) shows how class privilege and disadvantage shape the post compulsory education choices of young LGBT people, enabling and constraining the types of lives and identities that can be imagined and realised. This leads McDermott to conclude that the 'world *some* have won', toying with Jeffrey Weeks's (2007) title, is a case of some winning more than others. Clearly the 'world we have won' is not a uniform experience for all LGBT people.

Still, for some LGBT people, equality gains and new forms of inclusion have occasioned possibilities for participating openly in organisational life, without the fear of negative reprisals (Williams, Giuffre and Dellinger, 2009; Rumens and Kerfoot, 2009). In similar fashion to studies on class and sexuality described previously, this strand of organisational research reveals the unevenness in the experiences of lesbians and gay men at work, highlighting the narrow criteria by which the 'acceptable' homosexual figure can be distinguished from the 'unacceptable' in the workplace. The US-based research by Williams, Giuffre and Dellinger (2009) is striking in that respect, drawing on queer theory to expose the restrictions associated with disclosing and sustaining identities within workplaces where LGB sexualities are 'accepted'. One set of constraints concerns the discursive closure levied by prevailing heteronormative expectations about how LGB people should dress and behave, without attracting unnecessary attention to their sexuality, so as to minimise the risk of being accused of 'flaunting' sexuality at work. While some LGB employees found their visibility depended on their ability to conform to heteronormative sexual and gender stereotypes, others reported feeling 'normal'. Here particular constructions of 'acceptable homosexuality' involved, among other things, the expression of conservative politics, being in a monogamous long-term relationship and dressing 'professionally'. While Williams, Giuffre and Dellinger's (2009) study findings bear out Seidman's (2002: 9) assertion, that an increasing number of gay men and lesbians understand homosexuality as a 'natural, good part of themselves' and 'openly participate in mainstream social life', they suggest also that the normalisation of gay and lesbian identities in 'gay-friendly' organisational environments is not commensurate with a downgrade in the salience of homosexuality in the workplace. Put differently, the heterosexual/homosexual binary has a resilient hold on organisational life, reproducing the normative status of heterosexuality. As such, maintaining 'normal' gay and lesbian identities can result in a state of 'invisibility' or a 'gay-friendly closet', as Williams, Giuffre and Dellinger (2009) put it, in that becoming 'normal' means emphasising similarities and playing down differences with normative constructions of heterosexuality.

Further queer analyses about who and what is '(un)acceptable' in regard to organisational sexualities and genders are needed now, more so than ever before. Definitions of normality and abnormality, of what is acceptable and unacceptable, are subject to revision, contestation and alteration, presenting different opportunities and challenges for how individuals choose to live their lives. For LGBT people, the routine reproduction of heteronormativity in the workplace not only endures but continues to (re)produce existing problems as well as new ones, as it sustains gender binaries which support the representation of heterosexuality as the model of human relations to which individuals ought to aspire. This has harmful consequences for many people at work, not just in terms of conditioning the possibility of workplace homophobia and heterosexism towards LGBT persons, but also in how heterosexualities are normalised and the reproduction of narrow understandings about how men and women organise together. For example, organisational forms of heteronormativity leave unchallenged the assumption that all relationships between men and women are heterosexually structured, squelching the diversity of social relationships at work that may be understood and experienced otherwise (Rumens, 2011). One challenge for organisation studies scholars concerns how to avoid producing accounts of work life that (un)wittingly normalise heterosexuality. As Ashcraft (2009: 320) rightly argues, the tricky task here is to theorise both the distinctiveness and intersection of particular difference formations, without inadvertently extending binaries. This leads me and others, like Ashcraft (2009), to argue that queer theory holds much promise in that respect, particularly as the study of heterosexuality as an organising principle at work has been signposted as a serious but understudied subject in the organisational literature (Pringle, 2008). That being said, it is crucial to acknowledge that many queer theorists, like many organisation studies scholars, do not have a long pedigree of generating analyses of intersectional relations, despite the admonishments of those who rightly aver that sexuality and gender do not operate alone (Sullivan, 2003). Yet part of the process of undermining heteronormativity involves grappling issues of race, ethnicity, class and disability, to name but a few. Here, then, sensitivity towards acknowledging differences and how they intersect is potentially compromised when one difference is examined independently of the others and when notions of difference are subsumed under the term 'queer'.

In sum, then, problematising heteronormativity in the workplace encompasses concerns wider than sexuality and gender, requiring scholars to go beyond single-axis accounts of difference in order to denaturalise heteronormativity and craft 'queerer' accounts of organisational life. Future organisational research in this area must engage with other disciplines such as postcolonial studies, helpful to imagining what Warner (1993) calls a necessarily and desirably queer world. This notwithstanding, some green shoots of an imagined queer world of work can be observed in queer analyses of management and organisation.

Queering management

As is well argued, the emergence of queer theory represents a critical turning point in the study of sexuality. Challenging a naturalised ontology of sexuality by which people are organised and conveniently classified into sexual categories, queer theorists have denaturalised the idea that sexual categories reflect pre-existing internal differences between groups of individuals (Butler, 1990, 2004). Significantly, the capacity of queer theory to disrupt commonly held beliefs about the essence of sexuality and gender has wider relevance and application beyond the field of sexuality. For example, Lee, Learmonth and Harding (2008: 153) mobilise queer theory in order to make theory queer (in this case public administration theory), since it 'requires that we ask about the ontological status of 'things' that we might otherwise take for granted'. Indeed, it is difficult to imagine anything capable of evading queer theory's analytical grip, even those concepts at the heart of academic disciplines, as management is to organisation studies. The possibility of destabilising what has become so taken-for-granted about the concept 'management' has attracted some, but not nearly enough, scholarly attention over the last decade, despite a promising start in Martin Parker's (2002a) seminal article, 'Queering Management and Organization'. Parker was one of the first to articulate queer theory's capacity to denaturalise what we take-for-granted about management as occupation, person, practice and academic discipline. If management can be shown to be a social construction, historically patterned, it follows that we may wish to explore how we can 'do' management in other ways. There are valid reasons as to why organisation studies scholars ought to embark on such a venture. One concern for Parker is that our capacity to develop alternative ways of conceptualising organisations and modes of organising that do not engender 'considerable cruelty and inequality' are being stifled 'through the generalized application of managerialism as the one best way' (2002b: 184). Therein lies the nub of the problem: a lack of imagination at a time when a 'hegemonic model of organization', – a template that has a 'certain air of inevitability to it' (ibid.) – is reproducing more of the same. Imagining alternative ways of organising is a vital task if we are to break the stranglehold of managerially biased ways of understanding management. In that sense, queer theory can help us to question the common (business) sense that tells us managerialism is a 'good' thing and remind us that it is merely one way of organising among many. For Parker, when conceptualised as a form of radical social constructionism, queer theory might be used to reinvigorate debates about management and human organising, drawing attention to the idea that 'doing manager' is performative in the Butlerian (1990) sense, as something that is constructed through the continuous and iterative enactment of management norms. Crucially, this does not mean that management has no connection with sexuality and gender.

More than most, (pro)feminist theorists have exposed management as a gendered construct, typically imbued with historically and culturally specific values and meanings that relate to 'masculinity' (Kerfoot and Knights, 1993; Collinson and Knights, 1996; Wajcman, 1998). By comparison, much less has been made of the sexuality of management or, indeed, organisation, although there are some notable exceptions (Hearn et al., 1989; Roper, 1996; Pringle, 2008). Significantly, a small number of scholars have mobilised queer theory to examine how heteronormativity and management are linked, in ways that reproduce binary gender discourse, constraining current understandings of managers and management. From a queer point of view, the 'heteronormativity of management' is a burning issue, warranting more scholarly attention than it currently receives. For example, Lee, Learmonth and Harding (2008) develop a queer reading of public administration, an area of practice devoted to translating law into policy, and making policy work. Drawing on case study material regarding the effectiveness of sexual health promotion services for men who have sex with men, Lee, Learmonth and Harding point out how gay men employed in managerial roles unconsciously adopt a heteronormative gendered discourse to position themselves as effective managers. The research shows how the heteronormative dimension of a dominant managerial masculinity, with its emphasis on rationality and separation of the public from the private sense of self, offers subject positions that require gay male managers to 'do' management through a heterosexual male managerial identity. This is remarkable in the context of sexual health promotion aimed at men who have sex with men, where 'a gay identity is more or less compulsory for appointment to these health promotion posts' (2008: 158). Lee, Learmonth and Harding are at pains to point out how their study findings underline the normative power of a heteronormative managerial identity. A similar argument is made by Tyler and Cohen (2008) who queer management in terms of its linkages with normative masculinity and the desire for recognition, but from a different angle. Analysing the BBC comedy series *The Office* as a cultural text that exposes the performativity of gender and management, Tyler and Cohen argue that much of the comedy value of the TV series comes from the ways it ridicules and disrupts the performativity of management. The lead (heterosexual) male protagonist, David Brent, personifies this beautifully, as he routinely engages in an excessive reiteration of masculine norms and heteronormativity. As such, the ambiguities, insecurities and incoherencies of management and gender are thrown into sharp comic relief, denaturalising some of the ways in which management and masculinity have come to be seen as a 'natural' and uncontested feature of contemporary organisational life.

While the research reviewed earlier uses queer theory to contest the reified status of management, none of these studies offer an alternative, utopian vision of doing management. It is understandable how some commentators might regard this as a frustrating state of affairs or even a failure, especially in the light of Parker's (2002b) complaint about the paucity of debates on alternative modes of organising and management. On the one hand, the refusal to provide solutions or a 'best way' of doing management keeps queer theory from being appropriated into making yet another prescription of the type commonly dispensed in management textbooks. Since queer theory can be used to unsettle and denaturalise normative dimensions of management and organisational life, it follows that organisational researchers using queer theory would encourage the exploration of alternative ways of organising and doing management on the ground, without specifying and privileging 'one best way'. On the other hand, the organisational research that employs queer theory is limited, indicating barriers for exploring such alternatives and disrupting the 'normal' business of management. Queer inflected empirical studies of alternative ways of doing management have not yet caught hold, but they are badly needed, not least to help us understand how organisational members can make organisations queer places to organise.

Queer attachments in the workplace

Researching how individuals might construct queer identities, relations and subjectivities in the workplace requires delving into the undergrowth of organisational life, researching the minutia of people's workaday lives. Curiously, there is very little empirical research conducted by organisation studies scholars that uses a queer lens to re-examine what we take-for-granted about how people organise in the workplace. In my effort to shed light on the possibilities for individuals to queer identities, intimacies and relations in organisations, I carried out research on gay men's workplace friendships in the UK (Rumens, 2011). One recurring theme to emerge from the study data, worth elaborating here as an illustration, is the 'queer moments' conditioned within workplace friendships for revising heter-onormative discourses of male-female friendships. These discourses often construct male-female friendships as unavoidably sexual in nature and a dry run of romantic coupledom. Indeed, as friendship scholars note (Monsour, 2002; Rawlins, 2008), the mobilisation of a heterosexist notion of friend-ship as a distinct relationship from romantic or sexual relations is far from redundant, as evidenced in the contemporary studies carried out by many heterosexual friendship researchers. As such, the horizon of possibilities for exploring male-female friendships that resist prescriptively dominant heterosexual norms is obscured.

Through a process of queering, cross-sex friendships may be regarded as relationships that are (re)produced through and in meaning making proc-esses of signification. More generally, we can theorise friendship as a way of 'doing', insomuch as it does not materialise from an essential truth about human interaction but is an enacted practice. In this vein, male-female friendships are constituted through an iterative process of meaning mak-ing that is shaped by cultural norms about, for example, sexuality, gender and human relations. Butler's (1990) concept of the 'heterosexual matrix' is useful here because it refers to the constellation of norms that constitute a seemingly coherent relationship between sex, desire and gender. The matrix assumes heterosexuality to be the most 'natural' expression of sexuality, privileging a heteronormative 'truth' on male-female friendships (Rawlins, 2008). When male-female friendships jar with heterosexist norms that govern how such friendships are organised, they are at risk of becoming 'unintelligible' and, potentially, 'queer' (Tillmann-Healy, 2001). Indeed, in a heteronormative culture, cross-gender relations are said to be 'relatively scriptless relationships that lack clear guidelines' (Felmlee, 1999: 55), which require male and female friends to engage with norms on hetero-relations to establish and make sense of their attachments to each other. But, in a cultural context where the essential 'nature' of sexuality and gender norms is increasingly contested and understood as fluid, changeable and situated (Weeks, 2007), it is possible to understand male–female workplace friend-ships as potentially important sites for disrupting gender and sexual bina-ries. Here, then, queer theories enable us to aerate normative definitions of friendship so that we may, for example, fracture the binaries that shape the form, content and meanings of male-female friendships.

Saying as much is to recognise the opportunities available within work-place friendships for disrupting gender and sexual binaries as well as those that relate to relationships, such as friend/lover. Even the term 'cross-sex friendship', well established in academic discourse on male-female friendships, implies that boundaries between the sexes are clearly demarcated and that friendship occurs only once these boundaries are crossed. Other scholars have articulated the same concern (Monsour, 2002), but there are few who have conscripted queer theories in order to problematise such matters. As I have shown (Rumens, 2008, 2011, 2012), the workplace is one context where friends can engage in creative discursive activities and interactions that dislodge (hetero) sexual relations as the organising principle of adult male-female relationships. The insights derived from queer theories have been most illuminatory in that respect, by revealing instances of how work friends can rely on the intimacy and informality of friendship to disrupt heterosexist norms that suggest, for example, sexual desire is non-existent in gay men's friendships with women. At the same time, it is vital to acknowledge the concrete circumstances of specific work environments, which shape social interactions and the friendship choices made by individuals. In that respect, developing and maintaining 'queer friendships' in the workplace should not be understood as an entirely effortless endeavour.

The overwhelming evidence from my research is that versatility is needed by friends in order to move in and out of discursive identity categories. This may entail both friends making a conscious effort to resist the pull of heteronormative discourses that would categorise them and their friendship in ways not of their choosing. Developing male-female friendships that reach beyond the normative grasp of particular discourses requires energy and commitment on the part of friends themselves. Sustaining the queer aspects to friendships at work can be particularly hard, as these friendships are sustained in 'public' arenas, and thus susceptible to third party interpretations and objections. When constructed in relation to heteronormative discourses on friendship, the range of potential attachments within male-female friendships are circumscribed through restrictive binaries such as heterosexual/homosexual and friend/lover. As many interview-based conversations with gay men demonstrated, while friends may actively resist being categorised by heteronormative discourses they often put themselves and their relationship at risk of becoming unintelligible (Butler, 2004), or 'queer'. In these moments, it is possible to identify new emergent meanings constructed by friends themselves that unsettle heteronormative ideas about what male-female friendship means. Queer moments in friendship can bring into sharp relief the amorphous quality of friendship as a concept and performative practice, with possibilities arising for dominant friendship norms to be 'undone' and revised. However, one issue for friends who act on the queer possibilities within their friendships present is that 'crossing' the heterosexual/homosexual binary can be far from transformative. In composing new ways of relating at work, men and women can (un)wittingly normalise heterosexual relations as 'natural'. Needless to say, queer theory has a particular interest in how we (un)consciously disadvantage ourselves in terms of identities, relationships and behaviour (Warner, 1999).

For instance, it is possible to examine how and why friends draw uncritically on normative discourses, which have a pivotal role in helping some male-female friendships reach acceptance at and outside work. For instance, mobilising a populist and crude discourse of gay male sexuality as posing no sexual threat to women prises open opportunities for male-female workplace friendships to become established and normatively accepted. From one perspective, this is a costly strategy because it reproduces restrictive sexual and gender binaries, dealing a blow to action-based commitments towards challenging heteronormative discourse and practice in the workplace. In that sense, my research provides a more complicated slant on the notion of negotiating sexuality within 'cross-sex' friendships, which has typically been reduced to questions of heterosexual sexual attraction and desire (Rose, 2000). Constituted through and against normative discourses, it can be difficult to tell if some of the discursive activities friends engage in can be read as queering heterosexual behaviour and/or reinforcing the norms that underpin forms of heteronormativity. One way of managing such discursive tensions is for friends to actively understand each other as subjects who are sexual, gendered, racial, classed and so on (Rawlins, 2008). This is no small matter but critical reflection and mutual understanding is, in part, necessary for creating 'queer' workplace friendships that transcend heteronormative constraints. This leads to me to wonder what possibilities might exist and be conditioned by particular work contexts for fashioning queer relations that may, in turn, contribute towards queering our places of work. Here the file remains open. It is frustrating that such issues are not seen clearly by many organisation studies scholars, mostly because the dominant approach to understanding the world of work (including friendships) is welded to a managerialist model of privileging organisational interests and outcomes. So, as I approach the end of this chapter, what of the future prospects of queer theory for helping us to queer organisation theory and denaturalise heteronormative accounts of organisational life?

Queer theory and organisation studies: Prospects

To conclude, I return to the matter of queer theory and organisation studies. In this chapter I have pointed out that various scholarly discussions about queer theory such as the problems associated with mainstreaming in parts of the academy, whether it is intellectually moribund or whether we are now in a post-queer phase of theorising, seem remote and premature from those taking place within university business schools. While some organisation studies scholars appear to be playing catch up in that respect, by developing analyses that queer organisation and work, it is still the case that queer theory sits uneasily within organisation studies. However, this might not be such a bad thing. Its awkward positioning makes queer theory well placed to disrupt what we take-for-granted about organisation.

With little prospect of being mainstreamed within organisation studies in the near future, even in its critical fringes labelled CMS, queer theory has the potential to agitate and unsettle the legitimising function played by numerous business schools that protects the larger and long-term cultural investments made in the terms 'management' and 'organisation'. For example, it is encouraging to note recent attempts at queering classical management theory, as Fleischmann's (2009) queering of F. W. Taylor's infamous and highly influential principles of scientific management demonstrates. Nonetheless, although these initial efforts are welcome they are tentative and isolated, arguably of little threat to the dyed-in-the-wool managerialism that is present in countless management and organisation studies texts. More queer analyses are needed to trigger change, less on a seismic scale and, more as a series of on-going localised disturbances that disrupt the apparent coherence of organisation theory. Such small-scale challenges are powerful when they are persistent and unpredictable, relentlessly gnawing at concepts and ways of thinking about management and organisation that have become calcified. It is a decade ago since Parker (2002a) promoted the role of queer theory for exposing the production of knowledge within the academy and in business schools as political practice. Although progress in realising Parker's vision has been slow, it is worth reasserting the merit of such a queer project for organisation studies scholars.

Queer theory can expose the political contours of knowledge production within university business schools and, thus, of theory formation itself. Clearly, here as elsewhere, queer theory has the ability to 'mess up [... the] normal business in the academy' (Warner, 1993: xxvi). In regard to organisation studies, part of this activity involves rupturing artificial and exaggerated distinctions between 'mainstream' and 'critical' management studies, since both are implicated in the routine reproduction of heteronormativity. After all, the issue of heteronormativity is too important to be the exclusive intellectual property of CMS scholars, requiring the involvement of all those who inhabit the academy. This is no small matter and there is still much work to be done, on a range of fronts within organisation studies. Perhaps given the less congenial landscape for queer theory within organisation studies, there are still opportunities for queer theory to do its 'work', although there is every chance that queer theories, theorists and their supporters will struggle to cross the atriums of the most influential business schools in the UK and elsewhere. Still, queering business schools is a tantalising prospect, one that might condition the possibility of an alternative business school, as Parker suggests:

A university (or even management department) which dressed in drag, and recognized its own economy of secrecy and disclosure, its economy of repression and freedom, might be an institution that worked against itself in some rather playful and productive ways.

(2002b: 162)

Potentially, then, queer theory opens up an important and reflexive dialogue for organisation studies scholars, pertinent for the study of not only the 'traditional' objects of queer analysis such as gender and sexuality, but also organisation, management and organisation theory. Arguably, despite the scathing criticism delivered by some of its most outspoken critics elsewhere (Jeffreys, 2003), queer theory continues to retain an attractiveness that is, in large part, due to its appetite for asking awkward questions of the ontological and epistemological assumptions that underpin much of what we currently accept about studying organisations. This makes queer theory one of the more fitting candidates for revivification if we give credence to reports of its intellectual bankruptcy and death.

Bibliography

Adler, P. S., Forbes, L. C. and Willmott, H. (2007) 'Critical Management Studies', *The Academy of Management Annals*, 1(1), 119–179.

Adkins, L. (2002) *Revisions: Gender and Sexuality in Late Modernity*. Buckingham: Open University Press.

Ashcraft, K. L. (2009) 'Gender and diversity: Other ways to make a difference' in M. Alvesson, T. Bridgman and H. Willmott (eds) *The Oxford Handbook of Critical Management Studies*. Oxford: Oxford University Press, pp. 304–27.

Bendl, R., Fleischmann, A. and Walenta, C. (2008) 'Diversity management discourse meets queer theory', *Gender in Management: An International Journal*, 23(6): 382–94.

Bendl, R., Fleischmann, A. and Hofmann, R. (2009) 'Queer theory and diversity management: Reading codes of conduct from a queer perspective', *Journal of Management and Organization*, 15(5): 625–38.

Borgerson, J. (2005) 'Judith Butler: On organizing subjectivities' in C. Jones and R. Munro (eds) *Contemporary organization theory*. Oxford: Blackwell, pp. 63–79.

Bowring, M. (2004) 'Resistance is not futile: Liberating Captain Janeway from the masculine–feminine dualism of leadership', *Gender, Work & Organization*, 11(4): 381–405.

Bowring, M. and Brewis, J. (2009) 'Truth and consequences: Managing lesbian and gay identity in the Canadian workplace', *Equal Opportunities International*, 28(5): 361–77.

Brewis, J. and Linstead, S. (2000) *Sex, work and sex work: Eroticizing organization*. London: Routledge.

Brewis, J. Linstead, S. Boye, D. and O'Shea, T. (2006) (eds) *The passion of organizing*. Liber: Copenhagen Business School Press.

Burnett, L. (2010) 'Young lesbians explore careers and work landscapes in an Australian culture', *Journal of Lesbian Studies*, 14(1): 36–51.

Butler, J. (1990) *Gender trouble: Feminism and the subversion of identity*. London: Routledge.

Butler, J. (2004) *Undoing gender*. London: Routledge.

Collinson, D. L. and Hearn, J. (eds.) (1996) *Men as Managers, Managers as Men*. London: Sage.

Delbridge, R. and Keenoy, T. (2010) 'Beyond managerialism?' *The International Journal of Human Resource Management*, 21(6): 799–817.

Edelman, L. (2004) *No future: Queer theory and the death drive*. Durham: Duke University Press.

Felmlee, D. H. (1999) 'Social norms in same- and cross-gender friendships', *Social Psychology Quarterly*, 62(1): 53–67.

Fleischmann, A. (2009) 'Queering the principles: A queer/intersectional reading of Frederick W. Taylor's *The Principles of Scientific Management*' in M. F. Ozbilgin (ed.) *Equality, diversity and inclusion at work: Theory and scholarship*. Cheltenham: Edward Elgar, pp. 159–70.

Freeman, E. (2010) *Time binds: Queer temporalities, queer histories*. Durham: Duke University Press.

Gibson-Graham, J. K. (1996) 'Queer(y)ing capitalist organization', *Organization*, 3(4): 541–54.

Grey, C. and Willmott, H. (eds) (2005) *Critical management studies: A reader*. Oxford: Oxford University Press.

Halley, J. and Parker, A. (eds) (2011) *After sex? On writing since queer theory*. Durham: Duke University Press.

Harding, N., Ford, J. and Gough, B. (2010) 'Accounting for ourselves: Are academics exploited workers?' *Critical Perspectives on Accounting*, 21(2): 159–68.

Harding, N., Lee, H., Ford, J. and Learmonth, M. (2011) 'Leadership and charisma: A desire that cannot speak its name?' *Human Relations*, 64(7): 927–49.

Hearn, J., Sheppard, D. L., Tancred-Sheriff, P. and Burrell, G. (eds) (1989) *The sexuality of organization*. London: Sage.

Jeffreys, S. (2003) *Unpacking queer politics: A lesbian feminist perspective*. Cambridge: Polity Press.

Kerfoot, D. and Knights, D. (1993) 'Management, masculinity and manipulation: From paternalism to corporate strategy in financial services in Britain', *Journal of Management Studies*, 30(4): 659–79.

Landström, C. (2007) 'Queering feminist technology studies', *Feminist Theory*, 8(1): 7–26.

Lee, H., Learmonth, M. and Harding, N. (2008) 'Queer(y)ing public administration', *Public Administration*, 86(1): 149–67.

McDermott, E. (2011) 'The world some have won: Sexuality, class and inequality', *Sexualities*, 14(1): 63–78.

Monsour, M. (2002) *Women and men as friends: Relationships across the life span in the 21st century*. New York: Lawrence Erlbaum.

Ozturk, M. B. (2011) 'Sexual orientation discrimination: Exploring the experiences of lesbian, gay and bisexual employees in Turkey', *Human Relations*, 64(8): 1099–118.

Parker, M. (2001) 'Fucking management: Queer, theory and reflexivity', *ephemera*, 1(1): 36–53.

Parker, M. (2002a) 'Queering management and organization', *Gender, Work & Organization*, 9(2): 146–66.

Parker, M. (2002b) *Against management: Organization in the age of managerialism*. Cambridge: Polity.

Pringle, J. K. (2008) 'Gender in management: Theorizing gender as heterogender', *British Journal of Management*, 19(1): 110–19.

Rawlins, W. R. (2008) *The compass of friendship: Narratives, identities, and dialogue*. Thousand Oaks, CA: Sage.

Rohy, V. (2011) 'Busy dying' in B. Davies and J. Funke (eds) *Sex, gender and time in fiction and culture*. Basingstoke: Palgrave Macmillan, pp. 205–19.

Roper, M. (1996) 'Seduction and succession: Circuits of homosocial desire' in management' in D. L. Collinson and J. Hearn (eds) *Men as managers, managers as men*. London: Sage, pp. 210–26.

Rose, S. (2000) 'Heterosexism and the study of women's romantic and friend relationships', *Journal of Social Issues*, 56(2): 315–28.

Rumens, N. (2008) 'The complexities of friendship: Exploring how gay men make sense of their workplace friendships with straight women', *Culture and Organization*, 14(1): 79–95.

Rumens, N. (2011) *Queer company: The role and meaning of friendship in gay men's work lives*. Farnham: Ashgate.

Rumens, N. (2012) 'Queering cross-sex friendships: An analysis of gay and bisexual men's workplace friendships with heterosexual women', *Human Relations*, 65(8): 955–78.

Rumens, N. and Kerfoot, D. (2009) 'Gay men at work: (Re)constructing the self as professional', *Human Relations*, 62(5): 763–86.

Schilt, K. and Westbrook, L. (2009) 'Doing gender, doing heteronormativity: Gender normals, transgender people, and the social maintenance of heterosexuality', *Gender & Society*, 23(4): 440–64.

Seidman, S. (ed.) (1996) *Queer theory/sociology*. Oxford: Blackwell.

Seidman, S. (2002) *Beyond the closet: The transformation of gay and lesbian life*. New York: Routledge.

Skidmore, P. (2004) 'A legal perspective on sexuality and organization: A lesbian and gay case study', *Gender, Work & Organization*, 11(3): 229–53.

Starkey, K. and Tempest, S. (2008) 'A clear sense of purpose? The evolving role of the business school', *Journal of Management Development*, 27(4): 379–90.

Sullivan, N. (2003) *A critical introduction to queer theory*. New York: New York University Press.

Tatli, A. (2011) 'On the power and poverty of critical (self) reflection in critical management studies: A comment on Ford, Harding and Learmonth', *British Journal of Management*, 23(1): 22–30.

Tillmann-Healy, L. M. (2001) *Between gay and straight: Understanding friendship across sexual orientation*. Walnut Creek, CA: AltaMira Press.

Tyler, M. and Cohen, L. (2008) 'Management in/as comic relief: Queer theory and gender performativity in *The Office*', *Gender, Work & Organization*, 15(2): 113–32.

Valocchi, S. (2005) 'Not yet queer enough: The lessons of queer theory for the sociology of gender and sexuality', *Gender & Society*, 19(6): 750–70.

Wajcman, J. (1998) *Managing like a man: Women and men in corporate management*. Cambridge: Polity Press.

Ward, J. and Winstanley, D. (2003) 'The absent present: Negative space within discourse and the construction of minority sexual identity in the workplace', *Human Relations*, 56(10): 1255–80.

Warner, M. (1993) *Fear of a queer planet: Queer politics and social theory*. Minneapolis: University of Minnesota.

Warner, M. (1999) *The trouble with normal: Sex, politics, and the ethics of queer life*. New York: The Free Press.

Weeks, J. (2007) *The world we have won*. London: Routledge.

Williams, C. L. and Giuffre, P. A. (2011) 'From organizational sexuality to queer organizations: Research on homosexuality and the workplace', *Sociology Compass*, 5(7): 551–63.

Williams, C. L., Giuffre, P. A. and Dellinger, K. (2009) 'The gay-friendly closet', *Sexuality Research and Social Policy*, 6(1): 29–45.

13
Queerying the Public Administration in Italy: Local Challenges to a National Standstill

Chiara Bertone and Beatrice Gusmano

Introduction

Given the orientation to silence non-heterosexual experiences that informs centralised Italian legislation and policies, and following a European trend towards decentralisation, local administrations have taken on a fundamental role in LGBT policies, and developed partnerships with local LGBT organisations. Our analysis of these policies confirms the presence of a national as well as a more global trend, namely the fact that the 'urban safety' discourse has become a main source of legitimation for public intervention on LGBT issues, creating discursive boundaries that allow little space for a positive public representation of queer subjects and for the recognition of their agency. In looking at these boundaries, we draw upon the concept of 'speakability' which Cooper proposes in analysing local LGBT policies in the UK 'to identify a cluster of normative and epistemological practices' including 'the urge and capacity to speak, the extent to which a topic or field renders itself utterable, what can be legitimately said, and a talent for speaking' (2006: 928). In this chapter we show how the changes in the terms of speakability towards a discourse on 'urban safety'[1] imply a shift in the role of local administrations, from promoting rights, to meeting the needs of a victimised, normalised and individualised subject (Pitch and Ventimiglia, 2001). It also corresponds to a redefinition of the role assigned to the actors of civil society as partners of local governance: from bearers of claims, based upon conflictual political views, to shared interest groups.

Case studies were carried out to examine the only existing Italian local networks built by five administrations around LGBT issues (Naples, Rome, Bologna, Turin, Venice). A comparison between the case studies shows different possibilities for the construction of subjectivities in the development of local LGBT policies, depending on the local configuration of actors and on their strategies in moving across the boundaries in which the discursive framework and material structure of local policies confine LGBT issues (Cooper and Monro, 2003).

Among the conditions opening possibilities for resistance to an urban safety discourse, a crucial one is the room for action for strategic brokers working within the administration and whose main role is that of translating the claims of LGBT organisations into comprehensible demands for the municipality. By acknowledging rather than denying the political and conflictual implications of LGBT movements' claims, municipalities can contribute to the empowerment and recognition of an active, collective subject, making space for a public, positive representation of queer differences and presences.

Contextualising LGBT policies: The Italian case

Italy stands out as one of the few Western European countries in which LGBT rights are not yet recognised. This situation has deep roots in history, since denial more than repression has characterised Italian public regulation of homosexuality over the last century, implying an erasure of the non-heterosexual subject rather than its public construction as a 'counter-type' (Mosse, 1985). This orientation corresponded to that of the Catholic Church on sodomy that, although considered an unspeakable sin, was tolerated *de facto* (Dall'Orto, 1988). The persistence of denial orientation is particularly evident in the absence of any form of legal recognition for unmarried couples (homosexual and heterosexual), and for non-heterosexual parenthood. The naming of homosexuality as a possible ground for legal protection against discrimination also continues to be denied by law, with the exception of discrimination at work, an area where Italy has, albeit partially, complied with the European Directive 2000/78/EC, establishing a general framework for equal treatment in employment and occupation.

Given these historical conditions of the persistently low legitimacy of LGBT policies in Italy, the terms of the debate on familisation of homosexuality as a form of homonormativity, as it has developed in other Western countries, does not seem to fully apply to Italy. The access to 'ordinariness' for gay and lesbian subjects that changes in legislation on family life, in particular legal recognition of same-sex couples, have granted in other countries implies that the notion of the respectable citizen gets uncoupled from heterosexuality, while remaining deeply classed in its symbolic connotation and in its material conditions of access (Taylor, 2011a/b; Browne, 2011). In Italy 'respectability' still remains more linked to a strictly heterosexual – and intergenerational – notion of family. Analyses of the political debate on bills regarding the legal recognition of same-sex couples show that there is strong resistance to allowing discursive space even for a homonormative (Duggan, 2003), familised subject, despite the attempts made in this direction by LGBT movements. Citizenship in Italy is built strongly on the stability of family ties: social policies are structured on the assumption that individual welfare must be primarily based on solidarity support by family and kinship

(Saraceno, 1994; Naldini, 2003). These conditions, which Italy shares with other Southern European countries, have been identified as key factors in explaining these countries' low pace of change in family practices and legal regulation, with marriage still retaining much of its institutional strength. Questioning the primacy of heterosexual marriage by making space for a non-heterosexual subject, however familised it may be, still seems too much of a challenge to such stability (Saraceno, 2008).

Having failed to obtain results in expanding recognition of intimate ties, claims for legal change on the part of LGBT organisations have more recently focused upon anti-discrimination policies, and in particular upon legal recognition of homophobia as grounds for hate crimes (D'Ippoliti and Schuster, 2011). This has been interpreted as a move towards a safety approach, which sees the aggressor as scapegoat, erasing the structural dimension of oppression, and focuses on minoritarian subjects as victims, running the risk of overshadowing a more positive, assertive vision of their experiences (Pitch and Ventimiglia, 2001). Even the first Italian campaign on homophobia promoted by the Equal Opportunity Department of the centre-right government, which has been widely welcomed as a symbolic step towards breaking the silence of national institutions about homosexuality, actually reproduces, and even reinforces, the invisibility, or closeting, of the homosexual subject through a 'politics of in-difference' (Pustianaz, 2010), as recalled by its title 'No difference'. The silencing of the homosexual subject and the invisibilisation of the signs of difference which s/he bears have been interpreted as an expression of the notion of a homogeneous public sphere, supported by a highly influential Catholic discourse, withstanding cultural processes of individualisation and allowing little space for the recognition of difference (Trappolin, 2004). Moreover, the invisibilisation of differences also concerns differences between the same subjects of LGBT policies: in these policies this acronym generally tends to erase the specificities of the subjects included in it, and especially differences between sexual orientation and gender identity issues remain largely overlooked.

The little room allowed for a positive image of LGBT subjects might also be a reason for the marginal, albeit recently growing, impact of the discourse of diversity management in Italy, which was inspired by the work of Florida (2003), framing the struggle on discrimination in terms of economic utility, insofar as the safeguarding and management of diversity is viewed as a tool for promoting economic competitiveness. Despite the classed nature of this approach, and its individualising and privatising implications (Squires, 2008a), it still requires the positive recognition of difference for a subject – as gay or lesbian – carrying specific resources and competencies that have to be acknowledged (Monro and Richardson, 2010).

The construction of a homonormative subject – as well as the designation of boundaries between public and private spheres – results from the context-specific normative citizenship structure: even attempts to make space for representations of the privatised homosexual subject as consumer take different forms, in Italy, from those described in other contexts, like the US (Duggan, 2003) or the UK (Taylor, 2009). The 2011 campaign against homophobia subscribed to by mainstream LGBT associations shows how they have recently been trying to make space in public debate for a homosexual subject as a (middle-class) consumer, while denying a positive recognition of difference. Depicting same-sex couples in the act of enjoying traditional local food and wine – with the slogan: 'Civilisation. A typical Italian product' – this campaign embeds the homosexual subject in the Italian community, grounding entitlement to recognition upon her/his belonging to a culturally homogeneous national identity (De Vivo, 2011). This framing seems to resonate with a Catholic discourse privileging a communitarian representation of cultural homogeneity and social solidarity, concealing the classed implications of the notion of the 'normal' family. In this context, the attempts to develop more inclusive citizenship at local level find little space for proposing a positive representation of queer subjects and for the recognition of their possibility of agency and empowerment.

Neoliberalism, local governance and LGBT issues: Global trends, local declinations

In developing policies to fight discrimination on the grounds of sexual orientation in Europe, local administrations have taken on a fundamental role, developing partnerships with local associations – first and foremost LGBT organisations – and other levels of governance. As recent studies have shown, analysing this process in depth in the British context (Cooper, 2006; Monro and Richardson, 2010), this trend – beginning in the mid 1980s – is an expression of a neoliberalist process that is witnessing a transfer of responsibility from central government to local administrations and the outsourcing of services, with the consequent diminishing of the universalist, public nature of the welfare state (Brenner and Theodore, 2002). This process generates a welfare system that variably mixes public intervention, market and social solidarity, thereby decreeing the end of the monopoly of public authority and allowing the proliferation of partnerships. The strategy employed by local administrations is to forge partnerships with the private sector, effecting the shift from government, understood as the set of powers exercised by the state, to governance, or rather a multilevel, locally-based model of government, the result of synergies between institutional and social actors (Sabbatini, 2005). Furthermore, issues of the redistribution of goods, and hence of justice, referring to universalistic rights to enjoy common conditions of social reproduction are marginalised: the focus is trained upon needs rather than rights. The hegemony of an economist framework (De Leonardis, 2002) implies that entitlement to welfare provisions is granted on a moral basis (the subject of policies must be worthy) or according to the laws of the market. Being informed by the principles of subsidiarity and solidarity, welfare policies imply the positioning of problems and actions in the private sphere of family and intimate relationships, with justice issues involved in these actions delivered to the sphere of morality and conscience.

As a consequence, the conflictual dimension of struggles around the common good is banished from public discourse. In this new configuration of welfare mix, a negotiating approach to public action (Gaudin, 1999) produces actors involved in partnerships encouraged by the rhetoric of governance – as the only space of legitimacy available in the public arena – to turn into interest groups that must speak the economic language of instrumental alliances (De Leonardis, 2002). In the process of restructuring the welfare state, this type of consultancy becomes increasingly formalised, giving rise to partnerships in which the local administration capitalises on the resources in its area, promoting the empowerment of local communities. Studies on community activism (Larner and Craig, 2005) and on extra-parliamentary representation of gender (Squires, 2008b) point to the fact that the weight of managing partnerships is mainly borne by 'strategic brokers' (Larner and Craig, 2005). Literature shows how, in order to firm up the idea of activation, the competencies and knowledge of civil society activists, initially recognised as external consultants, start to be used by local governance. Strategic brokers are activists who assist the partnerships by fostering change through a network approach between associations and local administrations. There is a distinction between those who work in government agencies, as spokespeople for the needs of the community, and those who maintain their own profile as activists in associations, engaged in interfacing with the local administration. In both cases, however, strategic brokers spend a great deal of their efforts in networking, since policies are rooted in bargaining. Their expertise derives from the ability to translate silent voices into comprehensible demands for the local administration. Translation is understood here as 'a continuous process through which individuals transform the knowledge, truths and effects of power each time they encounter them' (Herbert-Cheshire, 2003: 456). At the same time, strategic brokers are increasingly required to make their political claims technical, or turn their contests into collaboration, erasing conflict from the discursive arena.

The implications of these developments for LGBT policies have been investigated in studies on the UK, a context where the neoliberal transformation of the welfare state is most advanced. Before this transformation, the first LGBT policies implemented in the UK were aimed at reducing direct and indirect discrimination by removing heteronormative assumptions from local authority policies and procedures and to support the development of the LGBT community through symbolic initiatives and public funding. This attention began to wane at the end of the 1980s, when more conservative tendencies began to take hold, also due to the AIDS moral panic campaigns, and the economy became the pivotal factor in political choices. The emergence of a homosexual commercial scene brought LGBT issues legitimately into local governance, economically interested in what was dubbed the pink pound – basically the spending power of affluent white gay men (Cooper and Monro, 2003). Linked to the more general concern with urban safety informing neoliberal policies is a further development, with the initiatives regarding homophobic violence getting the strongest institutional backing, allowing for the inclusion of LGBT policies into local planning. This local declination of LGBT policies shows the general shift from rights to needs in the construction of the subject of policies. Accordingly, LGBT associations shifted their focus from asserting a non-normative vision of sexual identity to demands on behalf of an individualised subject (Carabine and Monro, 2004). The development of public-private partnerships following the logic of governance could build upon this common framing.

Looking at the specific features taken by these processes in the development of local LGBT policies in Italy, our research focuses upon how the boundaries of speakability are negotiated, and resisted, by and between actors at the local level: strategic brokers, local government officials and LGBT organisations. The Italian case shows that some of these features of LGBT policies are shared across different countries, both as regards the agenda, with urban safety taking a central place, and the configuration of the actors. At the same time, specificities in the local declination of these same features are related to the Italian context of sexual citizenship.

Research design

In a national context characterised by the absence of specific norms protecting the rights of LGBT citizens, the study is based on identifying the strategies that local administrations could deploy to grant legitimacy to this policy area.[2] Case studies were carried out in 2010 to examine local networks built up in Italy by administrations around LGBT issues, in the cities of Rome, Naples, Bologna, Turin and Venice. These city councils were chosen because they are the only ones that have activated some forms of partnerships around LGBT issues. These case studies consisted in archive work, 12 focus groups and 18 in-depth interviews with key informants, including politicians, staff from the local administration, activists of LGBT organisations.[3] The local processes leading to the creation of the public/private partnerships and/or to the institutionalisation of a service dedicated to LGBT issues within City Councils were analysed. Specific attention was devoted to the role and experiences of strategic brokers,[4] and to the implications of their absence. Strategic brokers appear in fact to be crucial in defining the scope for action for LGBT organisations in the partnership, influencing the degree of depoliticisation of their claims-making and, on the other hand, the room for withstanding its transformation into lobbying.

The central focus of our analysis is represented by the identification of the terms of speakability that characterise the framing of LGBT issues in each case: we have explored the continuum between different definitions of policies, from promoting citizenship rights to assuming a paternalistic approach in meeting the needs of a 'minority', and the implications they have on the subjects' degree of agency. The different configuration of the actors involved in the local partnership in each city shapes different forms of negotiation and challenge to these discursive boundaries. In exploring them, we aim to outline the context-specific possibilities for public policies to escape from the 'politically sedative' (Duggan, 2003) articulation of an individualised and victimised subject, opening space for the speakability of a more active and/or queer subject.

Italian cities developing LGBT policies

Rome and Naples

The cases of Rome and Naples allow analysis of how local administrations with different political orientations, centre-left and centre-right, promoted a partnership with LGBT organisations notwithstanding the absence of strategic brokers within the administration. The Permanent Coordination Board between LGBT associations and the Naples City Council was created in 2007, as a response to some episodes of homophobic violence in the city. The Board is marked by a high level of conflict characterising the relations between the four organisations taking part in it, and the only common activity that it has carried out was a conference on homophobia organised in 2009. The Permanent Coordination Board on Gender Identity and Sexual Orientation in Rome started its activities in 2002 and was formally established in 2007; 17 LGBT organisations are included, but only a few of them actually take part in its activities.

In these two Boards a top-down approach to the development of the partnership prevails: it is the City Council that promotes and manages it, requiring LGBT organisations to adopt a non conflictual stance and to agree upon shared demands to be addressed to the administration. These expectations clash with the different views LGBT organisations have of the role of civil society within the partnership. According to the local administration, demands are supposed to be based upon the common belonging to a community and therefore upon shared goals; LGBT organisations are instead aware of the fact that the community expresses a variety of requests, and their claims express different, and often conflictual, goals. The partnerships result, however, in a shared basis of legitimacy for the development of LGBT policies, gathering consensus across the political spectrum, namely the fight against homophobic violence and the need for LGBT people to be secure. This framing, as we have seen, has become a priority in the national agenda of LGBT policies in Italy in recent years. Actually, this way of justifying LGBT policies is recognised by the actors involved, not only in these two cases but also in all the cities we studied, as perhaps the most effective strategy for achieving legitimation. The following two quotes, respectively from an LGBT activist in Naples and a city councillor in Rome, account for the political neutrality assigned to the security discourse:

> We tried to make ourselves known by taking advantage of a local situation which was fairly negative in terms of homophobia. So [...] we went knocking at the City Council door to say: 'We want to demonstrate in the streets and protest against homophobia. Are you on our side?' and the Council were with us.

> We had to somehow find a strategy for the institution [of the Board] in terms of rights, also because it was the period when people started talking about violence against homosexuals. [...] And so together with the associations we began to find out about their potential, and what message the administration wanted to communicate to the people of Rome. [...] There is everything within this goal: there is homophobia, bullying ... from schools to social and health protection.

Framed within the security discourse, LGBT policies can be justified in depoliticised, 'technical' terms, as an effective response to the needs of the population. Within these boundaries, the subject in whose name policies are defined is presented as a carrier for individual needs, a victim of discrimination and violence to be included as 'people like us who have made different sexual choices but which have no affect on everyday social, working and ethical life' (City Council, Rome). Confined outside these boundaries were the actions perceived as being more 'political', which even included Gay Pride parades, implying a visibility of critical bodies that would challenge the construction of a homonormative, victimised LGBT subject.

In Rome, the actions planned together by the Board and the City Council were expressly designed to exclude potentially controversial representations. Referring to awareness campaigns, for instance, some activists taking part in the Board have defined them as 'watered-down, the word 'gay' should not appear', 'there must be no kissing between couples of the same sex, our work has to be delicately balanced', showing their recognition that LGBT issues can obtain institutional legitimacy only if they are kept within strict discursive boundaries. In particular, LGBT organisations accept that any possible critical implication for the heterosexist order, regarding for instance the notion of the family, should be avoided.

At the same time, activists point to the dilemmas implied by the acceptance of these boundaries as regards the status of LGBT organisations themselves: by accepting a depoliticisation of their claims, their redefinition in 'technical' terms, they risk being transformed into interest based lobbies. The awareness about this dilemma represents a form of resistance to the rhetoric of the partnership at all costs. Other elements of resistance can be detected in the language used, when the political implications of the policies are highlighted, despite their definition in technical terms, as this comment by an LGBT activist about training courses for Rome City Council employees shows:

> Through this medium [training], which is highly technical [...] you are already carrying out an operation of protection for the community [...]. This on its own is a political result, not just technical and organisational.

However, there is little room for turning these elements of resistance into an effective redefinition of the agenda of LGBT policies by the City Council: it is rather the organisations that redefine their role. As we will see in other cases, the role of the strategic broker, which is absent both in Rome and in Naples, can be crucial in providing this space, allowing a translation of a conflictual claims-making process, where different subjectivities can emerge, into a political recomposition aimed at promoting the public good (De Leonardis and Bifulco, 2003). In these two cases, we find a risk of policy building on the logic of governance that has already been shown by other studies (Monro and Richardson, 2010): a further formalisation of the partnership (of the Boards in this case) is endorsed by the grassroots organisations themselves. The standardisation of procedures is seen by LGBT activists as the way to solve inter-organisational conflicts, allowing for the depoliticisation of their claims.

Bologna

In 2008 the Department for Education, Diversity and Gender Policies began to set up an Office for Diversity Policies. The aim was to cover all kinds of diversity, dealing in particular with those dimensions of discrimination recognised in European treaties, namely gender, sexual orientation and gender identity, that were not already catered for by other well-established sectors of the administration. Two public employees were transferred internally and assigned to the Office, and engaged in particular in equal opportunities, gender violence and LGBT issues. The development of local LGBT policies in Bologna relies on the presence of one of the employees that represents the strategic broker, a queer activist working within the administration, but operating in a context of low institutional legitimacy. Yet, the precarious institutionalisation of the Office weakened the continuity of its activities. Its only formal action was to establish guidelines for the City Council to constitute a Board of associations, which should appoint an advisory committee. Since 2010 the Bologna City Council has been under compulsory administration, and the process of partnership institutionalisation has been interrupted.

The relationship with local LGBT associations was also characterised by a top-down approach: the lack of pre-existing, independent coordination among associations resulted in a partnership imposed by the City Council, which could in no way replace a truly participative process. With regard to sources of legitimacy for LGBT policies, the Office's activities fitted into a pre-existing 'definition of the issue of violence in terms of security policies' that had informed policies on gender violence since the 90s; therefore, LGBT policies became formulated in terms of countering discrimination and homophobic violence. Networking with associations was also grounded upon this policy discourse: the only recent concerted action between the Office and a set of associations was a project of legal counselling against gender and sexual orientation discrimination. In managing these boundaries, the strategic broker played a key and, at the same time, very problematic role: given his double belonging, he brought out the partnership contradictions. On the one hand, in a time of serious conflict between radical and mainstream LGBT organisations, the tension between a necessarily partisan position within the movement and the strategic broker's institutional role became especially difficult to manage.

> I also tried, first, to find out if there were resistances, and it did not seem so, although it could be said that there was no enthusiasm either: however, I was given formal respect and legitimacy beforehand on the part of all the associations. [...] But I believe that, in more general terms, there was indifference and the absence of venues where this diffidence could be overcome: if there is no Board, everyone continues to act as if this Office did not exist.

At the same time, the strategic broker spoke about the emotional burden of furthering identity-related issues within an institution characterised by rigid bureaucracy, formal procedures, lack of knowledge – sometimes translating into open hostility – and the limits imposed by political forces that found it hard to acknowledge the legitimacy of LGBT policies.

> The motivation was of the highest order and this led to enormous disappointment [...] it was the outcome of the total investment that was made [...] which however was completely out of place in this context. [...] I don't know whether anyone less motivated [...] would have the strength to resist [...] this subjective implication is one of the contradictions [...] that are in some way implicit in policies based on subjectiveness. It's not easy to eliminate, and it's not just my problem: that reassures me, that I'm not going mad! [laughing].

The strategic broker was not credited with enough legitimacy, within the institution, to play a strong role of translation of the associations' political demands into institutional responses moving beyond heteroimposed boundaries. The failed institutionalisation of the Office shows, according to him, the limits of a strategy of legitimacy framing LGBT policies not as an object of political choices, but in technical terms as issues of citizens' protection: 'they were afraid, and officialdom hadn't got the courage to institutionalise us organisationally'. In a context of political discontinuity, these limits resulted in the fact that certain department policies, in particular, equal opportunity and gender violence, were transferred to the Promotional Activities and Projects Office in the Department for Family Services, while LGBT issues were banished again into invisibility.

Turin

Turin is the only case where we find a long-term institutionalisation of LGBT policies, thanks to the creation of a dedicated Office working in a context of relatively high legitimacy. The origin of this institutionalisation actually lies in the failure of a political struggle by LGBT organisations to obtain a register of civil unions from the City Council, due to the hostility of the Catholic component within the centre-left majority. This was considered too political an issue, since it questioned the notion of family. In this struggle, the conditions for an organised coordination of the major LGBT organisations had developed, leading to the constitution of the GLT Coordination Board, which explored other strategies of claims-making towards the administration. In this process, particularly decisive was the dialogue with the Equal Opportunities Councillor, who engaged in identifying existing opportunities to commit the City to develop LGBT issues, underlining that: 'public authority takes responsibility for the institutional response to these demands, detracting it from occasional voluntary work'. The negotiated common strategy was to work on the creation, in 2001, of an 'Office for overcoming discrimination based on sexual orientation and gender identity' (later renamed LGBT Office), to be based under the Gender Politics Sector. Currently, three people work in the Office in order to deal with training of public employees, activities with youth and schools and local and national networking.

In the institutionalisation of the Office, a sensitive political choice concerned the sector under which to establish it, which had to take account of the political opportunities for defining and legitimising its mission, defined here as 'protection choices':

> I made protection choices [...]: seeking out the area that I considered to be most sensitive and flexible [...] [The social policies] were profoundly orientated in the direction of topics of welfare responsibility while, even though this Department might have the task of setting in motion concrete support actions, it arose [...] from the subject of differences, which is profoundly cultural. So I thought I would protect it from finishing up in the welfare sphere, namely in the general area of adults in difficulty; at

the same time it was not yet strong enough to fit into a logic of cultural policies on citizenship rights.

Former Councillor for Equal Opportunities

Building a fruitful, strong partnership, the Office's activities have since been planned and carried out in synergy with the GLT Coordination Board that, in 2006, was renamed as GLBT Turin Pride Coordination Board. Now, it comprises 15 associations operating at regional level, including organisations dealing with diversity and secularism.

As part of the creation of an enduring partnership, great emphasis was placed on mainstreaming within the city administration, by the creation of a Piloting Group aiming to harmonise the city's various departments by promoting the intersectionality of LGBT actions. The Piloting group operates with a bottom-up approach: each sector's representative brings to the board the needs and issues that have emerged in his/her sector. The effective measures identified are then taken back to the sector, fostering and implementing good practices. Further attention to networking is directed towards vertical partnership with Turin Provincial Council and Piedmont Regional Council.

A fundamental part of the shared strategy for establishing the Office was the decision to build its legitimacy first of all upon research – to be carried out by independent academic experts – on the experiences of LGBT people in Turin, and on social attitudes towards them. This was felt to identify the most important needs and the areas of discrimination policies needed to address. The actors involved saw this emphasis on an expert-based definition of needs as the way to avoid political resistance within the City Council, by presenting the city commitment on LGBT issues not as the result of a political choice, inspired by a certain model of society to be developed, but as a 'technical' aspect. At the same time, both from within and from outside the local administration, they framed this reference to needs as part of a broader question of heteronormative citizenship. The mission of the Office was perceived as very clear in this respect:

> Act in such a way that [...] the entire public administration is able to accept and promote a culture for the elimination of prejudice within the city, as a result of which it opens facilities, modifies them and transcends what today we call the 'heterosexist look'.

LGBT organisations see the reference to the universal nature of citizenship rights as enabling presentation of LGBT policies not as a possible option, but as an essential duty for administrations, attributing strong public responsibility when it comes to guaranteeing and promoting these rights.

Asking the institutions to take responsibility for a scientific study, with a service dedicated to issues that are not those of a minority but regard citizenship in general, is a political project. [...] We said: [...] 'we want the city to do things for the community, to tell citizens that rights are part of our shared heritage'. [...] When you insist on the value of LGBT rights as rights that are not a question of safeguarding a minority, but a question of citizenship as a whole, then in my view you have found a key.

GLT Coordination Board

Given all their networking tasks, the ability of Office workers to build relations of trust and to communicate across very different logics is identified as crucial: as strategic brokers, they are required to translate community needs into demands that are consistent with administration tasks; at the same time, they are required to position themselves in a non-conflictual and impartial way. The relevance of this outstanding role emerged in the evaluations made for recruitment for the Office. After an initial period, it resulted in the choice of LGBT activists who, as city council employees, could be transferred to work full time at the Office. This double belonging, which is perceived by the administration as a resource, is however a source of tensions for the workers, who experience it as a burden leading to high risks of burnout. After some time, the employees chose to leave this double belonging, focusing only on their institutional role. Exploring the tensions leading to this decision, and more broadly the different meanings attached to the role of strategic broker, allows a grasp of some fundamental dilemmas of this position and their implications for LGBT policies. Recognising its importance for the effectiveness of LGBT policies, the actors involved came up with different readings of the strategic broker role: volunteer, militant, mediator.

Within the local authority, some associate the strategic broker with the 'volunteer' figure, which is highly evocative of the great tradition of social Catholicism in Turin. This implies a selfless commitment by the service workers and the construction of a needy, individualised subject of policies. In contrast to this meaning, the 'militant' evokes a commitment to promoting citizenship rights, rather than to supporting needy subjects.

Before somebody spoke of something of a volunteer action, but my inclination is to replace it with the word 'militant', just as we find, how to put it, personnel working with foreigners, rather than with the disabled, in a certain sense you go because it's somehow part of you, but I think that [you need] strong motivation. I think it is part of the experience of the employee of a public authority: [...] you perform a service for the citizenship and that's it.

At the same time, a positioning of the strategic broker in promoting a specific vision of the world is seen as unsuitable by the Office responsible:

There are militants in the services who have this attitude to some extent rather than political pressure: [namely] you have to change your perspective, in my opinion, you have to be prepared to listen and mediate more.

The strong legitimacy enjoyed by Office workers, due to the institution-alisation of their role and to the support network they managed to cre-ate, allows them to take up the role of 'mediators', capable of translating the demands, however conflictual and politicised, originating with LGBT organisations, into policies oriented to the common good (De Leonardis, 2002). This conception not only of the role of the strategic broker, but also of the public administration's responsibility in promoting an inclusive citi-zenship, implies a notion of partnership which does not necessarily require a depoliticisation and transformation of claims-making into interest group pressure. LGBT organisations recognise the positive outcomes of the media-tor role, rather than perceiving it as an imposition of the terms of speak-ability which they need to comply with in order to keep up a dialogue with the public administration.

With these bases, the LGBT Office has been able to develop a broad range of activities. Its aim has been to keep a bottom-up approach in identifying areas of intervention, by responding to the priorities defined by the Piloting Group. The Office has chiefly identified in training the key response to these requests. Training appears to be the main possible and feasible, long-term effective response, to the range of diverse needs of LGBT subjects: it is indeed justified as a cultural commitment to fostering the recognition of LGBT experiences and identities; as a tool to tackle violence (in particular to tackle homophobic bullying, a central topic for training initiatives in schools); and in terms of access to services. The Office, however, reframes this focus upon needs into a more comprehensive goal of social change, promoting citizenship rights and questioning heteronormativity. In this reframing, subjects are redefined through a collective process, which, by directly involving LGBT organisations in the planning and implementation of training, gives voice to an active subject, self-defining her/his experiences, needs and claims.

Venice

Venice is an example of the development of public policies on LGBT issues with strong commitment and organisational backing thanks to the politi-cal support of an influential councillor, but without the implementation of an institutionalised partnership with local LGBT organisations. The LGBT Monitoring Centre was assigned the task of identifying the most suitable tools to promote the civil and social rights of LGBT people. In particular, three areas of intervention were singled out: citizenship, LGBT culture, networks. The Monitoring Centre was created thanks to the strong commitment of the Councillor for Equal Opportunities, whose political influence secured great autonomy for experimenting new solutions for the organisation and the actions of the Centre. On the other hand, this process did not result in an institutionalisation of these experiences: despite having acquired great visibility and room for action, the Centre's life ended with the municipality's political shift in 2010.

Since it did not have to respond to a strong claims-making activity by local LGBT organisations, the Centre did not refer to a partnership that included LGBT subjects only, but developed projects with other local actors, following a logic of intersectionality (Monro and Richardson, 2010). In the lack of a structured partnership with LGBT organisations, therefore, the two employees did not play the role of translating claims from the LGBT movement into demands fitting the logic of local governance, but they rather promoted cultural activities around which to mobilise, each time, different local grassroots, artists and institutional actors.

As reported by the employees, the Centre tried to deal with the absence of institutionalisation, 'constantly negotiating for its own survival', but yet profiting from its relative agility compared to other organisational solutions. Although quite isolated within the administration's bureaucracy,

> in the meanders of spoken and unspoken censorship, [it could] invent survival strategies: [...] also important was the allergy to institutionalise processes, and we thought it very useful to operate on the edge between institution and city.

As regards the discursive frame characterising the activity of the Centre, the concern for LGBT security appeared rather marginal, due to the prevalence of a cultural approach to the recognition of differences and of an attention to the de-heteronormativisation of the public space: the fundamental strategy was 'to use cultural and artistic languages to speak about rights and homophobia, albeit indirectly'. Venice actually represents the public administration's first attempt, in Italy, to explicitly recognise queer approaches and practices, understood as an attempt to progress beyond the normativity imposed by mainstream narratives concerning LGBT inclusion. Thus, the subject which the policies refer to is not defined by identitarian belongings, but is contingently constructed on the basis of a shared goal, with the aim not just of expanding the basis of entitlement to existing rights, but rather of creating coalitions among marginalised subjects, those standing outside of the norm, as a strategy for revealing the partiality of the norm itself. Avoiding victimisation, this approach implies the empowering of subjects, recognising them as entitled to rights and actively participating in their construction. The choice of marking this subject as queer, thus refusing a definition based on identity, is also conceived by the actors involved as a way of resisting the exclusion of a positive construction of identity-based lesbian and gay subjectivity which characterises, as we have seen, Italian public discourse.

This frame corresponded, after all, to the local configuration of the actors: on the one hand, the absence of LGBT collective action allowed the Centre to avoid defining a subject in whose name policies are developed with well defined identitarian boundaries; on the other hand, the Centre itself did not engage in promoting consulting boards requiring grassroots organisations to act as interest groups, trying instead to enter a dialogue with contingent subjectivities. Such configuration, we will argue in the conclusions, places the case of Venice in the position of fostering the construction of coalitional subjects.

Conclusions

Our analysis of LGBT policies at the local level in Italy shows a trend towards the urban safety discourse becoming the main source of legitimation for public intervention on LGBT issues. This trend implies a shift in the role of local administrations, from promoting rights, thereby empowering an active and collective citizenship, to meeting the needs of a victimised, minoritised and individualised subject. It also corresponds to a redefinition of the actors of civil society, in the role they are assigned as partners of the local system of governance: from bearers of claims based upon conflictual political views and goals, they are encouraged to turn into interest groups, whose claims are based upon the common belonging to a community. The different case studies that we have carried out, however, reveal the local variability of these processes.

The cases of Rome and Naples depict the most linear representation of a close adherence to the urban safety discourse and to the depoliticisation of LGBT policies, both enforced by the top-down approach assumed by the City Council: the absence of a strategic broker strongly reduces the space for the actors to play a more active role in redefining the political agenda. In order to obtain a commitment by the local administration to implement LGBT policies, they comply, although often reluctantly, with the role of interest groups they are assigned.

In the case of Bologna we also find a top-down approach: the initiative is taken by the local administration grounding the fundamental legitimacy for LGBT policies upon the urban safety discourse and encouraging a practice of bargaining that wouldn't have been possible otherwise, given the conflictual relationships between local associations. The presence of a strategic broker in the Office for Diversity Policies, however, introduces elements of resistance to the strict compliance with the urban safety discourse, but his attempts to modify the political agenda and take up a role of translation of more politicised demands fails because of the low institutional legitimacy granted by the municipality to his role.

The long-term institutionalisation of the LGBT Office in Turin grounds its legitimacy upon the aim of political actors to make the City Council take responsibility for LGBT issues and upon the commitment to develop an equal partnership. Keeping a bottom-up approach in the definition of priorities and activities results in the unique possibility enjoyed by the strastrategic brokers to take up an effective role of translation of the associations' demands, however conflictual and politicised they may be, into policies oriented to the common good. Given these conditions, the room for action in defining the terms of speakability proves broader in the case of Turin: although demands are usually presented in terms of needs, in order to gain legitimacy, the Office reframes them into issues of citizenship rights, thereby giving voice to an active, collective subject, self-defining their experiences, needs and claims.

In the case of the Monitoring Centre in Venice, we find another strategy of resistance to the discursive boundaries shaping the national agenda on LGBT policies, with the marginalisation of the urban safety discourse in favour of a focus upon recognition of differences to be achieved by promoting cultural change. By referring to queer subjects, the aim is to break with the logic of inclusion based on identitarian belonging, proposing instead the construction of coalitional subjects, contingently formed on the basis of shared goals (Phelan, 1994). What makes the legitimacy gained by these activities precarious, however, is the fact that it derives from a rather isolated political support within the administration, rather than from active participation of LGBT organisations to a structured partnership.

In these cases, different possibilities emerge for the construction of subjectivities through processes of governance. In a context like Italy, public representations of LGBT subjects can already represent a strategy of resistance to the situated terms of speakability, concurring to break with a long tradition of silencing and invisibilising queer subjectivities, although some of them could appear as compliant to what in other contexts has been identified as a homonormative model. At the same time, in our analysis we could find some of the same processes that are in progress in contexts like the UK, where public recognition of an active, collective and empowered subject is threatened by the terms of speakability defined by urban safety and diversity management policies that respectively tend to victimise and individualise their marginal citizens, reducing their collective action into interest group lobbying. The consequence is that of undermining empowerment: the victimised subject gets confined in boundaries of speakability that deny her/him the agency for defining her/his priorities.

What our cases clearly show more generally, therefore, is that the terms of speakability of current LGBT local policies cannot be expanded just by the naming and staging of queer subjects by these polices, as it was in the case in Venice. They rather depend on the space, resources and legitimacy the actors involved in local partnerships find for practising collective and conflictual subjectivities; these conditions, however, challenge the very framing of LGBT policies implied by current processes of local governance.

Among the organisational conditions opening possibilities for resistance to an urban safety discourse and for the construction of non-victimised subjects, a crucial one appears to depend on the degree of legitimacy assigned to strategic brokers within the local administration. This legitimacy is grounded upon a political assumption of responsibility for LGBT issues and upon broad support by different departments of the city administration, as the one obtained by internal mainstreaming in Turin.

A second element concerns the strategic brokers' room for action within the partnership, and is given by the existence of an equal relationship between municipality and associations. Requiring the local administration's commitment to play an active role of translation, rather than imposing a certain definition of them, such partnership allows civil society actors to influence the discursive framing of policies, challenging the existing terms of speakability. By acknowledging rather than denying the political and conflictual implications of the organisations' claims, the local administration can contribute to the empowerment and recognition of an active, collective subject, making space for a public, positive representation of LGBT, and other, differences.

Notes

1. On 'urban safety' as a ground for developing local public policies and networks between local administrations, see for instance EFUS (European Forum for Urban Security).
2. For more information about the research, see Coll-Planas (2011).
3. For a detailed list of the interviewees, see the Annex in Gusmano and Bertone (2011).
4. In the empirical paragraphs, the strategic brokers interviewed are quoted by pointing to their role in the public administration rather than by their names.

Bibliography

Brenner, N. and Theodore, N. (2002) 'Building 'Euro-regions': Locational politics and the political geography of neoliberalism in post-unification Germany', *European Urban and Regional Studies*, 7(4): 317–43.
Browne, K. (2011) 'By partner we mean ...': Alternative geographies of "gay marriage"', *Sexualities*, 14(1): 100–22.
Carabine, J. and Monro, S. (2004) 'Lesbian and gay politics and participation in New Labour's Britain', *Social Politics*, 11(2): 312–27.
Coll-Planas, G. (ed.) (2011) *Combating homophobia: Local policies for equality on the grounds of sexual orientation and gender identity. A European White Paper*. Barcelona: Ajuntament de Barcelona, Direcciò Drets Civils.
Cooper, D. (2006) 'Active citizenship and the governmentality of local lesbian and gay politics', *Political Geography*, 25(8): 921–43.
Cooper, D. and Monro, S. (2003) 'Governing from the margins: Queering the state of local government', *Contemporary Politics*, 9(3): 229–55.
Dall'Orto, G. (1988) 'La "tolleranza repressiva" dell'omosessualità' in Arcigay (ed.) *Omosessuali e stato*. Bologna: Cassero, pp. 37–57.

De Leonardis, O. (2002) 'Principi, culture e pratiche di giustizia sociale', *Animazione Sociale*, 12: 11–21.

De Leonardis, O. and Bifulco, L. (2003) 'Partnership o partecipazione: Una conversazione sul tema' in F. Karrer and S. Arnofi (eds) *Lo spazio europeo fra pianificazione e governance*. Firenze: Alinea, pp. 67–84.

De Vivo, B. (2011) 'Trajectories of homonationalism in Italy', paper presented at *In and out of sexual democracies*, Rome: Facciamo Breccia, 28–29 May.

D'Ippoliti, C. and Schuster, A. (eds) (2011) *DisOrientamenti*. Rome: Armando.

Duggan, L. (2003) *The twilight of equality?* Boston: Beacon Press.

Florida, R. (2003) *The rise of the creative class*. North Melbourne: Pluto Press.

Gaudin, J. P. (1999) *Gouverner par contrat*. Paris: Presses de Sciences PO.

Gusmano, B. and Bertone, C. (2011) 'Partnership and legitimation in LGBT local Policies', in Cirsde and Turin City Council LGBT Office (eds) *LGBT local policies: Italy and the Piedmont case*. Torino: Città di Torino, 13–60.

Herbert-Cheshire, L. (2003) 'Translating policy: Power and action in Australia's country towns', *Sociologica Ruralis*, 43(4): 454–73.

Larner, W. and Craig, D. (2005) 'After neoliberalism? Community activism and local partnerships in Aotearoa New Zealand', *Antipode*, 37(3): 402–24.

Monro, S. and Richardson. D. (2010) 'Intersectionality and sexuality: The case of sexuality and transgender equalities work in UK local government', in Y. Taylor, S. Hines and M. Casey, M. (eds) *Theorizing intersectionality and sexuality*. Basingstoke: Palgrave Macmillan, pp. 99–118.

Mosse, G. L. (1985) *Nationalism and sexuality*. New York: Howard Fertig.

Naldini, M. (2003) *The family in the Mediterranean welfare states*. London: Frank Cass.

Phelan, S. (1994) *Getting specific*. Minneapolis: University of Minnesota Press.

Pitch, T. and Ventimiglia, C. (2001) *Che genere di sicurezza*. Milano: Franco Angeli.

Pustianaz, M. (2010) 'The threat of difference: Whose life is at stake in anti-homophobic campaigns', Paper presented at *Queer Crossings*, University of Palermo, 18–19 June.

Sabbatini, A. (2005) 'Governance', *La rivista delle politiche sociali*, 2: 407–23.

Saraceno, C. (1994) 'The ambivalent familism of the Italian welfare state', *Social Politics*, 1(1): 60–82.

Saraceno, C. (2008) 'Fare famiglia', *Parolechiave*, 39: 1–26.

Squires, J. (2008a) 'Intersecting inequalities: Reflecting on the subjects and objects of equality', *The Political Quarterly*, 79(1): 53–61.

Squires, J. (2008b) 'The constitutive representation of gender: Extraparliamentary re-presentations of gender relations', *Representation*, 44(2): 187–204.

Taylor, Y. (2009) *Lesbian and gay parenting*. Basingstoke: Palgrave Macmillan.

Taylor, Y. (2011a) 'Sexualities and class', *Sexualities*, 14(3): 3–11.

Taylor, Y. (2011b) 'Lesbian and gay parents' sexual citizenship: Costs of civic acceptance in the United Kingdom', *Gender, Place and Culture*, 18(5): 583–601.

Trappolin, L. (2004) *Identità in azione*, Roma: Carocci.

Index